D0515835

LONELY PLANET'S

ATLAS OF

Adventure

DISCOVER A WORLD OF **THRILLING** OUTDOOR ACTIVITIES

© Tom Robinson / Lonely Planet

INTRODUCTION

Y ou never forget the first time that you clamber into a sea kayak, fasten the spraydeck over your lap and set off on your maiden voyage on the open water, sensing the implacable power beneath your narrow craft and working with it rather against it. The same is true for embarking on any new activity or adventure in the great outdoors, whether that's clipping into a climbing harness for a first lesson on scaling rock walls, or packing some provisions and pedalling away on a bicycle towards a distant horizon.

There are numerous ways of exploring our awe-inspiring planet via land, sea or air, and the *Atlas of Adventure* aims to introduce as many of them as possible in more than 150 countries around the world. We tracked down our most adventure-loving experts, wherever they happened to be, and asked them to share their tips for the best places to try all the activities listed overleaf. This book is the result: an alphabetically ordered romp around the globe, highlighting the best outdoor pursuits you can enjoy in each country. We'll take you climbing in Thailand, mountain biking in America and sailing along the south coast of Britain. We've included everywhere it's currently feasible to set your intrepid foot, exploring the less trafficked corners of popular spots and venturing to far-flung places you may never have previously considered visiting. A few island regions – notably the Caribbean – have been tackled collectively.

The pursuits in the *Atlas of Adventure* range from hiking, biking and snorkelling to more adrenalin-charged experiences that will require some tuition before you try them – but our intention is to offer ideas for accessible activities for first-timers. However, we have also included profiles of iconic events and interviews with inspiring personalities from the outdoor sports world to show what might be possible with a bit of practice. It's easy to be intimidated by seemingly extreme feats but even the boldest biker, kayaker or mountaineer began somewhere and often the first step is simply deciding to try a new experience, one that might lie slightly outside your comfort zone, and giving it a go. Although we would urge all fledgling adventurers to seek expert tuition and equipment advice from accredited operators!

A desire for adventure is present in every traveller. And research has shown that learning a new skill or technique – whether that's how to make a clean paddle stroke in a kayak or clear a difficult descent on a mountain bike – is what helps keep our brains young and our bodies healthy. So pack your passport and your compass for a thrilling and rejuvenating journey around the world.

Canoeing in La Mauricie National Park, Quebec, Canada

GLOSSARY OF ADVENTURE TERMS

Abseiling Descending a rope using a braking device.

Bikepacking Cycle touring but on a mountain bike.

Bouldering Free solo rockclimbing (without ropes or other equipment) on large boulders rather than a vertical rock face, usually with crash pads to protect the landing.

Canyoneering The US term for canyoning (exploring a gorge or canyon, sometimes with ropes, often tracing a waterway).

Cat skiing Skiing (or boarding) in remote areas made accessible with the use of a snowcat

Coasteering Combination of scrambling, wild swimming and free solo climbing around the tidal zone of a coast.

Freediving Diving without scuba gear.

Glade skiing Off-piste alpine or backcountry skiing through trees.

Crag Rock face for climbing.

Deep-water soloing (DWS) Rockclimbing unroped above water, usually on sea cliffs, but sometimes above rivers or lakes.

Dirt-bagging Living cheap, by any means possible, in order to prolong an adventure experience.

Free soloing Climbing without ropes or other protection.

Freeride A discipline of mountain biking using stunts and obstacles on steep and technical trails. Also applies to snowboarding on off-piste, backcountry terrain, often performing tricks.

Gorge scrambling Canyoning (sometimes without ropes).

Hardtail Mountain bike with front suspension only, as opposed to a dual or full-suspension bike

Heliskiing Skiing or snowboarding after being dropped off by a helicopter.

Kloofing Canyoning in South Africa.

Long-period swells Sets of waves that have travelled great distances and offer good surf.

Long riding Big-distance horse riding.

MTB A common abbreviation for mountain biking.

Parahawking Paragliding combined with falconry.

Rappelling See abseiling.

Singletrack Tight, twisty and often technical section of running, riding or walking trail.

Skyrunning Mountain running on peaks over 2000m in height.

Sport climbing Rock climbing using permanently fixed anchors.

SUP Stand-up paddleboarding, where people use a paddle to propel a large surfboard.

Trad Climbing When rockclimbers place their own protection (anchors) while ascending.

XC Cross-country mountain biking.

GUIDE TO SYMBOLS

 4WD (four-wheel driving)

 Adventure racing

 BASE jumping/ skydiving

 Canoeing

 Caving

 Climbing & mountaineering (including bouldering)

 Cycling (road biking/touring)

 Stand-up paddleboarding

(Wild swimming)

 Diving & snorkelling

 Dune boarding/ volcano surfing

 Hiking

 Horse riding

 Ice skating

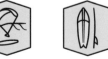 *Kayaking*

 Kitesurfing

 Surfing

(Wind surfing)

 Mountain biking (including bikepacking)

 Paragliding

 Rafting

 Running (trail/road)

 Sailing

 Skiing

 Snowboarding

Trekking (overnight & harder hiking)

Ziplining

© Philip Lee Harvey / Lonely Planet

Hiking the Routeburn track in Fiordland National Park, New Zealand

TOP10 ADVENTURE HIGHLIGHTS

Greenland

Iceland

Canada

Way out west, Moab in Utah attracts many mountain bikers, but don't miss the Sierra Nevada's trails.

U.S.A.

NORTH ATLANTIC OCEAN

Sea kayaking around British Columbia's Haida Gwaii, 50km south of Alaska, is sensational.

NORTH PACIFIC OCEAN

Bermuda

Madeira
Morocco

Mexico

Bahamas
Cuba
Belize
Guatemala   Jamaica Haiti Dominican Rep.
Honduras   Caribbean
El Salvador Nicaragua
Costa Rica
Panama

W. Sahara

Mauritania

Cape Verde   Senegal
Gambia   Burk
Guinea-Bissau   Guinea Fa
Sierra Leone   Gh
Côte d'Ivoire
Liberia

Venezuela

Colombia   Guyana Suriname
French Guiana

Ecuador

Dive at dawn, then ascend into Ecuador's Avenue of the Volcanoes for more explosive adventures.

Peru

Brazil

Ascension

Kiribati

Tokelau

Samoa
American Samoa

Niue
Tonga   Cook Is.

Fr. Polynesia

Bolivia

Saint He

Pitcairn Is.

Easter I.

Paraguay

SOUTH PACIFIC OCEAN

Uruguay

Chile Argentina

SOUTH ATLANTIC OCEAN

Chile's Torres del Paine is an adventure playground for hikers, bikers, climbers and kayakers.

Try kloofing in South Africa's incredible canyons, then explore the Drakensberg by bike or foot.

Antarctica

© Matt Munro | Lonely Planet © Don Johnston; Kseniya Ragozina; George Brits | Getty Images, © Lena Granefelt | Lonely Planet, © Aurora Photos / Alamy © Henn Photography; Andrey Danilovich | Getty Images, © Chris Ord

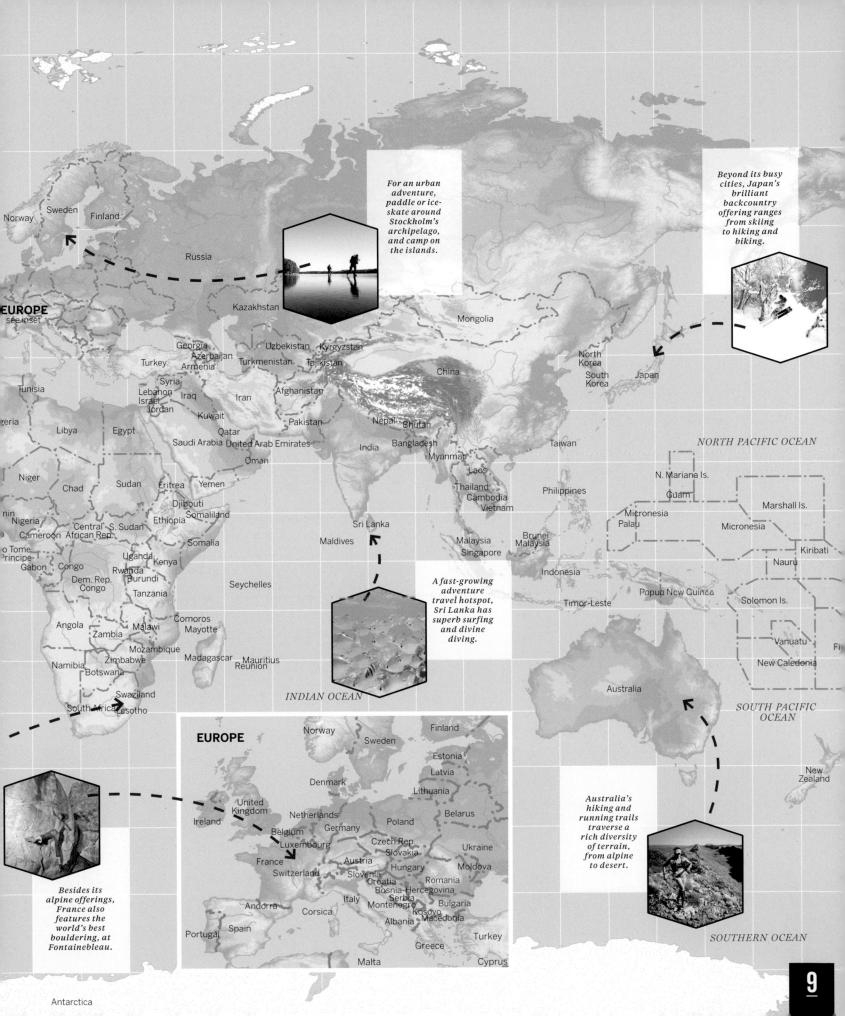

For an urban adventure, paddle or ice-skate around Stockholm's archipelago, and camp on the islands.

Beyond its busy cities, Japan's brilliant backcountry offering ranges from skiing to hiking and biking.

EUROPE
see inset

Norway
Sweden
Finland
Russia
Kazakhstan
Mongolia
Georgia
Azerbaijan
Armenia
Uzbekistan
Kyrgyzstan
Turkey
Turkmenistan
Tajikistan
China
North Korea
South Korea
Japan
Syria
Lebanon
Israel
Jordan
Iraq
Iran
Afghanistan
Tunisia
Kuwait
Pakistan
Nepal
Bhutan
Libya
Egypt
Qatar
Saudi Arabia
United Arab Emirates
India
Bangladesh
Myanmar
Taiwan
Oman
Laos
Niger
Chad
Sudan
Eritrea
Yemen
Thailand
Cambodia
Vietnam
Philippines
Djibouti
Somaliland
Nigeria
Central African Rep.
S. Sudan
Ethiopia
Cameroon
Somalia
Sri Lanka
Maldives
Malaysia
Singapore
Brunei
Malaysia
o Tome Principe
Gabon
Congo
Uganda
Kenya
Rwanda
Burundi
Dem. Rep. Congo
Tanzania
Seychelles
Indonesia
Timor-Leste
Papua New Guinea
Angola
Zambia
Malawi
Comoros
Mayotte
Namibia
Zimbabwe
Mozambique
Madagascar
Mauritius
Reunion
Botswana
Swaziland
South Africa
Lesotho

NORTH PACIFIC OCEAN

N. Mariana Is.
Guam
Marshall Is.
Micronesia
Palau
Micronesia
Kiribati
Nauru
Solomon Is.
Vanuatu
New Caledonia
Fi

Australia

SOUTH PACIFIC OCEAN

A fast-growing adventure travel hotspot, Sri Lanka has superb surfing and divine diving.

INDIAN OCEAN

Australia's hiking and running trails traverse a rich diversity of terrain, from alpine to desert.

New Zealand

EUROPE

Norway
Sweden
Finland
Estonia
Latvia
Denmark
Lithuania
United Kingdom
Netherlands
Belarus
Ireland
Belgium
Germany
Poland
Luxembourg
Czech Rep.
Slovakia
Ukraine
France
Austria
Hungary
Moldova
Switzerland
Slovenia
Croatia
Romania
Bosnia-Hercegovina
Serbia
Andorra
Italy
Montenegro
Kosovo
Bulgaria
Corsica
Albania
Macedonia
Portugal
Spain
Turkey
Greece
Malta
Cyprus

Besides its alpine offerings, France also features the world's best bouldering, at Fontainebleau.

SOUTHERN OCEAN

Antarctica

AFGHANISTAN

Mountainous Afghanistan is made for adventure, but the ongoing war and resurgent Taliban limit the options for adventurous travellers.

Afghanistan conjures a heady mix of encouraging and discouraging images: dusty mountain ranges, ancient ruins, heavily armed US troops, AK-47–toting Taliban. Travelling here is extremely dangerous, and warnings should be regularly checked and taken seriously, but one part of the country has remained relatively safe for the adventurous: the **Wakhan Corridor.**

Located in northeastern Afghanistan, the Wakhan Corridor is a remnant of 'The Great Game', the 19th-century contest of power between Britain and Russia. Stretching east–west for 350km, bordered by Tajikistan to the north, Pakistan to the south and China to the east, it was designed as a buffer between Russia's Central Asian possessions and British India. But the area's history goes back far longer – the valley has been used as a trade route since antiquity; past visitors include Alexander the Great and Marco Polo.

For modern-day visitors, the attractions are many. It's safer than the rest of Afghanistan (the few visitors who come here enter via Tajikistan) because it's largely cut off from the troubles that afflict most of the country. The Corridor is bounded in the south by the Hindu Kush – home to Afghanistan's highest peak, Noshaq (7492m) – and the Karakoram Range, and to the north by the Pamirs and the Panj River. It's a compelling geography for **trekking** and **mountaineering**, although the Wakhan is one of the poorest and least serviced areas of Afghanistan, so exploration is only for the most experienced and prepared adventurer. There are no established trekking routes, so travel with a guide (who usually provides yaks to carry gear).

An Afghan guide leads a trekker across a river in the Wakhan Corridor.

© Jan Bakker

ALBANIA

The dark horse of the Balkans, Albania combines a stunning coastline with a mountainous interior that presents a paradise for hikers and climbers.

S ince throwing off the Communist yoke in 1991, Albania has slowly modernised and opened up to the rest of the world. Its beautiful coastline – stretching 476km along the Adriatic and Ionian Seas – attracts most visitors, but the country's mostly mountainous interior has huge potential for hiking and climbing.

coast delightful, particularly along the **Albanian Riviera** in the south, where the 2000m-high ridgeline of Mt Čika and the Lighting Mountains provide a spectacular backdrop. Inland, white-water paddlers will find superb rivers, including the tight, twisting lines of the **Cemit**, the exciting rapids of the **Kir** and crystal-clear waters of the **Shala** – always with high mountain ridges looming above.

Hiking

Walking in Albania is characterised by dramatic landscapes – rugged mountainous terrain, deep valleys and powerful rivers – and trails often tiptoe past historic villages and ruins. The best trekking is found in the Albanian Alps, somewhat forebodingly known as the **Accursed Mountains**. Especially popular is the hike from Valbona to the village of Theth, which is overlooked by the gigantic 1000m-high cliffs of **Maja Harapit** (2217m).

Kayaking

Due to its Mediterranean climate, sea kayakers will find exploring the cliffs, coves and bays of Albania's

Climbing

Albania is not a well-known destination for climbing, but the country has great potential. In the south, **Gjipe** has sport routes that range from easy up to 8b on limestone cliffs that line a beach and a beautiful canyon. Just north of the capital, Tirana, the striped limestone walls of **Brar** canyon offer more quality sport climbing, although the long, steep routes here don't suit beginners. The hidden gem of Albanian climbing, though, lies in the north of the country: **Theth** is a 1000m limestone wall, the highest in the Balkans, with very few established routes and almost unlimited potential for adventure.

DON'T LEAVE WITHOUT...
Bagging the summit of Mt Korab. On the eastern border with Macedonia, Albania's highest mountain can be climbed in a day.

Hikers in the Albanian Alps, often poetically called the Accursed Mountains.

© Nebojsa Zabrdac | Shutterstock

ANDORRA

The principality of Andorra might be small, but for adventure seekers it packs a big punch.

Perched on high between France and Spain, the 'Country of the Pyrenees' is a semi-secret haven for in-the-know skiers, boarders, bikers, hikers and runners. What's more, Andorra's slopes and trails are comparatively uncrowded and prices are low.

Skiing & Snowboarding

Between them, Andorra's three ski resorts – **Grandvalira**, **Pal-Arinsal** and **Arcalís** – offer 98 lifts and 303km of runs, some starting at 2640m. Freeride 2km down the **Pic d'Arcalís** for thrills, or explore any number of randonnée routes, ski-touring or snowshoeing challenges.

Trail Running

Runners looking for a tough event will be salivating when they see the profile of the 170km-long **Ronda dels Cims**, one of Europe's most prestigious ultra marathons, circumnavigating Andorra via 16 of its 2000m-plus peaks. Not challenging enough? Try the **ELS 2900**, an invitation-only hut-to-hut mountaineering/sky-running event across Andorra's seven highest peaks, all over 2900m.

Cycling

Road cyclists can tackle the numerous cols of the **Vuelta a España**, while those looking for a sufferfest will be attracted to the **Col de la Gallina**, a 925m climb with grades of 20%. **Mountain bikers** should head to **Soldeu** or **Vallnord**; the latter regularly hosts UCI MTB World Cup races and is widely regarded as one of Europe's best bike parks.

DON'T LEAVE WITHOUT...
Exploring the Andorran section of the Haute Randonnée Pyrénéenne (a long-distance trail across the Pyrenees, linking the Atlantic and Mediterranean) through Parc National des Pyrénées.

ANGOLA

They say Angolans are fighters – but they are lovers, too. Travel here is much the same, an adventurous battle with untold rewards.

Just deciding to leap into the great travel enigma that is Angola is an audaciously adventurous choice, since the country has seemingly all-but closed itself off to travellers since peace broke out more than a decade ago. Landing a visa is a somewhat laborious and lengthy task – give yourself plenty of time, it's one of the world's most difficult places to get a visa for – but once you've successfully obtained permission to enter this extraordinary land, you are in for a real treat.

Hiking

Hike your way to Kalandula Falls, one of Africa's most spectacular waterfalls – stand at the crest of the cascade before navigating a precipitous path for a supreme view from the bottom.

4WD Exploration

Next, mount a 4WD expedition to the 9600 sq km **Parque Nacional da Kissama**, a coastal savannah where elephants, buffalo and endemic palanca antelopes seek shade under hulking baobab trees. Alternatively, voyage to the far south for remote exploration on a grand scale in **Parque Nacional do Iona**, a 15,200-sq-km extension of Namibia's Skeleton Coast National Park (see p200). It takes several days to traverse this ever-changing kaleidoscopic landscape of golden grasslands, crimson-coloured escarpments and expansive dune fields. Keep your eyes open and you'll see the 'living fossil' *Welwitschia mirabilis*, an alien-looking plant that lives for thousands of years. Other lifelong memory-making highlights include encounters with the ochre-coated Himba, one of Africa's most fascinating peoples.

ULTIMATE CHALLENGE
Only the bravest bicycle tourers include Angola on their itineraries, but those who do often rave about the most memorable two-wheeled trip of their lives, from cycling sandy roads to N'zeto to climbing the switchbacks to Serra-da-Leba Pass (1845m). Just be prepared for plenty of attention, not least from police who may be surprised to see you.

Exploring a steam cave on Mt Erebus, Ross Island.

ANTARCTICA

Any time spent in Antarctica, one of the planet's most extreme and inhospitable places, inevitably involves an adventure.

Antarctic travel has epitomised adventure for more than a century. For most of this time, the only way to experience it was to go with a government scientific programme or a hugely expensive private expedition. Fifty thousand tourists a year now visit, mostly sightseeing and wildlife watching, but it's still the one continent where you can't just take a cheap flight, turn up and do your own thing. Unless you skipper your own yacht to the ice, everyone has to rely on a commercial operator to provide the logistics – either just the basics for hardcore

exploration, or fully pampered glamping on ice. In between those extremes are two traditional means of polar travel – skiing and kayaking.

Far from the flat, monochrome void of the deep interior, the Antarctic Peninsula is beautiful and richly diverse. A melding of sea, snow and rock, enriched with wildlife and stories of human endeavour, it's no wonder most visitors consider it the trip of a lifetime. Weather governs everything here, but even with inevitable delays, most trips get plenty of time for active adventure. Ships and yachts visit constantly from November through late-March, but sea-ice conditions vary greatly year to year, and

© Aurora Photos | Alamy

this affects access to some locations. Skiing and climbing are best done in November and December, while January to February is better for kayaking and whale sightings.

Skiing & Climbing

The Antarctic Peninsula is basically one long mountain range dropping straight into the sea, flanked by equally steep islands poking out of the stormy straits and bays. Some of the larger islands have giant peaks – such as **Mt Français** (2822m) on Anvers Island and **Mt Parry** (2520m) on Brabant Island, which are both popular climbing and skiing areas – while dozens of lower islands and promontories provide easier days out.

Though barely any snow falls in the icy Antarctic interior, the maritime environment of the peninsula coast means softer, skiable snow on the mountain slopes. The skiing here is backcountry style. There are crevasses and the possibility of avalanches, but all outings are with well-qualified guides and even

skiers without huge experience can end up carving turns with an iceberg-strewn ocean as a backdrop.

Several established companies offer cruises with ski and mountaineering opportunities but the only ship-based option fully dedicated to ski adventures is Californian outfit **IceAxe Expeditions**, which runs regular trips at the start of every season. On most trips you can ski everyday, even in less-than-perfect weather, and you will encounter wildlife along the way, as the Zodiac navigates past seals and puts you ashore among penguins. Nights are spent safely aboard ship in well-catered comfort. A longer, tougher and more expensive option is aboard a yacht such as *Icebird*, the base for **Ski-Antarctica**, a company that has made numerous first ascents, descents and ski journeys on the coastal peaks and hinterland.

For those seeking to explore deeper into the big white void, **Antarctic Logistics & Expeditions**, incorporating the inland-Antarctic pioneers Adventure Network International (ANI), offers

*Above, King penguins coming ashore. **Right**, paddling on Paradise Harbour, Antarctic Peninsula.*

© Cedric Favero | 500px / © Andrew Peacock

two-week Ski Antarctica or Climb Antarctica programmes. These are separate to its long-standing operation on **Mt Vinson** (4892m), the continent's highest peak, and magnet for Seven Summiteers. Starting out of ALE's impressive Union Glacier camp, these trips offer the opportunity to make first ascents of lower peaks or take long, exploratory ski tours through the Heritage Range, a network of elegant low mountains with sweeping spurs and craggy ridges. Here, the weather is usually better but colder than on the Peninsula. After a four-hour flight from Punta Arenas, Chile, visitors spend some time at **Union Glacier** acclimatising and preparing for their adventure, before heading out with experienced guides on multiday adventures. For the climbing programmes, basic alpine experience at least is needed to make the most of the trip.

Sea Kayaking

Now the most popular adventure activity conducted by operators on the peninsula, kayaking offers visitors a way to fully immerse themselves in the landscape. Unlike planes and ships, a kayak brings

PULL OF THE POLE
Norwegian Roald Amundsen famously beat Brit Captain Scott to the South Pole by five weeks, arriving on 14 December 1911, and the planet's southernmost point continues to attract adventurers. In 2014, Canadian Frédéric Dion became the first person to ski to the Pole, and Australian cyclist Kate Leeming rode there on a fat bike in 2015.

you back to the pace of the place, in tune with the waves and the wind, powered only by yourself as you glide past icebergs to explore popular sites such as **Neko Harbour**, **Cuverville Island** and **Cierva Cove**, as well as hidden gems inaccessible to larger vessels. There's something intimate about moving around this blue world, plugged into to the fluid polar environment around you, spotting whales while penguins zoom underneath your paddle. Sea-kayaking options are available on several cruises as optional additions for an extra cost, but some operators, such as Southern Sea Ventures, run dedicated trips that will aim to paddle every day.

Diving

To enable even more immersion in Antarctica, some operators offer scuba options to certified divers with open-water and drysuit experience. A whole new underworld opens up: ice walls and caverns, historic wrecks, wildlife unseen from above and the truly unique chance to touch the ice from the inside – just watch out for the leopard seals as at least one diver has been drowned by an aggressive seal.

ARGENTINA

With the world's longest mountain range strung along its border for thousands of kilometres, Argentina is ripe for exploration and adventure.

The very word 'Argentina' evokes passion and extremes – think tango, Maradona, Eva Peron – but it is only as you stand among some of the world's most shapely and forbidding mountains, or teeter at the roaring edge of Iguazú Falls, that you realise the extremes here are natural.

The highest peak outside of the Himalayas rises in Argentina, not far from a vast expanse of flat, outback-like pampas the size of neighbouring Chile. The world's largest waterfall system thunders through rainforest, and glaciers crackle around the ankles of the Andes – almost 50 of them in one national park alone.

There are Argentine towns that are part of the lexicon of world adventuring – El Chaltén, Mendoza, Bariloche – and peaks that stir anxiety in even the boldest mountaineers.

The Andes form a serrated barrier along the country's entire western border – all 5000km of it. These peaks are shaped by some of the world's fiercest weather, with both the Roaring Forties and Furious Fifties slicing through the country. It's in the Andes that you'll find several lifetimes' worth of adventure opportunities beckoning: trekking, mountaineering, skiing, white-water rafting... even land sailing.

Trekking
With Andean mountain tops forming a 5000km spine along its shapely back, Argentina is perfect trekking country, and the best things happen at the pointy end.

Patagonia
Not for nothing is this place synonymous with adventure – here banshee winds, glaciers, cruel winters, frost and rain have carved an extraordinary and brutal landscape. The most famous trek in the land, the Torres del Paine, may be just across the border in Chile, but hike out from El Chaltén into **Los Glaciares National Park** and you might wonder how it could be topped.

Treks here lead up to Laguna de los Tres, a stunning lake pooled at the foot of the mighty Monte Fitz Roy, one of the world's pin-up mountains, its enormous and distinctive summit rock towering more than 2km above the water. Hop one valley south and there's a trekking route up to Laguna Torre and the Mirador Maestri, a vantage point that peers across glaciers to the needlepoint summit of Cerro Torre.

The most committing trek is a circuit of Monte Fitz Roy, traversing the Patagonian Ice Cap, the world's largest icefield outside Antarctica and Greenland. Hikers typically cross the range at Paso Marconi before snowshoeing or cramponing along the ice cap behind Monte Fitz Roy and Cerro Torre, returning towards El Chaltén over the Viedma Glacier and Paso del Viento.

The Lake District

The region around Bariloche offers equally good trekking, including a traverse of around four or five days through the spectacular **Nahuel Huapi National Park**, where you can expect to see Andean condors and craggy peaks above, and wind-pruned lenga forest and alpine lakes below.

The nearby **Volcán Lanin** towers over the northern Lake District, rising directly from a low plain to a height of 3776m. From most places, its heavily glaciated peak looks impenetrable, but a trekking route up the eastern slopes provides a strenuous (but not technical) course to an exhilarating summit.

Tierra del Fuego

In Argentina's deep south, a hop-off point for Antarctica, hikers can venture up into the rugged **Fuegian Andes**, which arc around the world's southernmost city, Ushuaia. Conditions are so harsh here that vegetation stops growing at around 600m, and unmarked routes provide a sense of remote exploration in keeping with the setting.

Mountaineering & Climbing

El Chaltén is a true mountaineers' town, but the prize peaks here – **Monte Fitz Roy** and **Cerro Torre** – beckon only the hardiest climbers. The finger-like Cerro Torre is considered one of the world's toughest climbs, with a history shrouded in controversy and mystery – it wasn't climbed until 1959, 1970 or 1974, depending upon which account you believe.

If, as is almost certain, these two mighty peaks are beyond you, 2248m **Cerro Solo** might appeal. Climbing from Laguna Torre, it's a straightforward

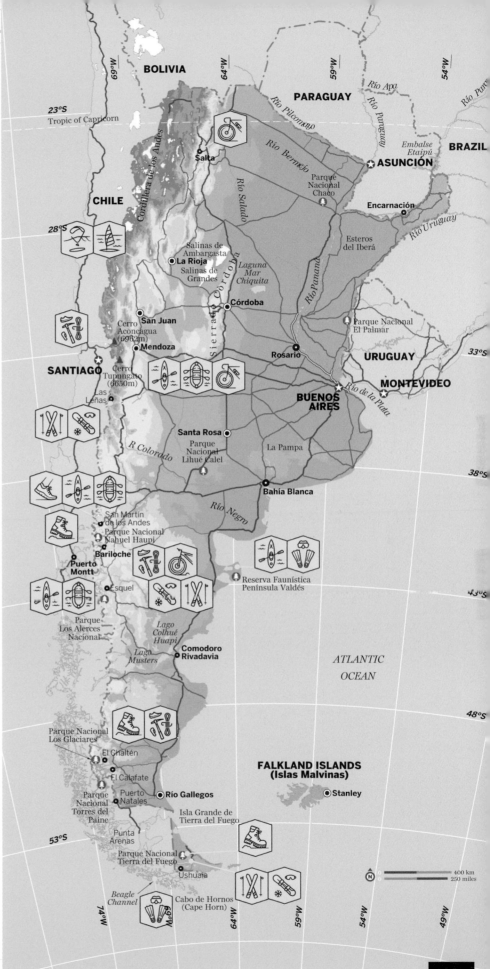

mountaineering ascent, including some glacier travel, to a peak that sits eye-to-eye with Cerro Torre and Fitz Roy – the views can be sublime.

Further north, rising above Mendoza, **Aconcagua** (6962m) is the world's highest mountain outside the Himalayas and it straddles the divide between trekking and mountaineering. The ascent of the peak, which is the second highest of the world's Seven Summits, usually requires a commitment of about two weeks. It isn't technical, but should not be underestimated as it has the mountaineering-style complications of extreme altitude and fiercely fickle weather changes. The most popular approach to the mountain is the Northwest Route through Plaza de Mulas, but the longer, more scenic and more technical approach is along the Vacas Valley and the Polish Glacier.

Unsurprisingly, there are many great places to rock climb across this craggy country. **Frey**, on the granite

spires of Cerro Catedral, above the climbers' haunt of Refugio Frey, is considered by many to be the finest climbing area in South America. The bulk of the climbs are graded around 5.9 to 5.12, and stretch up to 10 pitches. Rivalling Frey is **Los Gigantes**, about 80km west of Córdoba. The mountains here aren't high – up to about 2300m – but there are plenty of limestone crags and up to 100 (mostly) sport routes. As a bonus, you'll probably get to climb with Andean condors cruising overhead.

Skiing & Snowboarding

The ski season throughout Argentina typically runs from around mid-June to mid-October, and there are great options almost everywhere along the line of the Andes. Towards the north, about 500km from Mendoza, is Argentina's premier resort, **Las Leñas**. It's a see-and-be-seen ski field – pack as much après clothing as skiwear – but the dry climate makes it powder perfect. There are 33 runs, with vertical drops up to 1200m.

Head to Bariloche's popular **Cerro Catedral** resort and you may find that the skiing comes secondary to the scenery. One of the largest ski areas in South America, with a swathe of off-piste terrain, it sits beneath the stunning granite quills of its namesake mountain, the 2388m Cerro Catedral. Don't expect the powder of Las Leñas, but the infrastructure is great and there's more than 100km of slopes, mostly suited to intermediate and advanced skiers.

If the kudos of skiing at the world's southernmost fields appeals, head to Ushuaia and make for **Cerro Castor**, 26km from the city. Altitudes aren't high here, as the continent dips away into the Beagle Channel, but the powder on its 15 runs defies the elevation, and you can ski to 200m above sea level.

Every August, the nearby valley of Tierra Mayor is the scene of a pair of cross-country races: the 42km **Ushuaia Loppet marathon** and the 21km **Marchablanca**, which commemorates Argentine hero General José de San Martín's 1817 crossing of the Andes.

Trail Running

Hard mountains serve up hard events, and Argentina is home to a couple of arduous ultramarathons. The **Patagonia Run**, held in April, has seven distances, ranging from 10km to 145km, sending runners out from the town of San Martín

*Below, perfect trail running terrain above Nahuel Huapi Lake, Bariloche. **Right**, off-piste on virgin snow in the Andes.*

© Aurora Photos | Alamy

© Eric Schroeder | Getty Images

de los Andes through the stunning Andean scenes of Argentina's Lake District. It's a qualifying race for the Ultra-Trail du Mont Blanc and the 160km Western States Endurance Run.

At about the same time, also keep an eye out for **The North Face Endurance Challenge**. Involving distances up to 80km, it's held at changing locations, including Bariloche, San Martín de los Andes and Córdoba.

San Martín de los Andes is also the setting for **La Mision**, a four-day, three-night self-sufficient trekking event. It's less a race than a personal journey, 'to finish is to win' is its motto, taking participants through 160km or 200km of epic Andean terrain and sleeping wherever they decide to throw down their tent.

Whitewater Paddling

Rivers run like veins from the Andes, creating a wealth of whitewater opportunities. Mendoza is

DON'T LEAVE WITHOUT...

Sea kayaking at Península Valdés, where orcas famously beach themselves to hunt sea lion pups. Magellanic penguin colonies can also be seen here, and southern right whales breed June–December. Multiday trips paddle out from Puerto Pirámides.

one of the best rafting bases, with commercial trips running on four rivers, including the famed **Atuel** and the class IV **Mendoza** and **Diamante** rivers. For paddlers, Patagonia does what Patagonia generally does: provides masterful scenery that almost eclipses the activity itself. The milky, forest-wrapped waters of the **Río Hua Hum** (San Martín de los Andes) and the boulder-strewn **Río Corcovado** (Esquel) are especially beautiful.

Cycling
Touring

The roads of Argentina are a playground for the cyclist willing to explore, but for a truly memorable experience here let the *ripio* (dirt roads) guide you. Steer away from the tourist hotspots of the south, and head instead to the lesser frequented northeast regions of Catamarca, La Rioja and Mendoza.

Pushed for time? Dive right in at the deep end with a one-day off-road adventure on the old road from Londres to Tinogasta. Here, you'll pedal through dusty Wild West-esque landscapes: past flowering cacti, up long-forgotten switchbacks and along precarious ledges, which boast a stomach churning 1700m drop to the valley floor.

If you find yourself near the city of Mendoza, take the rough and ready Route 13 to Uspallata. Expect a tough slog and steep inclines to make the highpoint at 3200m above sea level. But the rewards on offer for such a challenging ride are plenty: swooping condors, snow-capped peaks, sublime sunsets and the remarkable 'hill of seven colours', just outside Uspallata.

Also not to be missed is a ride from the city of Salta to the vineyard mecca of Cafayate, via Cachi. The paved Route 33 winds steadily up to Piedra Del Molino pass at 3348m, before taking on a whistle-stop tour through the multicoloured mountains of Los Cardones National Park. Then it's on to the lunar landscapes of the Calchaquíes Valley, and (at last) a nice glass of *vino tinto* in Cafayate.

Mountain Biking
Strangely, given the landscape, mountain biking remains fairly undeveloped in Argentina, with little dedicated singletrack, yet MTB legend Hans

*Below, kitesurfing on Nahuel Huapi Lake, Bariloche. **Right**, the powerful torrent of Iguazu Falls.*

Rey rated a ride from **Tilcara** to **Calilegua**, in the country's northwest, among his top three adventure rides in the world. **Bariloche**, the thriving heart of Argentina's Lake District, is arguably the most established area, with a summertime mountain-bike park among the ski fields of Cerro Catedral; in 2016 it hosted a round of the Enduro World Series. Expect loose, dusty riding.

Land Sailing

When a lake has no water, your sailboat isn't going anywhere… unless it has wheels, of course. Across the clay surface of **Pampa El Leoncito**, 25km from the town of Barreal, *carrovelismo*, or land sailing, is big, with 'wind cars' recording speeds in excess of 100km/h across the smooth, 13km-long lake bed. Andean mountains tower to almost 7000m beyond the lakeshores, and the reliable evening *'conchabado'* winds can reach up to 80km/h, thus providing ample propulsion. Take a tandem joyride with a guide, or work your way up to driving your own single-seater.

Windsurfing & Kitesurfing

Wind is the driving force again at the well-named **Dique Cuesta del Viento**, or 'slope of the wind reservoir'. Set in a curious desert landscape – it gets rain just a handful of days each year – the reservoir is considered one of the premier windsurfing and kitesurfing destinations in South America, if not the world. Mornings here are deceptively calm (grab a sleep-in), but in the afternoon the winds are as reliable as clocks, particularly from October to early May. The reservoir is beside the town of Rodeo, 200km north of San Juan city.

Diving

Fancy diving off the southernmost continental tip in the world? Ushuaia has a number of great dive sites, including plenty of shipwrecks and swirling kelp forests through the **Beagle Channel** – needless to say, drysuits are the order of the day. At **Punta Loma** on Península Valdés, there's a great diving (or snorkelling) experience among a sea lion colony. For something very different, head to Bariloche to dive in the alpine **Nahuel Huapi Lake**, 760m above sea level. In the gin-clear waters you'll spot trout and explore an underwater museum of submerged log sculptures around Isla de las Gallinas.

© Mizzick | Shutterstock, © Matt Munro | Lonely Planet

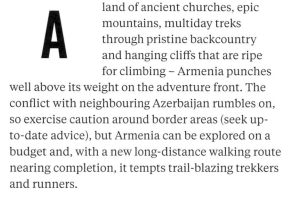

ARMENIA

Don't let this nation's diminutive size mislead you. Armenia is a country so steeped in history you'll feel like Indiana Jones just being there.

A land of ancient churches, epic mountains, multiday treks through pristine backcountry and hanging cliffs that are ripe for climbing – Armenia punches well above its weight on the adventure front. The conflict with neighbouring Azerbaijan rumbles on, so exercise caution around border areas (seek up-to-date advice), but Armenia can be explored on a budget and, with a new long-distance walking route nearing completion, it tempts trail-blazing trekkers and runners.

Hiking

The Transcaucasian Trail is a world-class long-distance hiking trail in the making, which forges a route across both the Greater and Lesser Caucasus mountains, connecting communities en route in a way that's never previously been attempted. The first section (due for completion at the end of 2017), will be the **Trails Of Tavush** in Armenia, with the focus on re-establishing four of the existing **Dilijan National Park** hiking trails and adding two completely new routes. The result is a five-day 75km trek on trails built to international standards, accessible to a broad range of visitors. The trail will connect cultural heritage sites and remote villages, providing new economic opportunities for isolated rural communities mostly overlooked since the fall of the USSR. The first walkers (and runners) to take on these trails will feel like proper pioneers.

Biking

For a country that's approximately half the size of Wales, you wouldn't expect there to be much in the way of adventurous cycle routes. But what Armenia lacks in geographical sprawl it makes up for in vertical ascent, with some of the toughest hill climbs you'll experience outside Tibet or Tajikistan. Road cyclists will relish the chance to explore forgotten offshoots and interesting detours along the Iranian border, while mountain bikers will find incredible downhill trails all within easy reach of the country's capital, Yerevan.

Climbing

Armenia boasts an exciting and established climbing scene, but also has an untapped reservoir of rock for potential pioneers to go new-routing on. Hells Canyon, an hour's drive from the capital Yerevan, is a popular limestone crag with excellent sport climbing in the middle-to-easy grades, as well as camping grounds situated picturesquely in the midst of the canyon.

UNCLAIMED ADVENTURE

Swimming the 32km width of Lake Sevan, one of the largest, high-altitude, freshwater lakes on the continent.

Armenia's powerful culture is ever-present on any adventure; Sevanavank Monastery on Lake Sevan.

© Justin Foulkes | Lonely Planet

AUSTRALIA

From plunging into the azure ocean surrounding the world's biggest coral reef to hiking through primordial landscapes dating back to Gondwana, adventure is everywhere in Australia – get among it, mate.

Australia's geography is built for epic adventures – it has massive inland deserts, sprawling mountain ranges, almost endless coastline and the world's biggest coral reef. Much of this geography is protected in national parks, which cover 4% of the world's sixth largest nation. To top it off, Australia is one of the world's wealthiest countries, a safe, friendly nation whose citizens have embraced adventure in all its many forms.

If Australians are besotted with one aspect of their topography, it's the 25,760km of coastline. On the weekends, roads are jammed with escapees from cities, all heading to their favourite beach to swim, surf, kitesurf, windsurf, kayak, dive or snorkel, or simply sunbake. While there are many iconic sections of beach, from Bondi to the golden sand of Bells, perhaps Australia's most famous section of coast is the 2300km off Queensland, which

holds the World Heritage-listed Great Barrier Reef. Although the reef has been damaged in recent years by agricultural run-off and climate change, it is still one of the wonders of the world.

Hikers – sorry, bushwalkers – will find incredible walking through some of the world's most unique landscapes, from the sometimes waist-deep muddy tracks of Tasmania to the rocky, sun-drenched peaks of the Larapinta Trail in Central Australia. More surprising, perhaps, to many visitors, is the quality of the backcountry snow sports scene in the higher reaches of the Southern Alps in the dark mid-winter, when you can practise telemark turns through snow gums and go snowshoeing over the range.

But whatever your adventure poison – be it climbing or kayaking, skiing or surfing, road cycling or mountain biking, trail running or camel trekking – you will find it here, usually in world-class form, and often without too many others around to break your solitude. Enjoy.

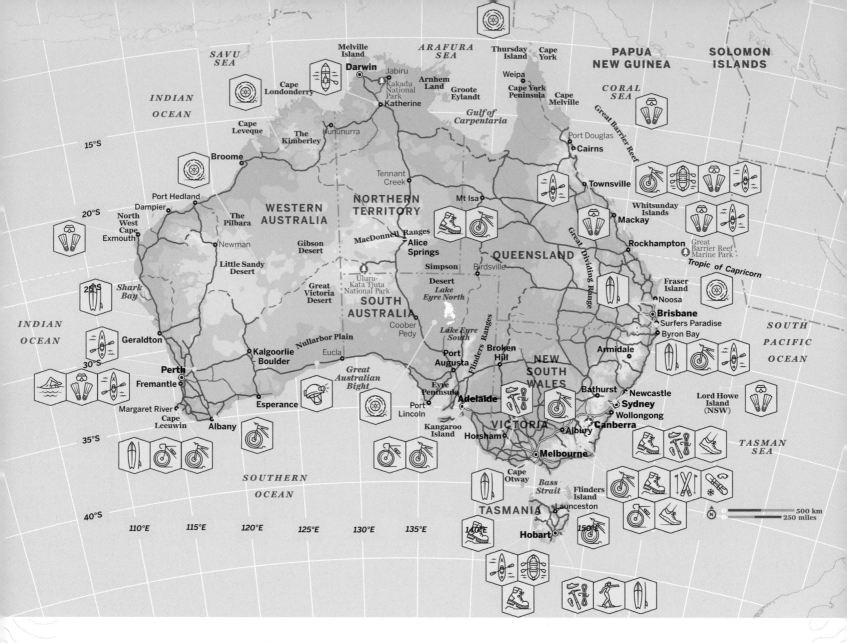

Mountain Biking

Australia is synonymous with sand, sea and surf, but the Lucky Country offers as much for mud-loving, landlubbing, trail-thumping bike riders as it does budgie-smuggler and bikini-wearing beach-goers and board balancers.

Mountain biking was born in the grit of Repack Road in Marin County, California, but it evolved in isolated pockets all over the planet, and the fecund rainforest cradle of Cairns produced perhaps the most anarchic and exciting offshoot brand of the mongrel sport.

Throughout the 1980s, on twisty tropical trails rudely scraped into the legs of Queensland's Tablelands, a mullet-topped posse known as the Minjin mob, led by Glen Jacobs (now one of the world's top trail builders), pioneered freeriding. When Jacobs lured the Mountain Biking World Championships to Cairns in 1996, riders were confronted with trails like they'd never seen before, and Australia bloomed as a major MTB destination.

A continent-sized country with a small population and immense tracts of raw wilderness – encompassing every sort of rideable terrain from desert tracks to alpine ridgelines and tropical rainforests, all largely uncluttered by historic buildings, private property and long-established rights of way – Australia proved perfect for purpose-building mountain bike trails.

Mountain resorts in the Australian Alps, faced

with an ever-shortening snow season as the globe warms up, have invested heavily in green-season activities, and mountain bikers are emerging as the grinning winners. The lifts at Mt Buller in Victoria and Thredbo in New South Wales (NSW) are now busy with bikers most of the year, and the downhill and cross-country trails in these places are world class.

Every state and territory has outback areas striped with singletrack, often dedicated purely to those on two wheels. Trail networks are typically well maintained by local clubs, marked, graded and free – just rock up and ride. Bike shops serving top gear and quality coffee are usually found nearby, and some offer rental bikes.

Wildlife encounters are common while bush biking. In the south you can expect up-close kangaroo and wombat sightings, while in the far north creek crossings have crocodile warning signs, big-as-your-face spiders make massive morning webs across tracks, man-sized roosters called cassowaries stalk the forests and even the flora fights back at every turn, with stinging trees and wait-a-while vines ambushing unsuspecting riders with Triffid-like fury. There's never a dull moment in the saddle here.

NSW & The ACT

The bush is never too far away, even when you're in Australia's major cities. The nation's capital, Canberra, welcomed the UCI MTB World Championships to **Mount Stromlo** in 2009 and the Capital Territory also has stunning riding at **Majura Pines**, **Sparrow Hill** and **Kowen Forest**.

Thredbo is the big pull card for pedallers, but the **Snowy Mountains** are liberally crossed with cracking trails between the high flanks of Mt Kosciuszko and Lake Jindabyne. Closer to Sydney, great riding can be found in the seductive embrace of **Royal National Park**, around **Manly Dam** and amid the eucalyptus-infused haze of the beautiful **Blue Mountains**.

Victoria

Mt Buller is one of the Southern Hemisphere's best MTB destinations, and the action continues across the Victorian Highlands, from **Mt Beauty** near the high-point of Bogong, to **Warburton** in the Yarra Ranges. Elsewhere, sensational cross-country trails roll through **Forrest**, a graded trail complex

in the Otway Ranges, close to the Great Ocean Road; the **You Yangs** near Geelong; **Wombat State Forest** in Woodend; and at **Lysterfield** on the outskirts of Melbourne, where dedicated MTB loops are a legacy of the 2006 Commonwealth Games. The **Yarra Trails** also wend wonderfully alongside the river that flows through the state capital.

South Australia

The **Adelaide Hills** have been luring mountain bikers for years, and the little outback town of **Melrose** in the Flinders Ranges is a dedicated MTB destination, with bespoke accommodation specifically for bikers and a Fat Tyre Festival every June.

Bikepacking in Wooroonooran National Park, Queensland.

© James McCormack

Queensland

Just outside the tropical city of Cairns, **Smithfields** has twice won hosting rights for the MTB World Championships. High above, on the cooler terrain of the Tablelands, a newer tangle of top trails have been built around a hub at **Atherton**. Australia's oldest mountain-bike event, the **RRR**, takes riders from the Tablelands to the beach at Port Douglas, while the **Crocodile Trophy**, an annual 10-day, 1200km stage race in North Queensland, is one of the world's toughest MTB races. Further south, Brisbane's mountain-bikers head to the trails in **Mt Coot-tha Forest**.

Northern Territory

In the rusty dusty **MacDonnell Ranges** around Alice Springs, in the country's Red Centre, you can enjoy some of the best desert trails on the planet – right up there with Moab, but without the crowds.

Tasmania

Australia's little island offers a stunning range of riding. The North–South Track on the flanks of **Mt Wellington** is a favourite for Hobart's mountain-biking community, while **Derby** in the northeast is the newest area to see a network of world-class singletrack being built. Ace events include the two-day **Blue Dragon** in the northeast and **Wildside**, a four-day epic along the rugged west coast from Cradle Mountain to Strahan.

Western Australia

The cream of Western Australia's MTB trails – including **Margaret River Pines**, **Albany** and **Dwellingup** – are linked together by the annual four-day Cape-to-Cape event, which traces the incredible coastline of Australia's southwest corner, combining hundreds of kilometres of singletrack with overnight stops in vineyards and boutique breweries.

DON'T LEAVE WITHOUT...
Riding Mt Buller's 40km Australian Alpine Epic Trail in the Victorian highlands – the only track in the country granted official 'epic' status by the International Mountain Biking Association (IMBA).

© Chris Putnam; Steve Thomas | Alamy

Road Cycling

Australia has kilometre upon kilometre of quiet country roads, a vast network of gravel tracks and dozens of traffic-free rail trails, making it a fantastic place to explore on two wheels.

At the more competitive end of road cycling's spectrum, the nation's many champion cyclists have trained on the mountain roads of **Victoria**. Climbs such as Mt Buffalo, Falls Creek, Lake Mountain and Mt Buller are ascents of Alpine proportions, lasting 20km to 30km, and feature in Victoria's annual 7 Peaks Challenge. The best hunting ground for hard rides is the High Country in the northeast. The state also hosts several sportives, including the week-long Great Victorian Bike Ride and the Giro della Donna.

Across the border in **South Australia**, Adelaide hosts the annual Tour Down Under, which sees the world's pro riders hit the hills in January. There's also excellent road riding in the state's wine regions (such as Clare Valley and the Adelaide Hills).

Similarly, in **Western Australia**, the best road cycling is found south of Perth and Fremantle in Margaret River, where there are plenty of places to stop, stay overnight and refuel on wine and cheese. Just make sure you're there in winter, when temperatures are more comfortable.

Bikepacking

To truly get a flavour of Australia, cyclists really ought to try bikepacking on the country's many unmade roads. These tracks need not be remote and it's often possible to overnight under a roof, should you wish, but it's definitely wise to pack provisions, water and a good map. These gravel roads open up incredible landscapes and facets of Australia, from Tasmania's primeval forests to the gold-mining heritage of Victoria.

An easy-going introduction to cycling in Australia can be had on the country's growing network of excellent rail trails, the longest of which is the **Great Victorian Rail Trail** at 134km. A bigger off-road challenge is presented by the epic long-distance (1070km) **Munda Biddi Trail** in Western Australia, from Mundaring (near Perth) to Albany in the state's deep south, which can be done it its entirety or bitten off in sections.

Above, lapping up the winding curves of the Great Ocean Road. Left, catching air at Mt Buller, which switches between ski resort and mountain bike park depending on the season.

Surfing

You can't discuss global surfing hot spots without pointing your board south towards Australia. Ever since Hawaiian legend and godfather of surfing, Duke Kahanamoku, rode a swell at Sydney's Freshwater Beach in 1915, Australians have taken to the sport as though they own it. And with more coastline than most other nations, why wouldn't they? It's no wonder Australia has produced more world-champion surfers than any other country.

With surf spots along all of the south, west and east coasts, finding a killer wave is no problem, and since most of the surfing population is anchored to metro areas, neither is finding an empty break if you are willing to travel.

Victoria

Bells Beach on Victoria's Surf Coast is the spiritual home of Australian surfing. When it's pumping, Bells attracts huge crowds to watch the local pros (and plucky blow-ins) take on moving-mountains of 5m and more rising over shallow reefs. Alternatively, try lesser-known **Winki**, only 100m north along the high-cliff coastline where, when the swell is running, you will be rewarded with faster, steeper and more barrelling waves. Other popular spots include the state's first National Surfing Reserve at **Phillip Island**, where you'll find world-class breaks such as Woolamai and Magic Lands (and quite a few great white sharks, due to the local population of fur seals).

Western Australia

The tiny village of Yallingup, 260km south of Perth, marks the gateway to **Margaret River**, known equally for its proliferation of wineries and surf breaks. Waves range from standard fun fare to monstrous water-walls only for the fearless. **Yallingup** itself is great for all-round surf. Serious surfers head further south to **Prevelly Park**, where swells rising up to 6m form perfect barrels racing across an offshore reef. Not a place for beginners. Nor is the famous **Boneyards**, located northeast of Cape Naturaliste and considered the best winter break for those crazy enough to take it on. Fact – Western Australia's coastline is jam packed with more top ten breaks than any other state.

Kalbarri, 590km north of Perth, packs a pretty good punch, its multitude of surf attractions include one of Australia's best left handers in **Benders**, a coral break for more experienced riders. Another lefty, **Lopes**, is a rock-reef break rated for pros or kamikazes only.

Tasmania

Like your surfing with mandatory tow-in? Located 30km off Cape Raoul, on the southeast coast of Tasmania, **Shipstern** was made famous by big name surfers Tom Carroll and Ross Clarke-Jones, who documented it in the film *Storm Surfers*. Regarded as one of the premier big wave targets in the world, this is near-death-wish stuff, the size, stepped formation of the wave face and prevalence of great white sharks giving it the reputation as one of the most dangerous places to surf in the world.

Queensland

Bagging a 'Burleigh barrel' at **Burleigh Heads** is a Gold Coast goal for serious surfers, while **Snapper Rocks**, which is a 45-minute drive from Surfer's Paradise, is another spot for the experienced, serving up a reliable right-hand point break. **Rainbow Bay** is perhaps better suited to grommies and greenies. Alternatively, **Noosa Heads** boasts five superb right-hand point breaks that are collectively regarded as one of the best spots in the world for longboarders.

New South Wales

The first world surfing championships were held at **Bondi** and **Manly** in 1964, but these are busy beaches. For a good city set, head to Sydney's **Northern Beaches**, where the 6km corridor between Dee Why Beach and North Narrabeen is considered the prime surfing belt. The Long Reef bombora known as Butterbox is in the middle and you can hopscotch around nearby to sample the waves from Mona Vale to Newport on to Whale Beach and up to Avalon. Lennox Head, near beautiful Byron Bay, is one of many surfing hotspots on the NSW coast, while further north, virtually straddling the Queensland border, **Duranbah Beach** (known as D-bah) has excellent right- and left-hand breaks.

Tearing up the waves at Byron Bay in northern New South Wales.

©Pete Seaward | Lonely Planet

Paddling

Australia is excluded from lists of the Earth's biggest islands, because it's a continent all to itself (which seems churlish), but if it was included, it would blow the rest right out the water. Since the legendary Paul Caffyn pioneered the route in 1981–82, several endurance kayakers have paddled right around this mighty southern land, a 1600km epic, but most mere mortals will be content to explore the country's cracking coastline one stretch at a time. Every state has long stretches of stunning shoreline, but there are several standout routes that all passionate paddlers want to tick off. It isn't about sea kayaking Down Under, though. If you know where and when to look, Australia offers sensational whitewater rafting and kayaking, and excellent multiday canoe experiences; there's a serious surf-ski scene, with myriad popular downwind races, and the SUP and outrigger cultures are vibrant.

Catching a wave at Manly, just a short ferry ride from the Sydney Opera House.

Victoria

The shoreline of **Port Phillip Bay** is ideal for exploration by kayak or SUP, with the area around the historic quarantine station on **Mornington Peninsula** particularly enjoyable. From here, experienced paddlers can pass Point Nepean and thread The Heads into the ocean proper. Out west, the **Surf Coast** has good downwind conditions for surfskiing, and kayakers can explore the **Twelve Apostles** off the Great Ocean Road. The **Murray River** forms the dividing line between Victoria and NSW, while the **Snowy River** rises beneath Mt Kosciuszko and flows through Victoria – both offer magical multiday missions. The coastline and islands around the mainland's most southerly point, **Wilsons Prom**, boast more premier paddling, with gin-clear water beneath your bow and several scenic campsites only reachable by boat or foot. Kayakers attempting to paddle to Tasmania start across the **Bass Strait** from here.

New South Wales

Superb sea kayaking is found all along NSW's shoreline, from **Byron Bay** and **Ballina** in the north to Eden's **Twofold Bay** on the southern **Sapphire Coast**, but simply paddling on **Sydney Harbour** is a very memorable activity, and one that's easily arranged with a rented boat. Surfski and SUP paddlers can make the experience competitive during the **Bridge to Beach** race, which starts at dawn beneath the famous Harbour Bridge and paddles past the Opera House to Manly Wharf. For something different, try the 111km **Hawkesbury Canoe Classic**, which takes place overnight. More leisurely canoeing trips can be enjoyed while exploring **Shoalhaven River** as it spills across the Southern Tablelands, while whitewater rafting trips shoot through **Barrington Tops National Park**.

Tasmania

Only highly experienced paddlers will undertake a crossing of Bass Strait or an expedition along the shores of the **South West National Park**, but more manageable and equally exquisite sea kayaking experiences can be enjoyed in **Wineglass Bay** in Freycinet, and around the **Tasman Peninsula** and **Bruny Island**. Whitewater can be found on several

© Blaine Harrington III / Alamy

rivers, including the **Lea**, and the **Tarkine** can be explored via the Pieman River. Tassie's big-ticket paddling journey, though, is the **Franklin River**, which takes rafters and kayakers through the Franklin–Gordon Wild Rivers National Park during a five- to 10-day lifelong-memory–making trip.

Queensland

From kayaking, SUPing or outrigging the **Coral Sea**, skirting the edge of the Great Barrier Reef, to running the **Barron River** or rafting the 45 rapids that punctuate the **Tully**, paddling in Queensland takes many forms. Two multiday experiences really stand out, though: the **Ngaro Sea Trail**, which wends its watery way through the wonderful Whitsundays, taking in South Molle, Whitsunday and Hook Islands, and incorporating some walking legs too; and the kayaking-and-camping trip along the coast of **Hinchinbrook Island**.

Western Australia

Local and visiting downwind junkies get their dose of adventure medicine during the annual race from Rottnest Island to Fremantle, **The Doctor**, named after the cooling breeze that pushes paddlers across the Indian Ocean. Elsewhere, kayakers share the river with power boats during the unusual two-day **Avon Descent**. More contemplative and wildlife-rich experiences can be had afloat amid the far-flung **Abrolhos Islands** off the coast of Geraldton, around **Ningaloo Reef**, and on the **Blackwood River**.

Northern Territory

Canoeing or SUPing up through the eight-stages of **Nitmiluk (Katherine) Gorge** is an immersive experience on every level, with camping possible on sandy beaches complete with slide marks from freshwater crocs. Multiday trips can be done, and if money is burning a hole in your paddling pants, you can even try heli-kayaking.

South Australia

Coorong's lagoons are best seen with an Indigenous guide, while **Port River**, close to Adelaide, has shipwrecks and mangroves to explore, and dolphins to meet. **Coffin Bay National Park**, **Kangaroo Island** and the 21-island archipelago of the **Sir Joseph Banks Group** are kayaking hot spots too.

© Australian Scenics | Getty Images

ICONIC EVENT
One of Australia's biggest annual paddling races, the Massive Murray Paddle (formerly Murray Marathon) is a 404km, five-day canoe and kayak race.

Paddling the tannin-stained waters of the Pieman River, Tasmania.

Climbing

The world's flattest continent is packed with enough vertical topography to occupy any climber for many lifetimes. Most famous are the Grampians and Mt Arapiles, though Australia has no shortage of other world-class crags. Sydneysiders luxuriate in their famous bay, but the city is bounded to the west by the towering bulk of the Blue Mountains and its paradise of cliff-lined valleys. In Tasmania, granite-like dolerite forms into endless cracks and, every so often, unique free-standing 'poles'. But climbing Down Under is more than just about rock, it's about the bush: giant gum trees, explosions of flowering wattle, mobs of kangaroos and that rare-to-find quality, solitude.

Victoria

Four hours west of Melbourne an anomaly appears. Rising from the wheat fields are what appear to be the ruined walls of a crumbling fortress, its ramparts crusted with moss and topped with a Telecom tower. Closer inspection reveals the walls are far from crumbling, but are formed from perfect silica-rich sandstone. And amid the labyrinth of buttresses, pinnacles and gullies roam climbers who spend their days climbing some of **Mt Arapiles'** 3000-plus routes. In the 1980s, Arapiles put Australian climbing on the map. A ragtag collection of ratbags and dropouts lived full-time in tents and spent their days competing for new routes. Soon, word spread, and in 1985 legendary German climber Wolfgang Güllich visited, climbing Arapiles' most famous route, Punks in the Gym (32/5.14a) – the world's hardest at the time. Arapiles is no longer at the cutting-edge, but it's still a place of pilgrimage for climbers at all levels, from those coming to repeat Punks in the Gym to absolute beginners.

Forty-five minutes east of Arapiles, the **Grampians** rise from the flat Wimmera plain. Set among its rocky ridges and valleys is near endless bouldering, and sport and trad climbing on perfect sandstone. Taipan Wall – a 70m-high tsunami of steep orange sandstone – is the crown jewel. Many climbers say it's the best cliff in the world, and if

Above, the stunning and aptly named Totem Pole rises 60m out of the ocean. Right, the immaculate red sandstone of Moonarie.

© Kamil Sustiak, © Craig Ingram | Alamy

one route were to epitomise Taipan's perfection, it would be Serpentine (29/5.13b), two pitches of sublime climbing up the proudest part of the wall. If the best route on the world's best wall isn't the world's best route, then what is? But Taipan is just the beginning, the 167,219-hectare park holds literally hundreds of crags and many thousands of boulders for climbers to explore. Best of all, most days your only companions will be soaring wedge-tailed eagles and the odd wallaby.

New South Wales

An hour west of Sydney, the hazy mass of the **Blue Mountains** looms on the horizon. 'The Blueys', as it's known to locals, is a contender for Australia's best sport climbing destination. Renowned for its crimpy orange sandstone, the sheer volume of rock is astounding. Most climbers come for the sport routes, but those seeking more adventure should abseil into the green depths of the mighty Grose Valley, exiting the 150m-high walls by climbing one of the hundreds of multipitch routes.

South Australia

In the desert, 400-suicidal-kangaroo-kilometres north of Adelaide, lie the **Flinders Ranges**. This ancient range holds one of Australia's best and least visited crags, **Moonarie**, an orange sandstone escarpment that sits on the edge of Wilpena Pound, a natural amphitheatre of mountains. The climbing here is something special, the red desert-polished sandstone is superb, while the big cliffs yield long, demanding pitches that are rendered just that little more serious by the remoteness and solitude of your surroundings.

Tasmania

About an hour from Hobart is the **Tasman Peninsula**, a rugged cape lined with massive dolerite cliffs. The peninsula holds a series of unique, narrow dolerite 'poles'. Most famous is the **Totem Pole**, a 60m-high, 4m-wide tower sticking out of a narrow gap between the mainland and a larger monolith behind it, the Candlestick. The first climber to reach its summit, the legendary 1960s hardman, John Ewbank, described it thus: 'Take a matchstick, change it into dolerite. Multiply it 1600 times. Stand it upright in a heavy swell, then swim away before it topples over.' The route is an adventure: after abseiling down to ocean level, climbers swing across the wave-torn gap, then climb 'the Tote' via two superb pitches. At the top it's not all over – getting off requires swinging 60m above the sea back to the mainland.

INTERVIEW: SIMON MENTZ
Climbing guide and co-author of the definitive climbing guide to Mt Arapiles, Simon Mentz explains the uniquely inclusive qualities of Australia's top climbing area.

'Even climbing-meccas such as Yosemite Valley barely offer climbs below grade 14 (5.7), yet Arapiles has hundreds of easier and intermediate climbs that are phenomenally good, offering varied climbing on quality rock with excellent natural protection. There isn't a better place in the world to learn to climb. And that quality continues all the way to the highest grades. Add easy access, pleasant camping, good bouldering and cliffs ranging from 10m to 110m, and it's clear that Arapiles remains the king of cliffs for climbers of all standards.'

Diving & Snorkelling

Australians have an intimate relationship with their oceans for good reason, and if you don't stick your face into a mask and dive beneath the brine during your time Down Under you're missing half of what this ridiculously diverse destination offers. The northeast coast, fringed by the planet's biggest barrier reef, inevitably steals the show, but sensational diving can be enjoyed all around the country's coastline. Much of it, however, is being seriously impacted by rapid climate change.

Queensland

The 2300km **Great Barrier Reef** shadows Australia's eastern flank, from Bundaberg to beyond Cape York. Sadly, the reef is experiencing serious grief, as sea temperatures and acidity levels soar, but outside stinger season (November–May, when jellyfish including the deadly irukandji make wearing a special suit while snorkelling annoyingly necessary) boats busily buzz across the Coral Sea from Cairns and Port Douglas, taking tourists to day-dive/snorkel sites such as the **Low Isles**, **Green Island** and the purpose-built pontoon by **Agincourt Reef**.

Inevitably, the best sites are more remote; places like Osprey Reef and **Cod Hole** (home to gigantic potato cod) require dedicated divers to fork out for multiday live-aboard trips, which feature numerous dives each day, and one every night – when the sub-aquatic animal world changes shift and the big boys come out for dinner. These range in price, with the quality of the on-board pampering scaled accordingly, but the diving is always exceptional, and it's the perfect way to earn extra qualifications.

Closer to Brisbane, **Stradbroke Island** in Moreton Bay offers excellent diving, including encounters with grey nurse sharks and mantas around Amity Point.

New South Wales

Sydney Harbour and the protected North Shore beaches boast brilliant snorkelling, especially **Shelley Beach** near Manly and **Bare Island**. Further out – 600km off the coast of Port Macquarie – **Lord Howe Island** is one of the world's best dive sites; situated at the confluence of five major ocean currents, conditions here

Butterflyfish feeding on the Great Barrier Reef.

© Jeff Hunter | Getty Images

are unique and there are 60 superb diving sites. Elsewhere, **Montague Island** has a huge colony of fur seals; **Jervis Bay** offers caves and hidden sponge gardens; **Solitary Islands Marine Park** is home to more than 550 species of fish; **Fish Rock Cave** near Kempsey has a resident grey nurse shark colony, while **Julian Rocks Marine Park**, by Byron Bay, is famed for whales, dolphins, leopard sharks and turtles.

Western Australia
While the GBR gets all the glory, **Ningaloo Reef** delivers ridiculous riches for divers and snorkellers, without all the on-land partying. Around **Exmouth** you can explore the reef from the shore, with no need to pay for boat charters. Ningaloo is rightly famous for whale sharks; snorkelling (diving isn't permitted) with these benign behemoths is an unforgettable encounter (just be aware: they arrive with eerie punctuality after the March full moon, which causes coral to spawn, reducing visibility during other dives). For tank-wearing purists, WA's premier site is Exmouth's **Navy Pier**, one of the world's best shore dives. You can also hang out with mighty manta rays in **Coral Bay** and snorkel alongside dolphins at **Monkey Mia**. Other premier WA sites include **Rowley Shoals**, the **Abrolhos Islands**, **Marmion Marine Park** and the **Montebello Islands**, while **Rottnest Island** – easily accessible from Perth – has superb snorkelling.

Victoria
Around Melbourne, within the protective arms of **Port Phillip Bay**, lie marine reserves and suburban snorkelling trails, and off **Portsea Pier** it's possible to swim with wonderful weedy seadragons. Just outside The Heads, **The Graveyard** has dozens of scuttled ships (including three J-class WWI submarines) to be explored, with penetration possible on some wrecks for more experienced divers. Out west, the waters off the **Great Ocean Road** and **Shipwreck Coast** are home to hundreds more sunken vessels and some challenging dive sites such as **Loch Ard Gorge**; this coast also features on the migratory route of numerous whale species. To the east, **Wilsons Promontory Marine National Park** is another outstanding diving area; aquatic locals here include fur seals, little penguins, octopuses, rays and sharks.

Tasmania
Across Bass Strait, Tasmania was once famous in bubble-blowing circles for its immense kelp forests, especially around **Eaglehawk Neck**, but over the past decade these have been decimated by rising temperatures. The area still offers sensational diving around the caves and canyons of **Waterfall Bay**, and the wreck of the SS *Nord*.

South Australia
In 1963, Rodney Fox was bitten almost in half by a great white shark while spear fishing off South Australia. You would think that might put him off the big toothy beasts, but no, he's subsequently made a career out of introducing other people to them. Go cage diving with Rodney around the **Neptune Islands** between SA's fin-infested Eyre and Yorke Peninsulas.

Northern Territory
The NT, despite its large population of saltwater crocodiles, does offer diving around **Darwin**, where there are reefs and wrecks, and you can submerge yourself in a glass box to eyeball a 4m croc in the Cage of Death at **Crocosaurus Cove**.

Exploring one of the most popular dives in Queensland, the wreck of the Yongala, near Magnetic Island.

A dive instructor on the Great Barrier Reef; the area is one of the world's best locations to learn how to dive.

© Matt Munro | Lonely Planet

35

and iconic forests of eucalyptus. From short but spectacular day walks to long distance tracks like the Bibbulmun, there's something for everyone, while Australia's famous wildlife – from bounding kangaroos to incredible birdlife – is never far off.

Tasmania

Often left off maps of Australia, Tasmania is not a place easily forgotten by bushwalkers. This small compact island, parted from the mainland some 12,000 years ago, holds epic bushwalking terrain. Most famous is the **Overland Track**, a 65km walk through the **Cradle Mountain–Lake St Clair National Park**. The rutted, muddy track is almost a rite of passage, leading walkers through a prehistoric landscape of Gondwanan myrtle-beech forests, buttongrass plains and alpine herb fields, all overlooked by spectacular dolerite sentinels.

Further south, in the **Southwest National Park**, the wilderness is possibly even more rugged and untamed. For our money, the **South Coast Track** is the pick of the hikes here (although the Western Arthurs traverse is more famous). Hikers are dropped off by prop plane at Melaleuca, then slowly walk back east along the famously muddy track, climbing the windswept heights of the Ironbound Range and passing a succession of pristine, deserted beachside campsites before reaching civilisation at Cockle Creek 84km later.

Central Australia

West of Alice Springs in Central Australia is the **West MacDonnell Range**, a series of spectacular mountains poking out of the desert landscape like the exposed spine of a fossilised dinosaur. Traversing this arid landscape is one of Australia's most unique walks, the 223km **Larapinta Trail**. It links razor-sharp ridges, dry riverbeds lined by gnarled gums, spectacular chasms and hidden oases of water and ferns – remnants of wetter epochs – all the way west to Mt Sonder. The landscape is harsh but beautiful, and as you pass through it you begin to appreciate the ingenuity of the local Arrernte people who have inhabited the area for 50,000 years.

Western Australia

Just east of Perth in Western Australia, the small town of Kalamunda marks the start of the **Bibbulmun Track**, a bushwalk that travels 1003km

Bushwalking

Americans hike, the English ramble, Kiwis tramp, but Australians bushwalk. And what a lot of bush there is to walk: 4% of Australia is protected in national parks, covering 280,000 sq km (an area larger than England) and spanning the vast spectral spaces of the deserts to the ancient Gondwanan forests of Tasmania and the low alpine terrain of the Great Dividing Range. The ancient, worn-down topography of Australia lacks really big mountain ranges, but it has everything else: a stunning, varied coastline, tropical and temperate rainforests, endless sand and gibber (stony) deserts,

Above, Dove Lake and Cradle Mountain sit at the start of the iconic Overland Track in Tasmania. Right, dawn breaks over the summit of Mt Anne in Tasmania.

© Catherine Sutherland | Lonely Planet, © Andrew Peacock

south to finish in Albany. Considered one of the world's great long-distance walks, the Bibbulmun takes walkers through the heart of the southwest, passing by giant granite boulders, towering karri and tingle forest, and coastal heathlands. While there are many 'end-to-enders', it's most often tackled in shorter sections.

The South and East Coast

The epic arc of the **Great Dividing Range** stretches for 3500km down the east coast of Australia, and in the folds of its dramatic topography there are many lifetimes of walking to be done. Forty-five national parks protect the range, many beloved

DON'T LEAVE WITHOUT...

Exploring Uluru, Australia's most iconic chunk of rock. While climbing to the summit is discouraged for cultural reasons, the hike around the base is incredible.

of bushwalkers. The most popular is the **Blue Mountains National Park**, just west of Sydney, where the steep, cliff-lined valleys hold everything from short, spectacular day walks to multiday off-track adventures deep in the park.

Further south, the **Australian Alps**, often snow-covered in winter, is another classic bushwalking destination, famed for its multiday hikes. In New South Wales hikers regularly climb Australia's highest peak, the modest **Mt Kosciuszko** (2228m). Further south in Victoria, linking the spectacular ridgelines of the Razorback and **Mt Feathertop** is a bushwalking favourite that can either be done as a day walk or linked into a longer multiday walk.

Trail Running

Wild, raw, brutally beautiful: Australian trails that are ripe for running range from undulating, deceptively tough coastal routes to precipitous and remote highland adventures that demand self-sufficiency.

Australia has undergone a trail running boom in the past decade, energised by high-profile festivals such as **Ultra Trail Australia**, which attracts 2000 competitors annually. Held in the **Blue Mountains National Park**, near Sydney in New South Wales, it uses highlight sections of the 44km **Six Foot Track**, which itself is host to another eponymous end-to-end outing considered an elder statesman of the now brimful event calendar.

Away from events, long-distance gazetted routes are key targets and include the **Great Ocean Walk** (100km, Victoria), **Cape to Cape** (135km, Western Australia), **Overland Track** (82km, Tasmania) and, for an epic arid desert experience, the 223km **Larapinta Trail** in the Northern Territory. A rural trail running hub of note is **Bright**, Victoria, where runners can pick up trails from the centre of town, leading to some of the biggest hill climbs going.

For those bound to metro areas, try Melbourne's **Yarra River Trails**, barely 3km from the CBD; or myriad wild routes through **Royal National Park**, right on Sydney's doorstep. The South Australian capital has the **Adelaide Hills**; Tasmania's capital, Hobart, features trail-striped **Mt Wellington** (1271m) as its backdrop – try the newly stitched 27km Kunanyi-Wellington loop, boasting 1300m of ascent – and **Canberra** is surrounded by singletrack.

ICONIC RACE

Broken Hill's Great Wheelbarrow Race features teams of competitors faithfully repeating the feats of early miners, who pushed their possessions great distances in wheelbarrows – in this case, 140km over three days.

© Chris Ord

Rogaining

Rogaining is a (relatively) new Australian-invented sport that has spread across the globe – think orienteering but with an endurance twist. Officially created in 1976 by members of the Melbourne University Mountaineering Club, rogaining is a cross-country navigation sport, like orienteering, but there are several key differences: orienteers follow a fixed set of checkpoints that must be tagged in order as quickly as possible, while rogainers (in teams of two or more) have a fixed period of time to collect as many checkpoints as they can. The checkpoints are each worth a certain amount of points and can be collected in any order, introducing a strategic element, as teams plot the most efficient route (competitors are given maps shortly before events). At the end of the designated time (World Championship length is 24 hours, but many races are shorter) – competitors have points docked for every minute they are late back to the 'hash house' (the HQ of any rogaine). The team with the most points is the winner.

Snowsports

Most people think it's all red dirt and enormous rocks surrounded by perfect beaches and baked by endless summers, but Australia has the third longest land-based mountain range in the world – the 3500km Great Dividing Range, which tracks the continent's eastern seaboard. And while its high point, Mt Kosciuszko (2228m), isn't on the scale of the world's Greater Ranges, the alpine environment is unique and spectacular.

Like the runs, the season is short and sweet, lasting June–August if you're lucky. Snow annually falls in the colder, more southerly states, and much of the riding is above the tree line, meaning it can get blasted by the wind. Because of this, drainage gullies and bowls provide the most reliable stashes.

There are a reasonable number of resorts, each with their own feel. In New South Wales you go from the gnarly off-piste action of **Thredbo** to sprawling **Perisher** – the country's largest resort offering something for all riders. In Victoria, only three hours' drive from Melbourne, **Mt Buller** boasts the most high-tech facilities. Further afield, **Mt Hotham** is renowned for steeps while **Falls Creek** has the prettiest village and a distinctly European vibe.

Resorts can be hectic, so for real adventure head into the backcountry where alpine touring skis or a splitboard will bring great rewards for those prepared to earn their turns. When the conditions are right you can have magical experiences cutting figure-8s off the Sentinel ridgeline in NSW's **Main Range** or getting freshies in the West Face chutes of **Mt Feathertop** in Victoria.

You may not get towering peaks and endless powder, but skiing in Australia has its own charm, especially when your tents are dug in among ancient, gnarled snowgums, frozen leaves glistening in sunset rays that burn the snow orange and yellow, and camp is filled with tired thighs, bright eyes and broad grins.

*Above, rogaining is growing in popularity in Australia. **Left**, tackling the Northern Territory's 223km Larapinta Trail.*

© Sputnik

Four-Wheel Driving

The vast inland deserts comprising 70% of Australia's landmass have a host of classic 4WD trips, many of which follow historic routes. One of the most famous is the **Canning Stock Route**, an 1800km track from Wiluna to Billiluna in Western Australia. Although Canning was a ruthless brute who mistreated local Indigenous people and his stock route never really took off, it's become a rite of passage for 4WDers. Other classic routes include the **Gibb River Road** in the Kimberley; South Australia's **Oodnadatta Track**; and the **Cape York Track–Old Telegraph Track** in Queensland.

Sailing

Deep in the green depths of Claustral Canyon in the Blue Mountains.

There's more to sailing in Australia than eating a faceful of icy sea spray on the Sydney to Hobart Yacht Race, one of sailing's blue riband events.

Island-hopping through the **Whitsundays** is an idyllic way to become more proficient; charters and sailing classes are widely available in this corner of Queensland. Sydney and its surrounds are also full of sailing schools and plenty of sheltered inlets.

Canyoning

Only a short drive from Sydney you can find yourself plunging down into pools, abseiling waterfalls and exploring a deep, green world amid the **Blue Mountains'** canyons. The difficulty and seriousness of the canyons vary, and you have to keep a close eye on weather conditions, but there is literally no more beautiful way to escape the summer heat.

Caving

The **Nullarbor Plain** – a vast, flat, inhospitable desert above the Great Australian Bight on the south coast of Australia – is the world's largest limestone karst system. Caving here is extreme: ultra-light aircraft are often used to locate entrances, before 4WDs are dispatched to get to the caves, which can then be explored. Permits are required to explore caves here, with only **Murrawijinie Cave** open to the public. And in **Mt Gambier**, South Australia, world-class **cave diving** can be enjoyed in deep limestone cavities amid farmers' fields (but only by highly experienced specialist divers).

Wild Swimming

Unsurprisingly, Australians are obsessed with open-water swimming. Many places have pier-to-pub races, but one truly iconic event is the annual **Rottnest Channel Swim**, a 19.7km epic from Cottesloe Beach to Rottnest Island in Western Australia. A new guided experience sees groups of experienced swimmers take on the 3.2km stretch of potentially lethal and tempestuously turbulent water between Point Nepean and Point Lonsdale at the mouth of Victoria's Port Phillip Bay, better known as **The Rip**.

Camel Trekking

Australia has the world's largest population of camels – an estimated 1.2 million, most feral – so it makes sense to use some of them to explore the country's many deserts. Get your taste of camel trekking (trekkers walk with the camels, which carry supplies) in the **Flinders Ranges** in South Australia.

© James McCormack

AUSTRIA

For a small country, Austria packs in plenty of adventure, particularly if you love your terrain rugged and mountainous.

Austria is often overlooked as an adventure destination; its mountains are not quite as high as its Swiss and French neighbours, the Grossglockner not quite as famous as the Matterhorn or Mt Blanc. But size isn't everything when you've got charm, lakes and lederhosen. And there are some pretty awe-inspiring escapades to be had. Where else can you paraglide over a city as magical as Mozart's home town of Salzburg, take a high-adrenaline descent of a summer tobogganing run (the Rodelbahn) or ascend a *Klettersteig* (via ferrata) on an upturned seabed such as the Dachstein massif? You can also find world-class rapids along the Ötztaler, epic ski

mountaineering in the Silvretta and follow in the dust trails of mountain biking legends at Leogang, or the Tour de France star Eddy Merckx in the Salzkammergut. If all this sounds too exhausting, well, Austria has a cure for that in the form of *Kaiserschmarrn*, a calorie-packed pancake that's more effective than any performance enhancing drug. Alternatively, order yourself an Augustiner beer, first brewed by monks, and say 'Prost' to that.

Mountaineering, Climbing & Skiing

It's easy to think of the Alps as a single homogenous chain of mountains, but zoom in and a myriad of chains comes to light. Even within Austria, there

Running ridges above Salzburg and a sea of clouds.

© Christoph Oberschneider | 500px

© gevision | Shutterstock, © Westend61 | Getty Images

are several mountain groups – from the Silvretta to the Stubaital, the Kaisergebirge to the Karawanken – each with their own fiercely proud identity, geographical characteristics and signature cheese. Austria's highest mountain, the **Grossglockner** (3798m) is a challenging ascent requiring crampons, rope, an ice axe and knowledge of how to use them. (The knife-edge summit ridge supplies one of those quite serious 'don't look down' moments.) Most of Austria's tallest peaks, however, are found in the **Ötztal**. It was here that the 5000-year-old mummified remains of Ötzi, the iceman were found. In winter the area becomes the playground of ski

tourers, and skiing off the Wildspitze (3770m), the country's second highest mountain, is high on every big-mountain skier's tick list.

For rock climbers, the town of **Innsbruck** is a magnet, surrounded as it is by many of Austria's best crags – some granite, some limestone – and home to most of its many rock stars.

Whitewater Kayaking

Seeing a landscape unfold from the perspective of a river offers a uniquely immersive experience; from a kayak, it's pure adrenaline-soaked adventure. Running rapids, crashing through walls of water

Above, Austria is one of Europe's best snowsports destinations. *Right*, riding spectacular singletrack in the Lower Tauern mountains.

and dropping narrow chutes arguably gives more fun (and terror) per 60 seconds than any other adventure sport, and Austria is home to some of the best class III to IV rivers in the Alps. The place to pay homage is the River **Inn**, which runs like an artery east across the country from the Swiss border through the Tyrol before turning north to Germany where it joins the River Danube. The river and its many tributaries offer epic kayaking and whitewater rafting. Take the **Ötztaler** – home to the annual Sickline Extreme World Championships, it boasts both class V rapids for pros and easier runs for those who just want a morning's madness on a raft. Most commercial runs finish up at **Area 47**, an extreme waterpark boasting an 80kph freefall slide, canyoning and cave abseiling – just in case you needed some more thrills.

Hiking & Trail Running

Austria's mountains have always been a popular destination for hiking holidays, and those narrow, undulating and twisting trails are equally well suited for the growing tribe of trail runners seeking challenging climbs and epic views, with a mountain

DON'T LEAVE WITHOUT...

Cycling *The Sound of Music* country. Aside from being the place where the musical was filmed, Austria's Lake District, the Salzkammergut, is cycling heaven, home to the Eddy Merckx Classic. Think lush Alpine meadows, crystal clear lakes and something else dear to the heart of every roadie – plenty of places for Kaffee and Kuchen.

hut never far from sight. The classic 120km **Stubaier Höhenweg**, which normally takes hikers seven to nine days, can be run in half that. Expect steep forest singletrack wending past thundering waterfalls, and soft and fast undulating trails that contour the hillsides to glacial scree and rock.

A shorter but no less dramatic mountain excursion is to cross the Ötztal mountains west to east from the famous **Gepatsch Haus** to **Sölden**. It's only 33km, but with two mountain ridges in between it demands deep lungs and quads of steel (and preferably a set of poles). Cold beer and glacial views don't get better than at Braunschweiger Hut (2758m) before the final descent to Sölden.

For ultra runners who love the big community feeling of events, Austria's answer to Mont Blanc's UTMB is the **Grossglockner Ultra Trail**, a 110km one-day race around Austria's highest mountain, which although not quite as hard, is just as epic, and way easier to enter.

Mountain Biking

If you take your mountain biking seriously, then it's probably best to leave the guidebooks and maps at

home and head straight to **Bikepark Leogang**. This World Cup venue is home to nine trails of varying difficulty and brag factor, from super steep downhill and flowing singletrack to North Shore-style runs. As a rule, the idea of going uphill in Austria is an alien concept, or at least something to be endured, normally on a wide fire track with your helmet slinging off the front of your handlebars before the real business of doing downhill begins. But suckers for pain and endurance will find happiness and joy in the 210km **Salzkammergut Trophy**, one of the world's toughest MTB marathons, which boasts 7119m of elevation as it takes riders around the World Heritage region of Hallstatt. Squeezed between lake and steep cliffs, Hallstatt is quite possibly Austria's most photographed village and home to one of the oldest salt mines in the world. The route also passes near the country estate where the court of Emperor Franz Joseph kicked off WWI.

Paragliding

Every two years, the world's top paraglider pilots descend on the city of Salzburg for the start of the **Red Bull X-Alps**, in which athletes hike and fly 1000km across the Alps to Monaco in as little as a week. All along its changing route are classic flying sites. The 1288m Gaisberg, which overlooks the city of Salzburg, offers some of the best city flying anywhere. Not only is it a short hike out of the city, it offers incredible views over its famous Baroque cathedrals as well as the soaring peaks of neighbouring Berchtesgaden. Not far to the southwest lies the aerial superhighway of the Pinzgau valley around Zell am See. Serviced by the Hohe Tauern mountains to the south and the Kitzbüheler Alps to the north, its reliable thermals make this a superb cross-country flying venue. Just don't mention the dreaded 'föhn', the notorious warm wind that makes flying all but impossible.

AZERBAIJAN

Explore an exotic land that falls between the cracks in most people's consciousness – between Europe and Asia, reality and fantasy.

U ntil beautiful Baku hosted the inaugural European Games in 2015, many westerners thought Azerbaijan was where miscreants were banished to in Harry Potter books – a reputation not entirely dispelled by the Land of Fire's 400 mud volcanoes and the odd perpetually burning mountainside. However, this deceptively modern nation, nestled between the Caucasus Mountains and the Caspian Sea, offers escapades aplenty, and it's the promise of more adventures rather than Dementors' cold kisses that keep people from leaving.

Hiking

Alti Agach National Park offers excellent ambling. Formed trails are few, but you'll find rivers and lush forest. Khizi Rayon is the country's least populated district, and the road into the park passes the semi-desert terrain of the **Candy Cane Mountains**. Look out for East Caucasian tur, a rare antelope.

Created by an earthquake in 1139, which popped the peak of Mt Kyapaz and disrupted mountain rivers, the seven hanging lakes known as the **Tears of Kyapaz** in Ganja are not to be missed (military checkpoints allowing).

There's also magical meandering to be done among the mud volcanoes, rock formations, caves and ancient carvings of **Gobustan**, 60km from Baku.

Mountain Biking

A purpose-built **Velopark** was constructed in Baku for the European Games' MTB events, but for a real wide-eyed ride on the wild side, explore the rocks, rubble and ancient petroglyphs in **Gobustan**. This Unesco World Heritage site at the southeastern end of the Greater Caucasus mountain ridge is ridden with ravines, mountains, relics and gas-stones.

DON'T LEAVE WITHOUT...
Trekking to visit Yanar Dağ (burning mountain), a natural gas fire blazing continuously on the Absheron Peninsula, jutting into the Caspian Sea near Baku.

BELGIUM

In Belgium, cycling enjoys quasi-religious status and riders are the heroes of bedroom walls. The savage routes of their races are open for anyone to attempt.

A small country, split between the Flemish-speaking north and French-speaking south, and squeezed betwixt the Netherlands, Germany and France, Belgium's distinctive character is fuelled by history, fine beers and chocolate, and hard cycling.

Road Cycling

Even in a country where all cycling is venerated, there's a hierarchy of events. Gent–Wevelgem and Liege–Bastogne–Liege are both classics with the power to create legends, but the **Tour of Flanders** dominates the high altar. Victory in the Ronde van Vlaanderen, as it's called in Flemish, deifies the rider. National holiday and cup final rolled into one, Flanders is where the gladiators of cycling do battle.

Waymarked routes give a flavour, but for the full Flanders feeling, and a chance to experience the brutality of 230km on closed-to-traffic roads, there's no beating the annual amateur **Ronde van Vlaanderen Cyclo** – a punishing test that might be better named Ronde van Vlaanderen Psycho, considering the risk to bike and bones it poses.

The Ronde van Vlaanderen's cult status stems neither from hills nor distance, even if it is infernally steep and interminably long. No, the event's true horror lies in its cobbled sections: bruising kilometres of ill-laid stones that turn the smoothest racing bike into a bucking bronco. Like evil trolls, the gaps between cobbles are wide enough to snatch a front wheel or pinch a puncture, while the moss, mud and camber can unseat the finest riders in a blink. Rumour has it that if conditions look too dry and easy, locals spread manure across the stones.

Survival myths abound – wear two pairs of padded shorts, fit an extra roll of handlebar tape, anything to mitigate the Magnitude-10-Richter vibrations clattering through the bike. Some say grip the bars with a concert pianist's lightness of touch, others suggest deflating tyre pressures to avoid bouncing from one stone to the next. The only consensus is that it's easier to contend with this hellish, pocked terrain when riding fast – try that when the gradient hits 20% on the Paterberg or rear-wheel traction vanishes on the iconic Muur-Kapelmuur.

Climbing

There's no mistaking Belgium for the Alps, but limestone walls in the **Ardennes** offer routes to challenge any crag rat. The Rochers de Freyr is the honeypot, with 15 crags and over 600 routes graded from French 3 to 8c. Access is free, but you must be a member of a UIAA-registered climbing club.

Paddling

Beguilingly wild, the **River Ourthe** carves through a deep wooded valley. It's brisk-flowing rather than whitewater, and kayak hire can include a bus ride upstream to let paddlers go with the flow.

© Visit Flanders

> **ICONIC EVENT**
> Bleak, blustery and bonkers, the De Panne Beach Endurance race is a 52km charge along wet sand beside the North Sea. There's a mass-start of 1300 riders on mountain bikes.

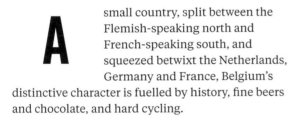
Testing bikes and joints on Flanders' notorious cobbles.

BELIZE

Belize flies under the radar of Central American destinations, but it's a pocket-sized powerhouse when it comes to adventure pursuits.

B ordered by Mexico to the north, Guatemala to the west and the Caribbean Sea to the east, Belize is the odd one out in Central America – the only nation where English is the official language, despite a melting pot of cultures spanning Maya, Mestizo and Garifuna. Off-shore lies the world's second-largest barrier reef (after Australia's great one), while inland you'll find jungle-strewn Maya ruins, remote treks and some of the craziest caves in the Americas.

Diving

There are few diving destinations in the world as magnetic as the **Blue Hole** on Belize's Lighthouse Reef. Seen from the air this deep-blue 300m-diameter watery pupil, rimmed by a shallower aquamarine iris, is the visual icon of diving in Belize. The descent into the sinkhole is relatively deep – up to 40m – and inky dark, despite the clarity of the water. The nerve-racking but exhilarating part is gliding beneath the limestone overhang and along the underwater walls. Most dives are sub 10 minutes, but it's an otherworldly underwater experience not to be missed.

Sea Kayaking

Kayaking around the reefs and cayes off the coast of Belize is sensational, but for a real adventure head out to far-flung **Glover's Reef Atoll**, a string of islands a two- or three-hour boat ride from the mainland. Formed by a submerged mountain ridge, the reefs and lagoons here are an unsurpassed paradise for kayakers, divers and snorkellers, while the chilled island lodges exude the ultimate castaway feel.

Caving

The 4.8km-long **Actun Tunichil Muknal** (ATM), Cave of the Stone Sepulchre, is a breathtaking

Diving the reef off St George's Caye.

© Douglas Klug | Getty Images

subterranean experience, taking you deep into the underworld that the ancient Maya knew as Xibalba. An obligatory guided tour, best organised in San Ignacio, will take you through freezing rivers, blackened holes, past walls of calcite flowstone and Maya artefacts, until you reach the spine-chilling calcified skeleton of the cave's namesake 'Crystal Maiden' – a centuries-old crystallised sacrifice of a young girl. It's tough going and you will get very wet, but you'll be kitted out with hard-hat, headlamp and led by an experienced guide into a world that leaves many people humbled and weak-kneed.

Cave Tubing
The Caves Branch River floods another underground network, **Nohoch Che'en Caves**, providing ideal conditions for cave tubing. After a short jungle trek, you climb into a rubber tube and float through the darkened caves, where stalactites and strange Maya paintings on the cave walls are illuminated by your

KENDALL BEYMER ON THE BLUE HOLE
'All divers find something to love on Belize's Barrier Reef, but the Blue Hole is unique. You stare at a wall for 40m, then it blows your mind by ballooning into a massive cavern, with the largest stalagmites I've seen.'
Kendall Beymer, Ecologic Divers, San Pedro, Belize

headlight. For a more extreme adventure, a guide will take you on a full day spelunking trip deep into the system, wading through streams, scrambling over rocks and emerging into the extraordinary Crystal Cave.

Ziplining
Flying through the jungle canopy on a zipline (flying fox) is a thrilling experience, and Belize does it well with at least six set-ups scattered around the country. Hooked to a safety harness you zoom from tower platform to platform, crossing rivers and canyons and climbing ever higher. Calico Jack's in Cayo features a canyon swing and a cable walk, while at Mayflower Bocawina you can fly down Belize's longest zipline then rappel down a waterfall. Perhaps the most remote zipline is at Blue Creek in the Deep South of the Toledo District, which is reached by a 40km 4WD drive followed by a jungle trek.

Running beneath Jomolhari (7326m) in the Bhutanese Himalayas.

BHUTAN

Enter the Land of the Thunder Dragon for a dizzying dose of precipitous adventure pursuits.

B hutan's policy of Gross Domestic Happiness, a principle officially regarded as more important than measures like Gross Domestic Product, may be the reason Bhutanese collectively sport a permanent smile (or maybe they just have an inside line on what a well-kept secret the nation represents for adventurers seeking raw and undeveloped experiences).

Trekking & Trail Running

The remote **Snowman Trek** is high on most trekkers' (and runners') wish lists. The 300km route snakes up gigantic valleys, climbing high over more than a dozen passes punching past 5000m, with the second half all completed above 4000m. You'll need to book through a trekking agency for a traditional trek package supported by a team of donkeys. Be prepared for long days on trail and the possibility of passes being snowed in.

Mountain Biking

MTB has been popularised by Bhutan's King Wangchuck, an ardent fan, and with trails linking many villages, routes are opening up. While most of Bhutan's cycling adventures are routed along dirt roads, there are some established singletracks, including fast and flowy **Jiligang**, in Punakha Valley; the 13km **Tharpaling trail**, beginning near a monastery and descending 1000m; and the 14km **Pho Chhu trail**, also in Punakha, which crosses one of the country's longest suspension bridges.

Paddling

With six major glacial rivers shooting off the steep flanks of the Himalayas, it's no wonder Bhutan excites kayakers and rafters. The **Paro Chhu** in Paro Valley and the **Upper Pho Chhu** in Punakha Valley both feature Class III–IV rapids, the latter pumping at 85 cubic metres per second. For experts, the **Mo Chuu**, also in Punakha, pushes the extreme of Class V and is for kayaks only, as it's too steep for rafts.

UNCLAIMABLE ADVENTURE

Bhutan's Gangkhar Puensum (7570m) is the world's highest unclimbed mountain. There have been historical attempts, but in 1994 the Bhutanese government closed peaks higher than 6000m to climbers, out of respect for local spiritual beliefs, so its virginity remains sacrosanct.

© Chris Ord

BOLIVIA

South America's poorest country is rich in natural wonders. Here anyone can scale the highest peak or pioneer a new route into undiscovered territory.

Known as the Tibet of South America, Bolivia's landlocked terrain is actually extraordinarily diverse. Its main city, La Paz, sits 3640m up on the Andes' vast Altiplano plateau, where the locals wisely chew or brew coca leaves to ease the punishing effects of altitude. But within hours of La Paz you can raft a lush jungle river, kayak the world's highest lake or bathe in desert hot springs. Among the foothills that fall away to the east are pristine cloud forests and semi-arid canyons hiding pre-Incan ruins and underground worlds, with the Amazon basin stretching far to the north and the near-impenetrable Gran Chaco plain bordering the south.

Mountain biking

Bolivia's Andean spine provides multiple downhill thrill-rides within easy reach of La Paz. Treacherous dirt roads, old mining tracks and ancient Inca trails plunge vertiginously from the parched Altiplano into the cloud forests of Amazon foothills where many first-descents can still be attempted.

By far the most popular route is the spectacular **Death Road**. From a chilly mountain pass north of La Paz, it's a 65km, almost non-stop descent through the cloud-line and countless overhanging waterfalls to the balmy subtropical town of Coroico, 3600m below. Once called 'the world's most dangerous road', a new highway on the opposite side of the valley means you'll now share the perilously

DON'T LEAVE WITHOUT...
Cycling the world's biggest salt flats, Salar de Uyuni, a disorientating, surreal and unforgettable experience. In the vast white expanse, you'll encounter Dalí-esque standing rocks, brightly coloured hot springs and miraculous colonies of chinchillas and flamingoes.

© flirom | Getty Images

Descending the notorious Death Road, 65km of almost non-stop downhill.

Cowboy country: the rust-red canyons of Tupiza are best visited on horseback.

the biggest draw for horse-riding explorers. This is old bandit country, where Butch Cassidy and the Sundance Kid famously laid low while being hunted by the Pinkerton Agency, and you'll feel every inch the outlaw trotting through remote gorges of majestic rock spires and cacti. You can follow in Butch and the Kid's hoof marks to the frontier mining town of San Vicente on a three-day trek through sweeping badlands, although you'll find no tombstone marked with their names in the eerie, edge-of-the-world graveyard where they were apparently buried after the famous shootout.

At the opposite end of the country, saddle up with the *vanqueros* (Bolivia's poncho-wearing cowboys) on one of the vast *estancias* (ranches) in the tropical **Reyes** pampas. You'll need to learn to lasso before heading out into the open grasslands on your steed to help round up livestock. Wading through piranha-infested lagoons, with the calls of howler monkeys and exotic birds overhead, you realise that this is a ranch experience like no other.

Hiking

The brilliant-white crowns of the **Cordillera Real** mountain range, which march in regal splendour from Lake Titicaca to La Paz, are the perfect place to try high-altitude trekking for the first time. Many of the summits can be reached on two- or three-day non-technical routes, from trailheads with quick road access. At just over 6000m, **Huayna Potosí** is the most accommodating (literally), with staffed huts up its glaciated eastern flank. But you'll still encounter some huge, heart-stopping crevasses on the way to the steep final snow climb, where some exhilarating ice-climbing takes you to the airy summit. The thousand-kilometre views, like the rarefied air at this height, are breathtaking.

Elsewhere, all manner of jungle hikes are possible among the cloud forests of the **Yungas** valleys that lead to the Amazonian gateway town of Rurrenabaque, where machetes and dug-out canoes can take you into the fecund jungle. But don't miss your chance to walk alongside dinosaurs in the **Torotoro National Park**, not far from Cochabamba. Among the dramatic canyons and caves in this high valley are great raised flanks of mudstone rock with the giant preserved footprints of unknown prehistoric creatures, marching up into the skies above you. Close by, the blind catfish of **Humajalanta Cave** and the lush swimming holes and waterfalls of **El Vergel** are waiting to be discovered in this wondrously timeless world.

narrow switchbacks that hang over dizzying 300m drops with few other vehicles.

But there are even wilder singletrack alternatives for experienced riders. From **Chacaltaya** (once the world's highest ski resort, before its glacier melted in 2006, leaving the rickety 1939 ski hut stranded in scree) you can thunder 4300m towards the jungle floor of the Zongo Valley. It's arguably the biggest one-day mountain-bike descent in the world.

Horse Riding

The miniature Wild West of rust-red canyons and rugged hills in the south, surrounding **Tupiza**, is

© Jess Kraft | 500px

BOSNIA & HERZEGOVINA

Untouched, unexplored and unspoiled, this conjoined, once war-torn nation on the Balkan Peninsula offers excellent adventures, without the crowds.

Since gaining independence in 1992, Bosnia and Herzegovina has rebuilt itself into an accessible destination, yet it remains beyond the radar of many travellers. With rugged inland mountains and a tiny coastline, it has short, cool summers and severe winters. Remnants of the war remain, including Sarajevo's intriguing suburban supply tunnel and the skull-adorned mine-warning sites in the mountains, but there are plenty of safe places to explore.

Canyoning

Water is a strong theme in a land with more than a thousand rivers and streams. Canyoners will love the crystal-clear waters and endemic flora of **Rakitnica**, which has an eight-hour guided trip suitable for beginners. The **Bijela** and **Unac** rivers both have canyons with more advanced routes.

Paddling

The winding waters of the **Una** present several potential adventures, including a three-day paddle from Kulen Vakuf to Bosanska Krupa. The **Tara** offers decent whitewater kayaking, as do the **Trebižat** and **Krivaja** rivers, while the emerald-green **Neretva** is better for beginners.

Trekking & Climbing

The Bosnian section of the **Via Dinarica** – a 1930km trail through the Balkans that can be split into short hikes – runs on old trekking paths, military tracks, trade routes and shepherds' crossings. Highlights include the spectacular 4m-wide natural arch of Hajdučka Vrata on Mt Čvrsnica, and 2067m Bjelašnica mountain, one of the country's top trekking destinations. Between the traditional and historic villages of Umoljani and Lukomir (Bosnia's highest village), there is a superb 8km section passing centuries-old water mills. Elsewhere, **Sutjeska National Park** offers easy access trails to mountain lakes and guided-only treks into nearby primeval Perućica forest, with giant 50m-high trees and a 70m waterfall. The mountains attract climbers too: the rocks at **Drežnica**, near Mostar, are suitable for beginners, while experienced alpinists can try ascending 2226m **Čvrsnica** in Herzegovina.

Mountain Biking & Skiing

An unsung MTB destination, Bosnia's **Dinaric Alps** offer myriad top trails for rough riders. Cycle the undulating 40km trail along **Ruište-Boračko lake** to Konjic or head to the **Bjelašnica** mountain resort for downhill action. In winter, Bjelašnica's slopes are enjoyed by skiers and snowboarders.

© marco wong | Getty Images

DON'T LEAVE WITHOUT...
Checking out the bridge jumping. Leaping from iconic Stari Most (Old Bridge) in Mostar is historically a rite of passage for local lads. For a fee, the city's dive club teaches tourists how to survive the jump, but be warned, the 20m plunge into the icy Neretva river is a dangerous business and definitely best left to the locals.

The leap from Mostar's Stari Most is not for the faint of heart.

BOTSWANA

Water either dominates the Botswanan landscape or is breathtakingly absent. The cycle of life this dichotomy creates is amazing to see, whether by boat, saddle or on foot.

Botswana is certainly not the place to come for mountain highs, but flatness is perhaps its greatest strength. As the Okavango River's waters reach the inland delta they are free to spread, breathing unprecedented life into 18,000 sq km of desert. This watery, wildlife-filled oasis, along with epic salt pans and vast stretches of the Kalahari, provide compelling challenges for human- or horse-powered exploration.

Mokoro Trips

You won't set any speed records when gliding through the myriad channels of the **Okavango Delta**, but in a *mokoro* (traditional dugout canoe) you don't have to – this is a thrill experienced in gloriously slow motion. Sitting just below water level, with your head among the vegetation, you're almost hemmed in by its wonder. Reach out and let the reeds roll slowly off your fingertips, gaze deeply into the maze to spot minuscule frogs and other wonders, or simply lean back and look up to a blue sky painted with the colourful calls and wings of the delta's birdlife.

Cycle Safaris

Elephants have been migrating across what is now the **Northern Tuli Game Reserve** for millennia, and now you can mountain bike in their giant footsteps. And, for sections of your journey, you'll likely be in close quarters with their living descendants (and even the odd lion or two). The four-day cycle safaris along the **Mashatu Wilderness Trail** run from March through November.

Horseback Safaris

Experienced riders can saddle up and take on astonishing environments in Botswana: wade wither-deep into the **Okavango Delta** while tracking animals between seasonal islands, gallop across the sun-baked **Makgadikgadi Pans** with migrating zebra and wildebeest, or venture into the **Central Kalahari**, land of the black-maned lions.

DON'T LEAVE WITHOUT...
Hiking into the sacred Tsodilo Hills to examine some of the 4000 prehistoric San rock paintings – it's an outdoor art gallery like no other.

A lioness in full predator mode, Duba Plains, Okavango Delta.

© Brendon Cremer | 500px

BRAZIL

Home to the planet's biggest river, most immense jungle and 7400km of Atlantic-stroked beaches – Brazil is a sensationally sultry centre of exotic adventure.

The world's fifth largest country tempts travellers with myriad adventures, from exploring epic kite-surfing conditions along the curvy Atlantic coastline to tackling trails, paddling tributaries and clambering up towering trees in the sweaty embrace of the Amazon Jungle – a wilderness so enormous it still contains lost cities and tribes that have no contact with the outside world. Seventy-six national parks provide great trekking and trail-running opportunities, while on- and off-road cyclists are well catered for, and rock climbers can explore cracking crags, including routes on Rio's iconic Sugarloaf Mountain.

Trail Running

Challenging routes can be explored all through Brazil's diverse national parks, but the annual **Jungle Marathon** is the ultimate Brazilian – and Amazonian – trail-running challenge. The race attracts ultrarunners from around the world who want to test themselves against Earth's biggest jungle, tackling swamps, river crossings, scorching heat and humidity, and the odd apex predator. Runners have to be self-sufficient (except for water), and choose between 127km and 254km distances. The night stages are particularly memorable as the jungle comes to cacophonous life and the Amazon glistens under bright moonlight. Armed guards patrol some sections of the race, protecting runners against panthers. Beware the anacondas as well.

Trekking

Walking in Brazil is all about variety. **Chapada Diamantina National Park** in the east is a forested landscape of dramatic tabletop mountains, spectacular waterfalls (Fumaça and Buracao) and caves. **Vale do Pati** is a 68km hike through the remote and sparsely populated interior highlands of Bahia, with overnight stays hosted by locals. Minas Gerais' **Serra do Cipó National Park** in the southeast offers mountains, waterfalls and wild flowers, and in the northeast you can trek across the lagoon- and dune-dotted lunar-like landscape of the **Lençóis Maranhenses National Park**. And, just an hour's drive from the favelas of Rio de Janeiro, verdant **Serra dos Órgãos National Park** could be on another planet; multiple walks can be enjoyed here, including to the park's highest peak, Pedra do Sino, 14km from the entrance.

Mountain Biking

Rio's Olympic mountain-bike course, **Deodroro X-Park**, opened to the public after the Games. The 5.4km-long track reflects Rio's culture and geography, with sandal-shaped dirt pits and coconut trees, a short climb to 'Flag Mountain' and a technical boulder-strewn descent. More groomed

Ipanema. For a bigger challenge, keen roadies can trace the 3000km coastline separating Porto Alegre in Rio Grande do Sul in the south and Salvador in Bahia in the north, a route that skirts Florianópolis' amazing beaches.

Paddling

To experience the headspins (insanely verdant fecundity, pink dolphins, potential sightings of capuchin monkeys, tapirs, three-toed sloths and caiman) and horrors (piranhas, humidity and horrendous insects) of the Brazilian rainforest, you need to travel along the water that powers it all. Multiday jungle-piercing **canoe** trips can be taken along tributaries of the Amazon, such the Urubu, which can be accessed via Manaus.

Sea kayaking is possible all along the Atlantic coast – including around Rio, offering a unique perspective of iconic sights such as Sugarloaf Mountain and Christ the Redeemer – but the Costa Verde in southeast Brazil, accessed via Paraty in the Bay of Ilha Grande, is particularly spectacular, with dramatic Jurassic Park-esque coastline vistas and even a tropical fjord: Saco do Mamanguá.

Just 74km from the megatropolis of São Paulo, the Juquitiba River washes the urban grime from wide-eyed paddle-grabbers during **white-water rafting** trips that are at their Grade III–V feistiest in November–March. Rafting can also be enjoyed on the Foz do Iguaçu, by the famous falls, and on Rio Novo in Minas Gerais, Tijucas River in Santa Catarina and Jacaru River in Para.

Surfing

Southern Brazil has the best surf, with epic oceanic swells hitting the Atlantic coast during the peak April–October season. Santa Catarina is the go-to state, and 40-beach **Florianópolis** is Brazil's surf capital. Hollow right- and left-handers are found at Santinho, Galheta and Praia, while Joaqunia and Meio da Joca both have powerful lefts and rights.

Itacaré, with its diverse coastline on the central coast of Bahia (Salvador) offers great surf. Boca da Barra has a right-hander stretching for up to 2km, while Corais and Itacarezinho form tubes, and Tirinica, short, fast-travelling hollow waves. **Arquipélago de Fernando de Noronha**, a volcanic archipelago 354km off Brazil's northern coastline, has some of the best surf northeast of Recife.

© José Eduardo Nucci; Cesar Okada | Getty Images

DON'T LEAVE WITHOUT...
Taking a tandem hang-gliding flight from Pedra Bonita over Rio de Janeiro, landing on a beach below. Check that the operator is certified by the Brazilian Hang-Gliding Association.

singletrack can be found at **Cemucam** in Cotia (São Paulo), where the 34km loop hosts the Brazilian mountain bike championships and 24-hour races. Those looking for an off-road journey can explore the 80km east–west traverse of sensational **Serra da Canastra National Park** in Minas Gerais, starting from the main entrance, São Roque de Minas, and finishing by the 186m-high waterfall Cachoeira Casca D'Anta.

Road Cycling

Starting at Flamengo and finishing with a 7km loop of Lagoa, the flat-and-easy Rio cyclepath can be ridden in a couple of hours and grants bikers an eyeful of everything the city is famed for: Sugarloaf Mountain, Urca, Praia Vermelha, Copacabana and

São Paulo has good surfing conditions just a couple of hours away on the state's northern coastline, where **Maresias** is well-known for its tubes. The area is also popular for **stand-up paddleboarding**, **bodyboarding** and **longboarding**.

Kitesurfing & Windsurfing

Fortaleza, on the northeast coast, is Brazil's kite capital, with the area from Cumbuco to Flexeiras offering perfect wind conditions of 20- to 26-knots. Favourable breezes blow June–January across beaches such as **Jericoacoara**. Nearby **Tatajuba** is a shallow-water spot that lays claim to some of Brazil's best winds, sometimes reaching 45 knots. **Barra de Lagoa**, south of Rio near Florianópolis, offers great conditions for beginners, with its flat lagoon.

Diving

Arquipélago de Fernando de Noronha, a 21-island marine park, has fantastic diving. Visibility can exceed 40m, and wildlife includes whales, lemon and reef sharks, clownfish, parrotfish and more. Closer to the mainland, **Banco de Panela** near Salvador is notable for wreck diving and marine life. While **Recife** is the place to go for shipwrecks – a hundred vessels are strewn on the seabed.

Climbing

Brazil offers great climbing, from world-class bouldering to 600m walls. São Paulo and Minas Gerais both have crags, but Rio is the urban climbing capital of the world. Its national park is home to an urban forest, with hidden crags and boulders, most of which are granite.

Minais Gerais in the southeast has mainly limestone and quartzite crags, and offers sport and bouldering. **Ninhos** (the namesake of the local town) is a classic route with overhangs, but to access the route you have to do an unprotected scramble.

For something different, score a toucan-eye's view of the Amazon by going **tree climbing**. Organised trips leave from Manaus and take punters up to 90m on giant ceiba and angelim trees.

*Below, multipitch climbing on Sugarloaf Mountain high above Rio de Janeiro. **Left**, golden hour SUPing in one of Rio's many bays.*

BULGARIA

Beautiful Bulgaria is bulging with adventure, be it beavering through bountiful mountains or diving below the blue waters of the Black Sea.

Bulgaria may be more famous for corruption than its incredible natural environment, but that is slowly changing. From the Balkan Mountains, which run laterally through the centre of the country, to the alpine ranges of Rila and Pirin in the southwest, and the Rhodope Mountains further east, visitors will find mountains and thickly forested valleys roamed by lynx, wolves and bears. Bulgaria's dynamic climate is perfect for paragliders, while on the coast the Black Sea is littered with exciting wrecks for divers to explore.

Hiking

There are boundless options for walkers visiting Bulgaria. One of the most dramatic and historic walks in the country is the three- to four-day trip from **Mt Musala** (2925m), Bulgaria's highest peak, passing alpine meadows, rocky cirques and glacial lakes to end up at the World Heritage–listed **Rila Monastery**, which was founded in the 10th

century and is one of Bulgaria's most famous sights. In nearby Pirin, **Vihren** (2914m) is another classic target for peak-baggers. But there are excellent networks of trails throughout Bulgaria, and walkers can explore between remote villages, ending long days with a glass of rakia (grape brandy) in one of the country's vast network of *hizhas* (hiking huts).

Climbing & Mountaineering

Climbing in Bulgaria is a revelatory experience; the country is dotted with numerous small but unique crags. Sport climbers should visit **Prohodna Cave** at Karlukovo, a bizarre limestone cavern with two entrances and two skylights in the roof known as the 'Eyes of God'. The area is not for beginners, with routes up to 8c+. **Lakatnik**, just north of the capital Sofia, is Bulgaria's most popular climbing area with 250 sport routes. Traditional climbers and alpinists will find their own piece of paradise amid the superb granite towers and crags gracing the **Rila** and **Pirin** mountains.

Above, snowshoeing in the Pirin Mountains. Right, the bulbous Dômes de Fabédougou.

© Stuny | Getty Images

Kayaking

While Bulgaria is riddled with rivers, many are too small for paddling – but there are a few exceptions. The **Kamchia** and **Struma** rivers are popular with guiding companies, and are excellent trips for beginners, while the tight, technical rapids of the **Devinska** and **Buinovska** are better suited to experienced paddlers. On the coast, sea kayaking trips are popular on the **Black Sea**, with plenty to explore, from beautiful beaches and towns to sea cliffs and Roman ruins.

Skiing & Snowboarding

With many peaks over 2500m, the **Rila** and **Pirin** mountains hold the country's best resorts. **Borovets** and **Pamporovo** are popular with Bulgarians and visitors alike, but one of the up-and-coming spots is found at the foot of the Pirin mountains – the historic village of **Bansko** (there are ruins dating back to 100BC). Bansko has 14 lifts covering two mountains, glorious forested runs and reliable snow (it also

has snow-making equipment). It is also one of the cheapest places you will find anywhere to try the ultimate skiing indulgence – heli-skiing.

Paragliding

A diverse landscape and dynamic weather patterns make Bulgaria one of Europe's best paragliding (and hang-gliding) destinations. There are many launch sites in the mountains, with **Sopot** in the Balkan Mountains being one of the most popular spots. Good flying conditions can also be found on the coast.

Diving

With marine history going back to antiquity, diving in the Black Sea is all about wrecks and historic sites. Divers can visit the remnants of the German WWII Black Sea fleet, from a battleship to minelayers and torpedo boats, or explore spooky sunken WWII Soviet submarines. North of Varna, there's an old Roman port at 12m, with the treasure of Alexander the Great rumoured to be buried nearby.

ICONIC RACE

With 5840m of ascent, the gruelling Tryavna Ultra takes trail runners 141km through the Balkan Mountains, past such highlights as the flying saucer–like brutalist Buzludzha Monument, built to celebrate communism then abandoned.

BURKINA FASO

Burkina Faso's rocky terrain will mesmerise and inspire action.

Bridging the gulf between the southern Sahara's sands and the green woodlands and grasses of the tropical savannah, Burkina Faso offers some enchanting surprises.

Hike among giants on Sindou Peaks – one of the country's most unforgettable sights, with its anthropomorphic rock features. The Dômes de Fabédougou near Banfora are just as intriguing; the great, bulbous outcrops resemble Australia's famous Bungle Bungles, but you'll have them to yourself. **Bouldering** and **rock climbing** are both good options, and afterwards you can head to Karfiguéla Waterfalls for a **swim** in one of the natural pools.

DON'T LEAVE WITHOUT...

Climbing Nahouri Peak, a cone-shaped karst that towers hundreds of metres above the surrounding savannah. The ascent is steep, but the 360-degree views from the top pay back your effort with interest.

© lalvarezg / Getty Images

CAMBODIA

Cambodia's past is populated by modern horror and astonishing antiquity, but this enigmatic country offers a present full of alluring adventures.

T hough tiny, Cambodia's burgeoning adventure scene is slowly opening thatched doors to the country's most remote corners, revealing spellbinding diving on remote reef systems, epic hiking through untrammelled jungle terrain and a diversity of Mekong River experiences.

Diving

Pretty gritty Sihanoukville is a fuzzy moustache on Cambodia's southwestern lip, known for its lively backpacker vibe, golden stretches of sand, and spectacular diving and snorkelling. Visitors hoping to go nose-to-nose with whale sharks can board a skiff bound for **Koh Prins**, some five-hours from shore, where unblemished soft coral, countless reef fish, turtles and exotic nudibranchs await. Cambodia's diving epicentre is comprised

of three main islands: Koh Prins (Big Island), Koh Moan (Chicken Island) and Naked Island. Caves, sheer vertical cliff faces and deep trenches are the hallmarks, but thanks to generally gentle underwater currents, even divers new to the sport can go deep into the blue. Night diving at the Anemone Garden is a feature experience on a grand scale – mingle with blue-spotted stingrays, energetic moray eels, rare bamboo sharks, catsharks and more. Many of the outer islands are uninhabited, but serve as excellent in-between getaway destinations for divers looking for an opportunity to recharge with sand between their toes and sunshine on their shoulders.

Trekking

Endangered gibbons provide a bombastic soundtrack to Cambodia's adventures, where the cacophony of raindrops on the jungle canopy in an

Ankor Wat at sunset; touring the site by bike is a wonderful way to get around.

© Danny Iacob | 500px

otherwise silent green world can seem as loud as any subway train. Hiking here involves walking through one of the world's few remaining wild frontiers.

Virachey National Park

Way, way removed from the banana-pancake trail, in Cambodia's remote northeast, lies humbling Virachey National Park, the largest parcel of protected land in the country. Here, the intrepid lace their boots tight, clutch machetes in sweaty palms and venture deep into the jungle, time-travelling to a world long forgotten. Far more rugged than the jungles in neighbouring Thailand, trails (where there are trails) can be punishing in difficult weather, but the rewards are great – some glimpse tigers and others spy on clouded leopards. Treetop ecolodges provide a unique experience for hikers looking to sleep eye-to-eye with gibbons and exotic birds. There are no vehicles inside the park – some areas have never been explored. One

multiday trek leads to grassy **Phnom Veal Thom**, with the only way back being by foot or inflatable kayak. This is an eight-day, seven-night adventure that reads like a Cambodian greatest hits collection: spot wildlife that includes gibbon, sambar deer and noisy hornbills, bathe in waterfall whirlpools, traverse rivers and streams, and overnight in hill tribe villages.

Banlung

Local guides (a must) can be arranged via Banlung, but overnight stays with local Kavet villagers serve as a cultural awakening for most visiting hikers, who find life in the jungle incomprehensibly challenging. Banlung, a frontier outpost, is the trailhead for many treks: a trio of towering waterfalls (Chaong, Katieng and Kachang) are 8km, 9km and 6km outside of town, respectively; the Yeak Laom Crater Lake (5km) features a loop trail that delivers

DON'T LEAVE WITHOUT...
Cycling around Angkor Wat, a 12th-century World Heritage–listed monument and the world's largest religious site, close to Siem Reap. Ride from crumbling tower to ancient pagoda to serene pond, basking in boundless positive vibes.

The mysterious cave temple of Phnom Chhnork.

intrepid hikers to a remote hill tribe village; and an impressive wat, Rahtanharahm, nestled in the foothills of the Eisey Patamak Mountains, is 1km from town. A trail from Rahtanharahm leads into the mountains, where a giant reclining Buddha looks out over the vast countryside.

Caving & Climbing

The 203 gruelling steps that lead up, then down – way, deep down – to the cave temple of **Phnom Chhnork** open up an other-worldly, subterranean realm. Phnom Chhnork is a short, 8km hop from the cosy town of Kampot, and features Funan-era shrines (5th – 7th centuries), monuments to the deity Shiva, and relics that pre-date even the great Angkor Wat. Say hello to the stalactite elephant that defiantly congests one of the passageways (for luck, of course). Nearby is the **Phnom Sera** cave system, home to so many ancient treasures that you'll enter feeling like Indiana Jones, if only for a day (entry fees are roughly $1, bullwhips are sold separately). Visit the caves at **Phnom Sorsia** if you're into bat caves. Kampot-based guides offer tours combining rock climbing, via ferrata, abseiling and caving, flecking your underground adventure with colourful anecdotes, legends and lore.

Paddling

The mighty **Mekong River** is the lifeblood of Southeast Asia, and kayaking the delta is guaranteed to raise your pulse. Lucky paddlers may spy the Irrawaddy dolphin, a gentle giant known to occasionally skim the surface alongside kayaks and skiffs. Given the breadth and scope of the Mekong, kayaking opportunities are near limitless in Cambodia, and you can spend days travelling from one remote village to the next, or a few hours paddling from a put-in in Phnom Penh. Fewer visitors explore the **Tonle Sap River**, but those who do are well rewarded. The Tonle Sap ecosystem is remarkable in its biodiversity (scientists have recorded more than 200 species of plants, 150 species of fish, the world's greatest number of freshwater snakes, a wide variety of bird species, many of which are endemic and endangered, and even the rare Siamese crocodile and the Mekong giant catfish). Outfitters have popped up throughout the country in recent years, though the bulk are clustered in the capital.

© Mark Andrews | Alamy

CAMEROON

Soaring summits, rolling hills and an endless array of paths to explore on foot, bicycle or boat – Cameroon is full of physical challenges and cultural rewards.

R ippling with hills and punctuated by active volcanoes of various sizes, including West Africa's largest mountain, Cameroon has incredible (and largely untapped) trekking potential. Most of the rivers and roads are untamed and make exciting (if hard) conduits for an exploration of the country's varied landscapes and fascinating culture.

Climbing Mt Cameroon

Who says you shouldn't play with fire? Climbing up West Africa's most active volcano is definitely a feat worth attempting. Dramatic Mt Cameroon, its slopes dotted with more than 100 cinder cones from recent eruptions (the last in 2012), towers 4095m above the Gulf of Guinea. Trekking over its basaltic lava flows to the top of West Africa should take two to three days, and is certainly not just a walk in the park – the trails start near sea level, so you're covering more than 4000m of vertical terrain in a fairly short distance. Take the Mann Spring route up and descend via the Guinness Route.

Cycling the Ring Road

Riding the **Ring Road** 367km through Cameroon's northwest highlands is as much of a cultural reward as it is an assault on your legs and buttocks. The rough, seldom paved and occasionally muddy route holds the greatest concentration of traditional kingdoms (*fondoms*) in Cameroon, as well as lakes, scenic hills and sharp mountains.

River Exploration

Kribi boasts Cameroon's best beaches, but pull yourself away for a motorised canoe adventure up the fast flowing **Lobe River**. Starting atop the Chutes de la Lobé you'll travel through thick, tortuous sections of mangroves before stopping at a pygmy settlement.

© szymanskim | Getty Images

ICONIC RACE

The Race of Hope (Course de l'espoir) is a 42km trail run to the summit of Mt Cameroon (4095m). Temperatures can vary from 40°C (start) to 0°C (finish).

Hiking through the craters of Mt Cameroon.

CANADA

Everything about Canada is big – mountains, forests, waterways and coastline – and the scope for adventure within this extraordinary natural landscape is immense.

The world's second-largest country backs up its physical size with an impressive array of outdoor opportunities, ranging from multiday hikes and paddling journeys to some of the world's most iconic cycling trails and epic alpine climbs. Perhaps the ultimate adventure challenge is thrown down by the monstrous 24,000km-long, close-to-completion Trans Canada Trail (TCT), the world's most extensive network of linked recreational routes – which joins east and west coasts and connects the Pacific, Arctic and Atlantic Oceans – and can be attempted by hikers, bikers, runners, horse riders and, in winter, skiers. You can, of course, bite off chunks, rather than attempting to eat the entire elephant all at once.

The sheer diversity of Canada's topography demands visitors take an adventurous approach. The west packs in terrain ranging from the craggy spires of the Rocky Mountains and steep forested coastal ranges to the dense forests and subarctic tundra of the northern provinces and the wild Pacific Ocean that pounds remote islands and the coast. Canada's interior is a mix of rolling plains and immense lakes, the far north and its remote islands represent a quintessential Arctic landscape, while the east offers drama of a different kind, with its abundant rivers and lakes, towering sea cliffs, more islands and a rugged coastline abutting the Atlantic.

Hiking

Canada is criss-crossed with trekking trails, including myriad multiday odysseys in remote areas, covering terrain that varies wildly from mountain ranges to lush, rich coastal rainforests, not forgetting the east coast's barren but majestic cliff-side rambles. Hiking here doesn't have to mean lugging a pack for weeks, though, because there are numerous day-hike options across the country. Heli-hiking is a brilliant option, as are lodge-based walking adventures, such as those found in the Bugaboos mountain range in eastern BC. These aren't cheap, but the price is offset by the fact you can be transported by chopper to a trailhead, walk for most of the day, then be picked up and flown back to the lodge for a shower, dinner and a few celebratory drinks at the lodge bar.

British Columbia (BC)

If you only experience one multiday hike, it's hard to beat the 75km **West Coast Trail** (WCT), a moderate-to-challenging seven- to nine-day ramble along the southwestern coastline of Vancouver Island, through the Pacific Rim National Park Reserve. It follows the route of an old rescue track that authorities (and survivors) used when the oft-wild seas of the Pacific Ocean smashed ships to pieces off the island's coast. The terrain lurches from long, sandy beaches to dense rainforest and rivers, through to root-filled tracks, old (and new) duckboard sections and more than 70 ladders that take you over the most challenging parts of the track – and also deliver you at day's end to your beachside campsite. It's a truly remote hike; the only reminder that the outside world still exists comes around the

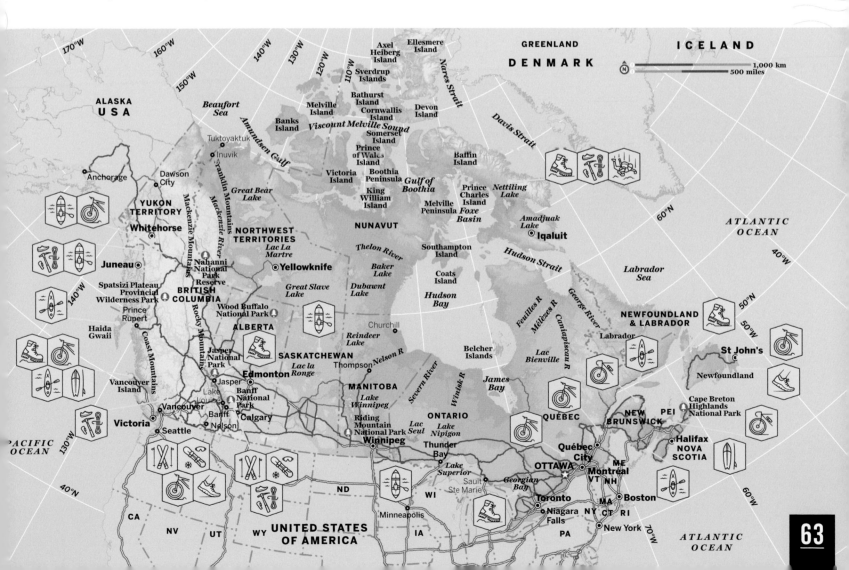

midway point, when Chez Monique's – a rustic café set right beside the beach and run by 78-year-old Monique Nytol – emerges like a mirage. Downing an ice-chilled beer and tasty burger in the middle of one of the world's most iconic multiday hikes is a memorable experience.

In the north of Vancouver Island, Cape Provincial Park boasts the **North Coast Trail**, a wonderfully wild and remote five-day hike that has all the appeal of the WCT but with far fewer people.

A very different walk can be tackled in BC's northwest, on the 53km **Chilkoot Trail**. This retraces the route used originally by the Tlingit First Nations people, then by desperate treasure-hunters in the late 1800s, lured from the world over by the siren call of the Klondike Gold Rush. The Chilkoot starts across the US border in Dyea, Alaska, travelling through coastal forest, before taking you back into Canada and northwest BC where you then start climbing high above the treeline into starkly beautiful alpine tundra through the Coast Mountains. The often snow-covered Chilkoot Pass (1074m) is a highlight; the crossing entails rock-hopping up a near-vertical pile of massive boulders to the top where, if you are not blown off by the howling winds funnelling through the pass, you can look back down over the terrain you've just ascended and wonder how the early prospectors managed it with all their gear. The

prospectors were required by Canadian law to carry with them an imperial ton of supplies in order to lessen the chance of them dying during the long, harsh winters. The landscape is sublime, as are the campsites along the trail.

Alberta

The **Willmore Wilderness**, in the central-west of Alberta, sprawls over 4597sq km and boasts an estimated 750km of trails. This remote park is probably Canada's best kept hiking secret – no roads enter, there are no bridges and no park entry fees. Walkers share this immense place with moose, bighorn sheep, mountain goats, caribou, wolves, and grizzly and black bears, in a landscape dominated by forest, huge mountains, glaciers, fast-flowing rivers and ridgelines up to 20km long. You can mountain bike and ride horses here, but off-trail hiking is what makes the park a standout. Ensure you are navigation-savvy, pack for all weather conditions, be bear-aware, and then look forward to as many days as you can spare experiencing some of the world's best wilderness hiking.

Next door, in better-known Jasper National Park, there are myriad magical trekking routes, including the 44km, 2- to 4-day **Skyline Trail**, which wends between Maligne Lake and Signal Mountain along an above-treeline track to dish up one of the Canadian Rockies' best backpacking adventures.

You're never far from amazing (and often terrifying) wildlife in Canada; a black bear and her cubs.

© Westend61 Premium / Shutterstock

Ontario

The 885km **Bruce Trail**, in Ontario's east, follows the rugged Niagara escarpment country, and is one of Canada's great long-distance trails. If you haven't got the required month or so to tackle the full version, there is the **Bruce Peninsula Traverse**, a cut-down, 10-day taster.

Newfoundland

On the eastern seaboard, on Newfoundland's west coast, you'll find the spectacle that is Gros Morne National Park, with its green-carpeted mountains, vast fiords, towering cliffs abutting the sea, and empty beaches. The **Snug Harbour to North Rim** two-day trek is superb, while for the more hardy and experienced, the **Long Range Traverse** beckons. This three- to four-day hike entails navigation along a barely discernible route. The rewards for all the effort (the second day entails a big climb up to the plateau) are epic views across the fiords from the massive cliffs, with (most likely) no other hiker in sight.

Quebec

Southern Quebec's **Les Sentiers de l'Estrie** runs 200km from Sutton (near the US border and Vermont) in the south to the township of Kingsbury in the north. There are campsites dotted along the trail, and you traverse two small mountains (Sutton and Orford) as you skirt the northern reaches of the Appalachian Mountains. In total, there are more than 6000km of public trails available with many on the Gaspésie peninsula, including a section of the International Appalachian Trail.

Nunavut

Canada's Arctic province and its mix of landscapes – rugged mountains, vast beaches, tundra – contain plenty of hiking. The 177km **Itijjagiaq Trail**, in Baffin Island's southern section, is more a route than a marked trail (there is a guidebook available), but there are nine huts along the way so it's easy to link these up via the rolling hills and valleys that comprise this spectacular region, full of huge waterfalls and epic canyons.

*Below, running the Four Lakes Trail in Squamish, BC. **Overleaf**, freeriding at Roberts Creek, just north of Vancouver, BC.*

Trail Running

With its topographic variety, Canada is a stunning trail-running destination. As you'd expect, ski/MTB resorts across Canada, such as BC's **Whistler**, offer fantastic singletrack trails. Newfoundland and Labrador's **East Coast Trail**, on the spectacular Avalon Peninsula, is an off-road running hot spot. Multi-use trails can be easily accessed at various points along the 300km route, offering running that takes you right out to the edge of the coastline, with the roar of the Atlantic Ocean for company.

The little adventure hub of **Squamish** in BC has become a rough running hotspot, with many trails of different distances, from the 6km Four Lakes Trail to the route of the Squamish 50, a tough 80km race.

La Chute du Diable (Devil's Fall) is a challenging route (345m of ascent) over often loose singletrack through La Mauricie National Park in south Quebec. Another tough Quebec trail is the 18km Johannsen-Sommets-Grand Brule loop, which starts and finishes at Tremblant, 1.5 hours' drive northwest of Montreal.

ULTIMATE CHALLENGE
Held in Quebec's Charlevoix region, the annual Ultra-Trail Harricana in La Malbaie has races for all abilities and ages, from beginner-friendly 5km and 10km routes to 28km, 42km and 65km challenges, and the big one: a 125km endurance epic through the region's mountainous terrain.

© All Canada Photos | Alamy

Mountain Biking

There is no one spiritual home of mountain biking – the sport is too diverse in its disciplines for that – but ask any off-road rider to nominate a dream trip, and expect to hear Vancouver's North Shore mentioned immediately. But there's more to Canadian MTB than freeriding, though...

British Columbia

Right on Vancouver's doorstep, the **North Shore** is globally acknowledged as the birthplace of freeride MTB. It consists of three separate forest-clad mountains – Cypress Provincial Park, Mt Fromme and Mt Seymour – which are striped with trails and loaded with features including steep, loamy flow sections, log runs, ravines, loads of slippery tree-roots, large boulder roll-overs and drop-offs, and any number of crazy timber jumps and narrow platforms, all winding through dense rainforest.

Since the heady formative freeride days that saw a youthful Wade Simmons and Brett Tippie getting big air off incredibly high ramps built among the forest's towering trees, 'the Shore' (as riders term it) has not mellowed, but it has perhaps become slightly more relaxed. There is now a bunch of new runs catering for beginners and intermediate riders, while the legendary trails – Empress, Boogieman, Pipeline – are still challenging riders.

British Columbia also boasts **Whistler Blackcomb**. Initially a ski-only resort, Whistler is now regarded as one of the world's premier MTB centres, thanks to the 1998 opening of Whistler

Mountain Bike Park. The green season now rivals the white months in terms of visitor numbers, with more than 100,000 riders flocking to the park to take advantage of the 47-plus trails that cover a total distance of more than 250km. The trails range from easy greens to challenging black runs, so it is just a matter of picking your poison.

Knitting all this together is the seven-day BC Bike Race (www.bcbikerace.com), with each stage dishing up around 1500m of ascent and descent across some of the best singletrack riding on the planet, including the North Shore, Vancouver Island and Whistler.

Yukon Territory

Further north, **Whitehorse** offers more than 700km within the city limits alone, the majority of it along sublime singletrack fringed by flaming fireweed. In midsummer, these trails bask under the midnight sun and the local clubs organise a 24-hour race where bike lights are banned. Nearby, **Montana Mountain** in Carcross has an MTB network built by the Tagish First Nation community, which is world-class (*Outside* magazine recently named the trails of Whitehorse and Carcross as the International MTB Destination of the Year, placing them above everything BC has to offer).

Quebec

Monte-Sainte-Anne packs in close to 150km of sublime MTB trails, spread across 115km of cross-country routes, 25km of downhill runs (this has hosted a round of the UCI Downhill World Cup) and 9km of enduro trails. The best part? It is right next to Quebec International Airport, so you can fly in and be riding the same day.

Newfoundland and Labrador

The pretty fishing village of **St John's** hides a thriving MTB community and spectacular trails. These range from muddy, steep, root-laden downhill trails, such as the aptly named Satan's Choice (a 200m descent in less than 1km), to beautiful coastal cliff-side rides, such as the moderate-grade Torbay to Flatrock Trail, that includes creek crossings and an awesome turnaround at Flatrock Point, looking over the Atlantic Ocean.

HOMEGROWN ADVENTURE HERO

Andreas Hestler, an Olympian who has ridden the North Shore for decades, explains the area's history and appeal: 'Until they started going big, it was just mountain biking for people who loved tech-gnar. As the movement to freeride began, and big bikes morphed to meet the requirements of what was being built and ridden, a schism occurred. Watching things take off – from ballsy huck-and-hope to the birth of an entirely new style of fluid riding based on huge stunts and jumps – was amazing. The skills that evolved drew a line. Years later, while that line is still drawn generally on size of drop and bike ridden, the Shore is still a place that challenges everyone who needs a little zing in their lives. Now the bikes level the field and bring everyone together within an 80th percentile, but you gotta love it or it's gonna bite you!'

© Scott Markewitz | Getty Images

Cycle Touring and Bikepacking

Canada is a fantastic destination for cycle touring and bikepacking, the increasingly popular off-road version of multiday pedal-pushing missions, with the near-24,000km **Trans Canada Trail** (TCT) the biggest of a bulging bag of brilliant bike-able routes.

The mountains and valleys of the **Cariboo-Chilcotin** region (in BC) and Alberta's **Rocky Mountains** are ideal for bikepacking. Options include following old trails and sleeping in huts on Vancouver Island, or taking it easier and cycling a rail trail with the family, staying at towns or lodges along the way.

Road cyclists up for a serious challenge can tackle the **Crossing**, a six-week, 6521km titanic traverse of Canada, from Vancouver to Halifax in Nova Scotia. For the less ambitious cycle tourer, it's hard to beat Prince Edward Island. Off the east coast, just above Nova Scotia and adjacent to New Brunswick, the island is easily accessed via vehicle ferry and has the brilliant **Confederation Trail** (itself part of the Trans Canada Trail), which runs 435km, from one end of the island to the other. Nova Scotia's **Cabot Trail** is another three- to five-day road route that has beautiful coastal scenery and is achievable with reasonable fitness.

For the ultimate remote riding escapade, check out the **Dempster Highway**, a 730km gravel-road extravaganza that takes riders from 40km southeast of the Yukon Territory's Dawson City, all the way up to the Northwest Territories' town of Inuvik, 200km inside the Arctic Circle. The riding is challenging – there are only two towns en route, so you'll need to pack plenty of supplies (including bear spray) – but the scenery and wildlife is epic; you'll move from dense forest and big rolling hills across and over the Arctic Circle into a lunar-like tundra-tussled landscape. The best time to ride is in July and August, when the weather is better and you'll enjoy 24 hours of daylight along the more northerly sections of the highway.

A 900km round-trip of Quebec's **Gaspe Peninsula** is a serious challenge, taking cycle tourers along coastal highways with epic ocean views and through the vertiginous Chic-Choc mountains and the even steeper peaks in L'Anse Pleureuse. The recommended route is clockwise from Mont Joli; average time taken is 14 days. Those with less time might ride the 500km section along the **Route verte** (which, in its entirety, is a 5000km cycle network right around Quebec) that skips the northern section's challenging mountains.

Above, bikepacking through the vast expanses of the Northwest Territories on the Dempster Highway. Left, downhilling at Whistler, BC.

© Robert Postma | Getty Images

© GROGL / Getty Images

Canoeing

Canada is synonymous with canoeing. The country's waterways were initially navigated in open boats by First Nations people. Later, European settlers used them as avenues of discovery and then trade routes. Now, Canada's many rivers allow modern-day adventurers to explore the country's more remote and wild areas. Rivers like the Yukon, Snake and South Nahanni are iconic and surprisingly easy to access, thanks to the many canoe-based outfitters and guiding companies.

Yukon Territory
The **Yukon River** flows right past the Yukon Territory's capital, Whitehorse, en route to the famous gold-rush frontier settlement of Dawson

City. There's only one seriously technical obstacle en route, Five Fingers Rapid, which isn't too challenging if you listen to advice and take the right line (it's a boat-eater if run wrong). You can hire canoes in Whitehorse and there are brilliant riverside (and island-based) campsites along the way. The classic two-week trip is best done in high summer, under the midnight sun, which is when the Yukon River Quest takes place. The annual race sees paddlers take kayaks, one- and two-person canoes, SUPs and voyageur vessels (large eight-person canoes, the traditional boats of French-Canadian fur trappers), along this 715km stretch of the river almost non-stop.

Less experienced paddlers can spend 14–17 days exploring 300km of **Big Salmon River**, from Quiet

Canoe touring on the South Nahanni River.

Lake to Carmacks on the Yukon River, cutting through the Salmon Mountains, or take on a section of **Wind River**, accessed via float plane from the put-in point of McClusky Lake, with journey's end 10 days later at Taco Bar or, for those wanting a longer trip (an extra three days), Fort McPherson. More experienced paddlers should check out the mighty **Snake River**, another floatplane-accessed (from Duo Lakes) paddle, offering more rapids (mix of grade I and II with intermittent III) and a far longer journey, of 500km to Fort McPherson.

Northwest Territories

Sensational **South Nahanni River** takes paddlers through some of Canada's most spectacular terrain as it wends through deep canyons inside Nahanni National Park Reserve and the Mackenzie Mountains, and it offers plenty of land-based activities along the way, including day hikes up nearby peaks. It's also quite a challenge for canoeists (rafters have an easier time) thanks to its intermittent rapids. Most guided adventures (canoe and raft-based) kick off at what is a major highlight of the journey: Nailicho (Virginia Falls), which drops 96m and is an incredible sight. From the base of the waterfall, you follow the river down for eight to 10 days, camping on the banks each night, until journey's end at the First Nations community of Nahanni Butte.

Ontario

This province's many canoeing destinations include two standouts (both part of the 42-strong list of Canadian Heritage Rivers). **Boundary Waters–Voyageur Waterway** (a mix of lakes and rivers that straddle Ontario's southern border and into Minnesota in the US) is both a brilliant adventure canoeing destination, and at the same time a memorable history lesson; this route was the main link between Montreal and Lake Winnipeg during the 18th and 19th centuries. It was used by fur-traders initially, and then explorers looking to punch through the wilderness and further on into the wilder west.

Contained within a provincial park of the same name, the **French River** is also rich in First Nations and Voyageur history. Initially used as a travel route by indigenous people, such as the Huron and Ojibwe (there are numerous archaeological sites along the river), it was later navigated by fur traders and explorers, including Alexander Mackenzie. The river packs in rapids, waterfalls, gorges and lakes as it makes its way 105km from Lake Nipissing to Georgian Bay. You can opt for day canoe trips, overnighters or the full French River journey.

British Columbia

For family-based canoe adventures, BC's **Bowron Lake Provincial Park** (in the Chilcotin region of the province) and its world-rated Canoe Circuit is a must. This circuit (book ahead, only 25 canoes are allowed on the circuit daily) is 116km, takes paddlers across six separate lakes (Indianpoint, Isaac, Lanezi, Sandy, Spectacle and Bowron) and takes five to seven days. For those with less time, there is the shorter West Side Trip. This involves you paddling from Bowron to Unna Lake. Both options are brilliant, offering stunning views across the Cariboo Mountains, the chance spot iconic Canadian wildlife, including bears and moose, and sublime lakeside campsites.

Saskatchewan

The **Churchill River** runs west–east through northern Saskatchewan before finally emptying into the Arctic at Hudson Bay, Manitoba. The river itself is comprised of a chain of lakes linked together by waterfalls and sections of rapids (which can be either run or portaged around; the river is suited to paddlers of all skill levels) and was used more than a century ago by Canada's Voyageurs. The most popular way to run the 105km Saskatchewan section of the Churchill is by putting in at Sandfly Lake and finishing at Otter Rapids, but you can opt for longer or shorter journeys. Most guides/outfitters are based in the township of Missinipe.

Quebec

No matter how far you want to paddle, **La Verendrye Reserve** (about three hours' drive north of Ottawa) and its 800-plus-kilometres of canoe routes (one-way and circuits) has myriad options, including the **Gens de Terre River** on its eastern border. This five-day, 79km canoe journey is classed moderate to difficult, with plenty of portaging. The last 50km, in particular, earns its 'difficult' moniker, thanks to technical rapids and travel through deep canyons with minimal egress points.

Sea Kayaking

It's not all about open boats and single blades, though, Canada also offers sensational sea kayaking.

West Coast

Kayaking around the coves and islands immediately off Vancouver is incredible – places such as **Bowen** and **Pasley Islands** – but for paddling bordering on otherworldly, explore **Haida Gwaii**, off British Columbia's northern coast, just 50km south of Alaska. This archipelago – dubbed Canada's Galapagos, owing to its isolation and resultant richness in unique land mammals and plants – comprises more than 200 mostly uninhabited islands that cop the brunt of the Pacific Ocean's tides and storms. Also home to the Haida people, the islands contain numerous historical and cultural sites, including the Unesco World Heritage Site of SGang Gwaay Llnagaay (Ninstints), with its Haida village remnants, carved memorial and mortuary poles. Campsites are found on most of the larger islands, usually just up from each beach,

Paddling in British Columbia.

tucked in under the shelter of dense forest. Due to its remoteness, the wildlife here is less bothered by human visitation, allowing you to get quite close (sometimes too close...).

Johnstone Strait, between BC's Vancouver Island and the mainland, is fantastic for wildlife-spotting kayakers, with a number of BC's resident orca pods often seen here. The paddling in this area is suited to all skill levels, allowing you to focus on spotting these magnificent marine mammals. A number of local outfitters offer multiday trips using semi-permanent campsites located at remote beaches along the island's eastern coastline. Nothing quite beats being woken by the sound of an orca or large whale exhaling just offshore.

East Coast

Canada's eastern seaboard also offers equally impressive adventures. Quebec's **Mingan Archipelago National Park** is a world-renowned kayaking destination, with numerous small islands, wind and water-eroded rock formations and myriad reefs and islets. Short paddling adventures are possible, but with 100km of navigable waterways linking the park's islands and islets, and camping allowed on a number of islands, multiday kayak escapades are a good way to explore. The western section of the archipelago is the most accessible, due to the number of island campsites, but you need to be relatively experienced as the changing winds and tides can be dangerous.

Newfoundland and Labrador boast around 28,000km of coastline, along with a multitude of bays, fiords, rivers, lakes and inlets. As well as the majestic coastline, kayaking here provides the opportunity to check out icebergs (the famous **Iceberg Alley** is found off the Newfoundland coast), beluga (and other) whales and the region's birdlife.

Nova Scotia is packed with kayak-friendly locations and epic landscapes; here you will often be paddling below dramatic sea cliffs that can reach 200m in height, or weave in and around some of its coast's rugged rock formations, channels and water-carved caves. The province's famous **Bay of Fundy** is dotted with sea stacks and caves for kayakers to explore, plus there's the area's huge 12m tides to experience.

© Don Johnston | Getty Images

Whitewater Paddling

Whitewater paddlers (kayakers and rafters) are spoiled for choice. The 1270km-long Ottawa River is famous for the volume of its rapids, with different sections of the river suited to kayakers and rafts. The **Main Ottawa River** offers the ultimate all-round experience, with class IV rapids combining with big holes, challenging chutes, waterfalls and calmer sections that pass river islands and beaches. **Middle Ottawa** is rated class III–IV while the **Lower Ottawa River** is ideal for both families and beginner paddlers, with its less intimidating class II rating.

A more remote rafting experience can be found on the **Tatshenshini River**, which starts in northern British Columbia, loops north into the Yukon Territory and wends back into BC before finishing in Alaska. Guided is the best option (unless you're highly experienced) and adventures can last 10–15 days. You'll paddle past an ever-changing landscape, from canyons cutting through the St Elias Mountains to glaciers (Walker and Novatak), via class III–IV rapids, before joining the Alsek River and floating past icebergs – and two more glaciers – on Alsek Lake for the last part of the journey.

With an abundance of freshwater, Canada is one of the world's best whitewater destinations.

© Thomas Barwick | Getty Images

Just north of Vancouver, Squamish is one of Canada's best climbing areas.

Climbing

The Canadian Rockies

Nestled between Alberta and BC, the Canadian Rockies contain climbing routes for all skill levels and disciplines. There are myriad famous mountaineering ascents, such as **Mt Robson** (the Rockies' highest) in BC, **Mt Columbia** (Alberta's highest) and the more accessible **Mt Temple**, which has a relatively straightforward route to its peak, but is still not for beginners (use a local guide for all these climbs). For those with little time, targeting Mt Robson and its surrounding peaks allows you to squeeze in (weather permitting) a few summits over the course of a week. Another bonus of having the Rockies as your climbing destination is the Alpine Club of Canada's backcountry hut system, making for a slightly more comfortable 'base camp' than most climbers are used to.

Bugaboo Provincial Park, in BC's Purcell Range, is within the Canadian Rockies and contains many brilliant granite spires, including the famous **Bugaboo Spire**. There are numerous trad-based alpine rock routes up this iconic peak, ranging from the four-pitch South Ridge to the more challenging 10-pitch North East Ridge. **Pigeon Spire** and **Snowpatch Spire** are two other peaks in the Bugaboos that are popular and worthy challenges. Banff National Park's **Mt Temple** is often dubbed 'the Eiger of the Rockies' due to both its grade and its location right next door to Lake Louise; getting to the top and looking down on the town itself is a surreal experience.

Northwest Territories

The remote **Cirque of the Unclimbables** (named in 1955 by climbers who couldn't see a feasible way up the sheer faces of the region's granite spires) is just outside Nahanni National Park. Only accessible via float plane into Glacier Lake, it will keep climbers busy with numerous potential summits, including the renowned Lotus Flower Tower alpine rock climb.

Nunavut

Big wall climbers can travel above the Arctic Circle to Nunavut's **Baffin Island** and challenge themselves on the immense sea cliffs that tower over the ocean, using the township of Clyde River on the east coast as a base and accessing these cliffs via boat. Alternatively, climbers can visit the Cumberland Peninsula and take on the famous twin towers of **Mt Asgard** or the west face of **Mt Thor**, claimed to be one of the world's largest uninterrupted cliff faces, with a vertical drop of 1250m. For serious rush-seekers, Baffin is also a big BASE and wing jumping location.

Squamish

Less remote are the soaring granite cliffs and moss-covered boulders of Squamish, an hour from Vancouver. Squamish boasts some of Canada's best bouldering and sport and trad climbing, with something for everyone from easy classics like **Exasperator Crack** (5.10c) to routes like **Cobra Crack** (5.14) – one of the world's hardest cracks – and **Dreamcatcher** (5.14d).

ICE CLIMBING

With a plethora of waterfalls, sheer cliffs and glaciers, the Alberta Rocky Mountains towns of Canmore and Banff are ice-climber heaven, with routes for all levels. Some are easily accessed from the roadside, such as famous 300m Cascade Falls (WI-3). The 230km Icefields Parkway links Lake Louise to Jasper, and is dotted with ice routes, including Bow Falls (WI-4).

A snowboarder going backcountry at Revelstoke, BC.

Snowsports

For many skiers and boarders, the wild, forested, powder-choked mountains of British Columbia and Alberta represent the pursuits' pinnacle.

Whistler-Blackcomb is the first Canadian ski experience for most, although the country's biggest resort is a victim of its own hype, and the slopes get busy. However, after a big dry dump, everyone from beginner to backcountry charger will be impressed by the size and variety of the terrain.

But further inland is where you're more likely to encounter Canada's 'white smoke'. Purpose-built family friendly resorts such as **Sun Peaks**, **Big White** and **Silver Star** are rarely too busy, and they all offer great skiing and a friendly vibe.

Trees underpin a large part of this difference. In many resorts, the Rocky Mountains don't rise above treeline, unlike the Alps, so pistes are cut through deep forests; elsewhere the trees may be gladed to allow you to enjoy tree skiing without getting wrapped around a 20m-tall pine.

Locals like to push boundaries, so smaller ski hills such as **Red Mountain** and **Whitewater** in southern BC offer some very challenging steeps and trees for those who want to test themselves. If you survive, head to their satellite towns (Rossland and Nelson, respectively), funky, bohemian enclaves that regularly win 'Best Outdoor Town' awards.

Continuing east, **Revelstoke** offers a unique mix of resort, cat and heli-skiing from one base, as well as the biggest 'vertical' in North America: 1713m.

Cat and heli-skiing is big in BC, with numerous operators running out of backcountry lodges dotted amid remote mountain ranges all the way from the US border in the south to the US border in the north, in the form of Alaska. It isn't cheap, but the vast fields of featherlight powder that will be made available to you make it a bucketlist adventure.

Other classic BC resorts include Kicking Horse, with some of the steepest chutes in the country, and Fernie, an attractive old mining settlement that just happens to have a selection of huge powder bowls waiting to be ripped apart above the town.

Alberta's **Lake Louise** is one of North America's most beautifully located ski resorts, sitting in the heart of grand, glaciated terrain and overlooking the dazzling blue waters of the eponymous lake and the gothic pile of Chateau Lake Louise.

The nearby resorts of **Sunshine Village** and **Mt Norquay** are also worth exploring, as is the spectacularly sited satellite town of **Banff**. The grandeur continues if you head north along the truly remarkable Icefields Parkway – one of the world's great drives – to the small ski hill of **Jasper**, where you'll realise that skiing in Canada is almost as much about the scenery as the slopes.

PROPER OFF PISTE

Snowshoeing has grown popular and many resorts have snowshoe (and XC skiing) trails through forested but not-too-remote backcountry. Or try fatbiking – Mountain bike meccas such as Whistler and Nelson now offer the winterised version on these balloon-tyred behemoths, and it's every bit as fun as summer biking.

© Rich Wheater; Ryan Creary / Getty Images

Dog Sledding

Canada's indigenous and European history is tightly entwined with trade, travel and exploration via pooch-power, and mushing is a central part of the country's culture. Reliving this historical partnership while being dragged at considerable speed (teams of six dogs can reach up to 30km/h) across distances of around 80km per day is an exhilarating experience. You will find dog-sled tours in most Canadian provinces and the chance to see how these dogs – and their owner/mushers – work as a team to transport you into the wilderness is something not to be missed. **Hautes-Gorges-de-la-Rivière-Malbaie National Park** (yep, it's a mouthful) is one of Canada's premier dog-sledding destinations thanks to its mix of mountains, cliffs, wild rivers and – at day's end – remote wood cabins, but you will find similar dog-sledding experiences in other provinces as well.

The best thing is, most dog-sledding guide outfits will show you how to harness up and then lead your own dog team, ensuring your childhood dream of reliving that Jack London adventure becomes an unforgettable reality. Just don't stop for the bears…

Below, dogsled racing is very popular in Canada. Bottom, bring a thick wettie – surfing at Long Beach, BC.

Surfing

It's not the first place that comes to mind when you think of surfing, but Canada's coasts, east and west, offer amazing wave riding.

Vancouver Island on the Pacific is one of the most spectacular surf destinations on Earth. Here, forested mountains swoop down upon golden sands and rocky coves, and long-period swells that have travelled all the way from the southern hemisphere roll ashore at spots such as Tofino and Long Beach.

Surfers are not top of the food chain here – bear, wolf and cougar prints can regularly be seen on the beaches, and orcas swim in these waters, so it's not just cold water you have to contend with. That said, the locals are among the friendliest surfers you'll meet. Winter brings steady swells – just remember to pack a hood, gloves and booties.

The same is true of Canada's Atlantic coast, where the surf scene focuses on the coast east of Halifax. Maybe it's the combination of icy seas and snow on the beach on a regular basis that makes Canada a warm and welcoming destination for surfers, and it's one you should certainly check out if you don't mind wearing a thick wetsuit.

© Jeremy Koreski benoitrousseau | Getty Images

Enjoying spectacular singletrack on La Palma.

CANARY ISLANDS

An autonomous archipelago of Spanish islands, scattered 100km off Africa's Atlantic coast, the Canaries provide the perfect winter activity base.

The subtropical climate and dramatically diverse topography of the Canary Islands attract flocks of migratory adventurers. The Atlantic waters that wash the archipelago provide world-class surfing, kitesurfing and windsurfing (on Lanzarote and Fuerteventura, in particular), and the sailing is excellent.

technical singletrack with guides from LavaTrax. Expect tyre-testing skin-scraping ruggedness, sweaty ascents and whoop-inducing descents.

Tenerife is a winter training base for several professional cycling teams, runners and triathletes – testament to the quality of the road riding and running – and Club La Santa on Lanzarote is a dedicated sport resort.

Cycling

Mountain bike trails gallop across the grit of **La Graciosa** and through the trees on **Gran Canaria**, but the best bumpy biking is on **Tenerife**. Here you can bus your bike up Mt Teide (3718m) – Spain's highest point and the world's third tallest volcano – and cruise to the coast, or explore sections of

Hiking

Little La Gomera is famous for top-quality hiking, but there are wonderful walking trails through pine and laurisilva forests, volcanic valleys and along coastal paths on Tenerife, and every island – even the lavascape of Lanzarote – has something to offer ambling explorers.

DON'T LEAVE WITHOUT...
Diving beneath the waves off Lanzarote to explore Europe's first undersea sculpture museum: Jason deCaires Taylor's Museo Atlántico.

© bbjiak | Getty Images

CARIBBEAN ISLANDS

Drag yourself away from the shore-side screen of palms and coconut oil and you'll find that the Caribbean offers a trove of unexpected adventure in beautiful locations.

Once known for its sun, sea and sizzling inactivity on the sand, the Caribbean has recently upped its game for active travellers, with a steadily growing number of adventure activities available beyond sailing. As you'd expect, watersports are massive, from snorkelling and SUP in calm and protected waters to world-class kitesurfing. On land there's hiking, canyoning and even mountain ultra-running. The most rewarding islands tend to be the larger ones – the bigger areas of the Dominican Republic and Puerto Rico simply offer more variety. However, the tall, volcanic islands in the Eastern Caribbean chain also offer excellent rainforest hiking, ziplines, waterfalls and plunge pools.

Diving

Coral like a thousand green molar teeth, barrel sponges large enough to sit in and networks of spiky staghorn flitting with sergeant majors and grunts, damsels and rock beauties... Caribbean diving is spectacular. The water is warm and visibility can reach 30m, some islands have purposely sunk wrecks, and even the smallest island has at least one dive operator. The best dive spots include **Tobago**, particularly its east end, famous for rays and large corals (one brain-coral is the size of a semi-detached house) that flourish on the nutrients brought on currents from the Orinoco (you need to be comfortable diving in currents). The **Cayman Islands** are known for their sheer walls, with corals as bright as cathedral windows. **Bonaire**,

A hiker surveys tooth-like Gros Piton on St Lucia.

© Justin Foulkes | Lonely Planet

one of the Dutch Leeward Islands off Venezuela, is famed for its colourful corals and sloping drop-offs. In the Bahamas they have made a speciality of diving with sharks, and off **Dominica** you can dive in 'Champagne' bubbles released by submarine volcanic activity. Also consider **Saba** and Jacques Cousteau's marine park off **Guadeloupe**.

Kitesurfing & Windsurfing

Due to constant tradewinds streaming in from the Atlantic, the islands have excellent kite and windsurfing. Winds are best from December to June, while the waves are bigger from December into the early part of the year, when you can perfect your freestyle. It's warm, of course, so a shorty wetsuit will generally do. And, as befits the Caribbean, easygoing communities have grown around the favoured spots, creating a great atmosphere in which to relax after a day spent being pummelled by the wind and waves. The best spots are at Cabarete on the north shore of the **Dominican Republic**, where winds hit the coast across the bay; at Silver Rock, on the southern tip of **Barbados**, where fluorescent kites and sails scoot back and forth from the lighthouse; and the enclosed bay near Vieux Fort at the south tip of **St Lucia**. Other favoured spots include the southern part of **Martinique** and Le Moule on the northern coast of Grande-Terre on **Guadeloupe**. Many of the smaller islands also have a small operator with a few rigs to rent, including **Antigua**, the **British Virgin Islands**, the **Cayman Islands**, **Tobago** and even glitzy **St Barts**.

Hiking

Almost all of the islands offer opportunities for hiking, usually for the day, particularly the larger Greater Antilles and the tall volcanic islands of the Eastern Caribbean. In places, old farmers' trails have been kept up, but often you hike to dormant volcanic peaks. For all the exertion, though, often these hikes are taken gently, with a guide's explanation as the centrepiece, detailing the extraordinary flora and fauna in the rainforest. Remember that many hikes culminate at a waterfall and rock pool, so bring swimming gear. Volcano climbs include verdant La Soufrière (1234m) in **St Vincent** and quiescent Mt Pelée (1397m) in **Martinique**, the Boiling Lake in **Dominica**, and

DON'T LEAVE WITHOUT...
Kayaking in Bioluminescent Bay, Vieques, Puerto Rico. Best done on dark, moonless nights, this is extraordinary. Paddle strokes set off weird white-and-green whorls of light (as millions of tiny dinoflagellates are disturbed, they emit a glow), fish zip away beneath you, tails flashing madly left and right, and manta rays move like glowing space ships.

the iconic, incisor-shaped Gros Piton in **St Lucia**. There are also rainforest hikes to see birds in the oldest forest reserve in the Western Hemisphere at the **Tobago** Main Ridge Forest Reserve. **Dominica** has a long-distance trail, 184km from one end of the island to the other, as do **Martinique** and **Guadeloupe**. In the **Dominican Republic** you can climb up to the Caribbean's highest peak, Pico Duarte (3098m).

Canyoning & Caving

Across the rainforest-smothered islands there are endless waterfalls, canyons and rivers for canyoning. **Puerto Rico**, the **Dominican Republic**, **Martinique** and **Guadeloupe** all have great canyoning, while there are options in **Dominica** and **Grenada**, too. For a gentler experience in the lower reaches of the rivers there is tubing. Or, if you wish to go underground, try caving in Puerto Rico.

Mountain Biking

Just a couple of islands have bike parks. Anse Chastanet, near the Pitons in **St Lucia**, has a handful of trails, as does the Toro Verde Nature Park on **Puerto Rico**.

Surfing

Despite the 4800km run-up for the Atlantic Ocean, there are only a few places with reliable, reachable surf. Two of the best spots are the east coast of **Barbados**, at Bathsheba (where you can watch the action from cafes), and at Rincon on the northwestern end of **Puerto Rico**.

Swimming

The Caribbean couldn't be much more inviting for wild swimmers. The best swimming event is the annual **Nevis to St Kitts** swim across the spectacular Narrows (4km of open water) between the sister islands. In the **Cayman Islands** (on Grand Cayman) you can swim with rays at Stingray City and, more bizarrely, it's possible to join the famous swimming pigs who live on Big Major Cay in the **Bahamas**.

Ziplines

Ziplines have now appeared all over the Caribbean – in **St Lucia**, **St Kitts**, **Antigua** and **Puerto Rico** (which claims the world's longest) – so you can see the rainforest close up, and suddenly find yourself flying across a 60m river gorge, before re-entering the trees.

Racing

Running in the Caribbean is hot, so expect events to start early in the morning. Several islands offer marathons (generally with a half and often 10km options) and some now have triathlons. They also offer some off-road runs and a few adventure races. **Martinique** stages the Tchimbe Raid and other ultra-runs, and the Guadarun is a six-stage race on six of the islands around **French Guadeloupe**.

Pigs may not fly, but they can certainly swim; the famous swimming pigs of Big Major Cay in the Bahamas.

© shalamov | Getty Images

CHILE

Squeezed between the spine of the Americas and the powerful Pacific Ocean, Chile may appear thin, but it's fat with adventure.

Chile looks impossible on the map – a sliver of land along the Pacific coast of South America – but its shape makes sense when you realise that the western border is the often-impenetrable Andes mountain range. It may only be 177km-wide on average, but Chile extends 4270km from north to south – that's a huge amount of latitude, making for gigantic geographic diversity. From blasted deserts to verdant volcanic slopes, fat rivers, vast lakes and stoic peaks, Chile provides a playground for almost any outdoor pursuit you can imagine.

Cycle the World's Driest Desert

The **Atacama Desert** in Chile's north is the world's driest non-polar desert, and it is ripe for an extraordinary cycle tour. Setting off from Arica near the Peruvian border and pedalling 1600km south to La Serena, this unique environment is as close to Mars as you can get without taking a six-month one-way space flight encased in a metal coffin – indeed it was here in 2016 that NASA tested the 'life-detection drill' that will one day search for life on the Red Planet. Cycling through this land is surreal and beautiful, its vastness is hypnotic and humbling. Divert to the coast from the Pan-American Highway and skirt the ocean to marvel at the juxtaposition of arid mountains rising straight out of the shimmering Pacific. Biking through barren landscapes of deep oranges and browns provides the gift of solitude and wonder, while frigid Atacama nights are best spent staring up at a blanket of brilliant stars unrivalled anywhere in the world. Once you become comfortable with the rhythms of such a trip, the desert turns out to be less of a place you survive and more one in which you can thrive.

DON'T LEAVE WITHOUT...
Skiing Portillo. The long-famed ski resort, clinging to the flanks of the Andes beside the spectacular road crossing to Mendoza, Argentina, blends groomed runs with steeps and big mountain slackcountry. It's South American resort shredding at its best.

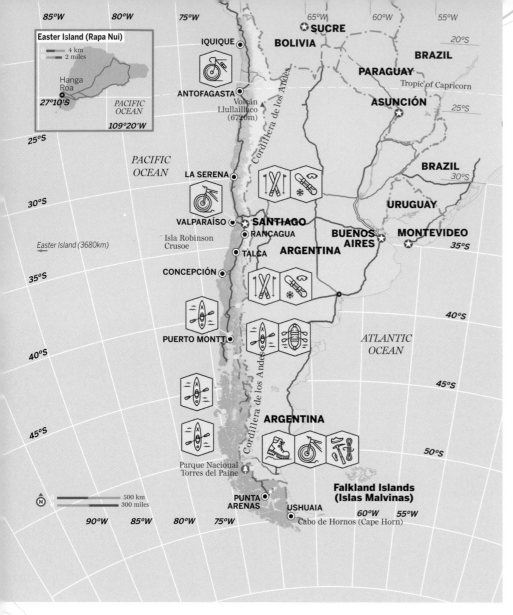

further south and explore the eponymous lagoon of **Laguna San Rafael National Park**, a gorgeous glacier-fed puddle. Or pull a paddle through the waters of **Bernardo O'Higgins National Park**, Chile's biggest protected area, where narrow fjords fold around the frozen feet of beautiful Balmaceda and Serrano glaciers, providing avenues of adventure for rugged-up kayakers.

And, of course, tasty-from-all-angles **Torres del Paine NP** is a spectacular place to sit in the cockpit of a kayak and explore lots of lovely *lagos*, ringed by frozen furniture and watched over by monstrous mountains. Peripatetic paddlers can reach parts of the peak-punctuated park that pedestrians can only wonder about and ponder while they wander.

Ski a Volcano

Imagine setting off amid thick native forest, skinning up the ever-steepening flank of a restless mountain to the majestic dome of an active volcano, the powerful fumes signalling you're close to the crater, before clicking into your bindings and cutting turns down a long, pristine, untracked powder slope. There are 500 volcanoes in Chile that are designated active, and you can ski them. With a pair or touring skis or a split board you can bag eight or so of Chile's volcanic peaks in just two weeks. If the full-on backcountry is not for you, then seek out a more user-friendly volcano experience by heading to **Volcán Pucon Villarrica**, a resort on the lower slopes of the perfect conical volcano **Villarrica**, from where you can tour to the smoking, open crater at 2847m. Being cold has never been so hot.

Paddle the Futaleufú

Making up for the dry north's aridity, Chile's south gets lots of rain. Combined with the country's precipitous pointy bits, that means fast-flowing water, and the more the rivers rage, the more raft-riders and playboaters beam. One of the best paddle pleasers is the Futaleufú – a river of gorgeous, vibrant turquoise water that slices through thick forest under the watchful eye of some big mountains – this Patagonian gem is a hell of a rafting trip. Though the river boils with enough class III and IV rapids to keep your pulse racing, portages are simple. The waterway is a popular playground for rafters and experienced kayakers, with some specialist companies taking intermediate

© Leon Werdinger | Alamy

ULTIMATE CHALLENGE

If you think your downhill MTB game is strong, then the Valparaíso Cerro Abajo will dial your ADVENTURE-O-METER up to 11. Held in the steep streets of the pretty seaside town of Valparaíso, the race bombs through alleys, stairs and purpose-made obstacles.

Kayak the Fjords

Similar to the coast of Atacama, thousands of kilometres to the north, **Pumalín Park** in the middle of the country is a protected area of wild mountains that plunges straight into the sea. Here, steeply walled fjords guard a majestic wilderness, much of which is completely inaccessible – unless you go by sea. Kayaking the fjords is a spectacular experience, offering a unique vantage point to witness and appreciate the glory that is Patagonia. Slicing through the water powered by your own steam, washing under big, cascading waterfalls as you look up at snow-capped peaks, pulling your kayak ashore at night on a secluded beach to set camp, soothing your tired muscles by slipping into natural thermal hot springs amid the rainforest – sounds wonderful because it is.

To boat a bit closer to the ice, point your bow

paddlers and upskilling them on the more technical sections. Another bonus of the Futaleufú is its very well developed camps, meaning when you are out of the water you can play cowboy on a galloping horse, try your hand at rock climbing or abseiling, fly fish for your dinner, hike through the wilderness or just hang around in stone hot tubs. Other whitewater hotspots include Río Azul and Río Petrohué in the Patagonian Lake District.

Hike South America's Biggest Trail

A monster is stirring in Chile: the **Greater Patagonian Trail**, a long-distance hike through the Patagonian Andes. At 1500km and growing, the trail is a work-in-progress which, instead of being guided by government, is the labour of love of hikers Jan Dudeck and Meylin Ubilla. The Swiss/Chilean duo are piecing together the GPT from beautiful existing

Rafting Patagonia's iconic Futaleufú river.

trails, neglected minor roads, the seasonal paths of herdsman and unmarked cross country sections. Some sections branch into multiple options where you can take to rivers and lakes on a packraft or sate your summit fever atop a volcano. The trail asks for no technical climbing or paddling skills, is broken into 18 sections that can be done individually and hikers can resupply at small towns along the way.

Torres del Paine

Way down in Patagonia is the jewel of Chile – the Torres del Paine National Park – home to one of the most iconic mountain silhouettes in the world. Aside from enjoying stunning kayaking, you can circumnavigate the park on foot or in the saddle (astride a horse or a mountain bike), enjoying some of the planet's most spectacular scenery at whatever pace suits.

Hiking

Those fleet of foot and short on time can run or ride the trails, but most visiting venturers prefer not to rush through such jaw-dropping backdrops, and opt to trek. There are myriad options – including **Mirador las Torres**, **Valle del Francés** and **Paso Los Cuernos** – but the classic circuit route is a 130km magical multiday mission. Travelling from hut to hut as you loop the loop, you'll note the proud Torres remaining the ever-present reference as you sweep past brilliant glaciers, Antarctic beech forests and pristine glacial lakes – habitats that support unique flora and fauna.

Climbing

The **Cordillera del Paine** massif is enough to strike fear and longing into any climber's heart. The region is famed for foul weather and extreme climbing with a hint of controversy, but though the reputation is warranted there is a surprising amount of accessible, moderate climbing in the park where even intermediate climbers with good mountain sense can get a taste of the extreme. Any time spent among the turquoise tarns, silent glaciers and towering granite horns of the park is unforgettable. Add incredible climbing and you've got the adventure of a lifetime.

Mountain Biking

If you like adventures with a little more wind through your hair, take your mountain bike. You can spend your time exploring repurposed sheep tracks or take a three-day round trip ride out from Refugio Las Torres along fireroads and double- and singletrack, which hops from smooth and flowy to teasingly technical, with switchbacks on the climbs and descents. The trails follow surging rivers and skirt still lakes that catch the reflection of the Paine Massif – your ever-present billion dollar view.

Below, Torres del Paine National Park is an adventure paradise. Left, climbing Torre Central, Torres del Paine.

© Thomas Senf, © Matt Munro | Lonely Planet

CHINA

China, home to a billion people, is also home to a billion possible adventures.

The Middle Kingdom is massive and as diverse in geography as it is in people. From the sculptured beauty of the rice paddies in the south to the vast, high deserts of Mongolia, and from the lofty peaks echoing with prayer bells around Shangri-La to silent, contemplative bamboo forests, whatever adventure you are seeking you can probably find it in China.

Trek Shangri-La

Shangri-La is as much a state of mind as a place, and though the location of James Hilton's paradise is disputed, the Chinese claimant offers much to the trekker. Head deep into Yunnan, into the mountains that border Tibet, and make for the secluded Yubeng village, which sits in the shadow of the holy Meili Xue Shan mountain range. Using this as your base, spend contemplative days of exploration where, made small in the arms of glaciated valleys and towering peaks, and caught up in the ancient culture, you'll find it impossible to not come away with an understanding of how trekking is more than simply walking. Ancient, resonant, ecstatic, imposing – trekking Shangri-La brings great reward.

Experience a Chinese Berm

China's middle class is booming and increasingly they want to splash their growing disposable cash on active lifestyle sports. Due to loads of mountainous and forested terrain, MTB parks and trails are being built across the country, including on the flanks of **Luofu Mountain**, where a mountain-bike trail network spans over 260 sq km of rugged terrain on the north bank of the Dongjiang, Panyu District. The Great Wall might have been built to keep people out, but the Great Berm is being built to keep them in.

Right, Liming in Yunnan Province is an emerging climbing destination.
Left, trekking in Yunnan Province.

© Aurora Photos | Alamy, © Garrett Bradley

Trail Run Hong Kong

On Mainland China there's an inconceivable number of running opportunities, but if you can swap scale for convenience Hong Kong has some great, accessible running. Despite its deserved reputation for skyscrapers, 40% of Hong Kong's 414 sq km is protected in nature reserves – and that means lots of trails. Among the myriad paths that traverse these parks, the region has four long-distance trails: **Hong Kong Trail** (50km), **Lantau Trail** (70km), **Wilson Trail** (78km) and the **MacLehose Trail** (100km). Hong Kong's environment really packs a diversity punch too, due to terrain that takes in thick forests, beaches, dense scrub, bubbling creeks and some impressive hills. When you think that pretty much everything starts at sea level and Hong Kong has three peaks over 860m, you can find enough vertical to get your thighs and lungs screaming. And because of the great access you are never that far away from a post-run plate of the world's best dumplings.

Cycle Touring

Unrelenting distances, horrendous roads, grinding mountains, cruel winds – what's not to love about cycle touring in China? Of course, you *can* arrange

UNCLAIMED CHALLENGE

Brave? Foolhardy? The world's best paddler? Leave your mark by dropping the boiling 'unrunnable' rapids of Tiger Leaping Gorge in Yunnan Province. Just 25m wide and 2000m high, the gorge funnels a torrent of water from the Jinsha River, a primary tributary of the upper Yangtze, into the narrow constriction to create epic rapids. Sections have been run, but no one has kayaked the full ferocious gamut of the gorge, which has a rep as a killer.

a cycle tour on a scale as epic as the country itself, something like pedalling the full 5000km from the Kazakh border to the Vietnamese border. Or you could bite off something much more manageable – say a jaunt through the bulbous karst towers of the southeast or a trip out from Beijing to the Great Wall, a site that's on everyone's bucket list. As a bonus, in places like Yunnan you will meet a surprising number of Chinese cycle tourists and get an opportunity to mingle with like-minded locals. For a priceless perspective that gets you down and dirty in a country's realness, it's hard to beat the one you get from the saddle of a bike.

Climb Sandstone Sentinels

The secret of limestone sport climbing in **Yangzhou** and **Getu** is long since out and the crowds have arrived, but there is a huge amount of rock in China and that means the potential for vertical adventure further afield is enormous. One such gem is **Liming** in Yunnan Province, around which extend valleys that are guarded over by huge sandstone monoliths. The giant orange and red faces are cracked by fissures that eat up natural protection, which makes them perfect for traditional climbing. When you're at the 'Chinese Indian Creek', try your hand at

© Lloyd Belcher, © Pawel Opaska / Alamy

the hardest traditional route in Asia, The Firewall (8b/5.13d), or better yet pick one of the many unclimbed peaks and put up your own new routes.

Hong Kong isn't on everyone's climbing radar, yet the sport has a long history here. The first routes went up after WWII but it was American superstar Todd Skinner's 1992 visit that sparked the modern era. Now HK has more than a thousand routes and its combination of readily accessible climbing and Big City culture makes it an alluring destination, particularly as a stopover on a longer climbing trip.

Scuba Dive the Lost City

There have been numerous environmental costs associated with China's rapid march to becoming the world's biggest economy: pollution, deforestation and the damming of rivers, but that damming has provided an unexpected wonder for divers. **Qiandao Lake** (Thousand Island Lake) was formed in 1959 when Xin'an River hydroelectric station was completed. As the surrounding valleys were flooded, they swallowed an 1800-year-old metropolis and created a unique wreck dive. The 'Chinese Atlantis', Shicheng (Lion City), was built during the Eastern Han Dynasty (AD 25–200) and is now a maze of white temples, intricately carved arches, towers, paved roads, houses and wonderfully preserved three dimensional reliefs of lions, dragons, figures and text all submerged 40m underwater. The Lion City is both a sign of the Chinese development mindset and a rare treat for divers.

Below, bikepacking through the Karakoram mountains. Left, in Hong Kong you're never far from some sweet singletrail.

COLOMBIA

Hosting terrain as untamed as the country's one-time reputation, Colombia's emergence from the travel wilderness means vast areas await exploration.

If you hear somebody describing Colombia as brutally wild, don't assume they're talking about the oft-maligned country's recent history. Colombia is rich in unexplored terrain, across Andean peaks and Amazonian jungle.

It's the only South American country boasting both Pacific and Caribbean coasts, more than 10% of its land is protected by national parks (compared to about 3.4% in the US) and it hosts the world's highest coastal mountain range: the Sierra Nevada de Santa Marta, topping out at around 5700m. At the foot of this range, in the stunning Tayrona National Park, it's possible to stand in the warm Caribbean Sea, peering up at snowcapped peaks.

In many ways, Colombia feels like a handful of disparate countries stitched together. The Caribbean coast exudes a languorous, sultry character that belies the fact that the country's most famous multiday hike is hidden right here in the tropical jungle. Inland, boisterous Bogotá sits in a high Andean valley, 2600m above sea level, making it the world's third-highest capital city.

South of Bogotá, the Andes split and fray into three high ranges that push up through the country, creating a wealth of hiking opportunities and a flurry of whitewater. Cross the Andes in the east and the country drops precipitously into the vast Los Llanos, a wildlife-rich area of tropical grasslands larger than Thailand, known as the 'Serengeti of South America'.

Colombia is undoubtedly one of the world's up-and-coming adventure destinations, because so much here is little known and yet utterly enticing.

Hiking

Machu Picchu has no monopoly on lost Andean cities. Hidden in jungle on the northern slopes of the Sierra Nevada de Santa Marta, **Ciudad Perdida** is the goal on Colombia's most famous hike. It's a five- or six-day walk through mud, waist-deep river

Exploring around the ruins of Pueblito in Tayrona National Park.

crossings, dense heat and a final 1260-step climb to the ruins of the ancient town. You can't do this hike independently; four trekking agencies in Santa Marta and Taganga have permit access.

Colombia's best alpine trek is the week-long **Güicán–El Cocuy Circuit Trek** through El Cocuy National Park, following a chain of stunning high lakes, waterfalls and mountain passes at altitudes exceeding 4500m.

For a got-there-before-the-crowds-did experience, arrange a day hike into **Caño Cristales**, flying into remote La Macarena and setting out on foot for what's been called the 'most beautiful river in the world'. The area only reopened to visitors in 2009 after years of guerrilla activity, but from around September to November the *Macarenia clavigera* riverbed plant turns brilliantly red and purple, adding swatches of colour to the yellow sand and clean blue water.

For another natural wonder, take a half-day hike through the open **Cocora Valley**, where the world's largest palm trees – 40m-high wax palms – sprout like hairs.

Cycling

Two words: Nairo Quintana. This powerful little climber earned his thighs in Colombia, making him a walking advertisement for the country's killer climbs. Quintana's home area of **Boyacá** is where wannabe-Nairos head, though the altitude – around 3000m – is taxing.

Medellín is arguably Colombia's finest cycling base, but you need to learn to love hills. The ride of note here – drawing hundreds of riders every weekend – is **Alto de Las Palmas**, climbing almost 1000m above the city and into the high Oriente valley, which is another cycling favourite. Combine Alto de Las Palmas and the **Vuelta Oriente circuit** and you have a classic ride of around 100km.

First, though, experience a Sunday cycle in **Bogotá** when, for seven hours, roads through the capital city close to motor vehicles and open to bikes. Known as **Ciclovía**, these weekly road closures began in the mid-1970s, pioneering an idea that soon spread worldwide. Today, approximately one million people take part in Bogotá's Ciclovía every weekend.

As you'd expect in a wilderness-strewn country that marries mountains with mad-keen cyclists,

© Kris Davidson | Lonely Planet

mountain biking is also popular. **Quindío's** coffee-growing valleys offer good trails, and from the highlands around **Medellín** you can explore trails that drop over 1000 metres, through cloud forests and down to river gorges.

Diving & Snorkelling

Colombia has more than 3000km of coastline – Pacific and Caribbean – so it's unsurprising that there's excellent diving here. The Caribbean has the real marine prizes, prime among which are the islands of **Providencia** and **San Andrés**, 700km off the Colombian coast but little more than 200km from Nicaragua.

Providencia sits atop one of the world's largest barrier reefs, while San Andrés, 90km to the south, has another 15km of reef. On the more laid-back Providencia, popular dive sites include Manta's Place, where southern stingrays glide, and Tete's Place, where fish life teems among fissures and caves. At Felipe's Place, a submerged statue of Christ stands 20m below the surface. On San Andrés,

*Below, a massive brain coral off San Andrés island. **Right**, trekking in El Cocuy National Park.*

Piramide is prolific with fish, octopus, moray eels and rays, while for wreck divers there are two sunken ships, the *Blue Diamond* and *Nicaraguense*, off the island's coast.

For aspirant divers, the town of **Taganga**, along the mainland's Caribbean coast, is one of the world's cheapest places to learn.

Whitewater Rafting

Kayaking remains a niche pursuit in Colombia, but there are several popular places for whitewater rafting. Almost midway between Bogotá and Medellín, the **Río Claro** carves through a marble canyon, where the rapids are only class I, making this a gentle and scenic float. At San Agustín, in the country's southwest, there are rafting trips on Colombia's longest river, the **Río Magdalena**, bumping through class II and III rapids, but **San Gil** is where it's really at. Colombia's adventure capital pulses with activity – paragliding, bungee jumping, caving, canyoning – but mostly the town is geared

© Aldo Brando; Daniel Garzón Herazo / EyeEm / Getty Images

HOMEGROWN ADVENTURE HERO
On 24 May 2001, Juan Pablo Ruiz Soto led the first Colombian team to summit Mt Everest. In April 2016 he took a team of Colombians to the top of Carstensz Pyramid, completing their Seven Summits. The former World Bank economist co-wrote *Alta Colombia: Splendor of the Mountain*, a book about Colombia's Andean highs.

around rafting. The **Río Fonce** offers a 10km run through class II and III rapids, while the **Río Suarez** provides the full water-rodeo experience, taking you into the maelstrom of class V rapids. It's pretty much furious water from the moment you launch, an hour's drive from San Gil, until journey's end at the confluence of the Río Suarez and Río Fonce.

Climbing

Suesca is rock-central in Colombia. Just an hour's drive north of Bogotá, the rural town is banded with a 4km-long line of sandstone cliffs towering above the Río Bogotá and a disused railway. The cliffs are about a 10-minute walk along the train tracks from town and feature more than 400 routes fairly well divided between trad and sport climbing. The cliffs reach heights of 125m and there's plenty here for all abilities – at the top end are climbs graded at around 7c+/5.13. There's a good climbers' scene at Suesca, with a campground at the base of the cliffs and a hostel-cum-climbing-shop nearby.

THE COOK ISLANDS

Paradisical punctuation marks on the mighty blue expanse of the Pacific Ocean, the Cooks offer a smorgasbord of tasty adventures.

People's preconceptions of the Cooks are typically based on the pages of luxury travel publications or honeymooners' photo albums, but beyond the idyllic lagoon of Aitutaki, this far-flung archipelago of coral-fringed islands have a seriously wild side, from caves with human remains to trails scaling rocky peaks and dive sites that plunge alarmingly into the Pacific abyss.

Diving & Snorkelling

The Cook Islands, of course, are actually the summits of near-as-damn-it drowned volcanoes, tip-toeing to keep their pretty heads above the ever-rising tide. Leave the shore by more than a few hundred metres, and the ocean floor is suddenly four kilometres below your thrashing feet. When boat diving from **Rarotonga** (the only island really set up for it) the dramatic drop-offs combined with great visibility are enough to give divers vertigo. Keep a close eye on your depth gauge, it's easy to get intoxicated by the feeling you're slow-motion BASE jumping. Outside the reef, expect hard corals and encounters with pelagic species including eagle rays, whitetip reef sharks, turtles and (in winter)

humpback whales. Inside the islands' lagoons, the snorkelling is superb and accessible to everyone, directly from the beach.

Paddling

According to local legend, the modern Maori population of New Zealand originated from the Cooks, with seven canoes travelling unimaginable distances across the open ocean. Paddling remains a traditional pursuit on the islands, and if you get the chance to try out-rigging, grab it. Otherwise, jump on a stand-up paddleboard or get yourself astride a sit-on-top kayak and explore the lovely lagoons.

Caving

The less-visited outer islands – including **Atiu** and **Mangaia** – are catacombed with mysterious caves. On Atiu, one cave is home to a unique bird that switches from sonar squeaks to standard-sounding bird calls as it emerges from the gloom. Both islands have caves containing human remains (some with signs that they didn't die in their sleep) that have been there for centuries. Cave tours – which are low tech (expect a torch if you're lucky) – can only be conducted by the families who occupy the land.

© Steve Allen | Getty Images

ICONIC EVENT
While the annual 32km Round Raro Run sticks to roads, the more interesting 8.5km Nutters' Run crosses Rarotonga's mountainous inland ridge on root-strewn trails, climbing to 653m.

Coral in a reef off the island of Aitutaki.

COSTA RICA

Misty jungles, Caribbean beaches, volcanoes, monkeys, sloths, toucans, world-class surf, cloud-forest trails, ziplines... pura vida adventures abound in this lucky land.

The world's an unfair place and rarely is this more obvious than in Costa Rica. The small Central American country has many times more than its fair share of natural splendour. *Pura vida* (pure life) is the Ticos' (Costa Ricans') spot-on national catchphrase. Costa Rica doesn't have an army, but it does have a spine of green mountains and smoking volcanoes, draped with lush rain- and cloud forests, and on both sides of the fortunate nation these lead down to mangrove swamps and long palm-fringed sandy beaches with seductive surf breaks. Wildlife abounds, from crocodiles to toucans, howler monkeys to sloths. You hate to use a cliche like 'paradise', but it's almost unavoidable here.

Unlike its neighbours, Costa Rica has a history of stability and prosperity; education and healthcare are the best in the isthmus and the tourist infrastructure is excellent. It's a little more expensive than its neighbours – a little bit more Americanised – but in return it's safer and easier to explore. It's the main ecotourism destination in Central America, with 25% of the landmass protected, spectacular national parks, and nature and marine reserves teeming with biodiversity – more than the US and Europe combined.

Costa Rica is a great place to come and do nothing. But also a great place to come and do plenty.

Surfing

Costa Rica spoils surfers rotten with more than 50 breaks – lefts and rights, beach and point breaks, reefs and river mouths – on both the Pacific and Caribbean coasts, and the water is warm all year round. And, for boardless breakchancers and beginners, practically every beach community offers hire and lessons.

Salsa Brava, on the Caribbean Coast at Puerto Viejo de Talamanca, is perhaps the most famous. Big powerful waves break over a sharp coral reef, making it better suited to the more seasoned surfer.

The secluded jungle beach of **Playa Pavones**, in the far southwest, is similarly renowned in surf circles and populated by more serious surfers who brave one of the longest rides in the world, the notorious three-minute left point break.

Surf is excellent along the Pacific Coast, with

Catching waves at Playa Santa Teresa on the Nicoya Peninsula.

© robertharding | Alamy

Playa Grande, on the northeastern Nicoya Peninsula, being another popular spot. A few kilometres south, the gentle surf at **Playa Tamarindo** suits beginners and the semi-experienced, while nearby **Playa Langosta** better befits the surf savvy. **Playa Guiones**, also on Nicoya, is blessed with consistent waves that tend to drop gently for newbies and intermediates alike, while more advanced surfers practise their tricks here too.

Playa Jacó, a straight line to the Pacific Coast from capital San José, is beginner friendly. Whereas neighbouring **Playa Hermosa** can get huge swells and changeable conditions and is better suited to the experienced.

Other popular surf hubs include the laid-back hippie haunt **Dominical**, the pristine beaches of **Mal País**, plus **Santa Teresa** and **Playa Hermosa**.

Hiking

From jungle treks to volcano climbs, the country's natural wonders are begging to be explored on foot. Cloud forests, for example, cover a mere 0.25% of land on Earth, yet can be easily experienced in Costa Rica. Rustling with wildlife, swathed in mist, exploding with mossy vines, ferns and rushing streams, it's proper *Jungle Book* stuff.

Monteverde

Reserva Biológica Bosque Nuboso Monteverde is one of the best parks in Central America, with an estimated 2500 kinds of plant, more than 100 mammal species and 400 vivid varieties of birdlife, including the colour-splattered quetzal. The park enjoys unique geographical conditions: humid trade winds from the Caribbean rush up wooded slopes to cool and condense into clouds loitering above the trees, creating a marvellously misty netherworld. The extra oxygen has helped foment potent biodiversity among the reserve's fecund flora, where orchids and bromeliads bloom. Ten short but well-maintained trails tiptoe through the lichen-wrapped tall trees, and you can stay overnight in huts.

Manuel Antonio

Pristine beaches, turquoise seas, bundles of wildlife, cliffside restaurants and tasty trails combine to make uber-green Parque Nacional Manuel Antonio the country's most popular national park – and it gets busy here in peak season. There are seven short trails and off-trail hiking isn't permitted, so it's mostly about wildlife spotting, waterfalls, surfing, feasting and watching the sun sink into the sea and setting the horizon on fire at the day's end.

Volcán Arenal

Volcán Arenal is another enticing hiking region. Not least because afterwards you can kick back in a volcano-heated pool to soothe aching legs. Well-marked trails cobweb the park, leading to waterfalls, crater lakes and lava flows. The two-to-three-hour Cerro Chato Trail climbs steeply through sky-bothering virgin-growth forest to reach the summit of Cerro Chato and a swimmable volcanic lake at 1200m.

Cerro Chirripó

Parque Nacional Chirripó's Cerro Chirripó (3820m) is the highest mountain in Costa Rica. Its summit is a popular two-day trek from San Gerardo de Rivas, passing through different climatic zones, from lush cloud forests to sparse rocky terrain. A stay at Crestones Base Lodge gets you to the summit for the next day's dawn. Though beautiful, it can be a challenging hike, only 16km in distance but with more than 2500m of climbing. However, seeing the sun rise from above the clouds is a classic *pura vida* experience.

*Above, canoeing is a great way to explore Costa Rica's often impenetrable jungles. **Right**, diving off Isla del Caño.*

Corcovado

Parque Nacional Corcovado in the south is home to an incredible 2.5% of the world's total biodiversity. You'll find deserted beaches, waterfalls, high tree canopies and teeming wildlife here. Humidity can reach 100%, however, and solo trekking isn't recommended, due to pumas, jaguars, crocodiles, swamps, wild rivers, snakes and more. This really is a wild place.

Bahía Drake

Neighbouring Bahía Drake also offers a beautiful and remote experience. Macaws and howler monkeys cause a cacophony in the canopy, while dolphins frolic in the marine reserve. A 17km trail between Agujitas and the San Pedrillo ranger station is a superb day hike, with some handsome beaches and plenty of wildlife spotting.

Diving & Snorkelling

While Central America's Caribbean coast is blessed with miles of unbroken barrier reef, making it one of the world's best scuba-diving and snorkelling destinations, Costa Rica's diving is trumped by Belize and Honduras to the north. But satisfactory snorkelling can be had off both shores, especially the southern Caribbean Coast, though conditions are variable. Other prime areas for fish-bothering are the impressive coral reefs at Bahía Ballena and Manzanilla. Bahía Drake is largely cut off from the rest of the country, so it's bulging with wildlife, with Isla del Caño the best place for meeting marine life while in snorkel and fins.

Ziplining

Squeal-inducing, ziplining canopy tours are to Costa Rica what bungee jumping is to New Zealand – the concept started here. The two main destinations for a jungle rush are around Volcán Arenal and Monteverde. A dozen cables zip across the Río Arenal canopy, and trips include waterfalls and entry to the resort's swimming pool and 13 thermal pools. Selvatura, in Monteverde, has 3km of cables, 18 platforms and a huge, intimidating Tarzan swing.

> **ULTIMATE CHALLENGE**
> Run the 400km La Ruta cycle route. Several have tried. Only a few have succeeded. The fastest known time is 81 hours.

Best of the Rest

If rafting's your thing, Costa Rica has top-notch **whitewater rafting** up to class V. Ride the wild torrents on the Reventazón and Pacuare rivers in the Valle Central, while you can find marginally less hair-raising options at Puerto Viejo de Sarapiquí.

The Arenal region is the **mountain-biking** hub, with a variety of tour options. With your own bike, the two-day Vuelta al Lago is an exciting annual mountain-bike ride around Lago de Arenal. Near the park entrance, a private network of bike-friendly trails follows the lava flow from the 1968 explosion. La Ruta de los Conquistadores is a multi-stage race that crosses Costa Rica from the Pacific to the Caribbean coast over three days and about 400km.

Kayaking is a great way to explore Costa Rica's rivers, lagoons and mangroves. Paddle to Golf Rica from Puerto Jiménez and you might have whales for company. Elsewhere, the mangroves of Bahía Drake are teeming with wildlife. **Trail running** is a growing sport here and, over six days each February, the Coastal Challenge takes runners on 240km of trails, up and down mountains, through jungles and along beaches in the country's southwest, including Dominical and Bahía Drake.

A keel-billed toucan; Costa Rica is famous for its incredible bird life.

CÔTE D'IVOIRE

Ironically, it's ivory that this country lacks, though you won't miss it while hiking through rainforests and up mountains, or surfing in the Gulf of Guinea.

Trekking is perhaps the country's most rewarding adventure activity, with two key hubs in the southwest: Parc National de Taï and the region around the city of Man. The former is relatively unknown, but at 5000 sq km in size it's one of the region's largest wildlife reserves, with some of the last standing primary rainforests in West Africa. The park has a variety of trails, including a route to the summit of sacred Mt Niénokoué (396m).

Man is further north, almost 100km east of the triple junction of borders between Côte d'Ivoire, Guinea and Liberia. Strike out to **climb** La Dent de Man (881m), a steep tooth-shaped mountain, or attempt Mt Tonkoui (1223m), the country's second-highest peak. If you stand on top of the latter, you should be able to see all the way into Liberia and right across Guinea.

You'll find Côte d'Ivoire's other adventure fix on its extensive 515km coastline, where the Atlantic waves set up perfectly for sensational **surfing** in several places, such as Dagbego in the west and the linked triumvirate villages of Assinie village, Assinie Mafia and Assouindé, close to the border with Ghana.

DON'T LEAVE WITHOUT...
Going looking for chimpanzees in Parc National de Taï, where the animals have famously been observed using tools.

CROATIA

With a sparkling coastline, spectacular canyons and a pleasant climate, this once war-torn land is now one of Europe's hidden gems for all adventure types.

The 1800km Adriatic coastline and its 1246 islands may be the star attractions of this Eastern European nation, but Croatia is also home to deep ravines and coastal mountains that make it perfect for climbing, hiking, biking and canyoning. Croatia was declared independent from Yugoslavia in 1991, but waged war with Bosnia and Herzegovina for four years. When peace was declared, its natural wonders and pleasant climate, coupled with burgeoning low-cost airlines, quickly turned it into a popular tourist destination. The Dalmatian Coast is dramatic, with steep cliffs rising from deep blue sea and islands scattered just offshore. It attracts yachts in droves, but also has great conditions for kiteboarding and windsurfing. The Istrian Peninsula offers a different kind of coast, dotted with vineyards, orchards and olive groves and a very Mediterranean culture influenced by its proximity to Italy. Inland, the karst topography creates spectacular landforms, caves and canyons including the unique waterfalls of Plitvice Lakes and the go-to climbing destination of Paklenica.

Hiking

Impressive mountains line the 100km trail from Zavižan to Paklenica, which can be split into stages, including the jaw-dropping 57km coastal **Premužić Trail** in **Northern Velebit National Park**, and the jewel at its end, **Paklenica National Park**, which holds 200km of mapped trails. Further north, near Jasenak, the hike to **Ratko's Shelter**, a unique cabin built into a cave, leads past a Madagascar-style karst landscape. Just to the south, **Plitvice National Park** offers a unique lush world of yellow rock waterfalls, rivers and sparkling lakes. In Istria, the half-day hike to **Vojak Peak** provides 360-degree views across the peninsula and islands – all the way to Venice on a clear day. In the south, **Biokovo National Park** has many marked paths offering expansive views of the southern Dalmatian coast. On the island of **Brač,**

DON'T LEAVE WITHOUT...
Trying the uniquely Croatian sport of Škraping. Taking place on Pašman island, Škraping involves navigating around a series of checkpoints in the fastest time possible while negotiating tricky obstacles and the razor-sharp sea-level limestone ledges that line the island.

the Adriatic's highest peak, Vidova Gora (778m), is a short trek from Boi, and like the island of **Cres** (further south) it's full of trails through hamlets, peaks, caves and beaches.

Climbing

Paklenica Gorge is the epicentre of Croatian climbing – and it's obvious why. The towering 300m face of Anica Kuk has a huge concentration of limestone sport climbing, from single to multipitches. The ideal time to go is April–October. Elsewhere, more than 1200 sport routes of various grades can be found near Pazin, Pula and Rovinj in **Istria**; the islands of **Hvar**, **Brač** and **Vis** all have single-pitch sport routes; **Split** has Marjan crag and **Dubrovnik** has climbing routes just above the old city.

Canyoning

Canyoning is also popular. **Vražji Prolaz** (Devil's Passage) offers an epic 2.3km of beginner-friendly wading and waterfall climbing a short drive from Zagreb. Further south, Zadvarje village is the gateway to the 2.5km **Badnjevica Canyon** – which starts with a 17m waterfall abseil into a 2m wide gorge with 30m- to 60m-high walls – and **Cetina Canyon**, which has cliffs up to 180m high and a 50m-high waterfall.

Trail Running

Istria has the country's most developed trail network. **Buzet** is its focus, with 24.8km of trails through abandoned villages and forested valleys. If steep canyons and wilderness are more your thing, Starigrad-Paklenica has trails in the **Velebit mountains** and there are plenty of routes in **Paklenica National Park** itself. Island trails are often more technical but **Cres**, **Lošinj**, **Brač** and **Mljet** are all good bets, with beautiful coastal singletrack hidden in pine forests and plenty of beaches with crystal clear water nearby to stop for a dip.

Even in Zagreb, **Medvednica mountain** is easily accessible, with plenty of soft trails and a big trail running community organising regular events.

Cycling

The 61km **Parenzana Trail**, which follows a disused railway through olive groves, vineyards and medieval towns in the Istrian mountains, is a popular touring route. The run between **Plitvice**

© Mikey Schaefer, © simonkr | Getty Images

Lakes, **Paklenica** and **Krka** national parks is another classic route.

The Dalmatian coast is perfect for cycling, with the 15km stretch between Starigrad and Seline, in the foothills of the **Velebit Mountains**, a highlight. The **Pelješac Peninsula** and the islands of Brač, Hvar and Korčula also have good routes.

Mountain biking

MTB is increasingly popular and **Losinj** is the place to go, with downhill trails good enough to feature on the UCI MTB World Cup circuit. Around **Split**, there's more riding, offering a mix of road and downhill trails.

Watersports

From the beautiful and historic Poreč Riviera and Rovinj archipelago in Istria to the crystal clear waters of the Elaphiti islets down near Dubrovnik, Croatia's coast is a paradise for **sea kayaking**. Inland, the Zrmanja and Krupa rivers in Velebit National Park, the Mrežnica river near Primišlje, the Krka river and Cetina Gorge provide grade 2-4 rapids and excellent kayaking and rafting. On the Island of Bol, just south of Split, the constant Mistral creates winds perfect for kitesurfing, and Zlatni Rat beach has designated areas, including a launch platform and lifeguard monitoring.

In southern Dalmatia, the channel between the Pelješac peninsula and Korčula creates similarly good conditions for **windsurfing**, while the calm Baćina Lakes provide 20 sq km of water for **SUP** fans, with seven different lakes, lotus flower fields and an ancient bridge.

Croatia is, of course, synonymous with **yachting**, and boats can be hired from Dubrovnik (south), Split (central) or Biograd-na-Moru (north). Late spring is an ideal time to go.

Below, mountain biking is increasingly popular in mountainous Croatia. Left, Paklenica Gorge is the epicentre of Croatian climbing.

CUBA

Cuba, the Caribbean's largest island, is one of the least developed. Just waking up from its communist past, the next adventure is now beginning.

Cuba is relatively undeveloped outside its main tourist areas, which means that, although it's absolutely ideal for exploration – with back roads to cycle and undiscovered towns to explore – logistics can be a bit daunting for independent travellers. For the most part, it's easier to travel with an established company or make sure that you have a good fixer on the ground.

Watersports

Around Cuba's 5646km-long coastline there are plenty of watersports opportunities, including **sailing**, **kayaking** and **kitesurfing**, at places such as Varadero.

Quality **scuba diving** – which, interestingly, was a favourite pursuit of Fidel Castro's – can be enjoyed in the archipelago of Jardines de la Reina and around Cayo Largo and Cayo Coco. Another top spot is Isla de la Juventud (The Isle of Youth), a marine reserve off the south coast of Cuba, which is sheltered from prevailing south east winds. Divers will find caves, drop-offs and wrecks to explore here.

Riding & Climbing

Road-cycling trips are a good way to see the country, and it's also possible to explore on **horseback**. Unusually for the Caribbean there is **rock climbing** in Cuba, in the mountains near Havana (Pinar del Rio, towards the island's western tip) and Santiago (the Sierra Maestra, where Castro had his rebel HQ). Technically, climbing is still illegal here, though that doesn't stop people doing it.

DON'T LEAVE WITHOUT...
Going canyoning. Wade, swim, jump and abseil down the rivers of the central Topes de Collantes mountains and the Sierra Maestra in the east.

CYPRUS

Encircled by the Mediterranean, and soaked with year-round sunshine, Cyprus offers plenty for solar-powered explorers.

Cyprus conjures images of sun-seeking holidaymakers baking themselves, but this island has a host of activities for those who love burning calories more than epidermis.

Cycling

With near-empty and perfectly surfaced rural roads running along coastlines and through mountains, **road cycling** in Cyprus is sensational. Grinding up the island's highest point – 2000m Mt Olympus In the Troodos Mountains – provides a challenging target, and the ride down is exhilarating. In summer, the mountains offer an escape from the heat, but winter or spring present perfect pedalling weather.

The island has superb **mountain biking** trails too: traverse 250km through the Troodos Mountains on dirt tracks linking villages, churches and wineries. In February–March, world-class mountain bikers and amped-up amateurs come to compete in the **Cyprus Sunshine Cup**, a series of races held over successive weekends along the island's singletrack.

Climbing

Rock climbing is increasing in popularity, with routes in several areas including the rugged Akamas peninsula and the pine-filled Troodos Mountains. Boasting 185 sport routes and 250 traditional, Cyprus has more than enough climbing for a dedicated trip.

Diving & Snorkelling

Surrounded by sea that seldom drops below 17°C, and with little tide, Cyprus is ideal for snorkelling and diving. The remains of the ferry *Zenobia*, one of the Med's three largest wrecks, lies in the bay of Larnaca.

DON'T LEAVE WITHOUT...
Kayaking through the sea arches and exploring the caves and historic coast of Paphos, birthplace of Aphrodite.

Climbing one of Český ráj's iconic sandstone towers.

CZECH REPUBLIC

This small central European state has a long tradition of the extreme, the novel and the downright nuts.

Castles, spas, beer and odd adventures... meet the Czech Republic. Bridging Western Europe and the Slavic east, the country has been washed around by the tides of history, drawn into one empire after another. Nowadays, Prague's perfect pilsner and rich culture bring flocks of tourists, while out in the countryside, hardy Czechs and action-seeking visitors get their adventure fix.

Climb with Knots

Among the sandstone tors of **Český ráj** (Bohemian Paradise) and Elbe Sandstone Mountains, Czech climbers shun modern metal protection for bits of knotted rope. They drop the monkey fists (their special knots) into cracks much like other climbers slot in a nut, only it's way more hardcore. The official story is that the knots used to protect the soft sandstone from damaging ironmongery, but maybe there is a little hangover of the inventiveness born of being shut behind the Iron Curtain for so long. If you want to earn your Czech climbing stripes, best leave your fancy metal protection at home and instead bring knotted lengths of rope and as much bravery as you can fit in your pack.

Cross-country Ski

The **Jizerská padesátka** is a 50km-long cross-country ski race with a pedigree stretching back to 1968. Traversing the Jizera Mountains on the border with Poland, the event tests the technique and lactic acid threshold of 7500 spandex-clad athletes. You could be one of them.

SPIRITUAL HOME OF...
Tower jumping. Czechs have turned jumping into an art form amid the stone formations of the Adršpach-Teplice Rocks. Jumpers hurl themselves terrifyingly between towers. Jumps are named and graded and even the easy leaps are not for the uncommitted.

© Standa Mitáč

DENMARK

Denmark is Valhalla for bikepackers, but in a country of contoured coasts and a burgeoning climbing scene, adventure comes in a variety of flavours.

Cycling is as intrinsic to Danish culture as Hans Christian Andersen. While not entirely flat, Denmark's rolling terrain so lends itself to pedal power that even those seeking escapades of another sort should consider travelling by bike. Beyond the mainland, the Baltic Sea has hidden treasures, including the spectacular white cliff-ringed island of Møn, which offers excellent mountain biking, hiking, sea kayaking and paragliding.

Cycling

Denmark's 26 aptly named Panorama routes combine sensational scenery with superb infrastructure, and link numerous government-sponsored campsites with comprehensive amenities to make this an ideal destination for **bike-touring**. The well-signposted routes seamlessly drift from the urban to the pastoral, where they wend through landscapes ranging from fairytale woodlands and lush orchards to rugged cliffs overlooking the steely Baltic Sea. No tour is complete without a ferry trip to one of Denmark's 443 islands, and if you enjoy off-road riding, check out the **mountain bike** trails on Møn.

Watersports

Whether you go **sailing** in Roskilde Fjord, **sea kayaking** around Fyn or pilot a **solar-powered dinghy** along Copenhagen's canals, waterways are nearly as plentiful in Denmark as cyclepaths. While Denmark's fjords don't rival its Scandinavian neighbours for scenery, they are teeming with wildlife and lined with quaint harbourside towns.

Klitmøller, on the northwest coast, offers some of Europe's best wind and waves for **windsurfing** and **kitesurfing**.

Climbing

Bornholm Island is home to an enthusiastic local climbing scene and some truly lovely landscapes. Bornholm boasts some exceptionally pretty bouldering, a well-developed trad scene on the sea cliffs, and an emergent sport-climbing sector at a couple of active quarries. Routes are short and anchors are scarce on the sea cliffs, but the combination of welcoming locals and plentiful Tuborg connoisseurs makes for a very pleasant climbing experience.

ICONIC ADVENTURE EVENT

Do an unusual lap of the Danish Parliament Buildings by taking on the annual Christiansborg Rundt, a 2km swim along the legendarily clean canals of Copenhagen.

Left, the forests of Zealand hold some superb singletrack. Top right, Tungurahua (5023m), one of Ecuador's many active volcanoes. Bottom right, a blue-footed booby; the Galápagos' rich wildlife draws many adventure lovers.

© Soren Svendsen | Getty Images

ECUADOR

Andean mountains? Check. Amazonian forest? Check. Life-affirming islands and coastline? Check. Too many adventures for just one trip? It's looking that way...

Adventure seekers in Ecuador are spoiled for choice – but you'd expect that in a nation where the topography plunges from snow-capped 6000m volcanoes through dense jungles riven with wild whitewater corridors to rolling surf breaks and biological reserves that inspired the theory of evolution.

Avenue of the Volcanoes

Perched at 2850m, the capital Quito is a good place to acclimatise before exploring the nearby Avenue of the Volcanoes. The nine volcanoes dotted north–south along the soaring Cordillera – some active, others extinct – all rise impressively above 5000m. Their ice-capped slopes are ideal for high-altitude trekking, some offering mildly technical climbing, but it is, perhaps, **mountain biking** that rings loudest. Indeed, riding down the slopes of an active volcano – most notably Cotopaxi, one of the highest active volcanoes on the planet – is now considered a quintessential 'Ecuadorian experience'. Thanks to a certain 'Biking Dutchman' (see panel), Ecuador is one of the first places in the world to offer travellers the ability to scream down a volcanic ash track from 4500m. For those who prefer **trekking**, the two- to five-day climb up Cotopaxi is physically challenging, and despite not being considered a technically difficult climb, you'll still earn the view, which encompasses all eight of the other volcanic peaks. There's **mountaineering** too, with technical climbing on Antisana (5704m), Illiniza South (5248m) and Chimborazo (6263m), the latter being the highest volcano (albeit inactive) in Ecuador, and climbable year-round.

Going Big in Baños

Ecuador's ever-erupting adventure epicentre offers everything for exhilaration seekers. Here you can go **bridge swinging** (note: we're talking a giant swing, not a bungee), take off for a **canyoning** tour, run **whitewater** rapids, go **rock climbing**, take on more

© Tristan Brown; Kseniya Ragozina | Getty Images

ANA LUCÍA NOBOA, THE BIKING DUTCHMAN

'We never thought that what started 25 years ago with five bikes and an old Toyota Land Cruiser would become such a trend! The famous Baños Puyo Descent and the Chaquiñán between Cumbaya and Puembo are two examples of the opportunities for cycling in Ecuador. Village trails and ancient pathways provide perfect fodder for mountain bikers, especially in the region of Baños, Quilotoa and Quito. There's a great multiday loop in the Quilotoa area, while outside Quito you can pedal between villages on old train tracks.'

mountain **biking** challenges and then celebrate your epic day in one of many local bars.

Amazonian Paddling

Whitewater fiends looking for Grade III and IV rivers should head to the jungle outpost of Tena for rafting, or sign up to a kayaking skills course to learn how to paddle the big stuff properly. Once you've mastered your recovery roll, point the bow towards more 'big run' rapids near Macas, Río Blanco or El Chaco.

Galápagos Islands

To get the most from a Galápagos gallivant, shun the flight and hitch a lift (as crew or passenger) on a boat leaving Esmeraldas. The thrill of the adventure is in **sailing** there across 1000km of open ocean, then ensconcing yourself in Puerto Ayora on Santa Cruz Island. Here, you can enjoy **surfing** at nearby Tortuga Beach (watched over by hordes of marine iguanas) and sublime scuba **diving** amid abundant ocean-life. The hammerhead shark dive at Gordon Rocks is particularly mind-blowing.

TOP TIP
If Galápagos is beyond your budget, explore the Isla de la Plata instead. Just 27km off the mainland, the islands offer exotic wildlife and great snorkelling.

Left, a short distance from Baños you can zipline over the Agoyán waterfall.
Right, camel trekking is a traditional way to traverse the Sahara Desert.

EGYPT

Long an exotic land of mystery, Egypt retains a strong pull on those seeking adventure.

W ater is precious in a desert land – witness the Nile's power in Egyptian culture – so although the desert has a strong pull, there are myriad aquatic adventures to be had in the land of the Pharaohs.

Diving

The spectacular **Blue Hole** in the Sinai Peninsula is one of the planet's most famous dive spots… and one of the deadliest. Only a few metres from shore, the submarine sinkhole is 94m deep and, according to legend, it's cursed by a young woman who drowned herself to escape an arranged marriage. The feature that has earned it the nickname 'Divers' Graveyard' is the Arch, a horizontal tunnel that bores 26m through the reef out to open sea, the entrance to which is at 56m – well beyond recreational diving limits. The temptation to explore the Arch has ended tragically for at least 40 people, but those diving within their limits will find a sensational site, as safe as any other.

Elsewhere in the Red Sea, the British supply ship SS *Thistlegorm* is a world-class wreck dive. Sunk in 1941, it lay undisturbed at 30 metres until Jacques Cousteau discovered it in 1956. Parts of the 131m-long hull have been peeled back to reveal the ship's innards and a bounty of World War II relics, including munitions, rifles, motorbikes, train carriages and trucks.

Camel Trekking

In the west of Egypt lies the vastness of the **Sahara Desert**, where, slowed to the ancient rhythm of the camel's march, you can get swallowed by the sands and by time. Striking out from a gateway town – in the north, Siwa with its crumbling fort, or Al-Kharga, Dakhla and Bahariya in the south – your camel train traverses barely discernible tracks across the shifting ground to connect vital oases. Out here, beyond the last outpost of human habitation, the desert is all contrast, permanence and transience, where in its very enormity the small details will sing to you.

DON'T LEAVE WITHOUT…
Kitesurfing. Due to consistent winds, plenty of sunshine and turquoise water, the Red Sea is a belter of a spot whether you shred on a kite already or are just looking to get your feet wet.

© John Coletti; 2630ben | Getty Images

EL SALVADOR

Perfect surf breaks, black-sand beaches, deep forests and the opportunity to scuba dive in a live volcano – El Salvador awaits the adventurous.

E l Salvador suffers bad press because of street-gang violence, but warnings miss the fact that most of the country is safe and inviting. The smallest nation on the Central American isthmus may be the only one without Caribbean coastline, but who needs that when you've got Pacific waves crashing onto black-sand beaches, ominous volcanoes and impressive national parks to explore?

Surfing

The Pacific Coast hosts a string of surf spots, with a heavy concentration of right handers. **Punta Roca** is said to have the best right in Central America and **La Bocana** has a left formed by a wide river mouth. Then there are loads of less-publicised, hush-hush waves that reward those prepared to dig a little deeper. The main swell season runs March to October (the rainy season), but there are rideable waves year-round.

Volcano Diving

El Salvador is a mountainous country and 22 of those mountains are volcanoes. **Ilopango**, just east of the capital San Salvador, blew its top in AD 260, and the massive eruption created the country's second largest lake. Diving in Ilopango you can see crabs, fish, algae and freshwater sponges, but the thermal activity is the real attraction. At one spot – La Caldera del Diablo (the Devil's Caldera) – you can see and feel the underwater volcanic activity with hot streams of water coming out between rocks.

Hiking

The highest volcano in El Salvador, **Santa Ana** (2381m), is just outside the capital. After a moderate hike, spend a few hours at the summit, smelling the sulphur, contemplating the juxtaposition of the blasted rocky earth and the vibrant turquoise lake, then be back down in time for a *pupusa* dinner.

DON'T LEAVE WITHOUT...
Bombing some downhill MTB. There is some sweet singletrack snaking through the forest near the surf break of El Tunco. Pack your body armour.

There's no need for a wettie in El Salvador; surfing at Las Flores, Usulutan.

© Paul Kennedy | Getty Images

ESTONIA

Where in the world can you pilot a dogsled in the morning, enjoy bog walking after lunch and go motor-paintballing for your evening's entertainment? Estonia, of course.

Charming to the core, with spades of scenery and bargains galore, Estonia is a three-season paradise for hikers and kayakers, and a snowy wonderland in winter. The adventure travel scene here is thriving, and includes some genuine oddities, including the anarchic sport of *Romuralli*, which sees motorheads in half-wrecked cars race around a track in dramatic demolition derbies, using paintball guns to up the ante.

Hiking

Two of Europe's best through-hikes cross Estonia. From the Gulf of Finland to the Gulf of Riga, the 375km **Oandu–Ikla trail** wends through woodlands and along elevated walkways in the unexpectedly pretty bogs. Doughtier adventurers will appreciate the 820km **Peraküla–Ähijärve trail**, which takes in shingle beaches, velvety pine forests and golden farmlands as it meanders southwards. Expect devine campsites and the company of elk, wolverines and moose. If a long hikes don't appeal, myriad day options are available, as are overnight trips to **bear-watching** huts.

Bog-walking

Mires cover a fifth of mainland Estonia, and play an important role in the country's folklore. During summer, strap on a pair of bog shoes (like snowshoes) and enjoy an amble around these mysterious peaty domains, which are 10,000 years old and boast unique wildlife. Top bog walks include **Lahemaa** and **Viru** in the north, and **Soomaa** and **Matsalu** in the south.

Paddling

Some Estonian bogs can also be explored by boat, and the town of Otepää once hosted an extreme snow kayaking race. An amazing aquatic adventure awaits anyone entering the Võhandu Marathon, a 100km non-motorised boat race from Lake Tamula in Võru to Võõpsu village, Põlva County, featuring forests and plenty of dam-fed rapids. Paddlers use canoes, kayaks, stand-up paddleboards, rafts, inflatables and pedal boats, but they must finish within 24 hours.

Snowsports

Skiing and snowboarding (cross-country and downhill) are popular, epitomised by homegrown freestyle skier Kelly Sildaru, who, aged 13, became the youngest gold medallist ever at the 2016 Winter X Games. **Kuutse Hill** in Otepää is the highest resort, while **Kütiorg**, part of the Haanja Nature Park in Võru County, offers the country's longest ski trail. The **Tartu Maraton** in Lipuväljak, Otepää, is a classic cross-country race that's been held for over 40 years. For something different, try **kick sledging**, enjoyed on frozen waterways such as Lake Pühajärv.

DON'T LEAVE WITHOUT...
Lashing half a dozen malamutes to a sled and careening through the woods. Outside of winter, this can be enjoyed on wheels.

The beautiful Endla Nature Reserve, a popular bog-walking area.

© Sven Zacek | Getty Images

ETHIOPIA

Comprising a landscape that swings from the 'Roof of Africa' to a volcanic desert depression that is among the hottest and lowest places on Earth, Ethiopia is extreme.

Trekking in the Simien Mountains is Ethiopia's signature adventure. This extraordinary mountain range rises out of the plains to reach 4550m atop barren Ras Dashen, the country's highest peak. For much of its length the range features an escarpment with a vertical drop of more than 1km, along the edge of which trails teeter, providing an airy experience. The trek *du jour* is to the summit of Ras Dashen, a stunning journey of about nine days, walking among the likes of gelada baboons and walia ibex.

As the source of the Blue Nile, Ethiopia unsurprisingly offers some excellent **whitewater rafting**. The Blue Nile itself has the full stable of rapids – Grade I to V – providing half-day floats through to two-week epics. The Omo River is the country's other notable rafting destination, known as much for its wildlife-viewing opportunities and interactions with tribal groups as its whitewater.

Ethiopia's greatest claim to fame is arguably its suite of world-record **distance runners**. The greatest of all, Haile Gebrselassie, famously trained in the Entoto Mountains overlooking Addis Ababa, and trails on the 3200m-high range continue to swirl with runners – if you want to run with the best of them, come to Entoto around dawn.

Emerging activities with enormous potential in Ethiopia are **rock climbing** and **mountain biking**. Near to Addis Ababa, about 30 climbing routes have recently been developed on a basaltic cliff named Armora Gedel that's being touted as Ethiopia's first sport-climbing cliff, while a network of unsigned mountain bike trails can be found in Menagesha National Forest on the slopes of Mt Wuchacha at Addis Ababa's edge.

ICONIC RACE

Chase the dust of Ethiopia's legendary runners through Abijatta–Shalla Lakes National Park in the Rift Valley, during the annual Ethio Trail run, held around August.

Left, hiking in the Simien Mountains. Top, gelada baboons are an intimidating but common sight in the Simien Mountains.

© Santiago Urquijo | Getty Images

FIJI

Adrift in the South Pacific, this fantastically friendly land of 'Bula'-bellowing beaming people welcomes those who want to explore beyond their beachside bure door.

More associated with beaches and sun than bikes and runs, and cups of kava over Strava palavers, Fiji actually presents multiple opportunities for outdoor activities beyond the obvious ocean-focused adventures. These clearly shouldn't be overlooked, however, as perfect paddling conditions and sublime diving on tropical reefs are available all around the islands. Inland activities include hiking and biking across wonderfully diverse and often challenging terrain.

Sea Kayaking

Almost every resort offers kayaks of the basic barge-shaped sit-on-top variety, and these are fine for a half-hour paddle. For a more serious expedition, however, check out Blue-Lagoon based Southern Sea Adventures, which operates multiday proper sea-kayaking tours through the Yasawa archipelago, island hopping, overnighting in traditional villages and camping on deserted atolls en route.

Mountain Biking

The best way to explore the interior of the islands, big and small, is in the saddle of a mountain bike, and Fiji offers a surprising number of off-road trails. On **Viti Levu**, the main island, you can cycle around the scenic foothills of Sleeping Giant mountain in Sabeto Valley, or have a crack at riding up Mt Tomanivi (nee Mt Victoria), Fiji's highest peak. On **Taveuni**, explore Bouma National Heritage Park and bike to the Bouma waterfalls for a wild swim, before pedalling to the International Date Line for a genuine time-travelling experience. On **Vanua Levu**, you can explore rainforest trails around resorts such as Namale, Koro Sun and Naveria Heights in Savusavu.

Hiking

Walking remains a primary way of getting around for many Fijians, and even remote paths are well maintained. Viti Levu has excellent trails for hiking and running amid fecund forests full of tropical birds, with standout experiences found in Koroyanitu National Park and amid the volcanic peaks of the Nausori Highlands, where the vistas erupt right in front of you. Bouma National Park on Taveuni has a trio of terrific trekking trails: the Vidawa Rainforest Hike, Lavena Coastal Walk and the Tavoro Waterfalls, where plunge pools offer a refreshing dip.

DON'T LEAVE WITHOUT...

Meeting the marine locals on Fiji's two truly unmissable wet experiences: the famous non-cage shark dive – where you can encounter up to eight species of big finned fellows, including bull and tiger sharks – and a swim with manta rays off Barefoot Island.

Paddling around the coast of Kadavu Island.

© Ron Dahlquist | Getty Images

Post-adventure, there's nothing better than a sauna and a chilly dip in one of Finland's many lakes.

FINLAND

Awash in lakes and Arctic expanses, Finland is where Europe goes naturally wild.

Wedged between Russia and Scandinavia's more-celebrated nations, Finland offers vast swathes of Arctic wilderness, seemingly endless forests and constellations of lakes (the country is 10% water). Its highest point might be just 1324m, but lack of altitude is no barrier to outdoor activity in this adventure-loving nation that gave the world the sport of Nordic walking.

Waterways are arguably Finland's defining natural feature, with almost 200,000 lakes speckling the country to create an extensive system of **canoeing and kayaking** routes. On the Väliväylä canoe trail you can paddle more than 150km along an old log-floating route at the southern edge of Europe's most expansive lake district. Finland's largest lake, Saimaa, is another excellent paddling destination, with an inland archipelago of islands creating infinite possibilities.

Hikers gravitate to the rather alarmingly named Karhunkierros (Bear's Ring) through Oulanka National Park, resting against the Arctic Circle. The 80km trail cuts through forest and gorges and, while mosquitoes are far more prevalent than the eponymous bears, the claw marks on the tree trunks will alert you to the fact that they're out there somewhere. The northern Lapland wilderness, with its midnight sun and brilliant autumn colours, beckons intrepid hikers. The prime spot is Finland's second-largest national park, Urho Kekkonen, where spectacular unmarked wilderness routes are dotted with huts.

The Åland archipelago is Finland's premier **cycling** destination, with bridges and ferries creating an easy hop across the flat islands. Closer to the mainland is the circular Archipelago Trail from Turku, a scenic road that has morphed into a cycling favourite.

While lack of elevation limits downhill skiing, **cross-country skiing** is huge in Finland, with most towns maintaining a network of trails (often lit) each winter. The best and most extensive cross-country networks are in Lapland – Ylläs ski resort alone has more than 300km of cross-country trails.

HOMEGROWN ADVENTURE HERO: NALLE HUKKATAIVAL

Arguably the world's best boulderer, Nalle Hukkataival is a professional climber who roams the globe climbing the world's hardest boulder problems. In 2016, he claimed the world's first V17 boulder problem, Burden of Dreams, in Lappnor, Finland.

© Simon Bajada | Lonely Planet

FRANCE

Besides being the world's top skiing destination, France has the high peaks of the Alps and Pyrenees, extinct volcanoes, canyons, ancient forests, sandy beaches, cols, crags and surf – it's an adventure paradise of otherworldly proportions.

Regularly attracting more than 80 million annual visitors, France is the planet's most popular destination (and 80% of French people holiday at home). Yet step off the beaten track and you'll have the place to yourself. With tens of thousands of kilometres of hiking trails, 39 World Heritage sites, seven national parks, five mountain ranges and over 3500km of coastline, there's more than enough to go around – whatever your adventure tipple. Cyclists follow in the tyre tracks of Tour de France legends, tackling the cols that make heroes out of mortals, while mountain bikers chew up the dirt along waymarked trails and throw themselves down custom bike parks that take over the ski resorts in the summer months. Trail runners scamper across mountains and valleys, climbers can explore some of the world's best bouldering and kayakers have dozens of stunning rivers scattered across the country to choose from. Where to begin?

Hiking

Containing around 180,000km of waymarked walking trails leading up hills, across mountain ranges and dormant volcanoes, along serpentine rivers and ancient pilgrim routes, and through vineyards and forests, France is a fantastically hiker-friendly country.

The FFRandonnée looks after France's long distance hiking trails, which come in three forms. *Sentiers de petite randonnée et de promenade* (PR for short), commonly found near towns and villages,

are France's equivalent of a 'footpath'. These day walks, which are typically 6km–15km, are marked by yellow stripes.

Sentier de grande randonnée de pays (GRP), indicated by yellow and red markings, are designed for walkers exploring a particular region or valley. They're often circular and can be done in one- to seven-day sections.

France's most famous footways, though, are the *Sentiers de Grande Randonnée* (GR), symbolised by red-and-white markings etched onto trees, posts and rocks. These are long-distance paths (typically 100km–900km) that cross large sections of the country, linking with GRP to provide a trail network of more than 65,000km.

Stopping to admire the grand Pic du Midi d'Ossau in the French Pyrenees.

© UKS_Mit / Getty Images

ENGLAND

Plymouth

NORTH SEA

Dover

Dunkirk

Calais

BRUSSELS

Cologne

English Channel
(La Manche)

Lille

BELGIUM

GERMANY

Dieppe

Arras

St-Quentin

LUXEMBOURG

Le Havre

Honfleur

Rouen

Reims

Metz

Bayeux

Ouistreham

Louviers

Strasbourg

Coutances

Caen

Lisieux

Nancy

ALSACE

Brest

Morlaix

Cancale

Évreux

PARIS

LORRAINE

Colmar

Dinard

Mont St-Michel

NORMANDY

CHAMPAGNE

Presqu'île
de Crozon

Carhaix-
Plouguer

Dinan

Chartres

Seine

Troyes

Belfort

Basel

Quimper

BRITTANY

Rennes

Orléans

BURGUNDY

Auxerre

Dijon

Besançon

Vannes

LOIRE VALLEY

Bourges

CÔTE D'OR

ITALY

Carnac

Belle
Île

Angers

Loire

LA SOLOGNE

Yonne

Nantes

Cher

Châteauroux

JURA

ATLANTIC
OCEAN

Montaigu

Poitiers

Vienne

Le Creusot

Montluçon

Rhône

Chamonix

La Rochelle

Aubusson

Lyon

Mont Blanc
(4810m)

Limoges

LIMOUSIN

Puy de Dôme
(1465m)

Clermont-
Ferrand

FRENCH ALPS

Angoulême

Puy de Sancy
(1885m)

St-Étienne

Grenoble

Alpe
d'Huez

Lacanau-
Océan

Dordogne

Puy Mary
(1787m)

MASSIF
CENTRAL

Bay of
Biscay

Bordeaux

Dune
du Pilat

Mende

Mont Lozère
(1699m)

Mont
Ventoux
(1909m)

Nice

DORDOGNE

Tarn

Nîmes

Avignon

PROVENCE

Biarritz

Adour

Toulouse

LANGUEDOC

Cannes

MONACO

Antibes

Pau

Tarbes

Carcassonne

Montpellier

Aix-en-
Provence

Marseille

St-Tropez

Cauterets

PYRENEES

ROUSILLON

Corsica
(50km,
see inset)

Vignemale
(3298m)

Monte Perdido
(3355m)

ANDORRA
LA VELLA

Puig
Neulós

LIGURIAN
SEA

SPAIN

MEDITERRANEAN
SEA

Barcelona

Perhaps the most famous examples are the great traverses, such as the **GR10**, a 900km mountain trail that spans the Pyrenees from the Atlantic to the Mediterranean, and the **GR20**, a 180km crossing of Corsica, said to be Europe's toughest GR trail.

Most routes are well signposted, but it's wise to take an IGN 1:25,000 map and/or one of the excellent 'topo-guides' produced by the FFRandonnée. Sadly, these are only published in French, but directions are simple.

The trails meander from village to village, so there's an abundance of accommodation and food resupply options. The mountain refuges are some of the best you'll find in Europe and *chambre d'hôtes* (like a B&B) are incredibly reasonable, making a week-long hike an affordable adventure.

Trail Running

With almost half a million active trail runners and more than 2000 annual events, France is a candy shop for a visiting *traileur* with a sweet tooth for going off-piste.

The country is home to some of the world's most prestigious races, including the 166km **Ultra Trail du Mont Blanc**, which starts and finishes in the Chamonix Valley, and veers into Italy and Switzerland as it loops Western Europe's tallest peak along the route of the Tour du Mont Blanc, climbing over 10,000m en route. Another blue-ribbon event that sits in any French trail runner's calendar is the **Grand Trail des Templiers** in the department of the Aveyron in the Midi-Pyrenees.

Chamonix valley might be the spiritual home of trail running in France, but the Pyrenees – Europe's second largest mountain range, which stretches 450km from the Atlantic Coast to the Mediterranean – is a veritable labyrinth of trails that will take your breath away. Literally. These peaks are home to some of France's most iconic and oldest trail races, from the **Trophée du Vignemale** (established in 1904) to the **Grand Raid des Pyrenees** – a 160km slog around the Haute Pyrenees that gives the UTMB a run for its money.

Elsewhere, the **SainteLyon** is an epic mixed terrain (50% trail, 50% road) 70km raid (run/walk/march) from Saint-Étienne to Lyon that's held overnight during the dark midwinter, and which has been going for over 60 years.

Be aware, though, that to take part in any running race (trail or road), competitors must supply a medical certificate from a doctor. Most locals sidestep this by joining clubs, which give them a licence and medical certificate valid for a year. A sneaky option for visiting runners is to join the Fédération Française d'Athlétisme, thus obtaining a 'Pass J'aime Courir', which requires just one medical certificate and lasts for a year.

Of course, it's not all about racing. Like elsewhere, trail running is a great way to explore backcountry routes that were originally built for hikers. France has gone the extra step, however, by supplying two-dozen-plus dedicated trail stations (*stations de trail*) spread throughout the Pyrenees and Alps, with way-marked routes specifically designed for trail runners.

Road Cycling

France seduces cyclists with impossibly picturesque villages, epic Alpine climbs, 100km/h rollercoaster

ICONIC RACE: THE MEGAVALANCHE IN ALPE D'HUEZ
The king of gravity enduro races, this mashup of downhill and cross-country riding starts above the snowline on Le Pic Blanc (3300m) and finishes 30km later at Allemont (720m).

Trail running at Lac de Chésery near Chamonix in the French Alps.

© Thomas Bekker | Getty Images

descents, forests, volcanoes, vineyards, gorges, beaches and mile upon mile of superlative cycling – not to mention the sheer pleasure of refuelling on wine, cheese and a fresh baguette.

For three weeks every year, the country showcases its attractions to riders of every persuasion in the **Tour de France**. The race's founder, Henri Desgrange, invented the idea of a Grand Tour in 1903. Ever since, France has been a nation of cycling connoisseurs, where locals will shout, '*Allez, courage!*' as you grind your way up a mountain, and where you're likely to be overtaken by a gnarled old rider wearing a woollen jersey and pedalling an ancient steel bike. Attention naturally focuses on the famed Alpine ascents: the Col du Galibier, the Col du Télégraphe, Alpe d'Huez and many more iconic mountains. And don't forget the classic climbs of the **Pyrenees**, such as the Col du Tourmalet, the Col d'Aubisque and the Hautacam, which tend to be on steeper and narrower roads, or stand-alone challenges such as the monster **Mont Ventoux** in Provence. These are all significant

feats for fit cyclists, but there are plenty of ways of attempting them with a little support: sportives such as the **Etape du Tour** or **La Marmotte** ensure food and water are available. And many tour companies take cyclists on rides such as the multiday **Raid Pyrenean**.

But France isn't only about the *grande montagnes*. The country has an overwhelming choice of easier challenges, such as following the route of rivers like the **Loire**, or exploring the more medium-sized hills of such regions as the **Auvergne** or the **Jura**. Or you can do what many cyclists do: pack the panniers of a touring bike with a bottle opener and a change of clothes and simply pedal from village to village, *auberge* (inn) to *auberge*, enjoying the good life.

Mountain Biking
Few countries offer such a feast of trails for mountain-biking (*vélo tout terrain*) enthusiasts as France. To escape the crowds and have a proper adventure, attempt one of the **Grandes Traversées VTT**, a series of 11 routes that roll across some of

ICONIC RACE: THE MARATHON DU MEDOC
Forget gels and energy bars, during this super eccentric (and gastronomically Gallic) marathon, competitors (often wearing costumes) are required to quaff wine and scoff cheese, oysters entrecôte and foie gras as they run the regulation 42km through the vineyards and châteaux of Bordeaux.

© Jean-Luc Armand | Getty Images

France's most iconic regions, from the Jura to the Pays Basque.

If that doesn't sound enough of a challenge, then you could attempt the **French Divide**, France's version of the Tour Divide, which uses dirt trails to join France's northern border with Belgium to the southern border with Spain, following part of the Saint-Jacques de Compostelle route and serving up a fantastic 2100km bikepacking challenge.

A network of 14 Alpine resorts straddles the France–Switzerland border, and during the green season many offer superb mountain biking. However, the **Porte de Soleil** is renowned as *the* mountain bike destination in Europe. With 650km of trails – spanning downhill, enduro and cross-country – as well as five bike parks and several mountain-bike schools, there's something here to suit every knobbly-tyre enthusiast. For an overview, enter the legendary **Pass'Portes du Soleil** in June, which is a huge three-day celebration of mountain biking that scoots around the French and Swiss sides of the resort.

Skiing & Snowboarding

Perhaps unsurprisingly, since Europe's biggest mountain range runs down the country's east flank and is readily accessible to a vast number of people, few nations in the world have embraced winter sports quite so enthusiastically as France. Seven of the world's 10 biggest ski areas are wholly or partly within the French Alps, including the daddy of them all, **Trois Vallées** (Three Valleys).

This mega-resort has enough skiing to keep everyone from beginner to expert entertained for a lifetime, with (depending on who you ask) between 500km to 600km of runs accessed via 183 lifts that can transport 260,000 skiers per hour. Add 1920 snow cannons, 76 piste bashers and some 2000m of lift-served vertical, and your mind soon starts to reel from the figures.

Many cold-season visitors to France are inevitably drawn to the world's original winter sports resort: **Chamonix**. From the phenomenal scenery – Mont Blanc's glacier-draped flanks rise almost vertically up from the valley in a display that never fails to impress – to the mix of winter sports enthusiasts from all over the globe (and a nightlife that reflects this), Chamonix remains the top-draw destination.

But skiing in France is not just about the Alps. The massively underrated French Pyrenees offer resorts such as **Grand Tourmalet** and **Saint-Lary**, which are world class on their day, despite relatively few skiers outside France having heard of them, and there are even small ski hills in the little-known **Massif Central**.

France's huge, interlinked ski areas such as **Trois Vallées**, **Paradiski** and **Espace Killy** were developed in the 1970s as something of a social experiment. While the tower blocks and apartments that make up so many of them are a far cry from traditional Alpine 'chocolate box' architecture, their frill-free design allowed (and still does allow) skiers on limited budgets to enjoy the thrill of experiencing some of the world's best slopes.

If money's no object, you can head to a resort such as **Courchevel**, which is renowned for its five-star chalets and hotels; mind you, most folks who stay in them are more interested in strutting around the bars and restaurants than hitting the slopes.

Should you hanker after 'traditional' you can still find that too. Resorts like the linked **La Clusaz** and **Grand Bornand** near the lovely lakeside town of Annecy, or **Bonneval-sur-Arc**, hidden at the end of a high valley in the Maurienne region, are attractive Alpine settlements with superb skiing on the dramatic peaks that surround them, while tiny **La Grave** offers some of the most challenging skiing on the planet.

© Magnus Kallstrom | Getty Images

Below, the French Alps are one of the world's most iconic skiing destinations. Left, technical riding near Chamonix, the capital of French adventure.

© Henn Photography | Getty Images

Snow Other

It's not all about skiing, though, as there are myriad ways to go adventuring here in winter. Val Thorens boasts the highest **zipline** in Europe, there's **ice climbing** in Chamonix, while in La Plagne you can go **bobsledding** on the course that was used for the 1992 Olympics.

Fatbiking is becoming increasingly popular in France, with resorts from Les Deux Alpes to Le Grand Bornand offering it as a winter alternative, and most resorts offer the more traditional winter sports of **cross-country skiing** and **snowshoeing** (the cross-country trails of Champagny-le-Haut are especially appealing).

Or if you really want to try something different, how about **ice diving** beneath the frozen Alpine lake at Tignes?

Climbing & Mountaineering

Few places on Earth get a climber's pulse racing like France. From the epic riddled peaks of the Alps, the endless limestone crags of the south, to the perfect sandstone boulders of the forests of Fontainebleau, it's no wonder French climbers rarely leave France.

Alpinism

When it comes to French climbing where else can you start but Chamonix? Nestled in the Alps near the border of Italy and Switzerland, **Chamonix Valley** is the beating heart of French alpinism. Close by, you will find many of the peaks of mountaineering lore: **Mt Blanc** (4808m), the ragged, jagged skyline of the **Aiguilles Rouges** and the golden granite of **Aiguille du Midi** (3842m). Aspiring alpinists can hook up with a guide, while hardened mountaineers can choose from a host of hard or historic (or both) routes. If you're not into getting cold and scared, do not despair, sport climbing and bouldering abound. End a day's climbing with cocktails in one of Chamonix's bars. And if you find the tourists of Chamonix too much, head south to the **Durance Valley** in the Hautes-Alpes. Here you will find everything from Alpine routes to sport climbing and bouldering.

Sport Climbing

Verdon or Ceuse? Gorges du Tarn or Buoux? Picking the best sport climbing destination in France is tricky. Many consider **Ceuse** and its immaculate pocketed limestone to be the best sport climbing crag in the world. Others think it is hard to go past the vertiginous gorge of **Verdon**, where committing abseils into the abyss leaves climbers perched above the thin turquoise ribbon of the Verdon river far below. Still others prefer the easy access and gorgeous limestone cliffs of **Gorges du Tarn**. But wherever you go, it will be amazing.

Bouldering

An hour south of Paris is the best, most famous and historic bouldering area in the world: **Fontainebleau**. Imagine all the things that would make for a perfect bouldering area – flat, sandy landings, endless boulders, soft-on-the-skin sandstone, unique shapes, densely concentrated problems – and you find it here. Originally considered a training ground for the Alps, *bleausards* (local climbers) have been bouldering here for more than 100 years, and it's considered a rite of passage to get burnt off by geriatric (but well-muscled) *bleausard*, who generally have all the classics wired. Best of all, you are never too far from a *café au lait* and croissant, while rest days can be sent touring the art galleries and museums of Paris.

Canyoning

There's a pleasure in canyoning that's indescribable. Only those who have done it can appreciate the sensations one experiences while jumping into mountain rock-pools, abseiling down waterfalls, clambering over rocks and sliding down chutes. With seven mountain ranges full of gorgeous gorges, plus a plethora of guides to show you the best spots, France is the sport's spiritual home.

Possibly the most exciting place to get your feet wet in France is the **Le Canyon des Ecouges**, one of Europe's most beautiful gorges, found half an hour from Grenoble in the High Alps. Equally impressive is the **Canyon des Oules de Freissinières** in the Écrins National Park, although you might want to have a few other 'easier' canyons under your belt before attempting this monster.

Paragliding

With close to a thousand paragliding sites, more than any other country, it's fair to say France is a veritable Valhalla for paragliders. Unsurprisingly, due to the high mountain thermals, ski lifts allowing

easy access to the take-off sites and a relatively stable weather pattern providing an average of 24 flying days per month, the Alps have the lion's share of sites, with **Lake Annecy** and **Chamonix** the most popular. Whether you're a seasoned pro looking to fly off the Aiguille du Midi or a beginner heading to the Col du Forclaz with its stunning views of Lake Annecy, there's something to suit all abilities. It's worth noting that most paragliding schools operate April–November, when the daylight hours are longest.

Serious enthusiasts should head to the small Alpine farming village of **Mieussy** in the Haute Savoie, which happens to be the birthplace of paragliding. And beginners will love **Dune du Pyla** on the Atlantic coast, where the largest sand dune in Europe provides a very soft landing.

Kayaking

Boasting more than 700 clubs and thousands of kilometres of rivers, France is blessed when it comes to paddlesports. For those looking for something extreme and beautiful, the 21km **Gorges du Verdon**, with ethereal green water and 700m canyon walls, is an enticing place.

Above, a paraglider soars above the Hautes-Alpes. Left, just south of Paris is the bouldering paradise of Fontainebleau.

© Tristan Shu | 500px

The surreal turquoise waters of the Gorges du Verdon are hugely popular with paddlers.

such, it's home to a huge surf industry, regular international surf contests and a large local as well as itinerant surfing population.

The attractions of the region are obvious – warm waters (summer sea temperatures are around 22–23°C), plenty of sunshine and consistent Atlantic swells, along with a hectic social scene and the chance to rub shoulders with surfers from all over the world. You may encounter some crowding and localism, especially at busy spots such as Biarritz, Cap Breton, Hossegor and Seignosse, but it's easy to avoid the worst of it by walking or driving up or down the coast from the main breaks.

The sport first took off in the early 1960s in **Biarritz**, where there's a varied array of waves including busy beach breaks like Grande Plage, classic point breaks such as Lafitania and the huge offshore reef of Belharra. Beyond this it's essentially beach breaks, such as **Lacanau**, as far as the Gironde estuary, some 300km north.

Further north still, **Les Sables d'Olonne** has a vibrant surf community without the hype and crowds you'll find in the south, while Brittany on France's northwest tip has a very different feel with colder waters and a more rugged coastline – the point and beach break set up around **La Torche** offers the classic Brittany surf experience.

Numerous marathon kayaking events take place, but there are two key events in France: the **Ardeche**, a mass participation 35km paddle race through Gorges de l'Ardèche, and the **Dordogne-Périgord**, where amateurs and professionals race side-by-side over various distances to Castelnaud-la-Chapelle.

Various whitewater centres provide ample opportunity for developing technique, but one of the best is in the foothills of the Pyrenees, at the **Stade d'Eaux Vives** in Pau, an artificial river where the World Canoe-Kayak Championships has been held on countless occasions and the French national squad train.

Surfing

France is one of the focal points of European surfing, with the area around Hossegor and Seignosse on the southwest Atlantic coast having some of the best waves on the continent. As

Kitesurfing

In France you'll find hundreds of zones spread all over the country, and 'le Kitesurf' is very much considered a mainstream sport. The country's 800km Mediterranean coast is stroked by the strong, dry winds of the Mistral and Tramontane, making it perfect kitesurfing territory. Within its 70 zones, the **Languedoc-Roussillon** is one of the most popular. And if you fall into the expert camp, then no trip is complete without visiting **Leucate** (which holds the annual 'Mondial de Vent' competition) and **Saint-Pierre la Mer**, where the French and Junior World Kitesurfing championships took place in 2016. Further up the coast, the **Provence-Alpes-Côte d'Azur** is busier, but the **Plage de l'Almanarre**, with its fabulous 5km sandy beach, is well worth a trip. On the Atlantic coast, there are plenty of choices, but one of best is **Lacanau**, which is suitable for all abilities and home to one of France's top beach breaks.

© Thierry Dosogne | Getty Images

FRENCH GUIANA

With 95% of the country cloaked by thick jungle and only a narrow coastal strip developed, French Guiana is ripe for exploration.

F rench Guiana is a curious place: the futuristic European Space Agency launch site positions it in the modern world, but that contrasts sharply with the untamed tropical Amazonia that dominates. For almost a century, this 'Green Hell' was the dumping ground for France's most unsavoury criminals, including Henri Charrière, better known as Papillon, the name of his popular autobiography. Today, for adventurous and wilderness-embracing travellers, it could be a 'Green Heaven'.

Trekking

Bursting with 1300 types of tree and a wealth of animal species encompassing 190 mammals (including jaguars), 720 birds, 480 fish, innumerable snakes, four types of caiman and more bugs than you could swat in a lifetime, the virgin jungles of French Guiana are prime survivalist territory. Wannabe Papillons could get dropped off in the country's heart, perhaps around the Approuague River at the Grand Kanori rapids, then push their way to the small settlement of Saül, eating what they catch and navigating by compass, but there are some established trails, which capital city Cayenne's tourist office can point you towards.

Paddle the Maroni

The Maroni River is the natural border between Suriname and French Guiana, an important waterway that provides access to the deeper regions of the rainforest. Make for Saint-Laurent-du-Maroni and rent a traditional dugout canoe, then cast off on the vast navigable network for a few hours or a few weeks, staying in tiny villages at night.

ULTIMATE CHALLENGE
What could be more romantic and adventurous than joining the French Foreign Legion? In French Guiana you could survive the Legion's Jungle Training Centre and as a bonus earn yourself French citizenship.

GABON

Gabon is draped in stunning landscapes and is so overflowing with biodiversity that hippos feel the need to escape the crush and go surfing.

S taggeringly, three quarters of Gabon is still covered by dense tropical rainforest. Those who are lucky enough to explore here will find lagoons, cloud-tipped mountains, rocky plateaus and rivers rushing down rocky canyons. And then there's the wildlife…

Hike with pygmy trackers to observe western lowland gorillas in Loango National Park (head to the park's beaches to see those wave-riding hippos) or walk to Langoué Baï – a forest clearing in Ivindo National Park, where gorillas and elephants congregate – after **paddling** a pirogue (canoe) to Kongou Falls. Then there's Mt Brazza to **climb** in Lopé National Park, and a perfect point break to **surf** at Mayumba.

THE GAMBIA

Like a tight-fitting glove, The Gambia surrounds its namesake river and proffers wildlife encounters and forests full of birds.

N o country in the world is as intrinsically linked to a river as The Gambia. This sliver of a nation – Africa's smallest country – owes its very existence to the River Gambia, and every experience here is linked to the waterway in one way or another.

Travel by **boat** in River Gambia National Park to encounter chimpanzees, hippos, manatees and hundreds of bird species. If the adventure urge is still calling, try petting some rather large lizards at the sacred Kachikally Crocodile Pool. Alternatively, **hike** through Abuko Nature Reserve to see everything from bush babies and porcupines to cobras and pythons.

GEORGIA

This mountainous region of Eurasia has a plethora of stunning alpine panoramas, sheer canyons and raging rivers that drain west to a 330km-long super-scenic coastline.

Georgia's Greater Caucasus Mountains extend into the north like the spine of a petrified dinosaur, holding many hiking and mountaineering opportunities. The Black Sea sprawls to the west, and numerous rivers promise remote rafting and kayaking adventures. Sunny Gudauri has 57km of ski runs including slalom, downhill and heli-skiing, and, reputedly, Europe's cheapest ski pass.

Mountaineering

The imposing **Bezengi Wall** (near the Russian border) is the ultimate mountaineering adventure arena: a serrated ridge roughly 13km long linking several of the Caucasus' highest peaks – including Georgia's highest, **Shkhara** (5201m). Most of the ridge crest is around 5000m with steep walls plummeting 2000m either side. Numerous gendarmes and cornices mean a difficult yet ultra-rewarding climbing. Another technical and stunning ascent is **Mt Ushba** (4710m); climbers approach from the south, journeying through isolated Svaneti, a series of medieval villages dating to the 9th Century.

Hiking

Hiking here means traversing enclosed high valleys, rocky gorges and rugged mountain passes, and sleeping in rustic, remote Middle Age villages. Highlights include **Chaukhi Pass**, **Keli Volcanic Plateau** (permit required) and Tobavarchkhili Lake in the Egrisi Mountains. The hidden **Khada Gorge** features historical towers and graves, and crossing the range to the west descends into Gudauri.

Rafting

Whitewater rivers abound in Georgia. **Rioni** (Grade II–V) houses Tvishi Canyon, a 16km paddle-basher with continuous whitewater. Another beautiful canyon (Grade III) is on the **Mtkvari**, which passes a 10th century fortress. The huge drowned cave-complex town of **Vardzia** (near Mtkvari) is a great base for sensational splash-fests. Several routes of varying difficulties put in from here. Jomardi Tours organises trips to all these places. Whitewater heroes (and those travelling with kayaks), feel the call of wild **Inguri** and its deep, spectacular canyons. Rapids here are extreme (Grade VI plus); it's rumoured the lower river section has never been paddled before...

© Maya Karkalicheva | Getty Images

DON'T LEAVE WITHOUT...
Paragliding over the Caucasus Mountains. With a range of launch sites countrywide, from 500m to 2500m high, paragliding the Caucasus is a serene experience that will linger long after feet touch terra firma.

Hiking in the Caucasus Mountains in the historic province of Svaneti.

GERMANY

From tough Teutonic trails to silky ribbonesque rivers just asking to be run, Germany is an underrated adventure powerhouse.

P oor Germany. With such Alpine scene-stealing European neighbours as Switzerland, France and Austria, the land of lederhosen often gets overlooked by those who favour active outdoor excitement over beerhall high-jinks.

But there are long-distance trails to be hiked and ridden, rivers to be paddled, cliffs to be climbed and adventures aplenty to be had, in the Rhineland massifs the Harz and Ore mountains and, of course, in Bavaria, Germany's most famous outdoor playground. Here you can ascend to a wintersports heaven, crowned by Germany's highest peak, the 2962m Zugspitze.

Poor Germany can offer rich pickings for those with an adventurous eye.

Hiking

In Germany, many long-distance trails offer a slice of everything: steep and serious terrain with mountain views, undulating tracks through forests, hiking paths linking historic villages and remote walks where you can still spot wildlife, including black bears and lynx.

Saxon Switzerland and the Thuringian Forest are respectively home to Germany's most scenic long-distance walks: the 112km **Malerweg** – known as the Painter's Way for its historical association with landscape artists – and the **Rennsteig** (168km), a ridge walk in the Thuringian Highland. The latter is not to be confused with the equally stunning 320km **Rheinsteig** from Bonn to Wiesbaden, a trail shadowing the Rhine and featuring challenging climbs and a variety of landscapes of both natural and cultural significance.

The Saxon-Bohemia region in the east is home to the **Kammweg**, a 289km hiking route that's one of Central Europe's oldest, while the 660km **Goldsteig** in eastern Bavaria is Germany's longest notable trail, its route traversing woodlands and riverscapes and overlooking a line-up of 1000m-plus peaks.

Other popular trekking areas include the **Harz** and the **Black Forest**. Those seeking more vertiginous challenges can, in summer, check out the multitude of routes crammed into and around the **Bavarian Alps**.

Climbing

One of the best sport climbers in history, Wolfgang Güllich (1960–1992), was German, so it's no surprise the country features world-famous crags that, while

The summit of Zugspitze (2962m), the highest peak in the German Alps.

© mikemcd | Shutterstock

Right, bouldering in the Frankenjura, Germany's best climbing area. Left, hikers traversing Herrenwieser See in the Black Forest.

not known for their size, are respected for their interest and difficulty levels. The region of **Südpfalz** was the crucible for Güllich's talent, with trad climbing, sport climbing and bouldering all on offer, and its topography boasting 120 towers and 200 massifs.

The limestone crags of the **Frankenjura** present more world-class climbing; the region is notable – in addition to its high density of traditional breweries – for more than 6500 routes, including the world's first recognised 9a (5.14d) grade climb, 'Action Directe'. Güllich specifically invented the now commonly used campus board training tool to build the strength required for the route, which features long dynamic moves off single-finger pockets.

The **Elbe Sandstone Mountains** are also well regarded by climbers. Free climbing is popular but via ferrata offers exposure for the non-experienced. There are an estimated 14,000 routes up the Elbe's more than 1100 freestanding pinnacles.

Road Cycling

Germany has more than 200 dedicated long-distance cycle routes, so the two-wheeled traveller is spoiled for choice. These well-signposted – often traffic-free – pathways offer a more adventurous way to hop between historic cities, or to explore areas of great natural beauty. Take your pick from a pedal through dramatic river valleys, along rugged coastlines, past crystal clear Alpine lakes, into dense forests and over imposing mountain passes.

If navigation isn't your strong point, then following the banks of one of Germany's many rivers is a great way to go. Popular rides include the 870km **Elberadweg** or the legendary **Danube** – a riverside route revered by cycle tourists worldwide. If history is your thing, then a pedal along the Rhine is a must. Be sure to add an extra few days into your schedule to explore one of the hundreds of medieval castles scattered along the banks of this trail, which runs from Kleve in the north west, to Lake Constance in the south east.

If you prefer your waters to be more of the ocean blue type than river green, then head up to the fringes of the Baltic Sea, where a 1095km **Flensburg-to-Usedom** trail skirts Germany's northern coast. The riding here is mostly on a flat paved surface, with some sections of sand or cobble to negotiate. Expect to encounter dramatic chalk cliffs, shallow sandy bays, windswept peninsulas, lush green forests and the Unesco-listed medieval towns of Wismar and Stralsund.

ULTIMATE CHALLENGE
Love lactic burn? Try the Zugspitze Trailrun Challenge. The 'shorter' event is a 16km/2195 vertical-metre climb from Ehrwald to the Zugspitze summit. The full marathon ups the ascent to 3965 vertical metres, while the masochistic 'double classification' tackles both.

© Juergen Wackenhut | Shutterstock, © Cody Duncan | Getty Images

Not to be missed are also some lung-busting rides on quiet trails through the mountains of the **Black Forest** in the south west of the country.

Mountain Biking

Although backroad-touring adventures such as the 860km Elberadweg are immensely popular, there is also a bevy of off-road options.

To find singletrack, rough riders gravitate to the regions of **Sauerland**, the **Eifel**, the **Harz** (which has more than 2200km of dedicated mountain-bike trails) and the **Black Forest**, commonly regarded a mountain biking paradise.

The 200km **Rennsteig Cycle Trail** travels through the Thuringian Forest Nature Park and the Slate Mountains, with 120km of the route on forest tracks.

Bikepark Winterberg is Germany's premier go-to for downhillers and freeriders. It features a multitude of creative obstacles and ranks among the best bike parks in Europe, the 9km of freeride trails being the biggest draw. And the **Palatinate Forest Park** is another forest gem, featuring 300km of pathways through west Germany's largest unified wooded area.

Snowsports

Riders will find 300km of trails in the Palatinate Forest Park.

Lying just below the Zugspitze, **Garmisch-Partenkirchen** is the epicentre of all things snowsports,

its credentials founded on hosting the 1936 Winter Olympics and 2011 Alpine World Ski Championship. It boasts 20km of pistes ranging from 700m to 3km, a snowboard park and 40km of cross-country (XC) trails. True XC adherents, however, will base themselves out of nearby ski village **Oberammergau**, which has 90km of routes, plus a few steep pistes on the slopes of the Laber (1683m).

For those seeking more intense thrills, the **Dammkar-tunnel** near Mittenwald on the opposite side of Garmisch-Partenkirchen, has a 40% incline that's one of Germany's most challenging.

Allgäu boasts 500km of downhill slopes, including some deep-snow off-piste skiing, and with 200 ski lifts it easily lays claim to being Germany's largest continuous ski field.

Paddling

There's plenty of water sloshing around Germany in the form of lakes, canals and some of Europe's greatest rivers – think the Danube and the Rhine – with more than 40,000km of predominantly flat water for paddling enthusiasts to explore.

Paddling the big rivers is popular, but you have to share with big cruisers. Perhaps the most appealing multiday paddle is in the **Müritz National Park**. Here you can pack supplies and meander through a mosaic of lakes, pitching the tent bankside at night. Similar paddle-camp explorations can be had in the **Spreewald**, south of Berlin; around Lake Constance (the second largest in Europe); and on the **Schleswig-Holstein lakes**, from Eutin to Kiel. Another astonishing Alpine puddle that can be explored by kayak or paddleboard is **Lake Eibsee** below Zugspitze in Grainau, Bavaria.

For something different, paddle the small **Altmühl** between the Rhineland and the Danube, which includes an underground tunnel section that was artificially constructed to supply the Rhine-Danube canal. Spooky but fun.

Though Germany can't hold a whitewater flag to many global destinations, it does have a few runs worth getting skirted up for, including the steep descent of the **Eistobel** on the Argen River in Bavaria. The **Gutach** in the Black Forest is another fast flowing, narrow and tough run. For guaranteed conditions, try the artificial whitewater of Augsburg Eiskanal in Augsburg – constructed for the 1972 Munich Olympic Games.

© Philip Koschel / LOOK-foto | Getty Images

GHANA

Walk among wild elephants and other iconic African species, paraglide off rocky ridges, and tour meteoric landscapes and traditional villages on horseback.

G hana may be famed for historic slave forts, but its coast is also lined with many beautiful beaches, some of which are ideal for surfing. And the rivers cutting deep inland flow through sections of fecund wilderness, which sustain impressive populations of African wildlife and provide memorable active safari experiences.

Foot & Canoe Safaris

With East and Southern Africa hogging the limelight, you'd be forgiven for assuming West Africa was not the land of classic wildlife safaris. But **Mole National Park** in Ghana is crawling with creatures big and small, and here you truly have the chance to take a step on the wild side. Head out on foot with guides for enthrallingly close encounters with elephants, buffaloes, baboons, kob antelopes

and more. And on canoe safaris, organised by the nearby Mognori Eco Village, you can marvel at crocodiles, monkeys and some of the dazzling 300 species of birds known to frequent the park.

For those not afraid of heights or the dark, **Kakum National Park** provides additional wilderness thrills – walk along its floating trail and stare into the lush tree canopy from a height of 40m, or take to the jungle floor for a guided night-time walk in search of leopards, bongo and giant forest hogs.

Horseback Explorations

The crater lake of **Bosumtwe** and the hills that surround it in central Ghana owe their formation to the massive impact of an ancient meteorite. Now carpeted with lush vegetation and dotted with traditional villages, these hills make for a captivating horseback journey. The loop around Bosumtwe should take about 10 hours.

DON'T LEAVE WITHOUT...
Filling your parasail and running off a lofty perch in the Likpe mountains to soar over the Volta region's waterfalls and forests.

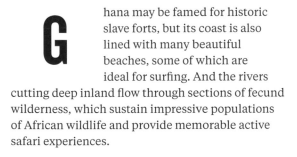

Foot safaris are a great way to see wildlife such as this bushbuck in Mole National Park.

© Mint Images · Frans Lanting | Getty Images

GREECE

From the island-speckled splendour of the Aegean to the majesty of Mt Olympus, Greece is a landscape ripe for heroics.

Lapped by sparkling emerald seas on three fronts, and surrounded by hundreds of islands, Greece boasts a bounty of aquatic adventures. But Europe's third-most-mountainous country also offers plenty of terrestrial escapades, amid terrain once considered the abode of gods.

Watersports

A lively afternoon breeze typically breathes across the Aegean, creating cracking conditions for **sailing**, **windsurfing** and **kitesurfing**. Lefkada is one of the best spots to hoist a kite, with Naxos, Rhodes, Karpathos and Kos also popular, while Paros hosts world-cup windsurfing action.

Sea kayaking and **stand-up paddleboarding** are both sensational ways to explore thousands of islands scattered across the Ionian, the Aegean and the Sea of Crete.

Diving & Snorkelling

Though world-class **snorkelling** has always been enjoyed around Greece, until 2005 **scuba diving** was heavily restricted – now bubble blowers have 16,000km of incredible coastline to explore. Chios Island is one of Europe's best dive sites, with decent visibility, warm water, amazing reefs, caves and wrecks. Volcanic Santorini has a labyrinth of canyons, swim-throughs and caverns, while the caves on Dragonisi Island, off Mykonos, offer the chance to encounter monk seals. For experienced technical divers, the wreck of the HMHS *Britannic*

(sister ship to the *Titanic*), which lies 120m deep off the island of Kea, is a big attraction, but far more accessible is a drowned German seaplane in 20m just off Naxos.

Hiking & Climbing

Spring is the best time to attempt any serious walking in Greece, where routes include sections of the European Long Distance Paths E4 (which traverses Crete) and E6. Elsewhere, wander among the mind-blowing monoliths at Meteora, stroll through the forests of Pelion or explore incredible archaeological ruins at Delphi or Dion.

Climbing to Zeus' throne atop 2917m Mt Olympus, Greece's highest peak, can be undertaken as a challenging two-day clamber from one of three trailheads. The precipitous route from Prióna, near Litóhoro, is most popular, taking walkers through a Unesco biosphere reserve and ascending the Kakí Skála (Evil Stairway). The final approach to the route's highest point, Mytikas, involves a technical climb.

Sport Climbing

Mountains and sea meet at Kalymnos. The small island exploded onto the international sport-climbing scene after being 'discovered' by Italian climber Andrea di Bari in 1996. Since then, the steep limestone crags with their iconic stalactites (or tufas) have lured climbers from across the globe. Besides the excellent rock, most climbs offer fantastic views and are conveniently located close to cute villages and pristine beaches.

DON'T LEAVE WITHOUT...
Exploring Greece's snow-sports resort at Parnassos. Here, from December to April, you can ski and snowboard. And when the white stuff melts, the resort offers great hiking, mountain biking and canyoning.

GREENLAND

Even in our modern age, the second largest ice cap on the planet remains a true frontier for intrepid explorers.

R emote and untameable, Greenland should rank highly on any self-respecting adventurer's bucket list. Famous for its sprawling Arctic landscape, much of the island is covered by a vast glacier. At the end of its inexorable march towards the coast, the ice gives way to a dramatic collection of precipitous mountains, spellbinding fjords and rustic villages.

Ski-exploring

The treacherous beauty of the Arctic has not diminished one iota since the Golden Age of Polar Exploration and little has changed since Fridtjof Nansen's landmark Greenland crossing in 1888. Modern explorers can follow in the footsteps of historical giants by pitting themselves against an

epic 500km traverse of the ice. Many expeditions begin in the east at **Ammassalik** and finish in the west at **Kangerlussuaq** (or vice-versa). Whichever direction you take, no trip would be complete without witnessing the haunting sight of the abandoned DYE2 missile detection station languishing deep within the frozen wastes. Adventure Consultants, Jagged Globe or Icelandic Mountain Guides can provide logistics.

Dogsledding

An even deeper homage to the history of the region is the continued practice of expedition dogsledding. Benefit from the experience of the Inuit people as they share this tradition dating back more than 5000 years. Dogsledding is a truly unique way for man and beast to bond as they explore the wild fjordlands around **Kulusuk**.

Climbing

From the waters of **Scoresby Sound** rise a series of jagged peaks. Rarely seen and climbed, these imposing granite monoliths are the stuff of legends for big wall climbers dreaming of first ascents. This is adventure climbing at its best – no guidebooks, no crowds and, in all likelihood, no possibility of rescue.

Ski mountaineers can put a feather in their cap with a short peak-bagging expedition around **Gunnbjørn Fjeld**. At 3694m, it's Greenland's highest mountain as well as the tallest peak north of the Arctic Circle. Weather permitting, an ascent of several subsidiary peaks would be a nice way to round out a week.

© RubyRascal; Mint Images · Frans Lanting | Getty Images

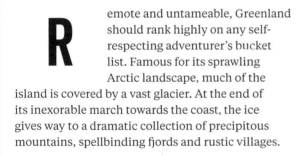

DON'T LEAVE WITHOUT...
Shooting the breeze across the frozen wilds while kite-skiing – the speed record for the Greenland Crossing was comprehensively smashed in 2015 with the aid of kites!

Top, tourists examine the glacier terminus at Scoresby Sound. Left, dogsledding is the traditional way to explore Greenland.

GUATEMALA

Paraglide around volcanoes, toast marshmallows in lava, raft canyons for days, explore jungles and Mayan ruins... this is the place to play at being Indiana Jones.

Central America's most mountainous country offers huge swathes of wilderness, wetlands, waterfalls, otherworldly crystalline pools, lush forests, fine coastlines with both black-sand and Caribbean coconut-fringed beaches, and many volcanoes, some still smoking. And perhaps most excitingly, its jungles are seemingly full of unexcavated Mayan ruins.

Volcano Trekking

From spirited multicultural Antigua, the former capital, the infectiously handsome landscapes of **El Altiplano** (the Highlands) stretch right to the Mexican border, offering a playground of peaks and mountains, lakes and ruin-rich jungles. From Antigua, guided hikes up Pacaya's (2552m) volcanic cone bring you to flowing lava, where you can toast marshmallows and catch superlative sunset views.

More satisfying volcano conquering can be had on nearby Agua (3766m) and Acatenango (3880m). Volcano-ringed **Lago de Atitlán**, described by Aldous Huxley as one of the most beautiful lakes in the world, has superb hiking trails – beside water and up mountainsides – linking traditional villages where men still wear traditional Mayan dress.

Rich in indigenous culture, the **Western Highlands** also offer excellent hiking, once again up volcanoes, and especially near Quetzaltenango. Volcán Santa Maria (3772m) towers over the town and offers wondrous views from the top, particularly at dawn, while Volcán Chicabal (2720m) bequeaths summiteers a pretty crater lake.

Best of the rest

Paraglide over volcanoes at Lago de Atitlán, where you can go **scuba diving** too – or kayak, bike or boat about. The lush tropical canyons of the Río Dulce make for an unforgettable boat ride or kayak trip. The country's up-and-coming **surf scene** is best tasted at Sipacate, which offers classes and rentals for beginners. Guatemala's world-class **whitewater rafting** ranges from one- to five-day trips, including reams of jungle scenery, visits to Mayan ruins, rapids up to Grade IV, waterfalls, canyons and abundant birdlife (on Ríos Cahabón, Chiquibul, Coyolate, Los Esclaves, Motagua, Nahualate and Usumacinta).

Mountain biking, **rock climbing**, **kayaking**, **paragliding**, **surfing**, **ziplining** and **horse riding** can all be done from Antigua. Elsewhere, the Verapaces are riddled with more caves than you could explore in a lifetime, and the Semuc Champey swimming hole looks like an elf kingdom that Tolkien himself might have dreamed up.

DON'T LEAVE WITHOUT...
Hiking 60km into Petén jungle to the spectacular ruins of El Mirador, a fascinating, largely unexcavated Mayan city. The vast Maya Biosphere Reserve is one of the most ecologically diverse regions in the world, home to giant anteaters, scarlet macaws, jaguars and pumas, plus hundreds of unique plants and trees.

Left, historic Antigua is close to a lot of adventure action. *Top*, a guide leads the way into the jungle of the Maya Biosphere Reserve.

© Justin Foulkes | Lonely Planet

GUINEA

West Africa is off the beaten track – and Guinea is off the off-beaten track – so take a step into the unknown in this compelling destination.

S pectacularly beautiful Guinea has a dark history of slavery, coups and dictatorial rule, and is only just emerging from the shadow cast by the 2014 Ebola epidemic. But what potential this place has for adventure, particularly in the highlands, home to deep canyons and big rivers dropping into cascading waterfalls. Hikers can explore mountains and forests on day walks, or attempt multiday epics.

Wild Trekking & Waterfall Chasing

Rising from the narrow coastal plain, the **Fouta Djalon** plateau not only provides the source for the Gambia and Senegal rivers (and much of the River Niger's waters), but also most of Guinea's activities. Hiking trails wend through its forest-clad valleys, over verdant rolling hills and past numerous waterfalls and escarpments. Camp or stay in small villages populated by Guinea's munificent people.

In the area around the village of **Doucki**, known as Guinea's 'Grand Canyon', you'll cross vine bridges, navigate through gorges and be bedazzled by the vistas. The village of **Pita** also provides access to great hikes and two dramatic waterfalls: **Chutes de Kambadaga**, a three-tiered fall that plunges into a jungle inhabited by monkeys and colourful birdlife; and the tall but narrow **Chutes du Kinkon**.

Chutes de Saala, reached on foot from the village of Diarai, is another good shout for a hike – keep one eye out for chimpanzees, or close both and take a refreshing plunge in the falls' cool waters.

BE THE FIRST OF YOUR FRIENDS TO...
Explore curious Corisco Island, a super-remote, white beach–fringed paradise off Guinea that's tipped to be a scuba-diving hot spot, now it has a hotel and airport.

GUYANA

This raw, thickly forested country of rich biodiversity is a magnet for intrepid travellers – hell, it even has a town named Adventure!

A small country renowned for attempts to protect its rainforests, Guyana is a premier wildlife-watching destination. Pack binoculars and bug spray, you're diving into the heart of the jungle.

Waterfall expedition

The spectacular, 226m-drop **Kaieteur Falls** is a must-see, and the best way is to cobble together your own adventurous expedition. With careful preparation travellers can link minibuses, boats (portaging for rapids) and hiking trails (BYO machete) into an unforgettable journey.

At the falls, carefully stand at the edge of the unfenced drop and peer down, before lolling about in the river mere metres from the lip. To raise the adventure ante, harness up and join 114,000-litres-a-second of H2O that drops the enormous face, by abseiling the falls. With the setting sun, thousands of swifts swarm in a murmuration before darting behind the cascade to nest, just one amazing sight in a bounty that includes giant tank bromeliads, golden rocket frogs, giant river otters and the magnificent scarlet cock-of-the-rock.

Range Riding

Play out your cowboy fantasies where the rainforest meets the savannah. Guyana has a long *vaquero* (cowboy) history, and though it's on the wane you can still saddle up and fully immerse yourself by volunteering at a working ranch, or simply spend time at Dadanawa, Guyana's biggest and most isolated farm. Time your trip to coincide with Rupununi Rodeo Festival and dive deep into *vaquero* folklore.

UNCLAIMED ADVENTURE
Just because the conquistadors, Sir Walter Raleigh and who-else-knows couldn't find El Dorado – the lost city of gold – doesn't mean you can't. It's got to be in that jungle somewhere, right?

HONDURAS

Trails through wildlife-rich jungles; wonderful whitewater rafting; superb diving; and a huge wilderness area calling out for exploration. Welcome to Honduras.

Honduras' two biggest tourist drawcards are the extraordinary World Heritage-listed ruins of Copán and the Caribbean wonderland of the Bay Islands. But elsewhere there's more than a dozen national parks, cloud forests, vast cave systems, huge lakes, volcanic islands, beautiful beaches and resplendent wildlife – all relatively less-trodden and super-cheap to experience.

Sometimes called Central America's Amazon, the remote untamed wetlands and jungles of La Mosquitia (also called Moskitia) has great allure for the more adventurous. Comprising almost a fifth of the country, this area has few phones and only basic accommodation and food. Getting around requires effort, but the traveller is rewarded with a genuine off-the-beaten-track experience in the marshy wetlands, savannahs and biosphere reserves protecting virgin tropical rainforest.

Diving and Snorkelling

Thanks to the world's second largest reef, off the Caribbean Coast, and a coastline that's dotted with white-sand-splattered and palm-tree-punctuated islands, the diving and snorkelling in Honduras is world-class. Bay Islands is the number one destination, and many people go here to earn their PADI scuba-diving qualifications relatively cheaply, amid turquoise waters, gleaming beaches, fresh seafood feasts and lively nightlife. Underwater, you're more likely to be dancing with sea turtles, rays, shoals of tropical fish, corals and sponges, and, if you're really lucky, the world's largest fish: the whale shark. Utila is the main hub and the best place to spot the extraordinary creatures, while the fascinating wrecks of the larger nearby island of Roatán offer a tempting alternative (it has superior beaches too).

Hiking

Parque Nacional La Tigra is only 22km from the capital, Tegucigalpa, but the cloud forest feels a world away. Day hike amid orchids, bromeliads ferns, deer and white-faced monkeys. Further to the northwest, you can go quetzal spotting, wander behind waterfalls, enjoy ancient Lenca ruins, explore 12km of caves, or enjoy a relaxing boat trip in beautiful, otherworldly Lago de Yojoa. The 17km lake attracts more than 400 species of bird.

Climb Montaña de Santa Bárbara (2777m), the country's second-highest peak, on a challenging hike through orchid-rich cloud forests, while quetzal spotting. Just north, the cloud forests of Parque Nacional Cusuco are another place where quetzals and parrots are spied amid the giant ferns of the Merendón Mountains, with five trails, swimming holes and waterfalls.

DON'T LEAVE WITHOUT...
Experiencing Central America's best whitewater rafting. Plentiful birdlife, wondrous scenery and Grade III–V rapids combine for a memorable experience at Río Cangrejal, in Parque Nacional Pico Bonito, where you'll likely see toucans. The park also offers excellent kayaking and hiking too.

Feeding time for grey reef sharks.

© Brandi Mueller/ Getty Images

HUNGARY

Most of Hungary resides below 200m altitude, but flat doesn't mean boring; there's plenty of fizz in the foothills, plains, rivers and caves.

Hungary's largest lake, Balaton, is a haven for kitesurfing and windsurfing and, in winter, ice aficionados ice-sail, windsurf and skate across it. The Buda Hills, near Budapest, offer good climbing and trekking, while the Matra Mountains house Mount Kékes (1014m), the country's highest point. Hungary also has an extensive network of forest cycle paths.

Caving

Hungary has a cornucopia of caves, mostly in the north. Clamber along narrow passages in a multilevel labyrinth within the **Pálvölgy–**

Mátyáshegy system, which has recently been linked with another network to form the **Szépvölgyi System**. At 28.6km, Szépvölgyi is Hungary's longest network, with 10 entrances, one of which is only 4km from Budapest's parliament building. Its intricate tunnels require expert guidance. Budapest itself has 44km of underground caverns, while the Buda Hills on Budapest's outskirts contain more than 150 caves. Also in the north, keep an eye out for the Hall of Cyclops in **Imre Vass Cave**, Aggtelek National Park – an area abundant in subterranean systems.

Hiking

The 1128km **National Blue Trail**, which starts on Írottkő Mountain (884m) on the Austrian-Hungarian border, stretches right across Hungary. Hikers pass centuries-old townships, the Danube River, various Hungarian peaks and the dripstone cave of Aggtelek. **Challenge hiking** – where walkers pit themselves against the clock – is popular, with events on most weekends.

Canoeing

More meandering than whitewater, Hungary's rivers offer numerous canoe capers. **Bodrog** (55km, two to three days) has mountain views and passes Sárospatak, a township with a historical castle. **Rába** (211km, seven to 11 days) is Hungary's wildest river, and is suited to intermediate/advanced canoeists. It has countless curves, pebble beaches and islands.

DON'T LEAVE WITHOUT...
Ice surfing on Lake Balaton. Attach a snowboard to a windsurf sail, pick a windy day and slide along Balaton's huge wintry expanse.

In winter, Lake Balaton is perfect for ice surfing.

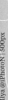

© Ilya @iPhotoN | 500px

ICELAND

Glaciers, terrain-tearing fissures, volcanoes, midnight sun and Northern Lights – an Icelandic adventure offers the chance to see the planet reforming before your eyes.

About half the size of the UK, with a population of just over 300,000, Europe's least-densely populated country has plenty of space, but Iceland is anything but empty. With three national parks in its arsenal, including the continent's largest, it boasts a landscape literally littered with earth-shuddering geothermal activity and blow-your-mind dramatic formations.

Pretty much straight from the capital of Reykjavik, you can go multiday hiking and wild camping on lava fields coated with centuries-old moss, venture to the edge of exploding geysers in the Geysir Hot Springs area or teeter on the tipping point of terrain-tearing fissures in Thingvellir National Park – above and below the water. For something even cooler, grab some crampons and get face-to-face with calving glaciers and dramatic ice caps at Vatnajökull National Park, or go on a mission with a more subterranean theme, descending into the dormant magma chamber of Thrihnjukagigur volcano.

Ski above the ocean at Hlíðarfjall, or jump in and ride the Atlantic waves that crash into the westerly Reykjanes peninsula. Then, when you've worn yourself out, head to one of the natural hot springs at Reykholt, in West Iceland, to refresh tired limbs in the 'new' Blue Lagoon.

Arctic Surfing

Reykjanes peninsula juts into the ocean just an hour's drive from Reykjavik (and right by Keflavik Airport). Ringed by volcanic reefs, the sheltered beaches here offer great surfing, and surprisingly – in summer at least – the water temperature isn't dramatically colder than in Scotland (still, you do need a good thick wetsuit with hood, gloves and boots). Beginners should head to Sandvik's black-sand beach, or join a surf camp. Organised surfing trips also visit the west fjords, Ólafsfjörður, and Snæfellsjökull Peninsula and national park.

Cave Exploration

From old lava tubes to glacial tunnels, caves once played a vital role in survival on Iceland, being utilised by farmers (and sometimes their cattle) to shelter from the elements, particularly in winter. Evidence of this can be seen in Víðgelmir, aka 'The Cave', near the town of Reykholt. Just shy of 1600m long, with a height of 15.8m and a width of 16.5m, it's the country's largest cave and contains evidence of habitation spanning back to the Vikings. Walkers can undertake a guided excursion inside, and those feeling more adventurous can go further, climbing between the stalactites and burnt-red boulders to find the end. Other spelunking options can be found in Tvibollahraun lava field (25 minutes from Reykjavik) and Thingvellir National Park, where Gjábakkahellir ('Little Girl's Cave') was formed some 9000 years ago.

Dive the Continental Rift

Armed with scuba diving (or snorkelling) gear and a dry suit, adventurers can explore the Silfra fissure in Thingvellir National Park. Here, what appears to be a rocky channel is actually the crack between two continental plates, so you can literally place one hand on North America and the other on Europe while checking out the incredible water clarity (100m+ visibility) amid the green 'troll hair' algae.

Hiking

Iceland contains boot-pleasing hiking terrain at all points of the compass. In the southeast sprawls vast Vatnajökull National Park, home to the eponymous 3000-billion-tonne glacier, Europe's largest chunk of ice. The frozen expanse of Vatnajökull partially or completely covers several volcanoes, including Öræfajökull, the summit crater of which protrudes from the ice to tempt climbers with Hvannadalshnjúkur (2110m), which is Iceland's highest point.

West is Snæfellsjökull National Park, which has a huge 1446m volcano with a massive glacier bunging its vent as its centrepiece, while in the southwest is Thingvellir National Park, where you can hike over volcanic erratics and old lava fields. The renowned 55km Laugavegur Trail between the hot springs of Landmannalaugar and the glacial valley of Þórsmörk is now commonly crowded, but the similar Sveinstindur-to-Eldgja hike is comparatively people-free and has cleaner mountain huts en route.

In the little-visited east is Borgarfjörður, where the Víknaslóðir (Trails of the Deserted Inlets) weave between abandoned villages and rhyolite mountains to offer multiday hikes. More challenging walks are found in the remote Westfjords region – from the end of the road at Krossnes it takes a week to reach Hornstrandir and the nature reserve at its terminus, and hikers need to be completely self-sufficient, but at the end they're rewarded with stunning red-sand beaches.

Paragliding

Within an hour of the capital you can see the volcanic landscapes from a different perspective – via a tandem paraglide. Strap on to an instructor and leap off the south coast to soar above waterfalls (while others merely walk behind them), glaciers and black beaches, gliding alongside the Arctic terns and skuas.

*Above, a hiker on Þórsmörk, a ridge named after the Norse god Thor. **Overleaf,** wild Icelandic ponies.*

© Max Rive | 500px

Horse Riding

Taking its unique credentials up another notch, Iceland is home to its own particular breed of horse. Still used for shepherding as well as leisure, these muscular, hardy, thick-coated equines even have an extra gait called the 'tolt', which is a smooth half-walk, half-run. Have a ride in the Víðidalur or Langadalur valleys, trek the historic Kjolur Trail that journeys between two ice caps from north to south, then go to the northwest, where every autumn you can join locals as they round up more than 2000 horses from the highlands to take them down to graze in the lowlands over winter. After an auction, join in the celebrations with traditional lamb soup and song.

Stand-up Paddleboarding

Veined with an abundance of rivers, pockmarked by lakes, gouged by fjords, and surrounded by a gloriously winding coast, Iceland has a fast-growing SUP scene. The most A-list location is Jökulsárlón glacial lagoon in the southeast, which has starred in two Bond films and *Tomb Raider*. Skimming around the edge of Breiðamerkurjökull glacier, you

DON'T LEAVE WITHOUT...
Venturing into a volcano. Iceland is home to the world's only volcano that can be explored from the inside: Thrihnukagigur, east of Bláfjöll Mountain, which hasn't erupted for 4000 years. Using an open elevator, subterranean explorers experience a journey into the Earth as they're lowered 120m into the magma chamber.

can paddle among the icebergs in what is now the country's deepest lake (a body of water that's still growing, as the glacier continues to recede).

Skiing & Snowboarding

Despite the name, Iceland doesn't get the kind of snowfall you might expect, and its few ski resorts are quite small. The biggest is Hlíðarfjall on the north coast, just above the country's second city of Akureyri, with 23 pistes served by seven lifts along with a reasonable selection of ungroomed areas. Despite its modest size, however, the surreal landscape and rare chance to ski above the ocean make Hlíðarfjall worth a visit. It's worth noting that midwinter skiing is not big in Iceland, due to almost 24-hour darkness; on the other hand, there's every chance you'll see the northern lights.

If the bug bites (it will) and you decide to explore more of this magnificent country on skis, ski touring and heli-skiing on the Troll Peninsula of the northwest and along the coast between Akureyri and Húsavík is becoming increasingly popular, and rightly so, since it features some of the wildest and most memorable winter landscapes on the planet.

INDIA

Rich in culture, colour, clamour, adventure and downright craziness, from the Himalayan peaks to the Keralan backwaters, India is as big on adventure as it is on mysticism.

Few countries in the world boast the geographical diversity of India. Crowned by the mighty mountains, valleys and foothills of the Himalayas, it's nirvana for adventurers seeking high-altitude trekking, mountaineering, paragliding, mountain biking, skiing, zorbing and rafting escapades. Further south, the deserts of Rajasthan are prime spots for nomadic camel safaris, while the deep south brings the coast into play, where you can try scuba diving, surfing, kayaking, or move inland for 'soft' trekking in the hills and wildlife sanctuaries of the Western Ghats.

Camel Safaris

Plodding through the desert on a dromedary is an evocative and romantic experience closely associated with the Indian state of Rajasthan. Jaisalmer – the 'golden city' – is the main base for exploring the **Thar Desert** and **Sam Sand Dunes**, while **Bikaner**, which has an annual camel market,

is a less crowded alternative. An overnight safari usually involves a 4WD trip into the desert, a few hours' camel trekking, and dinner cooked over a campfire while listening to camel drivers' songs, before drifting off under a velvety blanket of stars. It's possible to trek for days, weeks even, exploring distant desert villages while absorbing this remote way of life.

Deep in the mountains of Ladakh, about 120km north of Leh, the village of **Hunder** is the base for treks on Bactrian (two-humped) camels, said to be the offspring of animals that once plied the Ladakh–Xinjiang caravans. The Hunder sand dunes are rugged and starkly beautiful.

Trekking & Mountaineering

High mountain passes, deep valleys, glaciers and stunning snow-capped mountain vistas draw travellers to the hundreds of treks in the Indian Himalaya. The keys to a successful trek are timing (July and August are usually best at high altitude; May–June and September–October ideal in the

Camel safaris are the traditional way to explore the Thar Desert.

© James Farley | Getty Images, © Novarc Images | Alamy

An add-on trek is the steep pilgrimage to Hemkund, a sacred lake at 4300m. With sensational views of Uttarakhand's peaks, including 7800m Nanda Devi, the 3640m Kuari Pass trek passes through the Nanda Devi Sanctuary. The trek takes five days from Joshimath (Auli) to Ghat.

Ladakh & Zanskar
At 6121m, Stok Kangri, the highest peak in the Stok range, is popular as a 'trekkable' mountain – with an experienced guide and the right gear and preparation, even novice climbers can attempt this one. It can be done as a five-day group expedition from Leh.

Sikkim
One of the most coveted and testing challenges in all of the Indian Himalaya, the Kangchenjunga (Goecha La) Trek is an eight- to 10-day trek crossing the 4940m Goecha La Pass, with the reward being stupendous views of India's highest mountain, Kangchenjunga (8586m).

Western Ghats
India's best treks are not exclusively found in the Himalaya. In the far south, where Karnataka, Kerala and Tamil Nadu meet, the highland range known as the Western Ghats offers superb and relatively easy jungle trekking, with the added bonus of some of the country's best wildlife sanctuaries. Top trekking bases include Ooty, Wayanad, Munnar and the Coorg hills.

Skiing & Snowboarding
With some of the world's highest mountains and year-round snow at altitude, India has some excellent skiing and snowboarding, but the best conditions are found in Jammu and Kashmir, on the border of Pakistan, where unrest can flare. The few resorts have basic infrastructure and can't be compared to anything in Europe or North America. For ultimate thrills, try heli-skiing.

About 90 minutes by jeep from Srinagar, **Gulmarg** is India's top destination for high-altitude powder skiing. The solitary two-stage gondola carries you up to extreme boarding conditions or off-piste skiing.

Away from Kashmir, just above Joshimath in Uttarakhand near the borders with Tibet and Nepal,

© skaman306; Jitendra Singh | Getty Images

DON'T LEAVE WITHOUT...
Cycling rolling roads through the great, green tea-covered hills of Kerala.

foothills), meticulous preparation, securing a good guide, and sufficient acclimatisation for treks above 5000m. Top trekking bases include Manali in Himachal, Leh in Ladakh, Joshimath in Uttarakhand, Yuksom in Sikkim and Darjeeling in West Bengal.

Himachal Pradesh
The Pin-Parvati Trek offers six days of exhilarating mountain trekking from Barsheni in Kullu's Parvati Valley to the Pin Valley in Spiti, crossing the 5319m Pin-Parvati Pass. You'll need to be self-sufficient with tents and preferably trekking guides. Another option with amazing views is the four-day camping trek that takes you from Manali and the lush Kullu Valley across the spectacular 4270m Hamta Pass to the Chandra Valley in desert-like Lahaul.

Uttarakhand
If your timing is right, the full-day trek from Govindghat, near Joshimath, to the high-altitude meadows that form the Valley of Flowers National Park will reveal a wondrous carpet of alpine wildflowers surrounded by snowy Himalayan peaks. Somewhat frustratingly, the flowers bloom mainly during the monsoon between July and September.

Top, five-star views at Phyang Monastery, a short trek from Leh in Ladakh. Right, paragliders find idyllic soaring in Himachal Pradesh.

Auli is an accessible and popular resort hosting India's longest gondola and awesome views of Nanda Devi, India's second-highest peak.

Paragliding

Catch some thermals and admire the silent views of the mountains or the coast during a tandem paragliding flight. In Himachal Pradesh, the prime take-off points are internationally renowned **Billing**, or **Solang Nullah** near Manali. Adventure operators here can organise solo flight training too.

Further south, in Goa, the low cliffs of **Arambol** have long been a favourite for paragliding, while the latest launching point in Kerala is the helipad on the North Cliffs at **Varkala**.

Whitewater Rafting

Many people associate Rishikesh with yoga and The Beatles, but it's also one of India's most accessible bases for mountain whitewater rafting and kayaking, with dozens of operators and possible

HOMEGROWN ADVENTURE HERO
In 2016–17, Shilpika Gautam walked and stand-up paddleboarded the length of the Ganges River, travelling 2977km from Gaumukh to Gangar Sagar in the Bay of Bengal, while raising awareness about pollution. She broke the world record for the longest continuous distance SUPed by a female.

routes on the fast-moving **Upper Ganges**. The most extreme route is from Kaudiyala, paddling roughly 40km to Rishikesh on Grade III and IV rapids. Beach camps along the way provide a break from the raging river.

Other standout Grade II and III rafting trips are from Leh (Ladakh) and on the **Beas River** between Pirdi and Jhiri south of Manali.

Diving

Scuba diving has developed considerably in south India in the past decade, but the ultimate sites are a long way off the mainland around the **Andaman Islands**, 1370km to the east of Tamil Nadu, and **Lakshadweep Islands**, 300km to the west of Kerala. On the Andamans, Havelock Island has world-class and well-organised diving to coral reefs and the odd wreck. Lakshadweep, north of the Maldives island chain, feels even more remote and pristine thanks to permit restrictions on visitors. From November to May, visibility is up

to 40m and the vibrant coral reefs are positively glowing with marine life.

Surfing

With over 7500km of coast, India offers a wealth of beaches and breaks for boardriders, with the biggest waves rolling in during the pre-monsoon and monsoon season, May–September. The best surf is enjoyed from **Andaman** and **Lakshadweep** islands, in the company of turtles, but excellent conditions can also be found either side of the Indian Ocean-facing cape at Kanyakumari, including **Varkala** and **Kovalam** (both in Kerala), and **Auroville**, **Covelong** and **Mahabalipuram** (Tamil Nadu).

Backwater Kayaking

Kerala's backwaters are famous for houseboats and punted canoes, but adventurous travellers might want to explore the area's hub, Alleppey, under their own paddle power. A number of operators run guided kayaking trips through the backwaters, cruising through water-locked villages and narrow canals.

Gorgeous gorgonian coral off Havelock Island in the Andaman Islands.

INDONESIA

Hiking trails that crest the backbones of sulphur-belching volcanoes; surf that breaks on Asia's most remote islands; whitewater lines that descend into gorges unfathomably deep. You'd be forgiven for thinking Indonesia was Malay for adventure.

Indonesia is a massive archipelago nation, home to 17,508 islands, including the world's most crowded (Java, with some 141 million residents) and nearly 10,000 that remain uninhabited. Over 700 languages and dialects are spoken here, more than 300 ethnic groups are recognised and, as such, political, social and environmental harmony is often an amorphous thing. But it's this wild diversity – in culture and in topography – that makes Indonesia an adventure playground of limitless potential.

Here, you can spy on the world's largest dragons while trekking on the far-eastern Sunda Islands, or kayak the Sekonyer River in made-for-adventure Borneo while orangutans swing through trees overhead. You can hike to the rim of ill-tempered volcanoes in Bromo Tengger Semeru National Park, or dive some of the planet's most biodiverse reef systems as you explore Indonesia's 80,000km shoreline. Easily accessed but hard to comprehend, Indonesia is rocked endlessly by sweeping forces of nature and a chaos of cultures, and beckons the traveller with its alluring otherness.

Surfing

Surfers have been rocking Indo waves en masse since the 1960s, when epic crystal pipes were discovered by swell chasers. Today, Bali is one of the world's greatest big wave draws (with the crowds to match), but there are countless other breakers to catch along the south-facing islands. Monster winter storms churn up the ocean and send big surf barrelling for Bali, Sumatra, Java, Flores, Lombok, and more.

Surfing in **Bali** is more than the sum of sand and sea. The island has daily flight connections to many large airports, accommodation ranging from bohemian shabby to five-star chic, and a nightlife scene that's become an industry unto itself. Uluwatu, with its mind-bending entry cave and ancient temple overhead, is the grand dame of Bali surf spots, with the rips at Padang on the Bukit Peninsula not far behind. When conditions are right, waves at Padang are some of the fiercest on the planet. Beginners will have a better time at Kuta Beach, where the sand is soft and forgiving, and surf schools can help you avoid embarrassing wipeouts (maybe). Swells are at their peak during the dry

© Johnny Haglund | Getty Images

DON'T LEAVE WITHOUT...
Climbing ancient Borobudur. The world's largest Buddhist monument features massive temple spires that sprout from the Kedu Plain valley floor, all set against a backdrop of countless volcanic peaks, including the volatile Mt Merapi.

Hideaways and Pitstop are among the most popular waves to catch.

It may be hard to believe, but there are pockets of solitude on crowded **Java** – even at one of the planet's wildest waves. Plengkung Beach is host to G-Land, a monster on Grajagan Bay in Alas Purwo National Park in East Java. G-Land is known for its notoriously dangerous reef, impossibly long point and howling winds, and is most easily reached by boat charter from Bali. Surf camps here have been in operation since the 1960s.

Perhaps even more punishing than its name suggests, Apocalypse, rolling on tides aimed at a little island named **Panaitan**, located in the Sunda Strait between Java and Sumatra, is a real big boy wave. You don't have to risk your life at **Batu Karas** in West Java, the break here is gentle and there are plenty of surf schools willing to help you get on your feet. The namesake fishing village is a gem, and the vibe is generally relaxed.

Rafting & Kayaking

Rafting is big business in Indo, while kayaking has come on strong in the past decade, with smooth operations in Bali and West Java, and a burgeoning scene in Sumatra and Sulawesi.

Sumatra's Alas River is the gem of the whitewater scene. A 300km route that tears through Gunung Leuser National Park dishes Grade III and IV rapids, but what travellers really paddle for is the opportunity to spy orangutans (Gunung Leuser is one of only two remaining natural habitats), the critically endangered Sumatran rhino, tiger and elephant, and a stunning variety of native fauna and flora.

The **Citarik River** in **West Java**, which is a short drive from Jakarta, features a navigable stretch (15km plus) of water that even novice kayakers will be able to manage. During Java's wet season, the river runs substantially faster, making the Citarik a real challenge – and a particular rapid known as Cibaregbeg will turn your paddle-clutching knuckles white.

There are few whitewater rips in Bali; river cruising here is more of an introduction to the environment than anything else. That said, you can't beat the scenery; a ride along the Ayung River opens a world of rainforests, rice terraces, narrow canyons and more.

Indonesia's waves are legendary and its beaches aren't bad either; post-surf on the Mentawai Islands, West Sumatra.

season, from May through October, but note that this is the height of tourist season on Bali.

Among the surf set, **Nias** – an archipelago of 131 islands off Sumatra's western shoulder – is the ultimate destination. The 2004 Indian Ocean tsunami bashed one of the greatest breaks in the world, raised the underlying reef and made the wave even better. Sorake Bay is the flagship, but you had better come prepared for the challenge.

The **Mentawai Islands** offer even bigger gnarls, but they're difficult to reach (access is provided by private boat charter) and the surf resorts do equal damage to the pocketbook. If you can't put a price on adventure, then the Mentawais are for you. E-Bay, Beng Beng,

© John Seaton Callahan; Paul Kennedy | Getty Images

Trekking & Climbing

Indonesian rambling routes run the gamut from seaside cliff walks to demanding jungle expeditions; experiences here are limited only by your time and appetite for adventure.

Go wild with a visit to Padar Island in **Komodo National Park**. Starting on a beach of startling pink sand, you can summit Padar's serpentine spine in as little as three hours. Rewards include panoramic ocean views the entire way and the occasional staring contest with a fearsome Komodo dragon. Quiet Padar is an excellent counterpoint to the bustle of Komodo and Rinca.

Not far from the pastoral bliss of **Sumatra**'s Lake Toba, the world's largest volcanic lake, is the trailhead to the **Sipisopiso Waterfall**. With a drop of 120m, Sipisopiso is an iconic emblem of the Batak highlands, and while the hike itself is a breeze – think 600 steps, from top to bottom – the waterfall is a must-see. You can ratchet the difficulty by hiking

Whitewater rafting on the Bukit Lawang, North Sumatra.

to the pretty fishing village of Tongging for a chance to rub shoulders with locals.

If you've come to hike Indo, at some point you're going to climb an active volcano. Among the most impressive is **Mt Bromo**, a 2392m juggernaut with a stunning crater at its core. Rising out of the aptly named sea of sand, this is the centrepiece of the **Bromo Tengger Semeru National Park**, an otherworldly place of volcanoes, sulphur pits, canyons, caves, waterfalls and remote forests.

Climbing indomitable **Puncak Trikora**, formerly known as Wilhelmina Peak, will earn you a feather for your cap. At 4750m, Puncak Trikora is one of the three tallest mountains in Oceania, and a box to be checked on the Seven Second Summits list. The expedition to the summit begins at Lake Habbema,

and requires a two-day trek to the Semalak base camp. The final ascent can take eight to 12 hours, depending on weather conditions.

Diving

Positioned in the middle of the 'Coral Triangle', Indonesia is often quoted as having more biodiversity in its waters than anywhere else on the planet. Amid reefs, wrecks and volcanic sea mounts, it delights divers with an estimated 3000 species of fish. Sulawesi and Bali both offer brilliant resort diving, encounters with big pelagics can be had off Komodo, and around Raja Ampat you can drift across a kaleidoscope of coral. But for serious divers, a live-aboard multiday trip is the best option – Komodo is where most of these depart from.

Idyllic snorkelling in Bali.

Often overlooked, Iran has a six-month ski season and is incredibly cheap.

IRAN

If you announce that you're heading to Iran, someone will almost certainly advise you not to go. Ignore them – this is one of the most exciting countries on Earth.

Until recently, Iran, or Persia, was not somewhere that appeared on many people's travel radar. Now it is becoming increasingly accessible, and with that comes the opportunity to see the reality of a deeply misunderstood country. The Persian Empire, which once stretched from Greece to India, has left remnants everywhere: from the sprawling, majestic ruins of the ancient capital at Persepolis, to the World Heritage-listed squares and arched bridges of Esfahan. These sites alone are enough reason to visit, but Iran is huge – there's so much more to see, especially for those drawn to mountains, deserts, oceans and wilderness. Above all, this is a place defined by the hospitality and curiosity of Iranians – it might well be the friendliest country you ever visit.

Skiing & Snowboarding

If you've always overlooked the Middle East for winter sports, now's the perfect time to rectify that, because Iran is slowly becoming the ultimate alternative skiing destination, and it boasts a six-month snow season. The most popular resort in the country is **Dizin**, conveniently located on north-facing slopes in the Alborz mountains, just a two-hour drive from Tehran. It was constructed by the Shah (a keen skier) in 1969, and though the three-star hotel might be a little on the plain side, there are more modern chalets available and the chairlifts on offer do the job. The highest gondolas climb to 3600m, and the powdery snow – chest-high at times – is a match for just about anywhere in the Rockies or the Alps. Best of all, the season runs from November until late May and day passes cost between US$20 and US$25. What's not to love?

DON'T LEAVE WITHOUT...
Climbing to the highest point in the country. The peak of the volcanic Mt Damavand sits at 5671m and a trek to the top normally takes four days.

© Dudarev Mikhail | Shutterstock, © Henry Iddon

© Jean-Philippe Tournut | Getty Images

Breaking camp while bikepacking through Razavi Khorasan Province in northeastern Iran.

Dizin is recommended for beginner to intermediate skiers, whereas the nearby **Shemshak** is better for advanced skiers. **Pooladkaf**, in the south, is a good alternative as well.

Hiking

From the snowy summit of Mt Damavand in the north to the balmy flatlands of the south, Iran offers myriad landscapes for hiking enthusiasts. The **Alborz** are beautiful for high-altitude trekking, and you'll find rare flora and fauna alongside the challenging trails, plus hot springs, ancient castles and much more besides. The **Zagros Mountains** to the west are equally stunning, but a warning: leave plenty of extra time for stopping to drink tea with villagers. The Geopark on **Qeshm Island** in the south has incredible otherworldly landscapes and, if deserts are your thing, the **Dasht-e Lut** basin in the east is remote, relatively untouched and utterly wild; expect salt flats, wadis, vast plains and sand dunes up to 300m high. Local operators like Adventure Iran have a great knowledge base to help with your plans, and newer companies such as Persian Pursuits and Secret Compass offer exciting multiday itineraries.

Bikepacking & Mountain Biking

Iran has always been a crossroads of culture and trade, but it's also a popular route for touring cyclists on their way across Asia. Loading up panniers and pedalling across the country is the finest way to get a snapshot of life here and, with cheap kebabs in every roadside village, you'll never go hungry. Mountain biking is also increasingly popular, with both locals and visitors exploring the hills in search of new trails. As with hiking, the best spots are among the **Alborz** and **Zagros Mountains** – there's an abundance of dirt roads in these hills – and in the desert basins in the central and eastern regions of the country. If you are short on time, hit the great singletrack just outside **Tehran**, offering great views back over the capital. Most riding in the country requires some basic experience – with that, and the right attitude, this is the mountain biking playground you've always dreamed of.

Surfing

In the rarely visited provinces of **Sistan** and **Baluchistan**, a remarkable group of young Iranians are developing surfing culture along the coastline. The fishing village of **Ramin** is home to the country's first local surf club. Don't expect many facilities, but if you're willing to bring your own gear and share knowledge and experience with an enthusiastic community, then it might just be one of the most rewarding things you ever do. Contact the founders of We Surf in Iran to learn more.

IRELAND

Crashing waves hitting Atlantic shores, rugged landscapes and mercurial weather make Ireland a top destination for coastal adventures, testing endurance events and multiday walks, rewarded by end-of-the-day pints and pub music.

As the next-stop-America island on Europe's western extremity, Ireland is defined by the sea. Huge waves, towering cliffs and long beaches attract elite surfers, sea paddlers, climbers, kiters and open-water swimmers. In a country less than 500km long, the Irish have conjured up the innovative 2500km Wild Atlantic Way, which follows the coast-hugging roads and *boreens* (lanes) of the west coast to string together adventure-activity outfitters, spell-binding seascapes and welcoming bars. Ireland's waters have been a whale and dolphin sanctuary since 1991, so you'll be sharing the seas with a safari park of big marine wildlife, including humpback, fin and minke whales, seals and basking sharks. But don't overlook the interior, where winding rivers, wending trails, wild terrain, wind-whipped peaks and warm pubs combine to offer a thousand welcomes to the wandering adventurer, whether they're exploring on water, wheels or in rugged heels.

Paddling
Sea-kayaking

Ireland is a world-class sea-kayaking destination, with everything for the paddler from big surf to committing routes along colossal cliffs, as well as island hopping and deep sea cave exploration.

Numerous operators run trips that can include skills training, foraging for edible seaweeds, whale watching and night paddles lit up by otherworldly phosphorescence. For self-navigated trips there are a growing number of guides to Blueways paddling trails – such as County Cork's **Bantry Bay**, where there's a 9km loop between Whiddy Island and the mainland – while expedition paddlers can kayak to and between Ireland's many offshore islands. Making the open-ocean trip to the long abandoned early monastery and *Star Wars* location on **Skellig Michael**, 13km off the Kerry coast, is a serious adventure.

Canoeing

Ireland's two longest rivers, the broad majestic **Shannon** and the beautiful **Barrow**, both invite DIY canoeing and camping adventures. Along its 360km amble, the Shannon occasionally swells into expansive, island-studded lakes, Lough Derg and Lough Ree among them, while the four-day Barrow canoe trail takes paddlers from Monasterevin through six history-soaked, scenic and storied counties to the brine of the Celtic Sea.

Hiking

High ground and clinging bogs scattered across the island deliver challenging wild walking, though

---

ULTIMATE CHALLENGE

The world's 20th largest island presents paddlers with a satisfying circumnavigation challenge of 1500km (if they're prepared to make open-sea crossings between peninsulas and across bays). John Bouteloup, Franco Ferrero and Derek Hairon did the first loop in 1978. A year later, Irishman Tom Daly made the first solo circuit. Since then more than 50 paddlers have gone around. In 2015, Mick O'Meara set the 23-day record.

Ireland has relatively little open-access land, even in the hills. In compensation there are more than 40 national way-marked trails, plus 14 Munros to bag (peaks over 1000m), including the highest mountain Carrauntoohil (1038m) in County Kerry's Macgillycuddy's Reeks range.

The 130km **Wicklow Way** includes tracks through forestry, over bogs and across the Wicklow Mountains, passing the early Christian round-tower and monastery buildings at Glendalough, before – conveniently – dropping down into the heart of Dublin. The route has three Adirondack shelters so you can bivvy in the remotest woods and hills.

Just as rewarding is the **Dingle Way**, a 160km mountains-and-coast loop around Kerry's Dingle Peninsula. Detours from the trail will take you to the top of Brandon Mountain, around early ring forts and to the perfectly preserved stonework

Spectacular surrounds at Portrush, County Antrim.

of the Gallarus Oratory. Highlights of the hike are long stretches of beach, and paths around sea-nudging mountains that give you a balcony view to the Blasket Islands to the west. Dingle town is famed for live music (try Dick Mack's for talk, hot whiskeys and impromptu sessions), while the South Pole Inn at Annascaul is where Antarctic explorer Tom Crean retired to after expeditions with Scott and Shackleton.

Wild Swimming

Ireland has a long tradition and a contemporary enthusiasm for open-water swimming. The **Forty Foot** on the edge of Dublin Bay is mentioned in James Joyce's *Ulysses* and still attracts sea-swimmers year-round, while each August the capital's **Liffey River** hosts the world's second oldest continuously swum open race (400 competitors, no wetsuits, 2km course). Hundreds of coastal and inland swimming spots are listed on Irish outdoor swimming websites, with groups – 'pods' in local parlance – taking part in long swims in lakes, including 38km **Lough Derg**, or in the Atlantic. Sandycove Swimmers, based near Kinsale in County Cork, train by doing 1.8km laps of **Sandycove Island**. It obviously works – Irishman Stephen Redmond was the first person to complete the seven long-distance open-water swims that make up the Ocean's Seven, considered to be the goggles-and-Speedos equivalent to mountaineering's Seven Summits.

Adventure Racing & Ultra Running

It's been suggested that Ireland's embrace of adventure racing, ultra-running and other punishing outdoor challenges combines a celebration of a mythic warrior past with self-inflicted penance for the excesses of the country's recent boom and bust economy. With its rugged and varied landscape, and a mercurial climate that can hop between seasons in hours (but is rarely extreme enough to threaten life), Ireland has an exhausting calendar of idiosyncratic outdoor events.

Billed as Ireland's ultimate 24-hour test of endurance, **The Race** is run across the wilds of Donegal and – to ensure dreadful weather – held in March. The challenges include a 15km kayak, 166km of cycling, 5km of mountain running and 64km of

© Carl Bruemmer / Design Pics | Getty Images

road and trail running. All to be completed within 24 hours, non-stop and unsupported.

The **Art O'Neill Challenge** is inspired by the three Irish nobles who, in January 1592, escaped from jail in Dublin Castle and fled across the Wicklow Mountains to reach sanctuary in Glenmalure Valley. Now, annually, at midnight on a January night, runners and walkers take on the same challenge, navigating in the dark out of the city and over the Wicklow Mountains – often in storms, snow or rain – on the 55km trail to Glenmalure, while hoping to avoid the fate of the eponymous Art O'Neill, who died of exposure.

The **Kerry Way Ultra** (and Ultra Lite) sends runners 200km (or 58km) non-stop through some of the iconic tourist-tickling scenery around Killarney, its eponymous national park, and the Iveragh Peninsula, following the tracks and trails of the Kerry Way (another excellent national trail). If you have energy to spare you can appreciate standing stones, ring forts and long-shot panoramas of the Atlantic Ocean and the Macgillycuddy's Reeks range as you run.

Climbing

Irish rock climbers mainly focus on the granite of the Wicklow Mountains and the sea cliffs of Donegal and Kerry. Dalkey Quarry is a convenient playground for Dublin's climbers, with more than 300 routes, mostly single pitch, up to E7, and with great views over the city and out to sea.

Cycling

Busy, narrow roads are a cycle tourer's nightmare, so plan routes around remote peninsulas – such as Cork's Beara or Sheeps Head – or along the 124km **Grand Canal towpath** across the centre of Ireland from Dublin to the Shannon River. For mountain bikers there are challenging maintained routes in County Limerick's **Ballyhoura Forest**, including 98km of woodland path, tortuous singletrack, boarded stretches and technical rock trails.

Surfing

Ireland has Europe's biggest, best and most varied surf, and with a warm wetsuit you could spend a lifetime exploring its wild, rocky coastline. From Donegal in the north, all the way down the west coast, past County Cork to Wexford, this indented,

swell-battered coastline delivers waves to suit everyone from wild-eyed grommets to charging big-wave riders. For years, the classic rights and lefts of **Easky** in County Sligo were the focal point of the Irish surf scene, but now you'll see local wave riders all along the coast.

Bundoran remains the best place for a first taste of Irish surfing, with its superb array of beach and reef breaks. Some of the world's biggest and most challenging waves are found at the expert-only lefthand reef break at **Mullaghmore**, but the 'perfect' big wave is **Aileen's**, a 12m monster off the colossal Cliffs of Moher in County Clare, named after nearby headland Aill na Searrach (the cliff of foals) by the local surfer John McCarthy, who first rode it.

Canoeing on the River Barrow, Ireland's second longest river.

© Patrick Kinsella

ISRAEL & THE PALESTINIAN TERRITORIES

Sacred to the world's three great monotheistic religions, the Holy Land is not just a spiritual hub, it's also the perfect place for human-powered exploration.

Israel and the Palestinian Territories are at the heart of the paradox of the Middle East. Too frequently these days we only hear about the region for all the wrong reasons, but there are so many positive experiences to be had here – this is the cradle of all civilisation west of the Hindu Kush and a place which, for the adventurous traveller, offers a rich blend of unique antiquity, thriving modernity and the ultimate wilderness.

Hiking in the Holy Land

Lacing up your boots and strapping on a pack is not only the best way to escape crowds in major cities, it also offers the chance to see just how diverse the landscape is; from the cobalt-blue Israeli coastline to vast deserts in the south and terraced olive groves above the Jordan River. It is also a place where walking is an intrinsic part of the history, and you can quite literally follow in the footsteps of Abraham, Moses and Jesus. Hiking in Israel is well-established, with nearly 16,000km of managed trails. The longest and most exciting of these is the **Israel National Trail**, which runs from the Gulf of Aqaba in the south to near the Lebanese border. In the West Bank, the **Masar Ibrahim al-Khalil** (Abraham Path) takes hikers from rolling green hills to desert monasteries and wilderness in the south, connecting Palestinian communities along the way. Trails like these show the reality of a misunderstood place, and offer an unparalleled insight into the culture, hospitality and natural beauty.

Mountain Biking

This is a landscape that cries out for a mountain bike. There are hundreds of kilometres of dedicated singletrack, all of which encourage speed – look no further than either the **Israel Bike Trail** in the south, or the **Sugar Trail** that runs from Jerusalem to the Dead Sea.

Paragliding

If taking to the skies is your thing, then seek out the small but enthusiastic local paragliding community for the chance to fly over Biblical landscapes and, as a real feather in your cap, log flights below sea level. The 7 Winds school can help get you in the air.

ULTIMATE CHALLENGE
The Holy Land Challenge is a self-supported MTB race: 1367km of winding singletrack and dirt roads, powered by as much hummus as you can fit in your bag.

Israel and the Palestinian Territories have superb mountain biking terrain.

© Ilan Shacham | Getty Images

ITALY

With dramatic mountains, a divine coastline and delicious food, the boot-shaped country has all it takes to kickstart an adventure.

The combination of sunshine, mountains and the tasty carb-based diet makes Italy a mouth-watering prospect for the adventurous. From the drama of volcanic Sicily to the clear waters of Sardinia and the jagged peaks of the Dolomite mountains, the landscape will capture the soul of any adventurer. Where once it was religious pilgrims who endured risks and hardships to reach this great country, now it's cyclists and sea kayakers, climbers, divers, runners, hikers and mountain bikers making a beeline for the highs and lows of this spectacular outdoor playground.

Road Cycling

Walrus, handlebar, mutton chops – designing facial-hair topiary is a key element of **L'Eroica**. This fun event has swiftly become a classic, a tribute to the races on *strade bianche*, the white roads of gravel that thread their way through Tuscany's hills. Only traditional racing bikes can be ridden: steel frames, 'suicide shifters' (gear shifters on the downtube) and toe clips. Feed stations serve wine, cheese and cured meats; no flapjacks or gels here. Riders enhance the old-school mood with vintage woollen kit and, of course, a dandy moustache. The route is available to download and ride at any time of the year, or join the event in October.

Twistier than a nest of vipers, 48 hairpin bends lead to the top of the 2758m **Stelvio Pass**, in the

Old-school bikes, kit and facial hair are the order of the day during L'Eroica.

© Mario Llorca /Awakening | Alamy

Eastern Alps. The road climbs over 1800m in 24km at a lactic generating 7.4% average gradient; or take the 'easy' way up from Bormio on the western side, with a mere 22km of climbing. A Stelvio ascent demands a place on any cyclist's bucket list, but better still to link it with a ride up the nearby and equally fearsome **Passo di Mortirolo** for two epic challenges in a day. The annual **Gran Fondo Stelvio Santini** pairs the climbs into a festival of suffering.

There's nothing quite like riding from city to sea, especially when there's 296km between the start and finish. That makes the **Milan–San Remo** – across Lombardy and Piedmont to the Ligurian Riviera – the longest amateur cycling event in the world. Oh, and it's hilly, too. The route follows

> ## ICONIC EVENT
> The 24Hr of Finale features the camaraderie and challenge of 24-hour mountain bike racing – and adds an Italian twist: superb, sunny trails with views of Liguria's mountains and the Mediterranean, plus fine coffee and pasta.

the tyre tracks of one of professional cycling's five monument rides, but it takes place in summer rather than spring.

Brace yourself for eight lung-busting climbs on the **Maratona dles Dolomites**, a monstrous tour of the dinosaur-backed Dolomites, where the scenery is as spectacular as the ascents are spiteful.

Mountain Biking

Livigno's scintillating trails attract mountain bikers from around the world. Cable cars whisk riders 600m above the town before presenting a choice of downhill tracks peppered with jumps, drops, table tops and walkways. There's spellbinding scenery and a stoked après-ride life.

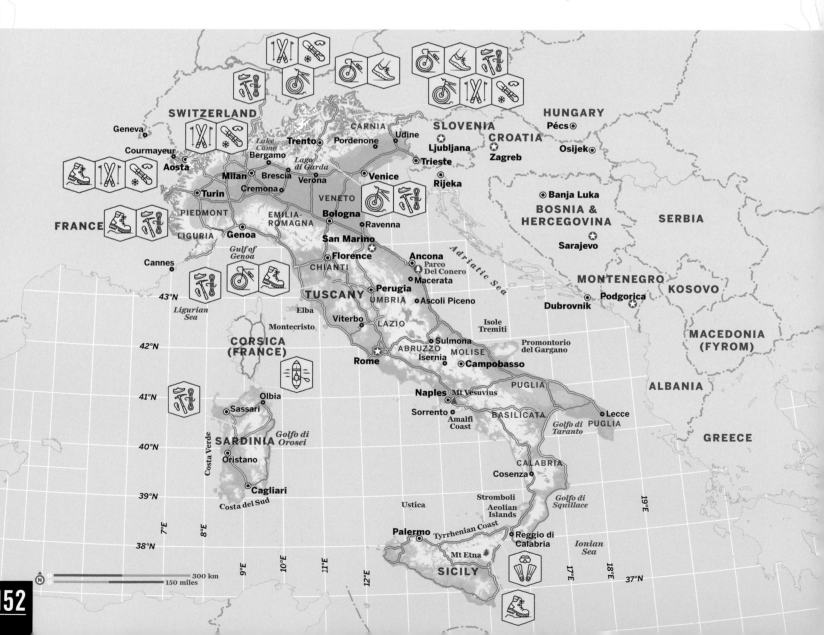

©blickwinkel | Alamy

Beyond the motor launches and villas of the *dolce vita* in **Lake Garda** lies a thrilling network of mountain bike trails. The unmissable downhill is the 20km plunge from the peak of Monte Altissimo di Nago to Torbole on the shore of Lake Garda. The Funivia Malcesine-Monte Baldo cable car takes the sting out of the climb, but no sedative can overcome the adrenaline of the descent.

The 58km **Sellaronda Mountain Bike Tour** in the Dolomites makes any shortlist of Italy's best one-day mountain bike adventures. It's the nerve-jangling summer alternative to the ski classic, using lifts to reach the four passes of Gardena, Campolongo, Pordoi and Sella, each of which is followed by dizzying descents.

Hiking & Peak Bagging

It might seem a somewhat curious motivation today, but the adventurous explorers of yesteryear were often fuelled by religion. The **Via di Francesco**, or Way of St Francis, is a classic pilgrim route, following the footsteps of the Roman Catholic friar on a month-long, 550km trek from Florence to Rome. The mountains of Umbria and Tuscany stand as a barrier between the two renaissance cities, the going softened by vineyards and olive groves. Question is, what to wear? Boots or sandals, wimple or Buff, habit or Gore-tex?

If you can't stand the heat... well, don't hike to the vast crater of **Mt Etna's** unpredictable volcano. It's not just the main cauldron of fire that makes this such an exciting 2900m peak; there are up to 200 active secondary craters capable of spewing red hot lava. It's about a three-hour walk from the Sicilian ski resort of Piano Provenzana to the top.

Half of Mont Blanc – sorry, make that **Monte Bianco** – is on Italian soil, just not the pointy bit (a source of some local debate), and Western Europe's tallest peak can be climbed from Val Veny, near Courmayeur, via the Gonella Hut and the Piton des Italiens route.

For a slightly less technical climb that still delivers a 4000m+ peak, try a two-day ascent of nearby **Gran Paradiso**, which at 4061m is the biggest mountain to stand entirely on Italian soil. Rising through the eponymously titled national park, it features via ferrata, wonderfully welcoming *refugi* (alpine huts) and a stunning summit ridge.

Tearing up the singletrack at Lake Garda.

Above, *ascending the Masara–Corda Rossa via ferrata in the Dolomites. **Right**, skiing at Sulden, a resort in the South Tyrol.*

preventing gravity from having its wicked way.

There are hundreds of via ferrata in the **Dolomites**, with ascents ranging from about 190m to a summit scaling 1200m. Harness buckled, helmet fastened and karabiner clipped on, novices can make their debut on the Grande Cir above the Gardena Pass, which has a sure-footed path and ledges, and jaw-dropping views.

For one of the greatest panoramas in the Dolomites, the De Luca–Innerkofler via ferrata serves up a spine-tingling view of the north faces of the Tre Cime di Lavaredo from Monte Paterno. The route throws in the excitement of WWI supply tunnels, so don't forget a headtorch.

The Dolomites is also a world-class climbing destination with many spectacular routes up to Grade 8c (5.14b). A little south, sport climbers will find some of Europe's most popular climbing areas at limestone Arco and Finale Ligure, while Sardinia is a compact but amazingly diverse climbing destination. Boulderers will find superb rock at Val di Mello and Varazze.

Trail Running

The shark-toothed profile of **The North Face Lavaredo Ultra Trail** (www.ultratrail.it), which starts in Cortina d'Ampezzo in the Dolomites, leaves no runner in doubt about what's in store over the 130km ahead. A mixture of wide tracks, rocky trails and savage ascents takes the breath away both literally and metaphorically. In 2017, it became one of the top six events in the Ultra Trail World Tour series, and the only downside is that because it's a non-stop race, the few hours of darkness will obscure some of the most delicious mountain scenery in the world.

The early spring **Santa Caterina Winter Trail** race in Stelvio National Park has a chilling difference: its 14km are on tracks covered in snow. That makes gear selection critical – hat or no hat, gloves or no gloves, tights or shorts? The need for running crampons is an easier decision. A total of 560m of ascent should raise the pulse and temperature, but expect your breath to billow in clouds of condensation.

Skiing & Snowboarding

From the Alps to the Dolomites, Italy – which lies in the shadow of some of Europe's most famous

If the via ferrata bug bites, it's possible to spend a week or more living amid the ridges and peaks of the **Dolomites**, hiking and scrambling from one mountain hut to the next, with the extraordinary thrill of watching the sun set and rise from what feels like the roof of the world.

Via Ferrata & Climbing

There would be no shame in adding brown trousers to a kit list when via ferrata is on the agenda. A legacy of WWI, via ferrata (literally, 'iron path/road') were routes forged to allow soldiers and supplies to pass through inaccessible mountain areas. The installation of fixed protection in the form of iron ladders, steps or cables, as well as narrow, gorge-spanning suspension bridges, made rock faces and summits accessible to non-climbers.

By clipping a lanyard and karabiner into the via ferrata, normal mortals can scale cliffs and giant walls normally reserved for the gods of climbing. Slip or tumble and the lanyard acts as a lifeline,

© imageBROKER | Alamy

© Michael Reusse | Getty Images

HOMEGROWN ADVENTURE HERO

Born in Bressanone, South Tyrol, in 1944, Reinhold Messner has crammed several lifetimes' worth of adventure into one life. He was the first man to scale all 14 of the world's 8000m peaks and the first to climb Everest without oxygen. His mountaineering exploits are all the more remarkable given his loss of six toes while climbing the Himalayan peak of Nanga Parbat in 1970, during an expedition that claimed the life of his brother, Günther. A purist in his approach to mountains – no artificial oxygen, no bolts, no communication – Messner started climbing at the age of five. His unquenchable appetite for adventure has also seen him cross the Antarctic, Greenland and the Gobi desert on foot. His Messner Mountain Museum, six interrelated thematic museums, is dedicated to the culture of the world's mountain regions.

mountains – has skiing to delight everyone from freeride charger to piste cruiser.

If you want to ski beneath (or on) **Mont Blanc**, head to **Courmayeur** on the Italian side, for conditions that are just as impressive as those found in Chamonix, with a much-reduced price tag. Or how about the Matterhorn? **Cervinia** lies on its southern flanks, but it's not as well-known because Zermatt in Switzerland sits beneath the iconic main face. Yet you can once again ski for considerably less in Cervinia than in Switzerland, and even slide over to Zermatt. A roadtrip down northern Italy's Aosta Valley links both these resorts, and other classics such as **La Thuile**, with its snow-sure north-facing slopes; unpretentious little **Pila** above the old Roman city of Aosta; and **Champoluc**, which has superb, uncrowded freeriding.

Another classic of the Italian Alps is **Livigno**, Europe's highest inhabited parish, which is not only snow-sure but also duty free, so the living – already cheaper than many other European Alpine countries – is even easier. Then there's the delightful **Dolomites**. Resorts like Cortina attract Italy's beautiful people, who strut along the piazzas and take long lunches at mountain restaurants, meaning the slopes can be surprisingly quiet. Check out the intermediate-level **Hidden Valley** – not only is it absolutely beautiful, it may be the only time you travel on a horse-drawn 'ski lift'. The Dolomites also boast the **Sella Ronda**, a circular network of runs around the massive **Gruppo Sella**, which links the resorts of Selva-Val Gardena, Corvara, Arabba and Canazei and – for intermediates in particular – is as good a day out on skis as you'll ever have.

Sea Kayaking

Adventurers with a passion to reach the places that others can't will revel in the isolated beauty of Sardinia's **Maddalena Archipelago**. More than 50 islets surround the seven principal islands, offering blissful opportunities to paddle beyond the reach of tourist crowds. The sheltered National Marine Park offers easy kayaking, even for beginners, the waters are clear and the sea is a retina-challenging turquoise. On the islands and islets, granite coves give way to sand – draw the kayaks onto the beaches and chill out with a swim, snorkel and picnic.

Diving

The grappa-clear waters around **Sicily** offer fabulous visibility for divers, while treacherous waters have littered the Mediterranean floor with fascinating wrecks. A cargo of stone and marble pillars that tumbled to the seabed in Naxos Bay resembles a Greek temple swallowed by the tide, while the haunting ruins of a WWII Italian merchant ship at Castellammare del Golfo now host teeming marine life. And at the shallow caves of Grotta Azzurra, glitterball light shines on corals, shrimps and rainbow fish.

Lipari, an island just off the north coast of Sicily, has a glorious coast to explore.

JAMAICA

Jamaica, the liveliest of the Caribbean islands, regales the adventurous with watersports galore and plenty to explore inland.

J amaica has a very developed tourism industry, including day trips to adventure parks that may feel a bit too 'organised' for independent-minded travellers, but the island is large and there's plenty to explore. There are all the watersports you can imagine – from SUP to kitesurfing – and inland there's superb hiking. What most people don't realise, though, is that Jamaica's rivers are just as exciting as the beach.

Watersports

Hotels all offer watersports such as sailing and kayaking. The best **windsurfing** and **kitesurfing** is at Burwood Beach near Montego Bay, where you can hire gear and get instruction.

Rafting

In Jamaica, river rafting doesn't mean whitewater, rather its diametric opposite: being punted gently on a bamboo raft. Try the **Great River** and **Martha Brae**, but definitely don't miss the **Rio Grande** – popularised by Errol Flynn – for 12km of heart-stoppingly beautiful countryside, with easy rapids and pools to swim in.

Wild Swimming

Jamaica's waterfalls are legendary. The best known, **Dunn's River** and **YS Falls**, are tourist traps (though still beautiful; go late to avoid the crowds), but on the back-roads are some spectacularly lovely rivers, falls and pools. Try **Mayfield**, the **Cabarita River**, the **White River** and **Reach Falls** (or ask at your hotel). Some companies offer tubing experiences. In the limestone **Cockpit Country** some rivers disappear underground and you can wade and swim to follow them.

Hiking

Reached on a path that climbs through rainforest and then stunted elfin forest – where agonised trees hang with lichen and moss – **Blue Mountain Peak** (2256m) is Jamaica's highest mountain. Hikes start at 3am from one of the high lodges, reaching the summit as dawn spreads its tentacles across the sky. There are also hiking routes in the **John Crow Mountains** and through the extraordinary **Cockpit Country**, an area of egg-box like, shaggy 150m-high verdant green hillocks.

Mountain Biking

Jamaica is home to some killer technical singletrack (best appreciated with the headphones playing reggae). Come during the seven-day fiesta that is the Fat Tyre Festival, but be quick, places sell out fast.

© Matt Munro | Lonely Planet, © Douglas Pearson | Getty Images

DON'T LEAVE WITHOUT...
Strapping on tanks and exploring the fringing reef along the northern coastline, where the water is warm and the visibility can be as far as 30m.

Rafting down the Rio Grande was popularised by film star Errol Flynn.

JAPAN

Japan is best known for its deep snow, but the entire country is an adventurer's dream. It's about time the world got in on the secret.

It sounds strange describing a country of 127 million people as a secret, but that's exactly what Japan is. At least in terms of adventure. Home to more ski areas than anywhere else on the planet – over 500 – Japan also has more mountains than Switzerland, more river systems than New Zealand, and more coastline than – you're hearing this right – Australia.

With 75% of the country covered by mountains – some of which receive the world's heaviest snowfalls – it was inevitable the secret would escape about the skiing and boarding. But it's only happened recently. Twenty years ago you could spend a week choking on Niseko's nipple-deep powder and see no other foreigners. Not one. However, word is yet to spread globally – or even within Japan – about how good other adventurous pursuits can be.

Road cyclists can find climbs to match any in Europe and mountain bikers can rip down singletrack through ancient forests. There are baby-blue waters rich with kaleidoscopic coral, crinkle-cut coastlines with amazing paddling, and – at the right time of year – near-empty barrels begging to be surfed. Deep ravines spill from the mountains, offering cooling waters for canyoners and paddlers in the summer, changing to waterfall ice for climbers in winter. Elsewhere in the mountains there are world-class crags. Skyrunners can spend days on vertiginous ridgelines. And the entire country is riddled with hiking trails of all lengths and levels of difficulty. Possibly best of all, after your adventure, you can soak in one of literally thousands of *onsens* (hot springs).

And it's all so accessible. Most activities can be enjoyed within hours of major cities and trailheads can often be reached by a public transport system of legendary efficiency. And, here's one more secret: Japan isn't as expensive as people believe. Especially if, like many adventurers, you're willing to dirt-bag it a bit.

Cycling
Road Riding

Let's say this straight up: Japan's road cycling is as good as its skiing. Over recent decades, the country has spent more money on roads than anywhere else, and the largesse has extended beyond major roads to tiny rural routes lucky to see one car an hour. Etched improbably into mountainsides, switchbacks have been stacked upon switchbacks and outsized bridges flung needlessly across gorges. Tunnels have been cut. Roadside concrete ramparts a hundred metres high dot the hills, and surfaces have been hot-mixed to mirror-smooth perfection.

Granted, traffic-choked roads still exist, but once out of the cities, head into the hills anywhere and you'll find a riding Shangri-La. Strangely, even among the Japanese, this remains almost unnoticed. Ascents of a vertical kilometre or more, which in Europe would be famed, here remain virtually unknown. Part of the beauty of Japanese cycling is the sense of discovery.

Nagano Prefecture is as good as it gets. Within it you'll find the Manza Line, with 107 switchbacks; the preposterously engineered Venus Line; and, at Norikura-dake, the country's highest paved road. Another recommended climb (in Yamanashi Prefecture) is the 2200m vertical ascent to Mt Fuji's fifth station.

For cycle touring, routes are better documented. Hokkaido is a favourite, where the landscape broadens out and there are sweeping vistas. Shikoku, too, is highly recommended. But seriously, the entire country has superb touring. There are great coastal routes as well.

Mountain Biking

Japan is littered with small forest paths, although purpose-built singletrack is rare. More rarely still is it publicised; trails are often kept deliberately secret. The rewards for sniffing out singletrack can be great, but foreign riders on short itineraries are best off with guides or hitting up MTB parks. Fujimi

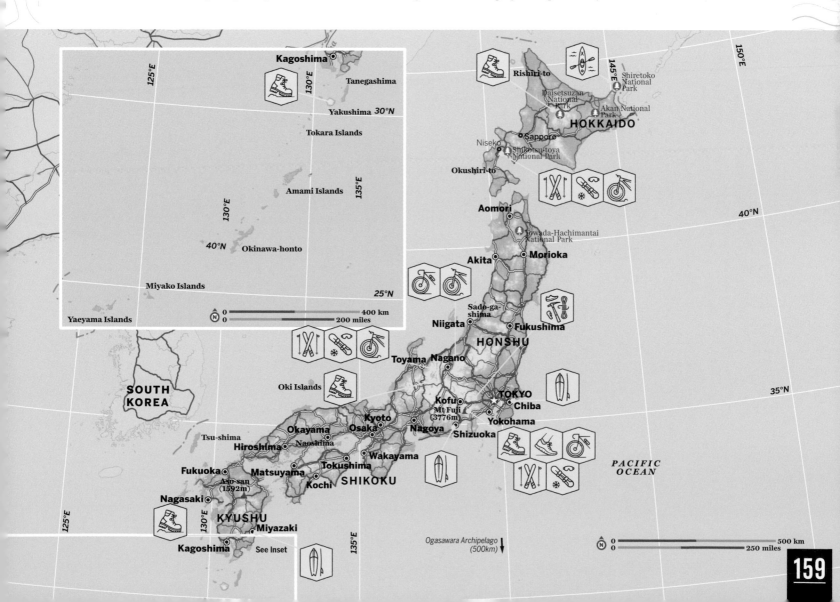

Panorama is Japan's largest, but other worthwhile destinations include Nozawa Onsen, Hakuba and Hokkaido's Niseko.

Snowsports

Mythology has it that skiing came to Japan in 1911, when Austrian Major Theodor von Lerch gave lessons on Mt Kanaya, but it was the 1972 Sapporo Winter Olympics that ignited the ski boom of the 1980s. There are now more than 500 operating ski areas in Japan and that doesn't account for the many decommissioned as the Japanese economy stalled and stagnated in the 1990s. Many areas shut and larger resorts turned to foreigners to fill lift lines. And the foreigners have come.

Flashy famous areas like Niseko and the Hakuba valley attract big crowds every season. They're slick operations with good facilities and, although Japan might not have the *steeps* (by and large the terrain is not uber steep), it definitely has the *deeps* – Niseko

gets up to 15m of snow. But given the number of resorts, wherever you are there's a micro resort nearby blessed with no queues, no crowds, no frills, and lots of deep snow.

Japanese society is well ordered and rules are well followed and that extends to the ski slopes. Foreigners can stare in hungry wonder at the untracked out-of-bounds that are just off-piste, but the Japanese patrollers will snag your pass if you do duck ropes. Such strict rule enforcement and the lure of untracked pow is taking adventurers into the slackcountry and beyond. Hiking for turns is exploding with the promise of dropping virgin fall lines luring punters away from civilisation.

A day on the Japanese slopes is more than just skiing, though. You might not be able to get a morning latte, but you can work your way through the befuddling options on the coffee vending machine. In the middle of the day you can stop halfway through a run, duck into a wooden inn and slurp down one of the best bowls of ramen you've ever had, before wiping your chin and clicking into your bindings for the afternoon session. When the turns are done, bookend your day by grabbing an Asahi from the beer-vending machine in the lobby of your *ryokan*. An infinite number of small things delight in Japan, but none more than the *onsen*, or traditional bath. There is no better way to finish a big day of riding powder than this ritual soaking. Seek out a traditional, public *onsen* for the full experience, strip off and figure out how to use the handkerchief-sized 'modesty towel' as your aching muscles recover. Not into public nudity? In places like Nozawa Onsen, take time out from stomping around marvelling at the architecture, the signs, the cartoon characters, by warming your frozen feet in a roadside foot *onsen*.

The people are polite, the food is delicious and baffling, the culture is endlessly fascinating, the snow is deep, the powder dry and the backcountry accessible. A snow trip to Japan is awesome.

Climbing
Rock

In such a mountainous country, it's unsurprising there's outstanding climbing in all forms. Japan's most popular crags are those at Ogawayama in Nagano Prefecture. Punching out of forested mountainsides, Ogawayama's dozens of granite

Below, riding the Avenue of Gingko Trees in Tokyo. Right, skiing deep, glorious powder at Niseko, Hokkaido.

© Patrick Foto | Getty Images

© Aurora Photos | Alamy

spires offer more than a thousand routes – trad, sport and bouldering, ranging from easy to cutting-edge. Not as large, but often regarded as Japan's best sports crags, Horai's limestone cliffs have routes up to 9a/5.14d. And the steep, heavily featured tufa at Futago-yama, in Chichibu on Tokyo's outskirts, hosts the country's hardest climb, Flat Mountain, a 9a+/5.15a. Other popular areas include Joyama (with 300 routes) and the basalt coastal cliffs at Jogasaki (550+ routes). Beyond Honshu, look to Honjo and Hieizan in Kyushu, and Ohdo in Shikoku.

And Ice

In winter, the epicentre of waterfall ice climbing is Akadake-Kosen Lodge near Yatsu-ga-take. There are more than just great ice routes by the dozen on the surrounding peaks; right next to Akadake-Kosen is Ice Candy, an artificial ice wall. And the lodge

DON'T LEAVE WITHOUT...

Skiing Mt Fuji. In Shinto it's the embodiment of nature itself, for Buddhists it's a gateway to another world. There is something special about skiing or boarding down the beautiful, conical Mt Fuji – the most iconic peak in Japan.

even has heated toilet seats, which – when it gets to minus 30°C or worse – are a godsend.

Elsewhere, if big routes appeal, Kai-Komagatake's O-ren-dani is a mini-but-multiday-expedition, offering 2000m of cold, deep climbing. For steep ice, Oyafudo drips with vertical pillars up to and over 50m. And for mixed climbing, Zao Ice Garden in Tohoku has superb routes to M9. In central Hokkaido, Sounkyo has roughly 15 routes ranging from WI3-6 and M7-8+, with the kicker being they're right next to the road.

Hiking

Across the entire archipelago, the hiking is both astoundingly good and – quite frequently – astonishingly rugged; finding routes without much climbing is often challenging, to the extent that *yama-nobori* (mountain climbing) and *haikingu* (hiking) so frequently mean the same thing they're usually interchangeable. Nowhere is this more the case than in the **Japan Alps**, where chains and ladders assist hikers up cliffs and along razor-sharp ridges on dizzyingly airy routes. The classic of classics is the multiday loop out of Kamikochi that encompasses climbing Yari-ga-take and traversing Daikiretto, offering a view of the Hotaka Range that's arguably the nation's best alpine vista, and that's saying something. In the same region, Tateyama and Tsurugi (The Spear) make fantastic, challenging outings. The Central and South Alps (particularly the latter) also offer tremendously rugged scenery. And, of course, there is Fuji-san.

Elsewhere, on the roof of Hokkaido, hikers can traverse the justifiably famed **Daisetsu-zan National Park**, a spread of volcanic peaks, alpine plateaus, waterfalls and lakes. Though not as jaggedly sharp as other Japanese alpine regions, it's more expansive country; swathes of meadows sit well above the treeline, making it one of Japan's best areas for alpine wildflowers. Kyushu, too, offers spectacular hiking into the volcanic zones surrounding Kirishima and Aso-san. And to Kyushu's south, on the island of **Yakushima** – home to Japan's first World Heritage listing – trails climb sharply through lush, emerald rainforests and thousand-year-old cedars to the summit of Miyanoura-dake.

Surfing

A surprisingly popular sport, with an estimated one million participants, Japan's surf scene tends to be focused north and south of Tokyo, in Chiba, Kanagawa and Shizuoka Prefectures, although crowds and wind-generated shorebreaks

Below, the short hike to Pinaisara Falls on Iriomote Island is very popular. Right, the mysterious Couple Stones at Yonaguni Monument off Yonaguni island.

predominate. But with good timing (read: hitting the right typhoon), waves of serious quality can be found both here and around the country, most notably at Kyushu's Miyazaki.

Skyrunning

With an abundance of airy alpine trails, it's not surprising skyrunning is exploding in popularity here. Okutama near Tokyo has great beginner trails, but fabulous routes all over the North, Central and South Alps can keep you above the treeline for hours, if not days. There's also a popular race series; events often fill up in hours, even months in advance. The Ultra Mount Fuji – which ascends 10,000m over roughly 160km – is the most prestigious, and is a stop on the World Tour.

Canyoning

Japanese rivers flow fast, short and steep. In the summer, up high, where they are more sequences of waterfalls than anything else, superb canyoning opportunities await, including first descents. Japan being Japan, it does things differently; while the rest of the world tends to descend canyons, *sawanobori* – literally 'stream climbing' – is more popular here.

Paddling

Out of the canyons, once the rivers flatten a little, rafting and kayaking opportunities abound. The sea kayaking can also be outstanding; although much coastline has unfortunately been concreted, there still remains an abundance of staggeringly beautiful untouched coves, sea-cliffs and islands. For good wildlife spotting on and off the water (including whales and bears), paddle around Shiretoko Peninsula, a Unesco World Heritage Site on eastern Hokkaidō.

Diving

Unsurprisingly, for an archipelago nation, many of Japan's islands offer excellent diving and snorkelling, particularly as you head south into the subtropics of Okinawa and its outer islands. In the waters of Yonaguni, one of the Yaeyama Islands, you can dive with hammerhead sharks during the winter, and explore a mysterious underwater monument that was discovered in 1986 and is known as Japan's Atlantis.

© Alex Munro Lonely Planet, © Chris Wilson / Alamy

JORDAN

From the mountains of Wadi Rum, to the wild uninterrupted desertscapes of Dana Biosphere Reserve and the protected coral reefs of the Red Sea – Jordan offers a real Arabian adventure.

Sandwiched between Syria and Iraq to the north, Egypt and Saudi Arabia to the south and east, and Palestine and Israel to the west, Jordan has, in recent years, suffered from its proximity to headline-hitting neighbours. However, those who venture to this mellow Middle East refuge will find not only a multitude of adventure activities to try, but also a dramatically diverse range of landscapes to try them in.

Hiking

For those looking to explore Jordan intimately, the 650km Jordan Trail tracks the ever-changing landscapes of the country, from Umm Qais in the north to Aqaba in the south. Partially waymarked, the route is divided into eight sections, takes about 36 hiking days, and passes 52 villages and all the iconic sites: the rock-hewn city of Petra, the moon-like terrain of Wadi Rum, the Byzantine ruins in Tel Mar Elias, the 12th-century Muslim castle at Kerak and the olive trees and farmlands of Carakale.

Diving & Snorkelling

It can get busy, but the hype around the Red Sea is justified. Under the waves, away from sprawling developments, a glorious cavalcade of colourful coral awaits at locations such as Aqaba Marine Park, where you can meet turtles, blue-spotted rays, snappers, barracudas and lionfish, and explore several shipwrecks, including a submerged M42 Tank.

Canyoning

Slicing through the desertscape near the Dead Sea is the 800m-deep Wadi Mujib. Here you can spend hours, days even, canyoning – sliding and slotting through the rock, rappelling down drops and navigating through this water-rich gorge, which sits 410m below sea level.

Rock Climbing

Nature's own Gaudí-esque sandstone architecture, which protrudes from the silt like the rump of a hibernating beast, makes many feet and hands itch with desire to clamber up Wadi Rum's *jebels* (mountains), and this place is irresistible for true trad and sport climbers. Mount the highest peak of Jebel Um-Adaami – from the summit of which you can gaze into Saudi Arabia – climb up one of the many Bedouin routes on Jebel Rum or scramble your way (rope-assisted) to the much photographed Burdah Bridge on Jebel Burdah.

Camel & Horse Riding

It's been more than a hundred years since Lawrence of Arabia traversed the deserts of the Valley of the Moon (Wadi Rum), but the thought of travelling over its blood-red sand by camel or horse, as he did, still holds allure. Most quadruped safaris start at the entrance to the Unesco Heritage Site, where Bedouin guides will take you beneath the orange cliffs, setting up camp under the shade of the rocks for half-day and multiday tours.

DON'T LEAVE WITHOUT
Going kayaking on the Dead Sea, which sloshes around at the lowest point on Earth, 400m below sea level.

Wadi Rum's monumental landscapes call out to be explored.

KAZAKHSTAN

Blistering desert, lofty alpine mountains, rolling grassland, blasted former military zones – Kazakhstan is the place for non-agoraphobic adventurers.

More than twice the size of Western Europe, this former Soviet Union powerhouse is a transcontinental country, where the vast open topography offers adventures for steppe-savvy, distance-hardened equestrian long riders and off-piste drivers.

Desert Off-Roading

Kazakhstan has vast and spectacular swathes of absolutely nothing. Scotland-sized regions are entirely devoid of humans – just endless horizons filled with scraggy scrubland, the odd ancient burial site and abandoned military outposts. In the country's centre is one such segment: the scrubby desert of the **Betpak-Dala**, roughly translating as the 'Steppe of Misfortune'. It's visited very occasionally by conservationists and hunters, but few travellers make it this far. However, several logistics providers (such as StanTours), will facilitate 4WD trips, if you're committed and well-prepared. The long-abandoned military base at Betpak-Dala's centre is a fascinating glimpse back into Cold War history. Other options for adventurous off-roading include the spectacular chalk cliffs of the **Mangyshlak Peninsula**, and a crossing of the former **Aral Sea** (now a bizarre ship-strewn desert).

Hiking

For a country that's predominantly pancake flat, there are some surprisingly good hiking trails – if you know which tucked-away mountain ranges to explore. Areas such as **Bayanaul National Park**, **Charyn Canyon** and the legendary **Tien Shan mountains** all have excellent single or multiday trekking routes, but perhaps one of the most interesting areas to explore is the fabled Blue Mountains of **Burabay National Park**.

Horse Trekking

The steppe's galloping animals were first domesticated 6000 years ago and the country has a deep affinity with its equine population. Many tour providers offer horse trekking, and the most interesting excursions for wilderness-seeking would-be longriders take place in the far northeast, in the **Altai mountains**. The three **Kolsai lakes** are an excellent choice for more time-pressed travellers, offering incredible alpine views from well-established horse trails, all just a few miles from the country's second city, Almaty.

Dramatic Charyn Canyon is best explored on foot.

© Serg_R i.500px

> ### UNCLAIMED ADVENTURE
> From the western slopes of the Mugodzhar Hills rises the Emba River. During winter it freezes, but each spring the meltwater begins running 647km across western Kazakhstan to the Caspian Sea. An intrepid adventurer could packraft the river's route to claim a likely first source-to-sea descent.

KENYA

With glaciers flanking jagged equatorial peaks and sea breezes blowing along its tropical Indian Ocean shores, Kenya serves up more than sweeping savannahs and safari dreams.

Cut by the majestic scar that is the Great Rift Valley, Kenya's landscape is as varied as it is beautiful. The steaming depths of Hell's Gate National Park offer rock climbers and cyclists the chance to rub shoulders with iconic wildlife, while undulating and remote terrain elsewhere provides surreal settings for horseback and camel safaris. Kitesurfers have more than 1000km of coastline to play with, and mountaineers, mountain bikers and trekkers will all be challenged by sacred Mt Kenya.

Horseback & Camel Safaris

There is watching the great migration, and there is being part of it... Imagine galloping on horseback alongside streams of wildebeest as they move across the savannah. Enabling you to be 'one of the animals', riding safaris provide an enthralling window into the wildlife of the Mara, Chyulu Hills and Laikipia Plateau. Multiday camel safaris, on the other hand, afford more of a cultural experience,

accessing the remote heartlands of the nomadic Samburu and Turkana peoples. You'll learn about bush lore, botany, ornithology and local customs.

Rock Climbing

Much like K2 is considered a harder climb than Everest, summiting Mt Kenya is much more challenging than topping Kilimanjaro. For starters, trekkers have no chance of reaching **Batian**, the mountain's lofty 5199m peak, which is the realm of experienced rock climbers – the push up the North Face route can last well over 12 hours, with technical pitches of 5.8 and 5.9. The 25m **Fischer's Tower** and volcanic gorge walls in Hell's Gate National Park are rewarding challenges for those with less climbing experience, as is **Tembo Peak** in Tsavo West National Park.

Trekking

Although it's not possible to reach the summit of Mt Kenya on foot, the mountain is still one of Africa's greatest trekking destinations. **Point Lenana**

ICONIC RACE

Kenya is famous for fast runners, and you might find out why during the Safaricom Marathon, a tough (and unfenced) course through the Lewa Wildlife Conservancy, where elephants, rhinos, zebras and the odd lion are the spectators.

© Saro17 | Getty Images

(4985m), which looks dramatically over the (fast retreating) Lewis Glacier to Batian, is the primary goal. Three routes, each taking several days, lead up to Lenana through challenging and varied terrain. And if you've come that far, go one mighty step further by taking on the spectacular **Summit Circuit**, a trail that encircles the mountain's main peaks between 4300m and 4800m elevation. Multiday treks with culture at the core are also an incredible experience, such as following Maasai guides through the **Loita Hills** in the Mara region.

Mountain Biking

Mountain biking in Kenya is as much about what's off the trail as on it. Nowhere is this better exemplified than in **Hell's Gate National Park**, where zebras, giraffes, impalas and buffaloes are all along for the ride. Large carnivores are very rare, though you may still be surprised how much space you'll want to give the others – they seem much bigger from your bike seat than from a 4WD. The rocky trails on **Mt Kenya** hold more of a physical challenge due to their

vertiginous gradients, and here it's the stunning landscape that takes centre stage.

Kitesurfing

With offshore reefs protecting its warm waters, and consistent, reasonably strong winds, Kenya's Indian Ocean coast is ideal for kitesurfing. Those with experience can wade off the white-sand beaches into the azure waters and let fly (literally), while learners can sign up at one of the schools located on Diani Beach south of Mombasa, or in Malindi on the north coast. Classes start on the beach, and once you've got the hang of manoeuvring the kite, it's into the water for body dragging.

Scuba Diving

The coastal hubs of Mombasa and Malindi both boast magical marine national parks, offering superb diving for experienced bubble blowers and beginners alike, with wildlife ranging from turtles and sharks to sea cucumbers and nudibranches, via thousands of tropical fish and corals.

Mountain biking at Hell's Gate National Park can throw up some unusual obstacles.

KIRIBATI

Little-known and seldom-visited, Kiribati is a divers' paradise.

Perhaps the world's most off-the-radar adventure destination, Kiribati is a dusting of tiny islands spread across a vast expanse of Pacific Ocean between (but a long way from) the Cook Islands and Hawaii. The country – comprised of 33 Micronesian atolls straddling the equator – is the first nation to ring in the New Year.

Diving

For a nation that's more water than land, Kiribati is, unsurprisingly, all about the sea. Diving is an emerging industry, which means two things: getting to a dive site and getting geared up is half the adventure, and once you're there you are virtually guaranteed pristine conditions all to yourself. **Kiritimati** (Christmas Island) offers great lagoon and ocean diving, while underwater adventures off **Tarawa** and the **Gilbert Islands** come with bonus WWII wrecks. There's an abundance of coral and sea life to meet, including sharks, rays, turtles and dolphins.

Surfing

For people sick of others dropping in on their waves, Kiribati is paradise, with its islands either side of the equator serving up good, deserted swells. Kiritimati, the largest of the atolls, has a 5km stretch of coastline with 24 breaks, eight of which are best left to experienced surfers.

DON'T LEAVE WITHOUT...
Going canoeing – it's a national pastime and the best way to explore Kiribati's myriad turquoise lagoons.

SOUTH KOREA

Peel South Korea back to the natural basics and the country is surprisingly raw and elemental.

The host country for the 2018 Winter Olympic Games packs an impressive adventure arsenal, with 80% of it covered in mountains and protected in 20 national parks.

Cyclists have benefited from a recent project to green the banks of four major rivers, which ended up laying down more than 2000km of bike paths across the country – you can now even ride more than 600km from Seoul to Busan purely on bike routes. Another cycling route circuits Jeju, the large island off the Korean peninsula's southern tip, while a 720km path along South Korea's east coast is also being constructed.

The **hiking** in Korea is exceptional, particularly on wind-blasted Jeju, where a series of trails known as Jeju Olle connect to make a 400km circuit of the island. Also on Jeju is Hallasan (1950m), a dormant volcano that is South Korea's highest mountain. Trails lead to the crater rim from four directions.

On the mainland, top hikes include Daecheongbong, the highest point among the peaks in Seongsan National Park, and an 18.6km urban hike across the hills of Seoul, following the line of the world's largest remaining city wall.

Jeju is also South Korea's premier **diving** destination. Offshore from Seogwipo, along the island's south coast, are colourful soft corals, vertical walls and enormous kelp forests in waters that mix tropical and temperate.

The Winter Olympics will focus attention on South Korea's **snowfields**. The country's oldest, largest and highest resort, topping out at 1458m on Dragon Peak, is Yongpong, which will host the Olympics' technical slalom and giant slalom events. Snowboarders favour the 22 slopes at Bokwang Snow Park, the closest resort to Seoul.

DON'T LEAVE WITHOUT...
Going diving off Jeju, South Korea's top diving destination, made famous by its hardy *haenyeo* women, who free dive for seafood. Offshore from Seogwipo, on the island's south coast, colourful soft corals and kelp forests can be explored.

KYRGYZSTAN

Rugged and mountainous, Kyrgyzstan is a land of contrasts and surprises, often called 'the Switzerland of Central Asia'.

Kyrgyzstan is primarily characterised by its dramatic alpine landscape – 80% of the nation is covered by the mighty Tien Shan Mountains and 40% is over 3000m high. This small country has plenty to offer the intrepid traveller, from vast grassy steppes to sub-tropical valleys and even deserts.

In the Saddle

A key stop on the Silk Road, Kyrgyzstan has seen all manner of travellers over the centuries. One of the best ways to explore the landscape is by traditional means – on the back of a horse, camel or even a yak. Local guides can take you on a cultural experience like no other, during which you'll stay in yurts and witness nomadic life that has remained unchanged for millennia.

Hiking & Climbing

If you'd prefer to use your own two feet, there are several lifetimes' worth of valley treks and alpine climbs. An hour from Bishkek, the **Ala Archa National Park** is famous for its wildflowers, and a good hike follows the Ala Archa River for around 18km. The park is also a prime location for skiing and mountaineering, with many options for ice, rock and mixed routes.

Kyrgyzstan has vast potential for alpine climbing. There are several high-altitude peaks with routes of great antiquity, some of which tip-toe above 7000m, the most famous being the massive marble pyramid of **Khan Tengri** (7010m). Most mountaineering opportunities remain untapped – so if the conquest of an unclimbed peak or the first ascent of a new line is your dream, look no further.

© kav38 | Getty Images

Climbing Pik Lenin (7134m), on the Kyrgyzstan–Tajikistan border.

ULTIMATE CHALLENGE

Bag three of the five summits needed to claim the title of Snow Leopard (a mountaineering accolade bestowed on climbers who ascend all peaks of 7000m in the former Soviet Union) – Pik Lenin (7134m), Pik Pobeda (7439m) and Khan Tengri (7010m).

A climber ascends the steep limestone walls of Vang Vieng.

LAOS

Though many landmines lurk in Laotian jungles, this mountainous, land-locked and river-filled country still offers an explosion of safe activities.

Laos is not a destination that encourages off-track, solo exploration (unless prosthetic surgery appeals), but it's still possible to visit isolated communities – some of which only received electricity in the 1990s – by foot or kayak with a guide. The luscious limestone forests in Khammouane Province contain the largest concentration of caves in Laos, including the 7.5km-long marvel of Kong Lor, which is studded with stalactite forests and an emerald green pool. Many rivers snake through Laos providing a buoyant economy through hydroelectricity, and many kayaking opportunities. The northern waterways of Nam Tha, Nam Ou and Nam Ha give glimpses of remote areas inaccessible by road.

Climbing

Rising like sabre-toothed tiger's teeth from the paddy fields, the karst formations towering around **Vang Vieng** feature more than 200 bolted routes for climbers of all abilities. Roughly three hours north of the capital Vientiane (which feels more Thai than Lao), Vang Vieng is a climbing hub for backpackers. Away from tubing tourists pickled on the Nam Song, riverside Sleeping Wall has climbs up to 25m high. Secret Canyon is a shady option in the dry season away from the sun's glare. Sector Calcaneus is particularly popular, a huge section of overhanging limestone climbable even in torrential downpours. A 20km *moto* ride from Vang Vieng, **Pha Daeng Mountain** also has some good overhangs. This is best climbed in the rainy season (June to October) because it's too hot in the dry.

DON'T LEAVE WITHOUT...
Scrambling up the 100 Waterfalls Trek. Accessed via Nong Khiaw village, ankle-tickling water is a constant chaperone for this 10km ascent that involves ropes and rickety bamboo ladders beside cascading waterfalls.

© Henn Photography | Getty Images

Ziplining

In the lush canopies of northerly Bokeo Province, the smallest and least populated province in Laos, the endangered black-crested gibbon isn't the only species flying from branch to branch. *Homo ziplineus* can be seen whizzing through the canopy of **Nam Kan National Park** (near Huay Xai) on ziplines up to 500m long. A series of aerial arterials criss-crosses through the park. It was built in 1996 by conservationists concerned by illegal logging, commercial cropping and excessive slash-and-burn practices in the area. These Ewok lovers also erected tree houses 40m high where happy zippers crash (not literally) at day's end. Best of all, zippers' coins contribute to the preservation of the black-crested gibbons' habitat. Sadly, no loincloths are provided...

UNCLAIMED ADVENTURE

Climbing Phou Bia (2817m). No recorded successful ascents exist of the country's highest peak, probably because the surrounding area is restricted and laden with landmines.

Kayaking

One of the best ways to reach isolated villages and connect with local tribes is to jump in a kayak. Dry season paddlers can expect mostly calm waters along rivers flanked with prehistoric trees, dangling creepers and traditional villages. Paddlers can bunk down for the night in some of these villages. Those going ashore will most likely attract a welcoming committee of grubby, smiling kids with holes in their clothes. Rice whisky could flow like the river at night; dawn chorus is a series of hacking coughs from pipe-smoking wizened women with toothless grins. Northern Laos is the best place for kayaking on the **Nam Tha**, **Nam Ha** and **Nam Ou** rivers. Head there during rainy season for whitewater and Grade II–III rapids.

LATVIA

The sublime mosaic of forests, lakes, rivers and pastures that form the Latvian landscape pique an irresistible sense of wanderlust.

A country with only one real bone fide city – beautiful Riga – Latvia's super low population density leaves plenty of green space for people to play around outside. The landscape is primarily a patchwork of small farms scattered among enchanting forests, which all appear to be marching towards the untouched white-sand beaches fringing a protected gulf within the Baltic Sea.

Hiking & Biking

Latvia's parks are celebrated by walkers for their biodiversity – deer, moose, lynx, bears and beavers are common, and birdwatching is popular. Autumn is ideal for walking, not only for the fiery hues of the forest canopy, but also for the mushrooms that litter the forest floor. The largest of Latvia's 700-plus conservation areas is **Gauja National Park**, with its iconic sandstone cliffs. The forest meets the sea at **Slitere National Park**, where the dramatic Cape Kolka offers a sense of isolation. **Mountain biking** is another way to explore myriad trails connecting various ecosystems.

Paddling

Kayakers and canoeists are spoiled for choice. For tranquillity and relaxation, the **Gauja River** will take you gently past a procession of scenic stone outcroppings. For more excitement, many smaller rivers become lively after the spring snow melt. Local boat hire companies can direct you to any number of active routes.

DON'T LEAVE WITHOUT...
Visiting Ventas Rapid – at 249m wide, it's Europe's widest waterfall (though certainly not its tallest at 2.2m).

LEBANON

Between the shining sea and rugged mountains, Lebanon is dramatic and beautiful.

B efore the civil war, Lebanon was known as the 'Switzerland of the East', not just because it was a banking hub but also for the peaks running parallel to the Mediterranean coast along the country's length. Reaching 3088m, and carved with deep gorges and sinkholes, these mountains make an attractive adventure playground.

Climbing

Looking to the success of their near neighbours in Greece and Turkey, Lebanese climbers have been quietly developing their own limestone crags, the best of which are in **Tannourine**, a secluded valley echoing with history, blessed by solid rock, friendly locals and plenty of bolts.

Trail Running

Walking tracks and donkey paths worn into the mountain sides over millennia have created huge trail running potential. The 470km **Lebanon Mountain Trail** – a miracle of environmentalism and civic pride in a land that has long suffered from sectarianism – takes in isolated peaks, hidden valleys and welcoming villages as it traverses the country's spine.

Snow Sports

Only an hour's drive from Beirut's choking streets you can strap into skis at **Mzaar** (2465m), the Middle East's biggest snow resort, which boasts vistas of colourful Bekaa Valley to the east and has westward views to the coast. There aren't many places in the world that you can carve on snow in the morning, then waterski in the ocean that same afternoon.

ULTIMATE CHALLENGE
Attempt the second ever ascent of superstar rock climber David Lama's hard route Avaatara (9a/5.14d) in the gobsmacking Baatara Gorge.

LESOTHO

A mountain kingdom stacked with top-shelf adventures.

W hether you tackle this destination on foot or approach it in the saddle, you'll find plenty of heady highs in Lesotho, the highest country on the planet.

Pony Trekking

Few people consider pony trekking a hardcore pursuit, but most soon change their tune after riding one of these robust little equine adventurers into Lesotho's mountains. Whether sliding down steep rock faces or carrying you along precipitous paths, the country's sure-footed Basotho ponies are astonishing. There are numerous opportunities for multiday pony treks across the country, in places such as Ts'ehlanyane National Park, **Bokong Nature Reserve**, and at both **Malealea** and **Semonkong lodges**.

Hiking

Don't expect waymarked trails for conventional trekking, but arm yourself with a compass, some confidence and a decent topographical map, and the kingdom is all yours to explore. That said, rugged and steep conditions underfoot in the **Drakensbergs** and **Eastern Highlands**, combined with harsh and very volatile weather conditions – think fog, thunderstorms and negative temperatures (even in summer) – can make it a hostile environment, so you should be both experienced and well prepared if you're going to take it on. Local guides come at a cost, but they provide immeasurable knowledge of the landscape, culture and language, which will add greatly to your experience.

ICONIC EVENT
Lesotho's singletrack trails are ripe for mountain biking, and the UCI class-1 Lesotho Sky Race – covering 390km (including 9000m of ascent) in six days, and limited to 100 riders – is a world-class event.

LIECHTENSTEIN

Famous for its riches and castles, little Liechtenstein offers a wealth of ways to spend your days outside.

B ordered to the west by the Rhine, this otherwise landlocked, mountainous principality is absolutely made for hiking, biking and skiing.

Green Season
Hiking

Liechtenstein is only 24km long, but it has more than 400km of walking tracks. The steep scree slopes of its highest point, **Grauspitz** (2599m), demand that hikers tap into their mountain goat genes to reach the summit, as there are no maintained tracks. The easiest ascent takes in the knobbly **Schwarzhorn**, then it's an adrenaline-pumping walk along a razor-thin ridge. The neighbouring peaks of **Falknis** (2562m) and **Naafkopf** (2570m) see more action due to maintained trails. Look over Germany, Austria and Switzerland from the summits. Summer offers the best walking; bring crampons and ice axes in winter.

Biking

Little Liechtenstein has 100km of cycle paths, wending from the Rhine valley into the Alps. There's mountain biking too: climb from Schaan to Gafadurahütte hut (1400m), explore Schellenberg mountain or trace Valorschtal Valley from Schönberg up to Malbun.

White Season

When winter hits, tobogganers, skiers, ice-climbers and snowboarders slide, slalom and skid to **Malbun**. Sub-zero Spiderman freaks can climb an odd, icy 20m man-made tower that looks as if it's a set prop from *The Lord of the Rings*. Cross-country skiers head to **Valünatal Valley** in Steg for tracks on easy (4km) and hilly (15km) terrain.

DON'T LEAVE WITHOUT...
Hiking up the hill to Vaduz Castle, along trails that ascend from the end of Egertastrasse. It's not normally open to the public, but your effort will be rewarded by royal views. Time your arrival for Liechtenstein's National Day, 15 August, when the prince invites all 36,900 of his subjects over for a beer.

LITHUANIA

The lowlands, coast and rivers of this pioneering place are best seen in the saddle or with a paddle.

The Baltic's southernmost country has a proud tradition of independence (it was the first to break free from Soviet control) and outdoor recreation. Locals love to explore their Curonian shore and wend through the wonderful wetlands, and welcome visitors to do the same.

Cycling

Lithuania's cycling infrastructure is becoming increasingly well developed, especially along the Baltic coast. The **Curonian Spit** in Kuršių Nerija National Park is a narrow, curvaceous peninsula separating the Curonian Lagoon from Lithuania's Baltic Sea coast, which boasts beautiful beaches and 60m-high dunes. Its northern half lies in southwestern Lithuania (the rest is Russian). A road spans the entire Lithuanian length of the spit, which bikers can do in a day, but it's worth absorbing the towns and nature reserves en route. Steed rental is in Klaipėda. From there, a 10-minute ferry ride terminates in Smiltynė, a village at the very north of the dunes. Pass through fishing villages, sculpture parks, heron and cormorant colonies, and onto the most scenic part: the Grey (Dead) Dunes, facetiously referred to by locals as the Lithuanian Sahara.

Kayaking

Heading east to escarpments and picturesque riverbanks, **Širvinta River** is ripe for kayaking. Spring finds the rivulet revving into life and waters flowing rapidly. Whitewater also froths (after heavy rain) in the narrow valleys of **Duksta** and **Zvelsa** with Grade II-plus rapids.

DON'T LEAVE WITHOUT...
Going down to the Lithuanian woods to get a surprise. In Juodkrante you can follow a trail across the Hill of Witches (populated by crow-monsters, devils and other folkloric frighteners) and in Žemaitija National Park you can explore (with a guide) the disused Dvina Nuclear Missile Base, which once pointed a nasty payload at the West.

LUXEMBOURG

With dense forests, rolling hills, gorges and river valleys – pint-sized Luxembourg packs in plenty of action opportunities.

Hiking

Venturing into the eastern Müllerthal region's woods feels like you're entering a fairy tale. Bizarre sandstone rock formations rise from the forest like elfin lairs, troll faces appear in the rocks, and stone steps look as if they lead to clandestine castles buried beneath moss. Gorges, rivers, castles, caves and sprawling vistas adorn the well-signposted 112km **Müllerthal Trail**. Many walkers depart from Luxembourg's oldest city, Echternach, and use Moersdorf, Müllerthal and Larochette as bases to stay along the way.

On the Belgian border, the Ardennes has high plains and steep sloping valleys to trek. Clervaux has more than 150km of picturesque trails. The **Escapardenne Lee Trail** tracks 53km up steep paths to rocky ridges, past Gringlee. The northeastern **Upper Sûre Nature Park** has a 700km network of hiking trails, not to mention some hilly cycling routes.

Cycling

Despite its diminutive size, Luxembourg boasts 600km of cycling paths (with another 300km in progress) and 700km of mountain-biking tracks. Follow a section of the country spanning river-hugging Saarland Cycle Path on the 36km **Römerrunde** route from Schengen for an easy ride. Knobbly tyre fans can tackle the short climbs and technical twists of the 26.5km circuit around picturesque **Larochette**, or the demanding 25km Clervaux circuit. Another favourite off-road route is the 35km **Bavigne-Boulaide**, which affords amazing Ardennes vistas.

DON'T LEAVE WITHOUT...
Paragliding off Gringlee (448m), near the tiny town of Lipperscheid, for curvaceous views of the River Sûre.

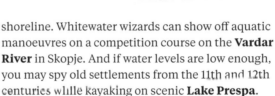

MACEDONIA

Thanks to myriad mountain peaks, the deepest lake in the Balkans and numerous caves, Macedonian adventure is alpine, sub-aqua and subterranean.

T his southeastern European country still feels like a secret destination, but here kayakers paddle across lakes and through whitewater carved canyons, divers explore submerged Neolithic settlements, skiers slide around the highest town in the Balkans (the 1350m eyrie of Kruševo), and hikers and bikers wend through wilderness areas populated with wolves, bears, boar, golden eagles and lynx.

Caving

At 1.2km, **Gostivar** is the country's longest cave and comes complete with an underground river and a 7m waterfall. **Bela Voda** (955m long) has a crystal-adorned cavern and an underground lake. **Solunska 4**, on Mt Karadzica, is Macedonia's deepest at 450m, with one single shaft plunging 250m. History and speleology juxtapose at **Pesna Cave**, which has medieval ruins near the entrance. And if your inner mole still isn't sated, the **Sopiste** karst region has around 50 caves.

Kayaking

Matka Lake is the place for canyon kayaking, where sheer cliffs and medieval monasteries flank the shoreline. Whitewater wizards can show off aquatic manoeuvres on a competition course on the **Vardar River** in Skopje. And if water levels are low enough, you may spy old settlements from the 11th and 12th centuries while kayaking on scenic **Lake Prespa**.

Climbing

Strewn like giant's marbles near **Prilep**, granite boulders test climbers' skills. Veer up the sheer limestone gorge at imposing **Demir Kapija**; scramble above **Matka Canyon**'s scenic lake; slab up at **Plocha**; contemplate red limestone crags at **Lake Ohrid**; and work your core on **Kadina**'s steep, 30m-long routes. Spring and autumn are best.

Hiking

Height-loving hikers can scale conical peaks in the **Jakupica Range**. Lake-loving peak baggers can climb Magaro (2254m) in **Galičica National Park** for views of lakes Prespa and Ohrid, which sandwich the park. And wild walkers wander through the gorges, pine forests, karst fields and waterfalls of **Mavrovo National Park**, from where it's also possible to hike/climb Golem Korab (2764m), Macedonia's highest peak, which straddles the border with Albania.

DON'T LEAVE WITHOUT...
Scuba diving off Lake Ohrid's dramatic tectonic shelf. Plunge into history, down into the depths of a Neolithic stilt village where 3000-year-old archaeological remains – such as ceramics, bones and tools – languish in the deep.

Fighting fierce rapids on the Treska River, Matka Canyon.

© Rade Lukovic | Alamy

MADAGASCAR

The world's fourth largest island, renowned for its incredible biodiversity, is a largely unexplored paradise.

Y ou can blame DreamWorks and David Attenborough if all you know about Madagascar is that it's the home of curious, charming lemurs and lithe-tongued, colour-changing chameleons. The wildlife – and indeed the plant life – is incredible, with 90% of it endemic to this island where life has evolved in isolation since it separated from India around 88 million years ago, but Madagascar is also an amazing adventure arena. The national parks protect monumental landscapes: mountains stretching to nearly 3000m, tooth-like granite towers and mysterious cloud forests, mangrove swamps and primary jungle riven by rushing rivers, razor-sharp *tsingy* formations and deep limestone caves. The country's 4828km coastline is no less promising – surfers rip up world-class waves, divers explore rich coral reefs, while kitesurfers and windsurfers harness some of the world's most reliable trade winds.

Hiking

It may have only one trail – the two- to three-day walk to Marojejy Peak (2132m) – but the World Heritage-listed **Marojejy National Park** leads walkers through evergreen rainforest to misty montane cloud forest and low alpine tundra. Twitchers can spot up to 118 species of birds, while the park has 11 species of lemur, including the beguiling (but critically endangered) silky sifaka.

South of Marojejy, on the **Masoala Peninsula**, there are more options, from short day walks to the gruelling seven-day trek from Maroantsetra to Cap Est. Again, the wildlife-spotting opportunities are off the scale, with 10 species of lemur, including the extremely handsome red ruffed variety, not to mention numerous delightful geckos, colourful chameleons and the exceedingly toxic tomato frog.

Other highlights include **Bemaraha National Park** and its bizarre 200m-thick plate of ancient, surreally eroded and razor sharp coral, known in the

DON'T LEAVE WITHOUT...
Going caving in Ankarana National Park, where you can explore some of its 140km of subterranean rivers and caves – just watch out for the cave-dwelling crocodiles.

Malagasy tongue as *tsingy*, which can be roughly translated as 'surface that cannot be walked upon'. The granite spires of **Andringitra National Park** are also another worthy destination, particularly for plant lovers, who can try to identify more than a thousand species.

Climbing

Rising above the tiny village of Andonaka in **Andringitra National Park** is a series of dramatic granite faces up to 800m high and streaked in black, orange and green. The big-wall face climbing of **Tsaranoro** – nearly all on bolts – is superlative, with routes up to 8c (the 10-pitch Mora Mora by Czech superstar Adam Ondra). The 14-pitch Out of Africa (7a) is considered by many to be the standout classic, but there are more than 50 free routes to do, with potential for many more.

Surfing

Warm Indian Ocean swells rolling up the Mozambique Channel create killer surf on the southwestern corner of Madagascar, particularly around the village of **Anakao** where there are least 18 breaks, 12 of which are world-class (most accessible only by boat). But surfers can find waves on all four corners of the island. Its remoteness and reputation for sharks (apparently exaggerated) have kept the crowds away, but that just means there's no one to drop in on your wave.

Kitesurfing & Windsurfing

Stroked by a powerful trade wind locals dub the 'Varatraz', northern Madagascar, particularly around **Diego Suarez**, is perfect for kitesurfers and windsurfers, who'll have the waters of the aptly named Emerald Sea all to themselves. Sakalava Lodge makes a great base for visitors, and they also hire out gear and offer lessons.

Diving & Snorkelling

Beneath the waves, the wildlife is almost as exciting as on land. Off the southwest coast you'll find the world's third largest coral reef system, **Toliara**, with 6000 recorded species including everything from prehistoric coelacanth fish to turtles and whale sharks. Further north, the **Nosy Be** archipelago also offers exceptional diving. May to December offers the best visibility (up to 30m).

Paddling

Pirogues are a tradition part of Madagascan life, and canoe trips are the perfect way to absorb local life and spot wildlife. Taking two-to-four days to paddle, the **Tsiribihina** and **Manambolo** rivers are two of Madagascar's most popular river journeys. Kayakers and rafters can also find more technical rivers such as the **Manankazo** and **Mazy**, while the sea kayaking off the east coast is superb, particularly around the **Masoala Peninsula** and around the **Sainte Luce Reserve** in the south.

Exploring the surreal limestone 'tsingy' formations in Bemaraha National Park.

© denniswdw | Getty Images

MALAWI

Malawi's loveable lake is a treasure trove for divers, while its mountains and high plateaus will undoubtedly put smiles on adventurers' faces.

Lake Malawi and its warm waters are as welcoming as Africa's most friendly country. And being full of fish seen nowhere else on earth, it's a remarkable place to don a mask and explore the depths. To the lake's south and west are a series of mountains and plateaus, providing memorable routes for hikers, climbers and mountain bikers.

Freshwater Diving

One of the world's best freshwater dive areas, **Lake Malawi** has about 500 species of fish, most of them endemic to the lake and from the colourful family cichlidae. Dive between September and December to witness the cichlids' complex mating rituals and mouth brooding.

Hiking

Malawi may be most famous for its eponymous lake, but it's the country's numerous mountains and plateaus that offer some of its greatest outdoor challenges. There is magnificent hiking on both the **Viphya** and **Nyika Plateaus** in the north, with chances to spot leopards and elephants atop the latter. The three-day descent from the granite domes of Viphya to the lake along the **Luwawa–Chintheche Trail** is also well worth the effort. The south has two prime hiking locales: the **Zomba Plateau**, which can be climbed from the town of Zomba; and **Mt Mulanje**, a 600 sq km massif composed of rocky ridges and peaks cut by several bowl-shaped river valleys.

Climbing

To take on the longest vertical wall in Africa – Chambe's 1700m West Face – pack your climbing kit and head straight for **Mt Mulanje**. Although nothing else matches it for sheer scale, there are other outstanding routes in the area. Climbing opportunities also exist around **Livingstonia** and on the **Viphya Plateau**.

ICONIC RACE
The 50km-long Luwawa International Mountain Bike Race follows a tough route along the rocky ridges of the Viphya Plateau in central Malawi.

An elephant assuming it has right of way in Liwonde National Park.

© Jonathan Gregson | Lonely Planet

MALAYSIA

Untamed rivers, colossal mountains, mystical caves and coral reefs heaving with one of the greatest profusions of sea life on the planet – Malaysia is an epic boots 'n' booties destination.

Malaysia's generously endowed topography features ancient tropical rainforests, raging river systems and dizzying mountain peaks that all give way to shimmering cerulean seas. But often it's what you can't see that yields the most gasp-inducing encounters. Beneath the water's surface a marine wilderness thrives, its explosions of colour and movement enough to rival Merdeka Day celebrations in the nation's capital. Underground, an elaborate network of caves and gargantuan bat-chirruping chambers lure non-claustrophobes down the rabbit hole. Unique in its geography, Malaysia is divided between two distinct land masses straddling the South China Sea: Peninsular Malaysia in the west, and East Malaysia on the island of Borneo in the east. Both are mountainous, densely forested and fringed by blinding beaches and reefs. The states of Sabah and Sarawak occupy the northern strip of Borneo and are the prime adventure hubs (it's here you'll find Mt Kinabalu and the country's

best diving), but Peninsular Malaysia has some choice offerings, too. From scaling granite peaks on off-the-map islands and exploring subterranean sights, to riding rapids through the rainforest and eye-balling hammerhead sharks – there are many contrasts to keep the adrenaline firing in Malaysia.

Diving

Described by undersea explorer Jacques Cousteau as an 'untouched piece of art', **Sipadan** is one of the world's top dive sites. The protected island, off the east coast of Borneo, cradles one of the richest marine ecosystems on Earth, thanks to the deep-water currents that flush the reef with nutrients. Perched atop an ancient volcano, Sipadan has an undersea topography that is truly mind-boggling. Sheer coral walls encircle what is essentially a scrap of beach and rainforest, dropping 600m into the Celebes Sea abyss. Swarming this eerie underwater precipice are turtles, manta rays, hammerhead sharks, tornadoes of barracudas and more than 3000 species of fish. There are 13 main dive sites

your nerve and a 20m-deep lagoon to fin around. Visibility is between 30m and 60m year-round and marine life abounds, so your adventures are limited only by your air consumption.

Off the coast of Peninsular Malaysia, the **Perhentian Islands** are an easily accessible dive destination that's kinder on your wallet, and a worthy alternative to getting your mask and tank wet at Sipadan. The two islands are a springboard to more than 20 dive sites, including several wrecks and enough hard and soft corals, pinnacles, bommies and sea critters to drown a marine biologist's Instagram feed.

Paddling

Stand-up paddleboarding on mirror-smooth lagoons is for sissies... riding a turbid inland swell is a true test of your paddling prowess. Twice a day, the **Batang Lupar tidal bore** courses through the port town of Sri Aman upstream from where the river spills into the ocean off Sarawak. This natural phenomenon is rated one of the world's top 10 tidal bores and peaks during dry season king tides, when it's game on for paddle boarders and surfers who come to participate in the annual tidal bore festival, **Pesta Benak**.

Brace yourself for a wild ride on the **Singor River** in the northwestern state of Perak. Malaysia's most notorious white-knuckle run packs a mean gauntlet of Grade III–VI rapids, two waterfalls and plenty of dunking, drenching and river scrambling thrills. For the best and fiercest of Malaysia's many rafting runs, the Grade III–VI **Padas River** in Sabah, with its twisting, churning, foaming rapids, is also a must put-in point.

Climbing

First climbed in 1999, the **Dragon's Horns** on Tioman Island off the east coast of Peninsular Malaysia have beguiled climbers for years. Summiting the 700m-plus twin granite spires is strictly for the experienced and entails hiking your gear through thick jungle, followed by a steep, cruxy granite climbing and, often, a night spent bivvying on the wall.

Don't let the location put you off – the Lost World of Tambun may be a theme park, but its greatest assets are made by Mother Nature. Tucked inside the Ipoh park's sprawling grounds in the state of

Above, a school of bigeye trevally off Tioman Island. *Right*, exploring Gua Tempurung, one of Malaysia's longest caves.

to furnish your logbook, but you'll need hours of bottom time to do Sipadan justice. If you have trouble pulling yourself away from the water, no bother, you can sleep on it aboard a converted oil rig at Seaventures Dive Resort.

Diving purists who regard eating, sleeping and surface intervals as onerous distractions from the water should check out **Layang Layang Island**. This stand-alone dive resort northwest of Sabah occupies a man-made island on a remote atoll in the South China Sea that was once a naval base. There's not much to do above water and no fumbling day-trippers to contend with below water, just 13 coral reefs to explore, some serious drop-offs to test

© Reinhard Dirscherl | Getty Images, © shaifulzamri | Shutterstock

Perak are about 50 rock-climbing routes, the most prized being a shimmy up the **Needle of Tambun** – a 60m-high, freestanding limestone pinnacle.

Hiking

Malaysia's mighty monolith, **Mt Kinabalu**, is a peak-bagger's must-do. The 4095m mountain is one of Southeast Asia's tallest, and the target of Sabah's most exhilarating, lung-sapping, heart-pounding expedition. The 8km, non-technical climb is normally tackled over two days, setting off before dawn on the second day to arrive at the summit for a scintillating sunrise above the clouds. To extend your journey and get off the beaten path, the via ferrata – the world's highest – is a worthy add-on adventure, taking you across the Panalaban rock face via a network of rungs, rails and cables.

Thrusting 45m in the air, The Pinnacles on the slopes of Gunung Api (Fire Mountain) are a just reward and a highlight of **Gunung Mulu National Park**. These giant limestone blades pierce the canopy in an otherworldly Edward Scissorhands-forest deep in Sarawak's jungle. The hike here is almost as epic as the landscape, and is well worth the buckets of perspiration that you will expel on the steamy ascent. The two-day trek starts gently enough, but soon you'll be racking up 1m elevation for every 2m you climb. The last section is the ultimate thigh-burner: a near-vertical trail that requires clambering up ladders and ropes in a gruelling hand-and-foot slog.

Caving

Mulu has geological wonders underground too. There are plenty of show caves to explore but none compares to the big granddaddy: the **Sarawak Chamber**. This cave – considered the largest in the world by surface area – could comfortably accommodate 40 Boeing 747s. To get here you'll need to camp overnight, walk or wade through a river that tunnels through a 50m-high chasm, traverse a series of fixed ropes, and climb up a giant boulder that will deposit you inside the cavernous chamber.

ICONIC EVENT

Urban BASE jumping is often a clandestine pursuit, but not in the Malaysian capital, where once a year more than 100 BASE jumpers hurl themselves off 300m-high Kuala Lumpur Tower during an annual extreme sports event called the KL Tower International Jump Malaysia.

MALDIVES

Welcome to an aquatic paradise in the midst of the Indian Ocean where the tide is rapidly rising.

Experience these adventures while you can; the Maldives' highest point is only 2.4m above sea level and most of the country's 26 atolls and 1000 coral islands are expected to be underwater by the century's end.

Diving & Snorkelling

Tropical water and ubiquitous coral provide world-class diving conditions, and bubble blowers can stay on liveaboard boats or shack-up at resorts on the many atolls. From here, underwater options are endless: cruise the current along the Kuredu Express off **Lhaviyani Atoll**, check out the caves and swim-throughs at **Fotteyo Kandu** (Vaavu Atoll) or look for moray eels amid the fan corals at **Broken Rock** (South Ari Atoll). Snorkellers can spy everything from vividly coloured Napoleon wrasse to sweet lips, parrotfish, turtles, dolphins, reef sharks and manta and eagle rays. Visibility ranges from 20m to just outstanding, but when it gets murky it usually means there's plankton around, which brings in humongous-but-harmless whale sharks.

Surfing

There are no beach breaks, so surfers need to be skilled, but the Maldives has some of the world's best reef breaks. They're spread across three main zones, which peak at different times due to position and monsoonal moods: **Male Atolls** (best March–October), **Central Atolls** (May–August) and **Outer Atolls** (late February–April/late August–October). The southern atolls, more exposed to swells sweeping right up from the Roaring Forties, get bigger waves.

DON'T LEAVE WITHOUT...
Perfecting your stand-up paddling skills at Chaaya Dhonveli and Lohis (Hudhuranfushi), which both offer superclear flatwater lagoons for SUPing around in, while marine wildlife scoots beneath your board. Surf to get among if you feel more confident.

MALTA

One of the Med's best adventure islands, the real Malta remains a mystery to many.

Malta, along with the smaller islands of Gozo and Comino (famed for its Blue Lagoon) that make up the Maltese archipelago, offers an enticing mix of super-clear water and a fine array of reefs, caves and wrecks for wild swimmers, divers and paddlers,

Diving

The archipelago has a wide variety of easily accessed shore dives in locations that vary from natural harbours and sheltered creeks to sea cliffs, suitable for everyone from beginner to expert. Classic dives include the shallow 12m **Ghar Lapsi** on Malta's south coast and **Lantern Point** on Comino's southwest tip, which has an underwater tunnel at 15m, but continues beyond 40m for more experienced divers.

Paddling & Board Sports

Sea kayaking is a great way to explore the picturesque coastline, especially the numerous sea caves. **Windsurfing** is popular, particularly around Qalet Marku on Malta's north coast, and **SUPing** is also taking off, while in winter there are even days when the occasional **surf** spot will work.

Climbing

An abundance of sea cliffs and steep inland valley crags provide some great climbing, usually with spectacular sea views. Most crags are single pitch, although multipitch routes can be found, and at many locations you'll find a selection of bolted routes and some naturally protected lines. Seek out shady north-facing crags such as **Victoria Lines** in summer, and warm, sunny south-facing crags in the wintertime.

DON'T LEAVE WITHOUT...
Exploring Malta's history by mountain bike. Rubbly trails and rough roads criss-cross the island, linking treasures ranging from Neolithic temples to the walled medieval city of Mdina. There's a very lively downhill MTB run from the historic hill village of Wardija.

The 556m-high summit of Le Morne Peninsula is a popular target for peak baggers.

MAURITIUS

One-time home of the luckless dodo, this idyllic Indian Ocean island has a surprisingly rugged adventure scene that's far from extinct.

C ast-away, far from the coast of Africa, well east of Madagascar, Mauritius might be famous for luxe hotels, flash weddings and swim-up bars, but beyond the fancypants hotels it's an exotic natural playground, ridged with massive mountains, lashed with trails and ringed by lovely lagoons.

Watersports

Bel Ombre, in the island's southwest, perfectly catches the prevailing tradewinds that once pushed pirates and explorers around these shores, and this is the epicentre of Mauritius' colourful kite-surfing scene. Mostly protected by reefs, which create lagoons ideal for SUPing and snorkelling, the island has one sizzling surf break at Tamarin Bay, which was made famous by the 1970s film *Forgotten Island of Santosha*.

Hiking & Trail Running

Mauritius is dissected by myriad singletrack trails and it's a dream destination for trail runners and wild walkers. A trekking highlight is the rainforest-cloaked **Black River Gorges National Park**, threaded with verdant trails, splattered with waterfalls and vibrant with wildlife including flying foxes, endemic Mauritius kestrels and pretty pink pigeons, a surviving cousin of the dodo. Also explore the 15km hike from Le Pétrin to Grand Rivière Noire along the Macchabée Trail, or take the 16km path from Plaine Champagne to Bel Ombre.

Climb Le Morne

A towering 556m-high rock edifice, typically topped with clouds and always enveloped in a slightly eerie aura thanks to the dark tale that sticks to its flanks, Le Morne is a Unesco World Heritage site because of its importance to Creole culture. Here, in the 19th century, a group of escaped plantation slaves – having spied an approaching posse of officials – threw themselves from the summit rather than face capture; a tragedy compounded by the fact that the group were actually arriving with news of abolition. The approach crosses private scrubland; access is unimpeded and independent hikers are rarely challenged, but to stay legit, engage a man called Yan from Trekking Ile Maurice, who guides clamberers to the minor summit several times weekly. Ascending to the true summit is more technical and requires rock-climbing equipment and skills, plus more involved logistical planning/ permission. The view, though, is as stunning as the backstory is sobering.

ICONIC EVENT
The Dodo Trail is an annual off-road sky running race that takes competitors across the mountainous spine of Mauritius, with the marquee distance 50km. Part of the African Sky Running Championships, its elevation profile is brutal.

© Mark Read | Lonely Planet

MEXICO

Mexico is a big, diverse country sandwiched between two oceans and ribbed with mountains. For adventure enthusiasts, it offers the whole enchilada.

A vast land with a wild history written in heart-blood and gun smoke, Mexico – the Nahuatl word for 'Aztec homeland' – is the most populous Spanish-speaking country in the world and the sixth largest country in the Americas in terms of total area. With terrain that ranges from desert to rainforest, mountains to ocean, monkey-balls hot to glaciated, it's a diverse nation brimming with potential adventures. The rich cultural history – Mexico has more World Heritage sites than any other country in the Americas – and its tradition of warm hospitality make it a favourite for travellers. With whitewater rapids and placid aquamarine oceans, near-perfect waves and miles of deserted trails, steep limestone blades that touch the sky and volcanoes so tall they sport ice pitches, this is the land of the free-ranging adventurer, which has everything an intrepid traveller needs to stay busy for a very long time.

Climbing
El Potrero Chico, 'the little corral', is a circular enclosure of uplifted limestone fins and spires situated just outside the sleepy pueblo of Hidalgo, Nuevo Leon, about an hour northwest of Monterrey. In the late 1980s, climbers from Texas stumbled into this craggy enclave and set to work, bolting climbs and building relationships with locals. Today, El Potrero Chico is one of the best winter sport climbing venues in the world, with more than 600 routes up to 600m tall. Climbs here range from 5.8 to 5.14 with a majority of moderate, multipitch sport climbs such as the 23-pitch Timewave Zero (IV 5.11a A0). Those looking for more challenge will find it on Sendero Luminoso (V 5.12d), a 600m route with 10 pitches of 5.12, considered one of the best multipitch sport climbs in the world.

Mountaineering
El Pico de Orizaba or Citlaltépetl (Star Mountain in Nahuatl) is the highest mountain in Mexico and the third highest in North America. The peak's height is a subject of debate but most sources put it at around 5610m. It's a beautiful mountain – a rocky, ochre volcano capped with white glaciers looming above the town of Tlachichuca on the border of Veracruz and Puebla. Most climbers start at the Piedra Grande Refugio (4270m) and tackle the Jamapa Glacier, a walk-up with one section of 35-degree ice.

The soaring limestone walls of El Potrero Chico are popular with North American climbers looking to escape winter.

© Rich Wheater | Getty Images

Those looking for a more technical climb will find it on the Serpent's Head, a Grade 3, 10-pitch ice climb on the mountain's west side.

Trail Running

The trail running in the **Barrancas del Cobre (Copper Canyons)** of southwestern Chihuahua was made famous in Christopher McDougall's best-selling book *Born to Run*, a lively account of some of the sport's quirkier characters, such as the late Micah True (AKA Caballo Blanco). But running was endemic to the region long before *Born to Run*. The native people who inhabit the canyons have a centuries-old tradition of running, both as a means to travel long distances over rugged terrain inaccessible by horseback, and as a sport. The Tarahumara, or Rarámuri as they call themselves – a name that means 'those who run' – play a game called *rarajipari*. These inter-village races run by two teams kicking a baseball-sized ball made out of a madrone or oak knot can go on all night and

cover 50km to 60km. For obvious reasons, the Copper Canyon is a magnet for trail runners. This system of six distinct canyons is deeper in places than the Grand Canyon of Arizona, and the myriad trail systems wind through oak and Andean poplar forests to the more tropical figs and palms found lower down.

Surfing

Surfers looking for consistent swell will find it along the **Nayarit coast** of western Mexico where, even in the summer off-season, you can find left and right breaks offering long rides. In winter months the ocean can pump the swell to triple overhead, and surfers bob among surfacing humpback whales while waiting in a rather competitive lineup. Sayulita, a quaint town of about 6000 people located 40km from downtown Puerto Vallarta, is a justifiably famous river-mouth break and home to some of the sport's best practitioners. That said, there's a beginner-friendly spot called Punta

DON'T LEAVE WITHOUT...
Kayaking and snorkelling off Isla Espíritu Santos in Baja. You'll see angelfish, parrotfish and rainbow wrasse, and swim with young sea lions.

© Luis Javier Sandoval | Getty Images

Mita that offers perfect rights for those interested in learning and/or mellow longboarding. The breaks known as San Pancho and Lo de Marco offer swifter left-breaking waves for those who like to rip. Looking for some solitude? Hire a *panga* (boat) to take you out to a distant reef break. In recent years, Sayulita has morphed from a surfer haven to a still-cool, eclectic get-away where surfers rub elbows with upscale tourists and native Cora and Huichol craftsmen. There's an upside to the popularity: cheap board rentals, internet cafes, great food right on the beach and English-speaking doctors.

Snorkelling & Diving

If Mexico was a scorpion's tail, **Isla Holbox** ('Black Hole' in Mayan), would be the tip of the stinger. Located in the Yucatán, in the far southeast, the 41km-long, 1.4km-wide island sits just offshore, separated from the little town of Chiquilá by a shallow lagoon. It's a sleepy place, with only a few cars, golf carts and mopeds, but from June through September the warm waters swarm with whale sharks, the world's biggest fish. It's against the law to dive with these 12m behemoths – Holbox is part of the Yum Balam Biosphere Reserve – but you can

Divers enter the dark waters of Chac Mool cenote on the Yucatán Peninsula.

snorkel, and the experience of swimming with so huge a life form is unforgettable. Whale sharks don't eat people, they eat plankton, so you're not in any danger cruising alongside these slow-swimming gentle giants. Because there's no reef, you won't see many brilliantly coloured fish, but the lagoon is host to sea turtles, manta rays and dolphins.

Another special feature of the Yucatán are its many submerged caverns called cenotes. Many of these can be dived or snorkelled, particularly along the Mayan Riviera, but pick an operator with care.

An uninhabited volcanic island chain situated almost 400km southwest of Cabo San Lucas, the **Revillagigedo Archipelago** is sometimes referred to as the 'Galápagos of Mexico'. This World Heritage site hosts many endemic species, but the best action takes place out in the surrounding ocean where divers swim with big fish: manta rays, sharks, dolphins and, between January and May, humpback whales. The islands are a Mexican Biosphere Reserve, and the only way to visit is to charter a deluxe 'liveaboard' boat.

Kayaking

North Americans flock to Baja California with good reason, but apart from the partying in resorts, the sheltered waters of the **Sea of Cortez** offer superb sea kayaking. Exploring the stunning islands of Loreto Bay National Marine Park, a Unesco World Heritage site, is the best place to start. Here you will find calm waters, abundant wildlife (including whales), crystal-clear water, rugged cliffs to traverse and sandy beaches to stop off on.

Further south, **Jalcomulco,** a quiet town nestled in the rugged Sierra Madre mountains about 30km from Xalapa, has some of Mexico's best white water – the Pescados section of the Rio Antigua. Jalcomulco is also a great jumping off point for dozens of other, more obscure and challenging river trips. Veracruz has more than 40 rivers that cut across the mountainous terrain and offer narrow, steep paddling through medium- to low-volume water, offering world-class whitewater rafting and kayaking for all levels.

UNCLAIMED ADVENTURE
Somewhere north of Mazatlán, in a cavern at the headwaters of the Rio Presidio, Pancho Villa cached $25,000,000 in gold and silver. Find it.

Exploring the bays and inlets of Isla Espíritu Santo, Sea of Cortez, Baja California.

Snorkelling cerulean waters off Palau.

MICRONESIA

Whether above or below the turquoise waters, adventure is never far away in this vast, far flung collection of islands.

Micronesia comprises a collection of more than 600 islands spread across five independent states: Palau, Kiribati, Nauru, the Marshall Islands and the Federated States of Micronesia. Together, they form an idyllic Pacific playground where ancient ruins can be found within the dense jungle and sunken wrecks lie beneath clear, warm waters.

Pohnpei – diving, surfing & jungle trekking

If you only have time to visit one island, this is a sound choice. Below the water you'll find an incredible array of coral gardens; on the surface a barrelling winter swell at **Palikir Pass** ranks among the world's best right-hand surf breaks; while on land, deep verdant jungle covers the mountainous terrain, where the tangled growth has hidden the **Nan Madol** ruins for almost four centuries.

Beran – kite & windsurfing

From November to March, when the trade winds blow across Beran in the Marshall Islands, some of the very finest kitesurfing and windsurfing can be found. Wind speeds reach 15–20 knots on average, but even calm days are full of promise, because the **surfing**, **deep-sea fishing** and **diving** are also world-class.

Palau – diving

For the ultimate diving experience, Palau can't be beaten. Prides of lion fish prowl around the corals that cling to the masts of the ***Chuyo Maru***, a wreck that rests in the northern Rock Islands after it was bombed into Davy Jones' Locker in April 1944. The **Blue Holes** in the southern Rock Islands – also known as Chelbacheb – are another enchanting dive destination. This World Heritage site features up to 300 coral and limestone islets, home to everything from manta rays to dolphins and sharks.

DON'T LEAVE WITHOUT...

Snorkelling Palau's Jellyfish Lake, a landlocked lagoon filled with millions of stingless jellyfish. It's as close as you'll ever get to swimming through a giant lava lamp.

© Leon Werdinger | Alamy, © Reinhard Dirscherl | Getty Images

MONGOLIA

With its sprawling plains, Mongolia is one of the most sparsely populated countries on Earth, and it remains the spiritual home of horse riding.

Parts of Mongolia's landscape are so barren that new arrivals could be forgiven for thinking they've arrived on Mars. Simply taking a cross-country bus is a hardcore adventure, but don't be misled, behind this confronting first impression is a country with a heart of gold – one of the most exhilarating places you could ever explore.

Riding with Eagle Hunters

Every first weekend in October, some of Mongolia's best hunters gather in the far western town of Ölgii to celebrate their practice of hunting with golden eagles. Riders and their birds of prey compete to catch animal pelts that are dragged along the ground, with awards presented for accuracy and speed, as well as to the hunters sporting the best traditional Kazakh dress. As five flights now leave from Ulaanbaatar to Ölgii each week, the festival has become something of a staple in travellers' calendars.

The festival may be a spectator experience, but getting in the saddle yourself is the best way to explore this horse-obsessed country. Tour providers facilitate traditional horse-trekking escapades right across Mongolia – from the interior's Khangai Mountains to the wild northern border regions with Tuva. However, if you're seeking a truly authentic experience, then it is possible to hire a translator in Ölgii and go to the festival (or its smaller companion in Altai) and directly arrange to ride with the eagle hunters. Be warned, luxuries will not abound on such an outing, and it'll be tough riding all the way, but the hardship is well worth it for the reward of seeing these magnificent hunters out on a real ride rather than posing for tourists' cameras.

Far left, bikepackers ford a river during a traverse of the Khangai Mountains. Left, a Kazakh golden eagle hunter from the Altai Mountains.

© Cass Gilbert, © Timothy Allen | Getty Images

Packrafting

The compact nature of packrafts – easily storable in backpacks and bike panniers alike – means that they are one of the most attractive ways of exploring the Mongolian countryside without having to lug a canoe around. From the Kherlen to the Tuul, Orkhon to the Khovd, there's enough rivers in Mongolia for anyone with a decent background in rafting to get excited. It's certainly an experience unlike any other, floating down a river untouched by humankind beneath ultramarine blue skies, breath crystallising in the cold winter's air with the iciest of water flowing beneath your inflatable. You'll see Bactrian camels grazing, birds of prey hovering overhead and even hear the howls of wolves at night. These journeys will stay with you for a long time.

Bikepacking

If horses aren't your thing and you'd prefer to ride a dual-suspension steed across the steppe, swap heels for wheels and set out on a bikepacking tour. Mongolia is a bikepacking paradise: 90% of its road network is unpaved – not that you have to stick to roads, there are no fences, and when roads end you can simply pedal across the grassy, open steppe – while the warmth and hospitality of Mongolians, who'll often insist in welcoming visitors into their *ger* (yurt), is legendary. Most cyclists start out from the capital, Ulaanbaatar, with a popular route being a traverse of the nearby Khangai Mountains.

Paragliding

Soaring through the sky, with eagles as your companions, paragliding in Mongolia is simply surreal. Depending on where you spread your wings, watch as pine forests, the verdant grassy steppe or the soaring sand dunes of the Gobi Desert race past beneath your feet. The best time to fly is from August to September, but local information on conditions is essential – try contacting the Paragliding Club Mongolia on Facebook.

DON'T LEAVE WITHOUT...
Galloping across the wild and wide open steppe on a genuine Mongolian horse.

Steep climbing in the Khangai Mountains.

© Cass Gilbert

MONTENEGRO

Plunging canyons, virgin forests, a curvy coastline and jagged mountains sit side-by-side in this beautiful, compact country where bears and wolves still roam.

For a comparatively small nation – about two-thirds the size of Wales – Montenegro packs a lot in. Dashing peaks, plunging gorges, twisting canyons, virgin forests, glassy glacial lakes, a craggy coast, beautiful beaches, historic towns, welcoming villages and ruined fortresses, and all in a Mediterranean climate. You can go from the sun-blessed coast to the lakes, canyons and accessible peaks of the northern mountains, or perhaps the untamed forest of Biogradska Gora further south, in less than four hours. (Although there are mountains near the coast, too.) Think of Montenegro as a mini European New Zealand, with bears and wolves, where women still hitchhike and doughnuts are a popular breakfast option.

Hiking

Montenegro is named after the Black Mountain in rocky **Lovćen National Park**, near the Adriatic, a lofty and rocky park that bequeaths hikers huge views and houses an impressive mausoleum of national hero Njegoš. The coast offers gentle, wildflower splattered walking trails between beaches such as those on lazy **Luštica Peninsula**, while in World Heritage-listed **Bay of Kotor**, the historic town sits at the end of an emerald-coloured fjord like a fairytale kingdom.

However, World Heritage-listed **Durmitor National Park**, in the country's rugged northeast, is the biggest draw for dawdlers. The atmospheric 39,000-hectare park boasts 18 brooding, mirror-like glacial lakes, including its poster girl, the Black Lake, protected by several imposing snow-capped peaks. A colour-coded network of well-maintained trails cover the park, which has bears and wolves (though they're rarely seen), joyous waterfalls, tinkling streams and daisy-dotted alpine meadows. Meanwhile, armchair alpinists can get up close to snowy peaks that would normally require mountaineering experience and equipment. (Some mountain huts are available for overnight stays.)

The 1600-hectare **Biogradska Gora National Park**, further south, is one of Europe's three remaining primeval forests. A 17km loop takes in

ICONIC RACE
Negotiate a triathlon course through a Unesco World Heritage site during Montenegro's OceanLava Triathlon: swim around the Bay of Kotor, cycle the coastline beneath the mountains and run through historical Dobrota.

Rafters on the Tara River, found at the bottom of the 1200m-deep Tara Canyon.

a couple of sizeable peaks and a large glacial lake.

Away from the national parks, **Orjen**, **Bjelasica** and **Prokletije** mountains have well-maintained trail networks. The more experienced trekker might consider the 138km Coastal Marathon Traversal, from Herceg Novi to Lake Skadar on the border with Albania, via three mountain ranges.

Rafting

Rafting the **Tara River**, in Durmitor National Park, has become Montenegro's most popular adventure activity. At 1300m deep, Tara Canyon is only 200m shallower than America's Grand version. There are rapids, but trips are more about experiencing the splendour of the dramatic cleft in the landscape, than about the vessel doing somersaults. May is potentially the spiciest time, though, when the last of the snow melt gets frisky. The two-day, 82km trip is the classic, with one-day options also available.

Kayaking

There can't be many better settings for a kayaking trip than the dramatic fjord of the **Bay of Kotor**, with craggy peaks towering over the red roofs of handsome Kotor. The largest lake in southern Europe, **Lake Skadar**, shared with Albania, is the other main option for commercial kayaking trips. More experienced rapid riders might be tempted by the **Morača** (includes Grade IV and V) and the less boisterous **Lim River** (though it still has some Grade V). Parts of the **Tara River** can be kayaked too.

Diving

In Montenegro's cerulean blue waters lie thousands of years' worth of shipwrecks, plus caves, shelves and sea turtles, with visibility usually between 10m and 25m (mid-May to September is best). Don a wetsuit at **Herceg Novi**, **Dobrota**, **Pržno**, **Ulcinj** and best of all, **Budva**.

Paragliding

With its many tall bits of pointy rock-cum-inviting launch pads, Montenegro is an ideal destination for paragliding. The most popular spot is **Brajići**, 760m above Bečići, which has expansive views across the water to Sveti Stefan and St Nicholas Island. The less experienced can go to **Lapčići** for tandem paraglides.

Cycling

All those mountain passes mean Middle Aged Men In Lyrca (MAMIL) will find plenty of steep climbs to grind their way up. A network of marked routes is being established, including the mammoth 14-day 1276km **Tour de Montenegro**, circling the country with 30km of climb (ouch). The shortest route is five days and 262km. If you've only got one day free, enjoy **Lovćen National Park** on a loop track from Cetinje. If you prefer off-road, Lovćen is also criss-crossed with well-marked **mountain-bike** trails.

Skiing & Snowboarding

With all these mountains there's plenty of cold play to be had on the slopes. The ski season lasts from December to March, with **Kolašin** being the most popular region. **Durmitor National Park**'s up-and-coming scene has three slopes catering for all abilities, all close to Žabljak. Cross-country skiing is best in **Durmitor** and **Lovćen**.

© malivoja | Getty Images

MOROCCO

Long an exotic destination for artists, exiles and explorers, modern Morocco has plenty to offer those seeking outdoor action.

Westerners have always had a dreamy fascination with Morocco, a country sitting at the confluence between geographies and cultures. They have come equally to escape as to seek adventure. From exotic cities bursting with history and labyrinthine souks marked by coloured silks, fragrant spices and stinking leather hides, to sparse deserts, lonely mountains and crashing surf – there is action of all kinds to be had. In-between adventures, get scrubbed clean in the hammam, drink oceans of mint tea and bear witness to a glorious country.

Trek the High Atlas

The **Atlas Mountains** stretch across the Maghreb, 2500km from Tunisia through Algeria into Morocco, where they rise proudly before the Atlantic Coast to the highest point in North Africa – **Jebel Toubkal** (4167m). The range marks a massive climatic bulkhead between the ocean and the arid expanses of the Sahara. The traditional lands of the Berber, the mountains are rent by fertile valleys and dotted with secluded villages making them perfect for trekking. After a hot day of walking mountain passes, perching on a rocky outcrop high above a small settlement as the sun sinks and the call to prayer echoes up the valley is an experience you won't forget.

Ride the Trade Winds

The same trade winds that fuelled global commerce for centuries by propelling ships across the seas now bring travellers to Morocco. The coast around the

Above, the mudbrick village of Hdida in the High Atlas is a popular stop for trekkers. Overleaf, the old and the new; a surfer at Essaouira.

© Lottie Davies | Lonely Planet

Essaouira gets lashed by consistent Atlantic winds, making it a magnet for windsurfers and kitesurfers. Sandy beaches ensure easy take-offs and on-water conditions range from long, gentle waves with light breezes for beginners, to blustery gales whipping over 2m waves for the more experienced. Essaouira's coastal side and medina are still partially defended by ancient ramparts that once protected this important trading city. Inside the defences, the world feels far removed and surfers can scoff sumptuous barbecued seafood cooked in the open-air market, watching Moroccan life unfold.

Camel Trekking

A camel ride is a joy that captures all your senses; the taut feel of the beast's skin, the heady mix of pungent smells, the swishing of sand broken by a grumpily

DON'T LEAVE WITHOUT...

Climbing in Todra Gorge. For 40 years climbers have been establishing routes in this 300m high limestone cleft. Comprising a sleepy village, pretty stream and grades from very soft to very hard, there is something here for everyone.

bellowed roar, and the hypnotic rocking as your mount shuffles across the barren earth. One of the best camel treks is to **Erg Chigaga**, a long stretch of towering dunes, some as high as 60m. There's plenty of time to settle into the camel's rhythm as you traverse the sandy seas for five days from the lonesome oasis of M'Hamid El Ghizlane to the dunes.

Mountain Biking

If riding big obdurate beasts is not your thing, swap four legs for two wheels and go mountain biking. The High Atlas provide a spectacular, culturally rich backdrop to challenging riding, with everything from fast and flowing trails to steep and technical singletrack. You can opt for a self-supported trip, or you can take up the services of one of the many operators offering fully supported tours.

MOZAMBIQUE

Head into untrodden hills, kitesurf the sublime shores or dive beneath azure waters for a constant parade of aquatic life, large and small.

With 2470km of tropical coastline, it's not surprising that Mozambique's waters are full of underwater treasures of the living variety. The beaches, some of the world's most spectacular, aren't just for lounging on either, they are also great venues for kitesurfing and surfing. Inland there are several mountain ranges and massifs for hiking – none better than the Chimanimani.

Diving

If you're familiar with the staggering beauty of Mozambique's beaches, you'll understand how truly epic the country's aquatic life must be to lure anyone away from the sand and into the clear depths of the Indian Ocean. Dip beneath the surface off **Ponta d'Ouro** and you'll likely encounter whale sharks, manta rays and turtles (loggerhead and leatherback). Step directly off the beach in **Tofo**

and your dive will quickly put you in the range of giant mantas, more whale sharks and smaller, fascinating creatures such as frogfish and seahorses. Meanwhile, in the **Bazaruto Archipelago**, dolphins, some 2000 types of fish and elusive dugong add to the kaleidoscope of creatures. The reefs of **Quirimbas Archipelago** add yet more pristine sites for divers to explore. Between the months of June and December, southern right whales enter the picture, with humpbacks also seen between July and October.

Hiking

Want a raw mountain experience, the type in which you need to carry everything in and out with you? Well, the rugged **Chimanimani** mountains straddling the Zimbabwe border fit the bill perfectly. Climb up through green and wooded valleys to rounded, rocky summits, the highest of which is Mt Binga (2436m).

DON'T LEAVE WITHOUT...
Kitesurfing off Vilankulu – its shallow, gently sloping seafloor and favourable winds make it an ideal location between late August and December.

Diving off Barra Beach, near Tofo in Inhambane.

© kasto80; Tim Rock | Getty Images

MYANMAR (BURMA)

A vast, strange world just beginning to shirk the oppressive shirt-tugging of the ruling military junta, Myanmar is a cultural marvel and an adventure darling.

Flit between thousands of centuries-old pagodas as you play hide-and-seek with tangerine-robed novice monks; be humbled by some of the most remote mountains the Himalayas have to offer; teeter over the edge of spectacular cliffs with precariously perched golden stones; be among the first to dive reef systems so remote and so pristine that even octopus are surprised to swim upon them. The realities of a new democratic age are only now taking shape in this most faraway and foreign land, but the whole of the country seems eager to welcome in the world and showcase one of Asia's most unique and spellbinding destinations.

Trekking

Hkakabo Razi is a towering gut-check to Myanmar's reputation as a sun-bleached Southeast Asian getaway destination. Reaching a staggering 5881m, this may be Southeast Asia's highest peak (nearby Gamlang Razi also lays claim to this particular distinction), while the whole of **Hkakabo Razi National Park** dishes out epic alpine experiences for adventurous amblers who aren't afraid to get a bit of elevation under their walking boots. Few people will have the constitution or the fortitude required to actually summit Hkakabo Razi – the first ascent was only achieved in 1996 by legendary mountaineers Nyama Gyaltsen (from Myanmar) and Takashi Ozaki (from Japan) – but don't let the mountain's indomitable Himalayan reputation dissuade you from a visit; the temperate and subtropical regions of the park sport remarkable wildlife viewing opportunities, river systems that have recently been opened to kayaking and rafting outfitters, and robust trekking opportunities from Putao, the village basecamp. Offering an insight into Myanmar's cultural diversity (the country has 135 distinct ethnic groups), Putao is home to several indigenous peoples, including the Taron, a pygmy tribe who number fewer than a dozen individuals.

A cyclist takes in one of Bagan's many temples.

© worklater1 | Getty Images

Biking

Biking **Bagan** is quite simply one of those quintessential experiences that you will keep locked in a trunk in your memory's attic forever. Imagine pedalling dusty dirt roads on a fixed-gear jalopy as the sun sets on the horizon, 10,000 ancient spires scraping the belly of the sky for as far as the eye can see, colourful hot-air balloons sharing rarefied air with pink and purple clouds overhead. Bagan by bicycle is a charming experience if there ever was one. Dusty New Bagan (not to be confused with crusty Old Bagan) is an excellent place to procure a mechanical steed on which to explore the **Bagan Archaeological Zone** and its trove of wonders spread across the plain, including the remains of more than 2200 Buddhist temples, pagodas and monasteries, mostly built between the 11th and 13th centuries. Stock up on supplies and sundries at New Bagan's morning market before you set out pedalling, and explore until you're red in the face (don't forget your sunscreen and hat).

DON'T LEAVE WITHOUT...

Learning how to paddle a skiff with one leg across Inle Lake. Fishermen here are famous for paddling their watercraft with one leg while they toss their large nets into the water with both hands. It's even more difficult than it looks.

Diving

One of the world's most remote undersea environments was off-limits to foreigners until 1997, when **Lampi Marine National Park** was finally opened to visitors (with the help of Thai officials and entrepreneurial dive shops). Located off the west coast of the Kra Isthmus (which Myanmar shares with Thailand) in the Mergui Archipelago, Lampi's idyllic oceanic allure is perhaps best represented by Shark Cave, a breeding ground for grey reef, bull and nurse sharks. Hallmark encounters in the marine park include sea turtles, the rare harlequin ghost pipefish, manta rays and even whale sharks (these behemoth softies migrate through these waters from January through to April). South Twin Island and Rocky Peaks are well known among macro-fanatics (spy nudibranchs and sea slugs), while Black Rock and Burma Banks sport beautiful reef systems and robust wildlife. Trips are best arranged via dive operators on the Thai side of the border.

NAMIBIA

Ocean and desert collide in this southern African nation, to provide adventure playgrounds of water, sand and rock, with each as vast (and wild) as the other.

Namibia's landscapes are epic, both in terms of sheer scale and natural beauty. Imagine singing sands and dunes that climb to over 300m in height and look more like works of art by Gaudí than anything produced by blowing winds. Now picture yourself hiking across their undulating crests and looking across an ocean of mammoth waves frozen in sand. If you feel like boarding down one of those waves... well, that's an option too. But the Namib Desert, which gave the country its name, is more than just a huge sandbox – it's also tortured mountains and rocky canyons. These captivating environments are ripe for explorations on foot or mountain bike. And soaring inselbergs such as Spitzkoppe are great places to cling to if you have a penchant for rock climbing. Flanking the entire country's west, running almost 1600km from South Africa to Angola, is a wild coastline with a history for sinking ships (how else did you think the Skeleton Coast got its name?). But with a surfboard in hand, you'll find nothing but joy along these remote shores. Namibia: a playground for sure.

Dune Boarding

The **Namib** is the world's oldest desert, but there's a new way to experience its dunes: on a board. Not far from Namibia's coastal town of Swakopmund, one of Southern Africa's top adventure-activity capitals, there are mountains of sand that provide perfect slopes to carve down. When you first set eyes on the dunes towering hundreds of feet into the blue African sky, you'll begin to buzz with anticipation, though it's wise to conserve a little energy – your journey of joy starts with some hard work: a hike up to your launching point. With board, gloves and goggles in hand, you're eventually staring down over some serious off-piste action. Now strap in, lean further back than you're used to (if you're familiar with snowboarding) and let loose! Once you've had your fill, try the lie-down 'schuss' option, which will see you hit speeds of 80km/h. Alter Action runs daily dune boarding trips from Swakopmund.

Hiking

Between hard rocks or atop a soft place, hiking in Namibia offers adventurous extremes. These can vary from short explorations of large dune

Tearing up the surreal dunes of Swakopmund.

© Klaus Brandstaetter/Getty Images

fields – most spectacularly around **Sossusvlei** in **Namib-Naukluft National Park** – to more serious endeavours such as the five-day trek through the rocky depths of one of the world's largest canyons. Due to soaring summer temperatures and the remoteness of the **Fish River Canyon** floor, hikes in the latter are restricted to May through mid-September. The enchanting and incredibly challenging 85km route from Hobas to Ai-Ais follows the sandy riverbed past huge boulder fields, startlingly dramatic scenery and a series of ephemeral pools (perfect for dips to beat the heat).

Other notable hikes include four- and eight-day loops through the **Naukluft Mountains**, which offer a more subtle charm than the Fish River Canyon. Speaking of 'note-able', it's possible to make the ground beneath you sing (well, hum) – usually in notes E, F or G – while hiking the crests of dunes south of **Swakopmund** or north along the Skeleton Coast. The unique mineral composition of Namib's sand in these areas causes it to loudly resonate when disturbed.

Surfing

With nothing standing between Brazil and the coast of Namibia, there is no shortage of large south Atlantic swell to rip it up on. And with sharks, seals, sand storms and incredibly remote breaks, there is certainly no shortage of adventure either. A great place to get your feet wet is in the coastal town of **Swakopmund**. The waves of choice are at **Nordstrand** near Vineta Point – it's an exposed reef break that is particularly good at high tide when the swell angle is from the west-southwest. **Tiger Reef**, at the mouth of the Swakop River, is another solid option. There's an exceptionally long left-hand point break at **Bocock's Bay**, a remote spot some 160km north of Swakopmund. The surf here, formed

DON'T LEAVE WITHOUT...
Skydiving over the stunning meeting point of the baking Namib Desert and cold swells of the southern Atlantic. Take the leap at Swakopmund.

over a soft sandbank, is incredibly consistent and you'll likely have it all to yourself. **Cape Cross**, 30km south from here, has some sweet waves too, though you'll be sharing the water with tens of thousands of seals. April and May tend to be the best months for surfing in Namibia, though any time between March and October is rewarding. Shark numbers boom in the off season when most mating occurs.

Mountain Biking

Imagine Moab. Amazing, right? Now imagine it sitting empty. Welcome to Namibia! Not only is there a profusion of compelling trails and dramatic scenery – rollercoaster singletrack through the moonscapes outside of **Swakopmund**, tricky jeep routes around the dry riverbed of the **Huab** and memorable descents down the **Auas Mountains** – but you can also spy incredible African wildlife from

your saddle, such as rare desert-adapted elephant and black rhino. With almost no vehicular traffic on the country's graded gravel roads, multiday mountain bike expeditions are a fantastic option.

Climbing

Rising like a mirage above the desert plains of southern Damaraland, the behemoth 1728m-high inselberg that is **Spitzkoppe** has long inspired climbers and earned it the moniker of 'Matterhorn of Africa'. Although first summited in 1946, its granite flanks continue to call out to hardcore climbers bent on tackling the nation's most challenging peak, such as American climber and soloist Alex Honnold. Some of the lower rounded domes offer thrilling scrambling for those who aren't as keen to tackle the vertical pitches. At night, camp below it all for a celestial show like no other.

The granite dome of Spitzkoppe rises out of the desert plains in southern Damaraland.

NEPAL

In Nepal, everything is extreme, from the altitude to travellers' emotions.

©Andreas Strauss / LOOK-foto; Bartosz Hadyniak | Getty Images

Westerners travel to Nepal to chase dreams: to climb the world's highest mountain, to trek a rugged Himalayan circuit, or to see one of the last of the endangered white rhinos. What they discover when they get there, beyond staggering geography, exotic fauna and boundless adventures, are people who exude an unwavering grace and hospitality.

Nepalis, many of whom are Buddhist, truly live by the oft-said phrase: 'The guest is God.' They go out of their way to offer whatever they have, from a cup of yak-butter tea and a spot near the fire in their home, to a willingness to risk their lives to help a foreigner in distress, even on the top of Everest.

In 2015, a 7.8-magnitude earthquake devastated Nepal, killing 9000 people and causing $5bn worth of damage. The epicentre, near Kathmandu, destroyed centuries-old temples and left its mark on almost everything. In outlying regions, mudslides swept away entire villages. Foreign aid was slow, but Nepalis helped each other: Dwarika's, one of the most historic hotels in Kathmandu, built 'Camp Hope', a tent city that housed 331 displaced people. Fortunately, the earthquake affected only 15% of the country's most iconic trekking routes.

In Nepal, be prepared for an adventure that will push you out of your comfort zone – both physically and mentally – and may change your life.

Trekking

It's impossible to fathom the scale of Mt Everest until you arrive at the 5335m-high Base Camp and realise you can't even see the summit of the world's tallest peak. Its 8848m triangular mass is hidden behind Nuptse (7861m) and Lhotse (8516m). But the

A trekker stops to gaze up at the flanks of Mt Everest.

trek to Base Camp is still worth every step. Reserve two weeks to make the 124km round-trip from Lukla. The distance isn't great, but the elevation gain is almost 2500m and it's wise to take it slow in order to acclimatise. Arrival in Lukla – the world's most dangerous airstrip, a 527m strip of asphalt that drops off a mountainside – is dramatic. From here, trekkers enter Sagarmatha National Park, sharing the centuries-old path to Namche Bazaar with porters carrying anything from cement to cans of beer, stabilising the load with tumplines around their foreheads. The trek follows the rushing Dudh Kosi River, crosses hanging bridges and passes through small villages. Above Namche Bazaar, the

air gets thin, white peaks jut into a bright blue sky, and the path continues to wind slowly up through seven villages, including Pangboche, home to an ancient Buddhist monastery. It's tempting to push through on the final day, but save time and energy to climb Kala Patthar (5643m) from the last village of Gorakshep. The view to the summit of Everest and Ama Dablam (6812m) will literally take your breath away.

While Everest Base Camp is a very popular option, myriad other treks can be explored. Help breathe life and tourist dollars back into Langtang – a region 64km north of Kathmandu that was devastated by the 2015 earthquake – by trekking the newly

INTERVIEW: MAYA SHERPA

Nepal's legendary female mountain guide has climbed Pumori, Cho Oyu, Ama Dablam, K2 and Mt Everest (twice). She's also a mother.

What are Nepal's most beautiful regions?
'All are beautiful in their own way. If you like big mountains, the Khumbu is the most spectacular, especially around Gokyo Lake. If you like to see more culture and fewer tourists, the Kanchenjunga, Makalu and Dolpa areas are very nice. The far west of Nepal is a largely undiscovered treasure.'

Which is your favourite peak?
'My first climb was Ama Dablam and this was hard. I had no good equipment and no experience. My shoes were too big because I borrowed them from a tourist, my crampons didn't fit, and my clothing was too cold. But I just kept going. I am most proud of my summit on K2 because, for climbers, this mountain is an icon.'
Any tips for first-time travellers to Nepal?
'Have a relaxed attitude! Allow time to mingle with locals.'

© JenniferJuliet / Shutterstock

© Saro17 / Getty Images

opened Tamang Heritage Trail. This round-trip nine- to 15-day circuit passes through the heart of the Tamang community of Tibetan Buddhist horse traders, considered to be the oldest tribe in Nepal. In addition to interacting with people from an ancient culture, trekkers climb to 4100m, pass through rhododendron forests, and have stunning views of Manaslu Massif, Langtang, Ganesh and Jugal Himal. Camp or stay in village tea houses along the way.

Paragliding and Parahawking

The laid-back resort city of **Pokhara**, 204km west of Kathmandu, is Asia's Chamonix – an action-sports hub where locals launch like lemmings from precipitous ridgetops. The mountainous topography, consistent thermals and access to a relatively soft emergency-landing pad in Phewa Lake, make this the perfect place to have a go at paragliding. Try flying with experienced experts like Avia Club Nepal, which has a roster of experienced

international pilots. All you have to do is take in the astounding views of the Annapurna Range, including Machapuchare (6993m), which juts from the cloud like a shark's fin and is off-limits to climbers because it's believed to be home to Shiva, the Hindu deity.

For a more intense thrill, consider **parahawking** (www.parahawking.com), the hybrid sensation that combines falconry with paragliding, where the birds find the best thermals in return for rewards. The sport is a win-win for all involved: humans get to feed a massive raptor mid-flight and the rehabilitated, non-releasable Egyptian vultures enjoy an opportunity to spread their wings.

Mountain Biking

A relatively new sport to Nepal, mountain biking has experienced some local resistance because many footpaths remain the only means for villagers to get around. However, because of new road

*Left, parahawking in Pokhara. **Above**, mountain biking in the Muktinath Valley. **Overleaf**, the glacier-fed Marshyangdi River is popular for rafting.*

construction around the iconic 241km Annapurna Circuit, Nepal's second-most famous trekking area has become more accessible to mountain bikers. A particularly popular spot is the **Kali Gandaki Valley** in Lower Mustang, which was once a famous trade route between India and Tibet and separates Dhaulagiri (8167m) from Annapurna I (8091m). Here you find everything from technical singletrack on ancient footpaths to sandy roads and tough, steep climbs. The views to the surrounding Himalayan peaks are worth the gruelling grind.

Newly arrived riders can acclimatise in the **Kathmandu Valley**. Shivapuri Nagarjun National Park is a beautiful 159 sq km oasis north of Kathmandu, where ancient paths connect Buddhist monasteries to mountain villages. From the hilltop

ULTIMATE CHALLENGE
Sure, climbing Everest is tough, but during Yak Ru, a 240km, five-stage mountain-bike race, there are no Sherpas to share the load. The race tops out at 5416m, and riders have to deal with blizzards, dust storms, heat and rocky descents.

nunnery of Nagi Gompa, mountain bikers can ride to the top of 2732m Shivapuri Peak or descend a ridgeline into the village of Gokarna.

Paddling

Nepal contains eight of the world's 10 highest peaks, so naturally it has long rivers ripe for rafting and kayaking, such as the iconic **Sun Kosi**, which originates in Tibet before flowing through Nepal into the Ganges River. On this eight-day journey expect Grade V thrills through gorges, and pristine white-sand beaches for camping. To raft the **Tamur River**, paddlers must first trek three days and over a 3000m pass, all with a backdrop of Mt Everest. For a shorter trip, try the **Bhote Kosi River** four hours north of Kathmandu, which offers 25km of Grade IV+ river.

THE NETHERLANDS

It might be flat, but this eccentric bike-obsessed country offers several surprising challenges, including underground cycling and mud trekking.

Dutch ingenuity and lateral thinking have produced numerous unusual activities, and, indeed, inactivities: the *paalzitten* (pole-sitting) record is over 52 hours. Infinitely more exciting, the pursuit of *Fierljeppen* involves pole vaulting over wide, watery ditches.

Wild Ice Skating

Peaceful ice-skating on canals, rivers and lakes is an obsession here. Sadly, it's a rare year that's cold enough for even short skate tours, while the apogee of the Dutch ice-blading tradition, the famed 200km **Elfstedentocht** race-tour through Friesland's 11 historic cities, has run just 15 times in over a century. When there is ice thick enough to bear around 16,000 participants, though, this one-day event can attract well over a million spectators – even though it begins within 48 hours of being announced. The record time is 6 hours and 47 minutes.

Elfstedentocht by other means

However, you can also complete the Eleven Cities tour by kayak or canoe, on foot or inline-skates, or by bike. Self-guided, independent trips are easy,

while a popular organised cycling tour has attracted 15,000 participants every Whit Monday since 1947. With a midnight cut-off time, the non-competitive 235km event attracts everyone from roadies to riders on commuter clunkers, recumbents, tandems and penny-farthings.

Hiking

To create a challenge in their otherwise flat and urban surrounds, the Dutch have invented **wadlopen** – literally, 'mud walking'. You can join groups to race the North Atlantic tides that ebb and flow, exposing and covering the mud flats of the Wadden Sea that separates the mainland from the five inhabited Wadden Islands. For the most extreme test of floundering, trotting and wading, take on the 18km of thigh-deep mud, seal-scattered sand bars and swirling water separating Terschelling from the mainland.

Nijmegen's **International Four Days Marches**, the world's largest multiday military marching event, celebrated its centenary in 2016. Nowadays civilians far outnumber military teams in this endurance walking challenge, which can involve yomping up to 50km a day for four days.

DON'T LEAVE WITHOUT...
Going cave biking. In the Sibbergroeve marl mine in Valkenburg, you can cycle a 10km circuit of underground tunnels.

A windmill provides the perfect Dutch backdrop for ice skaters on a frozen canal.

© Feng Wei Photography; Nisangha | Getty Images

NEW ZEALAND

The land of the long white cloud is also a country of endless trails, boundless beaches, charging rivers and epic horizons, punctuated by imposing peaks.

Despite tourism bodies and marketing people doing their utmost to recast this country as Middle Earth over the past decade or more, New Zealand isn't in the middle of anything. Teetering on the outer edge of the Pacific Ring of Fire, isolated at the southern extremity of the planet, whipped by weather that is utterly unforecastable, buckled by the soaring Southern Alps and sitting pretty and unpredictable atop multiple fault lines in the Earth's crust – this two-island nation is still physically fidgeting and shape shifting beneath the restless feet of its populace.

And what people this elementally powered place has produced. There are only four and a half million of them, but you'll always find a Kiwi at the very forefront of each new adventure pursuit and thrill-chasing trend, leading the way, surfing the wave and rolling the dice as they jump, run, ride, climb, spin, slide, plummet and paddle down, across or up whatever obstacle or opportunity they've decided to take on. The British did their utmost to claim him, but the first person to stand on the roof of Planet Earth, alongside Nepali Sherpa mountaineer Tenzing Norgay, was a dyed-in-the-wool New Zealander. And Edmund Hillary had learned his trade well in his own backyard, on the frozen and unforgiving slopes of Mt Cook.

Visitors to New Zealand are often overwhelmed by the extreme arena they're suddenly flung among. You can barely go round a corner here without coming across something – a glacier, fiord, volcano, waterfall, mountain, gorge, surf-stroked bay, vividly coloured lake, thermally heated beach or bubbling puddle of mud – that will literally take your breath away. It's borderline ridiculous. And because of the country's position on the globe – a long-haul flight from absolutely everywhere else – you often get to explore the more eccentric corners of this extraordinary environment in relative solitude.

New Zealand is the place where the wildest dreams of everyday adventurers become a reality. Whether you consider yourself a tramping-camping-trailblazer, someone who gets their kicks in the saddle or with a paddle, a climber, skier or aspiring expedition zorb pilot – this is the country to come to in order to push your ability and ambition to the outer limit.

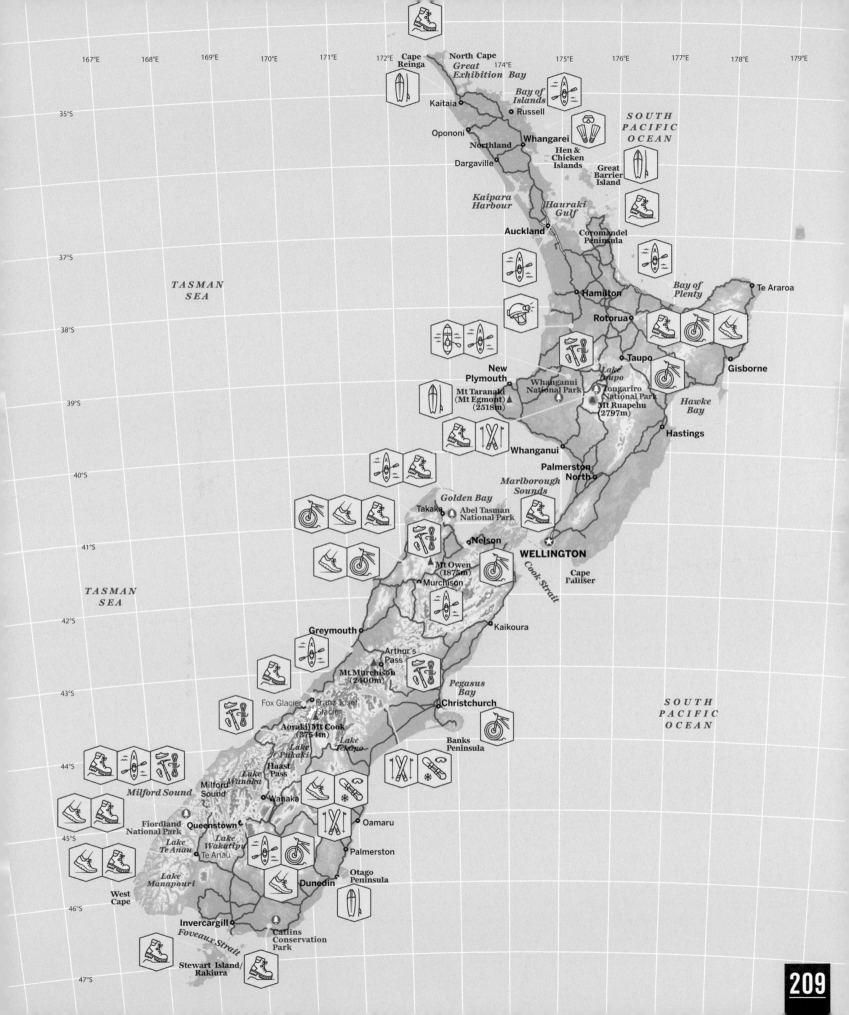

167°E 168°E 169°E 170°E 171°E 172°E 173°E 174°E 175°E 176°E 177°E 178°E 179°E

35°S

TASMAN SEA

36°S

37°S

38°S

39°S

40°S

41°S

TASMAN SEA

42°S

43°S

44°S

45°S

46°S

47°S

SOUTH PACIFIC OCEAN

Cape Reinga
North Cape
Great Exhibition Bay
Kaitaia
Bay of Islands
Russell
Opononi
Whangarei
Northland
Hen & Chicken Islands
Dargaville
Great Barrier Island
Kaipara Harbour
Hauraki Gulf
Auckland
Coromandel Peninsula
Hamilton
Bay of Plenty
Te Araroa
Rotorua
New Plymouth
Mt Taranaki (Mt Egmont) (2518m)
Whanganui National Park
Lake Taupo
Taupo
Gisborne
Tongariro National Park
Mt Ruapehu (2797m)
Hawke Bay
Hastings
Whanganui
Palmerston North
Marlborough Sounds
Golden Bay
Takaka
Abel Tasman National Park
Nelson
WELLINGTON
Cape Palliser
Cook Strait
Mt Owen (1875m)
Murchison
Greymouth
Arthur's Pass
Mt Murchison (2400m)
Kaikoura
Pegasus Bay
Christchurch
Banks Peninsula
Fox Glacier
Franz Josef Glacier
Aoraki/Mt Cook (3754m)
Lake Pukaki
Lake Tekapo
Haast Pass
Lake Wanaka
Milford Sound
Fiordland National Park
Wanaka
Oamaru
Queenstown
Lake Wakatipu
Lake Te Anau
Te Anau
Palmerston
Otago Peninsula
Dunedin
West Cape
Lake Manapouri
Invercargill
Foveaux Strait
Catlins Conservation Park
Stewart Island/Rakiura

SOUTH PACIFIC OCEAN

209

Mountain Biking

New Zealand isn't just a hotbed of mountain biking trails, it's an actual hotbed in places – the whole central North Island sits on an active field of volcanoes and vents. Further south, the landscape is dominated by the jagged teeth of the Southern Alps as they stretch from Fiordland to Wairarapa, and ribboned right across this wild landscape are some of the world's finest MTB trails.

Rotorua

Rotorua is as famous for its network of singletrack as it is for mud pools, steam vents and Maori culture. Also known as the Redwoods, **Whakarewarewa Forest** is a labyrinth of trails so buff you could almost ride a skateboard down them. With a mixture of native, redwoods and pine forest, there are almost 160km of mostly hand-built trails in this forest with something to suit everyone from the hardcore to beginners. Best of all, a dedicated shuttle services one of the forest's high points, so if pedalling is

not your thing you can still rack up plenty of berm time. Find Eagle vs Shark and you will have the ultimate flow-defining initiation to the forest. When you're sick of perfection, challenge yourself on the raw beauty of Kataore, which drops down to the stunning Blue Lake.

Directly across town you'll discover the flowing lines draped down Mt Ngongotaha at the **Skyline Rotorua MTB Gravity Park**. Start with Hipster, ride it fast, then step it up to session the jump lines all the way to Mr Black... but don't let the Surgeon's Table end your adventure early. Refuel at Zippy Central Café – the Southern Hemisphere's most bike-friendly cafe and a great place to plan an adventure ride like the 35km **Moerangi Trail**. This is a true backcountry sojourn and the ancient trees of the Whirinaki Te Pua-a-Tāne Conservation Park are as close to the Jurassic-era as you can get. Or head east and pick the eyes out of the **Motu Trails** with a descent of the Pakihi Track – 21km of trail ecstasy. No Rotorua MTB mission is complete

ICONIC EVENT
Crankworx is the planet's biggest mountain bike and ride-culture festival and the Rotorua iteration each March is a resounding success with a distinct Kiwi accent. Mountain bikers from around the world converge on 'Rotovegas' to ride and watch the downhill and slopestyle action, framed by local trails.

without a journey to the summit of **Rainbow Mountain**, 20 minutes' drive south of town. It's a flowing climb with enough raw volcanic energy bursting out of the ground to take your mind off the pinches. From the summit, Te Ranga will deliver you all the way to Kerosene Creek. This hot creek flows over a small waterfall and into a hot pool. Jump in and soak in the thermal properties of this geothermal treasure. You'll have earned it.

Taupo

Just over an hour's drive from Rotorua, Taupo is renowned for its beautiful lakeside trail, its geothermally active MTB park, and numerous backcountry and day rides all accessible from the town's bustling cafes, bike shops and restaurants. The **Great Lake Trail**, part of the New Zealand Cycle Trails, is a masterpiece. Ride the Waihaha to Waihora section first and arrange to have a water transfer to Kawakawa Bay, where you can follow the 71km trail all the way to the finish at Whakaipo Bay Reserve. For a perfect half-day of exploring, **Craters Mountain Bike Park** offers around 50km of singletrack set beneath pine trees, but if you'd prefer to notch up another adventure ride, then pack some food and hit the 38km out-and-back **Te Iringa** trail, overnighting at Oamaru Hut. **Tree Trunk Gorge** and **The 42 Traverse** are also worthy day trips for the seasoned masochist. Or limber up for the 85km **Timber Trail** that starts at Pureora Forest Village and weaves its way through the giant podocarp trees and across swing bridges.

Tasman

Nelson is encircled by developed networks and epic rides – with **Codgers Mountain Bike Park** based right in town. This 18km network is a great starting point to get acquainted with the region's terrain. It is also the staging arena for Nelson's iconic **Dun Mountain Trail**. Allow a day to ride this 43km epic that winds up along the route of New Zealand's first rail line through forest before popping out on Coppermine Saddle, an exposed alpine ridge near the summit of Dun Mountain (878m). This is where the fun begins: a 10km singletrack descent that will have your arms pumped and your eyes watering all the way to Maitai Dam. Spin out the final 11km along the Maitai River into Nelson, or veer off at Milton Street and ride to the door of another local icon: the

Sprig & Fern Brewery. Try the trails of **Silvan Forest** and **Sharlands** before heading northwest towards stunning Abel Tasman National Park where, on the southern edge, you'll find **Kaiteriteri Mountain Bike Park** – a network of 30km of groomed trails that radiate out from a high ridge back towards the postcard-perfect bay. Golden Bay is separated from Nelson and Kaiteriteri by Takaka Hill, which cradles **Canaan Downs Loop** within its peak – a 12km purpose-built ride that meanders around the grassy faces of the bowl.

*Left, Nelson has world-class riding just out of town. **Below**, amid nikau palms on the Heaphy Track.*

maintained trails sprawling the length of the skyline directly above the city. Traditionally, each ride began with a climb to the 450m-high summit – a warm-up grind – but, in 2016, the **Christchurch Adventure Park** opened, with a 1.8km chairlift delivering riders and bikes directly into the feeder trails for the park's descending trails, heralding a new era in the quaky city's MTB obsession. Wheeling west of Christchurch, directly into the Southern Alps, you'll find Castle Hill – home to the **Craigieburn Trails** with more than 30km of drool-worthy singletrack flowing through an otherworldly alpine landscape. Link the Hogs Back with Sidle 73, the Dracophyllum Flat and Coal Pit Spur track for 24km of singletrack bliss. For more isolation, seek out the **Poulter Valley** out-and-back track in Arthur's Pass and aim for a night in the six-bunk Trust/Poulter Hut.

Queenstown

Dubbed the 'Whistler of the South' by travelling pros, Queenstown's transformation from ski town to mountain-bike resort has been mesmerising. It always harboured pockets of singletrack brilliance – with the Seven Mile network, Fernhill Loop and the Moke Lake and Moonlight Trail – but when the gondola off Bob's Peak opened for bikes, the town went MTB mad. Skyline Queenstown takes riders from the heart of the bustling tourist town 450m to the top of **Queenstown Bike Park**, where 30 world-class trails beckon. With views across the town, glistening Lake Wakatipu and up to the jagged horizon of The Remarkables, these trails are among the most picturesque in the world, but you'll want to focus on where you're going... Warm up on Hammy's then try Vertigo, Original and, if you're feeling bold, link Hobbit and Killer Bee. Finish the day by riding directly to the bars and restaurants at the end of the trail. A post-ride visit to the craft-beer nirvana of the Atlas Bar on Steamer Wharf is obligatory. Still in Queenstown, take a shuttle to the top of **Coronet Peak** and head into Rude Rock – a ribbon of trail so perfect you'll have to ride it again. Link it up with Zoot Track and drop all the way back to the shuttle, or slip over the saddle into the Skipper's Pack Track and kiss goodbye to caution. And, during summer, **Cardrona Bike Park** offers yet more vertical, with New Zealand's highest and longest runs (one 10km drop boasts 1000m of vertical descent).

Queenstown's gondola takes mountain bikers up to the trails of the Queenstown Bike Park.

Starting from the western edge of the Canaan Downs Loop, the **Rameka Track** is one of New Zealand's singletrack highlights. This native bush descent flows like magic, linking trails that will take you all the way into Golden Bay, some 800 vertical metres below.

The final jewels in the Tasman mountain bike crown are the **Heaphy Track** – a winter-only, two- to three-day 78km adventure ride that wends all the way to the West Coast – and the **Old Ghost Road**, an 85km tramping and MTB route that traces an extinct mining track.

Canterbury

The Port Hills have long been Christchurch mountain bikers' ritual escape – 40km of well-

© Jonathan Gordon | Alamy· © Narratom Y! 500px

Tramping

Kiwis don't walk, hike, trek or ramble. They tramp. And the terrain they tramp across is so stunningly diverse and jaw-droppingly dramatic that you'd scarcely believe it all exists within the same small country. There are countless cracking day walks across the islands that comprise New Zealand, but the country's truly terrific topography demands more extensive exploration, and multiday tramping adventures are ideal.

The excellent Department of Conservation (DoC) maintains trails and operates a network of campsites and backcountry huts that extend all across the country. Huts vary from unmanned basic shelters, usually with pot-bellied stoves and wooden bunks, to plusher serviced shacks with resident rangers. Tickets can be bought individually, and they're excellent value, but those planning on spending an extended period tramping NZ's trails should invest in a Backcountry Pass, which provides unlimited access to most huts.

The exceptions are huts on the nine designated 'Great Walks', one of which – the Whanganui Journey – is actually a river experience that must be paddled in a canoe or kayak, with no walking whatsoever. Even putting this anomaly aside, the notion of reducing NZ's immense trail offering to single digits would be completely ridiculous, if it wasn't for the fact that it's proved to be wildly successful as a tool for marketing the country as a walking destination.

And, with so many tourist trampers trying to tick off the nominated nine tracks to the exclusion of all the thousands of other routes that are great walks in

A hiker takes in Lake Te Anau from the Kepler Track, Fiordland.

all but name, canny Kiwis have effectively reserved some of the best backcountry trails for themselves.

Whole areas – such as the Catlins at the bottom of the South Island – have remained beneath the rambling radar. This region, which is rich in wild paths that thread forests and trace a curvaceous coastline, going via waterfalls and sea lion colonies, would be well trafficked in most countries. Here you'll likely have routes like the 24km two-day **Catlins River–Wisp Loop Track** to yourself.

Even in footfall-heavy areas like Fiordland, where bunks in huts on the perennially popular 53.5km **Milford Track** (the original Great Walk) can be booked-out many months advance, alternative routes such as the 56km **Hollyford Track**, or a 61km circuit created by combining the **Greenstone** and **Caples** tracks are comparatively quiet. Another option in NZ's stunning South West is the demanding four- to five-day 62km **Rees–Dart Track** in Mt Aspiring National Park, which creeps over Cradle Saddle and passes the Dart Glacier.

Other great non-Great Walks include the 75km **Hillary Trail** through the Waitakere Ranges and along Auckland's West Coast; 70km **Queen Charlotte Track** in Marlborough Sounds; and the 48km **Te Paki Coastal Track** around Cape Reinga.

But the Great Walks shouldn't be viewed too cynically. In the early 1990s, these trails were assessed as NZ's best for a number of reasons, including their tramping credentials, infrastructure and ability to inspire people to explore the islands' full range of terrain, from the lunar-like landscape of the volcano-vaulting 43km **Tongariro Northern Circuit** to the sensational sandy beaches of the 60km **Abel Tasman Coastal Track**.

And while Milford might be busy much of the year, the 32km **Routeburn** and 60km **Kepler** tracks – both beautiful Fiordland flings – offer as much quality minus half the trail traffic. Two Great Walks are positively quiet. On the North Island's 46km **Lake Waikaremoana Track** it's often possible to bag the first hut, an exquisite eyrie on the escarpment overlooking the lake, all to yourself. And on oft-overlooked Stewart Island, which dangles from the South Island's toe, gentle 32km **Rakiura Track** offers intrepid trampers a good chance of spotting wild kiwi birds.

In 2018, a 10th Great Walk becomes the first addition to this pantheon of paths in 25 years. The 45km **Pike29 Memorial Track** is a three-day tramp from Blackball to Punakaiki on the South Island's wild West Coast, passing through freshly opened parts of Paparoa National Park with overnight stays in new huts on Moonlight Tops and above the Pororari River valley. The route features an 8km spur to Pike River, where 29 miners (commemorated in the walk's name) were killed in a 2010 accident.

For the time poor, New Zealand's best day walk is arguably the 20km **Tongariro Alpine Traverse**, but if you can squeeze in one multiday tramp, the epic 80ish-km **Heaphy Track** is a 'best-of'. The ancient Maori hunting trail links surf-soaked beaches with mighty mountains, via rainforests and sub-alpine tussock grasslands. Mind out for mountain bikers in winter, and *powelliphanta* (carnivorous snails!) all the time.

ULTIMATE ADVENTURE

Walk New Zealand's length along the Te Araroa (Māori for 'Long Path'), which snakes 3000km from Cape Reinga at the top of the North Island to Bluff at the bottom of the South Island, via volcanoes, beaches, mountains, forests and cities.

© Naruedom Yaempongsa | Shutterstock

Climbing
& Mountaineering

From the ragged peaks of the Southern Alps to the surreal Dalí-esque limestone boulders littering Castle Hill basin, New Zealand is a superb, diverse and supremely beautiful climbing destination, where more often than not you'll find yourself climbing in complete solitude, the mountains your only companions. The South Island is the headline act, holding most of the country's highest alpine peaks as well as its best bouldering and cragging, but the North Island has climbing charm too.

South Island

For high drama, it's impossible to start anywhere but the Southern Alps. Stretching for 500km down the spine of the South Island, the range holds the country's highest peak, **Aoraki/Mt Cook** (3754m), and its most aesthetic, **Mt Aspiring/Tititea** (3033m). Despite its relatively low height, Aoraki is still a significant challenge for climbers (it's the country's most deadly peak), with high levels of glaciation, tempestuous weather and a lot of technical climbing involved. It's definitely not for the inexperienced, but those with the skills can partner up or hire a guide from companies like Adventure Consultants. Aspiring is generally easier and less dangerous, but there are also plenty of smaller peaks that provide excellent challenges.

At the bottom of the South Island, in Fiordland, the less well-known **Darran Mountains** is another excellent alpine climbing destination, with committing but rewarding technical winter climbing and superb alpine rock in summer. The Darrans also hold some of New Zealand's best sport cragging, with the mostly weatherproof (Fiordland annually gets 6–8m of rain) crags of the **Cleddau Valley** holding some of the finest overhanging granite that you'll ever get your hands on. Check out Babylon and Little Babylon, but be aware that there is nothing for beginners.

At the other end of the isle, **Paynes Ford**, just south of the small hippy/tourist town of Takaka (which has great cafes for rest days), is another classic sport climbing spot and the country's most popular summer-climbing destination. Crowds of climbers gather in the nearby Hangdog Campground, from where they walk past a sensational swimming hole (complete with over-water climbing) to beautiful limestone edges overlooking verdant fields.

The jewel in New Zealand's treasure trove, though, is the bouldering at **Castle Hill**. Just 90 minutes' drive from Christchurch, Castle Hill basin – dubbed by the Dalai Lama as one of the 'spiritual

Left, Earland Falls on the Routeburn Track, Fiordland. Below, climbing at Whanganui Bay on the North Island.

© Tom Hoyle | Getty Images

centres of the universe' – holds a clutch of boulder fields scattered across grassy slopes and surrounded by a crown of snow-capped peaks. The blobby, white-limestone boulders have been weathered into incredible shapes that are perfect for climbing – and people visit from all over the world to grapple with the area's notorious sloped mantles. Spittle Hill and Quantum Field are the most popular fields, but the highly featured boulders of Flock Hill (which is on private property and is closed during lambing season) are really the crème de la crème.

North Island

The North Island may be the poor cousin of the South Island when it comes to climbing, but the potential here should not be underestimated. Perhaps the best of the North Island's many crags are the rhyolite crags of **Whanganui Bay,** on the western shore of Lake Taupo, which offer great sport and trad routes.

There's also a host of other crags, from the historic bouldering of **Baring Head** near Wellington to the sport and trad climbing found on the volcanoes of **Mt Ruapehu**, **Mt Ngarahoe** and **Mt Tongariro**.

Below, climbing the sculpted limestone boulders of Castle Hill. Right, Cathedral Cove on the Coromandel Peninsula.

Paddling

From charging rivers to waterfall-fed fiords and surf-sculpted ocean bays, New Zealand is a paddle-toting traveller's wet wonderland.

North Island

Auckland – home to the **King & Queen of the Harbour** downwind race, which sees surfski and SUP paddlers take on a 26km course across Hauraki Gulf – also offers more sedate sea kayaking, around the bays and islands. The city's **WERO Whitewater Park** has the world's highest man-made waterfall (4.5m).

Further north, in the **Bay of Islands**, you can lose days paddling the coast and camping in secluded bays, sometimes accompanied by dolphins. Self-supported trips are possible, but there are also commercial operators offering everything from short day jaunts to multiday trips.

Between Tauranga and Rotorua, the **Kaituna River** – home to the world's highest commercially rafted waterfall, Okere Falls (7m) – is one of New Zealand's most iconic whitewater runs. The **Bay of Plenty** coastline offers a range of options for sea kayaking; check out the beach at **Mount Maunganui** or north around **Waihi** and Cathedral Cove on the **Coromandel Peninsula**.

South Island

The golden-sand beaches and granite cliffs of the **Abel Tasman** offer a huge range of options for multiday exploration, while the township of **Murchison** is the best place in New Zealand to base to yourself for Grade II–IV whitewater. There are several rivers within 30 minutes of town, including the scenic Middle Matakitaki, a stunning Grade-II run.

On the South Island's wild West Coast, sandwiched between the Pacific Ocean and the soaring Southern Alps, the heavy rain-fed rivers are fast-flowing and ever-changing. Base yourself in **Hokitika**, and bring your wallet, as this is the home of heli-kayaking. Arrange a flight and be prepared for some edge-of-your-seat kayaking – most rivers start steep (Grade IV–V), and ease as they come towards the coast. Highlights include the **Hokitika, Arahura**, **Perth** and **Whitcombe rivers**.

Around Queenstown, the **Lower** and **Upper Shotover** are famous for their whitewater. Paddlers can even float through the 170m long Oxenbridge Tunnel before hitting the G4 Cascade rapid. Nearby, The **Kawarau** offers a range of Grade III–V whitewater, and the Dog Leg section takes you underneath the AJ Hackett Bungy Bridge, but be sure to make the take-out or you'll be scouting the Grade V Nevis Bluff – definitely not for everyone.

Stunning Milford and Doubtful Sounds in **Fiordland** are among New Zealand's most iconic drawcards and their shores, featuring giant granite walls and gushing waterfalls, can be explored by sea kayak. Intrepid paddlers can follow the Hollyford River out to the West Coast, then south and back into Milford Sound – a trip that demands experience and careful weather monitoring.

DON'T LEAVE WITHOUT...
Taking a canoe along the 145km Whanganui River from Taumarunui to Pipiriki on the North Island, a journey that takes about five days.

© Tom Hoyle; © Pete Seaward | Lonely Planet

Trail Running

New Zealand is to the Southern Hemisphere what the European Alps is to the Northern – trail-running dreamland. Its two main islands feature singletrack routes that dive into, around, up, along and over the gnarly nation's immense topography. You're never far from epic trails here. From seaside rollercoasters, ancient forest forays and placid riverside runs, to active volcanic adventures, golden tussock traverses and Southern Alps ascents – there's no lack of variety in the challenges on offer.

Queenstown and nearby **Wanaka** are the South Island's trail-running hubs, with easy access to endless rugged alpine tracks and ridge runs aplenty, while the trails around North Island's **Rotorua** and **Tarawera** – home to New Zealand's biggest ultra event – are sublime.

Even Aucklanders can't complain, with the **Waitakere Ranges** on the doorstep only a 40-minute drive west.

Almost all long-distance tracks feature huts en route, making multiday missions achievable. The **Kepler**, **Routeburn** and **Heaphy Tracks** (all Great Walks) are favourites, while newer targets that have the thriving local trail running community amped up include the **Hillary Trail** and **Old Ghost Road**.

> **ICONIC RACE**
> The Tarawera Ultramarathon sends runners from Rotorua to Kawerau in the Bay of Plenty, skirting lakes and passing waterfalls, with 102km, 87km and 62km options.

Skiing & Snowboarding

Resorts
New Zealand has a fistful of world-class snow resorts, each with a unique flavour, catering to whatever kind of cold play floats your boat. Want to ride an active volcano under the threat of eruption? Then **Mt Ruapehu** on the North Island is for you. The Southern Alps are peppered with resorts and blessed with excellent mountain towns in **Wanaka** and **Queenstown**. Friendly folks, great food, raging parties and gravity-fuelled frenzies. Whether you're shooting craggy chutes of **The Remarkables**, riding the rollercoasters of **Coronet Peak**, carving **Treble Cone** with the jaw-dropping views across a rocky elephant's hide to Lake Wanaka, or inverting in the terrain park at **Cardrona** – New Zealand on piste is on point.

Club fields
If you want a quintessential Kiwi snow experience, head to the club fields – quirky, small, privately owned mountains run like co-ops. Facilities are basic – likely no groomers and you might have to help with cleaning and cooking – but the vibe is friendly, tickets cheap, queues short and your chances of laying down untracked turns are high. Adventure is the name of the game: a sign on the drive to **Mt Olympus** reads 'Carry chains and courage', and though some – like **Craigieburn** and **Broken River** – offer serious challenges for advanced skiers, you don't have to be an expert to enjoy **Mt Dobson** or **Round Hill**.

'Lifted' riding
Don't want to wait in the lift line with the other chumps? New Zealand has heaps of helicopters and in a few short minutes you can punch through the inversion layer into bluebird skies and have one of the best days of riding of your life, dropping into bowls of virgin pow. Wow.

Earn your turns
Real adventurers like to earn their turns. Fortunately, there is loads of back- and slackcountry riding in New Zealand. Classic alpine ski touring can be done hut-to-hut around **Mt Cook**, in the Tasman, Murchison, Mannering, Aida, Fox and Franz Josef glacier regions. To hone your skills, join one of the great ski mountaineering courses on offer.

Black-Water Rafting

Beneath the small town of Waitomo in the King Country region of the North Island exists a labyrinth of caves with a subterranean river running through it. This being New Zealand, that presented the perfect conditions for a new sport to be created, and some 25 years ago black-water rafting was born. A number of options now exist, but a typical five-hour adventure finds people abseiling into an inky dark cavern such as Ruakuri Cave, floating along the underground waterway atop an inner tube – viewing glow worms along the way – and combining the experience with some caving and scrambling before emerging back into daylight.

Diving & Snorkelling

It may not have the Great Barrier Reef, but New Zealand boasts some of the planet's most interesting dive sites. These include **White Island Volcano**, where you can explore an active volcano underwater, checking out gas-burping fumaroles; and **Poor Knights Islands Marine Reserve**, 800m off Northland, rated by Jacques Cousteau as one of the world's top ten dive sites, with huge caves, arches, tunnels and sheer cliffs to explore, excellent vis and myriad marine species. Also see the wreck of the *Rainbow Warrior*, Greenpeace's flagship, which was sunk in Auckland Harbour by French saboteurs in 1985 while preparing to protest against France's nuclear testing on Mururoa Atoll, and now rests in peace in the Cavalli Islands, surrounded by the wildlife she was fighting to protect. On the South Island, **Milford Sound** presents divers with a challenge, with a 5m layer of freshwater (provided by epic rainfall) sitting above saltwater, making the establishment of neutral buoyancy a refined art.

Surfing

A combination of the huffing, puffing Roaring 40s and super swell coming off Antarctica means surfers in New Zealand rarely wait long for a decent wave, and those in the South Island in particular are treated to consistent conditions along uncrowded points, reefs and beach breaks. Top spots include the left-hand point break at **Raglan** near Hamilton on the North Island, and **Piha**, a black-sand beach with powerful breaks on the West Coast. The **Catlins** in the far south offer secluded conditions and encounters with fur seals.

Queenstown Capers

Few countries can boast an adventure hub quite as full of energy as the South Island's Queenstown, nestled in-between the ankles of the Southern Alps. From here, you can do just about anything, from **bungee jumping** off Kawarau Gorge Suspension Bridge and **jet-boating** on the Shotover and Dart rivers, to **canyoning** in the local gorge.

ICONIC RACE

Home to several adventure races, including GodZone (the world's largest expedition-length adventure race), New Zealand's signature multisport challenge is the Coast to Coast. It sees competitors leave Kumara Beach on the West Coast of the South Island, and pedal, paddle and run to New Brighton on the East Coast.

Runners competing in the annual Tarawera Ultramarathon.

© Graeme Murray | graememurray.com

NICARAGUA

World-class surf, spectacular jungle hiking and the chance to sample volcano boarding make this criminally underrated country a must visit for the adventurous.

Under-the-radar Nicaragua comprises lumpy volcanic landscapes, absurdly big lakes and beguiling lagoons, immaculate cloud forests, breathtaking beaches, Caribbean fishing villages and surf hangouts. The jungles are home to parrots and monkeys, toucans and armadillos, plus a crazy number of orchids. Satisfyingly, the tourism industry here is embryonic, providing a pleasingly unpolished experience.

Volcano Boarding

Central America's quirkiest adrenaline activity requires a 50-minute drive from the colonial city of León, and an hour's uphill hike, which brings you to the summit of still-active Cerro Negro (728m). The fine black volcanic ash on the 41-degree slope is perfect for boarding. You simply place backside on board and let gravity do its thing. Boarders can be at the bottom again in less than three minutes, a little blacker of face and clothes, and a little wider of grin.

Surfing

Wave riders will find nirvana on Nicaragua's southern Pacific Coast, especially at the Tola beaches. Set in a lush valley, the easygoing former fishing village of **San Juan del Sur** is the perfect hub, with perky nightlife and an easygoing vibe.

To the north, check out **Maderas** for a slow wave in 2m-deep water; or **Majagual**, **Marsella** or **Octal**. Going south, **Hermosa** has no less than five breaks; the much-photographed dazzling sands and charismatic cliffs of **El Coco** house yet more world-class surf, while **Yankee** and **Escameca** are also ace.

Hiking, Climbing & Wild Swimming

Mark Twain exploded with appreciation of **Isla de Ometepe**'s huge twin cloud forest-cloaked volcanoes in *Travels With Mr Brown*, and the Aztecs were also fans of this unique island. **Lago de Nicaragua**, the largest freshwater sea in the Americas after Canada's Great Lakes, used to be filled with seawater, and swordfish, freshwater sharks and other aquatic curios still live here. Some 1700 prehistoric petroglyphs can be found on the island, plus waterfalls, beaches, natural swimming pools, howler and white-faced monkeys. After some mishaps on the challenging all-day ascents of the active, conical Concepción (1610m) and more jungly and wildlife-rich Maderas (1394m), it is mandatory for hikers attempting both climbs to take guides.

Elsewhere, **Volcán Mombacho** is another popular volcano climb (home to 87 species of orchid) and there are more flat-headed peaks to clamber up near **León**. The mountains around **Estelí** and **Matagalpa** also offer excellent hiking.

DON'T LEAVE WITHOUT...
Exploring the excellent diving and snorkelling around the Corn Islands on the Caribbean coast, with wrecks and reefs accessible from the beach.

NIGERIA

Big in size and population, diverse in environment and culture, and dangerous in parts, Nigeria rewards the intrepid.

Even without the dangerous unrest in the north, Nigeria is bold and brash – a big culture melded from many ethnic groups and home to a heaving capital city constantly redefining itself. The land is as diverse as the people – mountains dressed in thick jungle give way to open savannah; river deltas and steamy mangroves stand in contrast to desert dunes. It's hard to pin Nigeria down, and that's part of the attraction.

Trekking

One of the country's best treks is an eight- to 10-day march through the large **Gashaka-Gumti National Park**, taking in the summit of Chappal Waddi – the Mountain of Death, which, at 2419m, is Nigeria's highest point. More expedition siege than fast-and-light mission, the slow pace through dense forest will afford you plenty of time to spot wildlife, perfect considering the park is home to myriad beasts including buffaloes, lions, elephants, waterbucks, roan antelopes, giant elands, black and white colobus monkeys, baboons, oribi klipspringers, hippos, crocodiles and the largest chimpanzee population in Nigeria. Pack your binoculars.

Lonely waves

Loneliness is generally a negative, but not when it comes to surfing. Having a break of tubes to yourself is the dream, and when the conditions are right, Nigeria can deliver. With the eyes of the international boardriding community only just now being trained on the country, intrepid surfers are starting to uncover great waves on the long Atlantic coast.

ICONIC RACE
The Obudo Ranch International Mountain Marathon, with a prize pot of US$250,000 (the richest mountain race in the world), involves a 11.25km dash up Mt Obudo. Get training.

NIUE

This tiny coral atoll passes most travellers by, so you'll have the stunning limestone escarpments and reefs almost to yourself.

With a circumference of just 73km, Niue is one of the world's smallest nations, but it punches well above its weight in the adventure stakes, with superb watersports and great hiking and biking. The island is topped with tropical rainforest and ringed by dramatic limestone cliffs.

Caving

You are not going to find any long, white-sand beaches on Niue, but what you will discover is a whole lot more intriguing: a myriad of forgotten caves, arches and chasms. Niue contains one of the most extensive cave systems in the South Pacific, some of which can be explored independently while others require local guides.

Diving & Snorkelling

Niue has stellar water visibility, ranging from 30m right up to an eye-popping 100m. Numerous 'sea tracks' lead away from the main roads to turquoise water and pristine coves (some of which were traditionally reserved for Niuean kings), caves and coral reefs, and each nook and cranny is teeming with colourful fish. For non-divers, the natural pools at Matapa and Snake Gully are both sensational snorkelling spots. Between June and October, if your luck is in, it's sometimes possible to snorkel or dive alongside humpback whales and with spinner dolphins.

Kayaking

Join a group and paddle along the Alofi coastline, or rent a kayak and plot your own adventure – perhaps a circumnavigation of the island.

ICONIC RACE
The annual two-day Ride the Rock mountain-bike race takes place in May or June. Hook along 8km speed stages across the centre of the island, or smash out a 60km circuit of the entire country, tearing along cracking coastal trails.

NORWAY

Epic fjords, giant-harbouring mountains, troll trails, hanging lakes and an Atlantic-carved coastline – Norway's mesmerising landscape is perfect for all outdoor adventures.

Despite a history intrinsically entwined with seafaring escapades – from far-venturing Vikings to polar pioneer Roald Amundsen and *Kontiki* expeditioner Thor Heyerdahl – adventurous Norwegians have plenty on their own doorstep to explore. Outdoor life is highly valued here, and the right to roam (and ride, ski, camp and forage) is protected by *allemannsretten*, a traditional concept enshrined in law by the 1957 *Outdoor Recreation Act*, so you can hike, bike and slide across mountainsides and around fjords all over the country – on the extensive backcountry trail network or completely off piste – scoffing cloudberries and pitching your tent where you please. If you don't want to camp (and winter gets pretty chilly) the Norwegian Trekking Association operates some 500 cabins around the country, ranging from fully serviced to quite basic, which provide comfortable and affordable accommodation. And when you've seen the mainland, Svalbard awaits.

Hiking

Beautiful paths stripe the country, but **Innerdalen** is often heralded as Norway's most spectacular valley. Presided over by peaks including the dramatic Innerdalstårnet (1452m), a magnet for climbers, the vale also features forests, ridgelines, waterfalls and lakes, all linked together by sensational trails. Not far from Innerdalen, you find the **Romsdalseggen ridge**, a day hike going from Vengedalen to Åndalsnes. A daily bus provides transport (July–September) from Åndalsnes to the starting point. Norway's most iconic hike is to the distinctive **Trolltunga** (Troll tongue), which cheekily pokes out of a mountainside 700m above lake Ringedalsvatnet. It's a 10-hour-plus return hike from Skjeggedal to the tongue, which you can then stand upon... if you dare. Another precipitous place that attracts walkers is **Preikestolen** (two hours hike from Preikestolhytta), a clifftop above a super sheer 604m drop into Lysefjorden, opposite the Kjerag Plateau in Forsand, which is a popular launching pad for BASE jumpers.

Skiing

Norway is the home of the Telemark turn, and everyone here skis, which is why they're all in such rude health. Downhill resorts can be found scattered through the Norwegian Alps at **Hafjell** near Lillehammer, **Trysil** (near the Swedish border) and **Geilo** (between Oslo and Bergen), and the **Sunnmørsalpane** (Sunnmore Alps) bring together snowy peaks and the Atlantic Ocean in a partnership perfect for ski touring. But the elevation

ICONIC EVENT
During the 54km Birkebeinerrennet race from Rena to Lillehammer, 17,000 people honour a historical event from 1206 (when an infant prince was smuggled through the mountains to protect him from assassins), all carrying the weight of a baby on their back.

isn't massive, and it's cross-country skiing that keeps the locals in shape. In popular areas such as **Sjusjøen**, 'classic' ski tracks are ploughed and fields are floodlit, all free of charge. Long-distance routes, such as the 170km **Troll-loipe** (troll trail) from Rondane National Park to Lillehammer can be tackled over several days (overnighting in huts) and events are very popular, none more so than the **Birkebeinerrennet** (see box, left).

Mountain Biking

When the snow melts, skis go away and Norwegians bust out their mountain bikes. Access to terrific trails is outstanding across the country, and there's a wealth of wild riding to be enjoyed, including trailheads at **Holmenkollen**, **Frognerseteren**, **Sørkedalen** and **Sognsvann**, right outside Oslo. If you're after something more groomed, try the flowing singletrack at **Tungvekteren** in Arendal, or give the downhill runs a blast at **Hafjell**, which has hosted MTB World Cup events. There's also a two-wheeled version of the Birken, called the **Birkebeinerrittet**, which sees thousands of riders hurtling along an 86km dirt-road route from Rena to Lillehammer, carrying the weight of that baby prince on their backs.

Road Cycling

Norway's roads are exceptional, and cycling the 36km **Atlanterhavsveien** (Atlantic Ocean Road) is an unforgettable experience. One of Norway's 18 National Tourist Roads, it's signposted from the fishing village Bud to Kårvåg, with the section between Vevang to Kårvåg hopping over seven brilliant humpback bridges, linking the mosaic of islands off the country's west coast.

Paddling

Norway's savagely serrated Atlantic coast challenges sea kayakers to come and explore. Steep-sided fjords provide wind cover, and the west coast is dotted with multiple islands, many forming sublime summer getaways for locals. **Smøla**, an island 150km west of Trondheim, is renowned for its superb paddling, and boat hire and guiding is readily available. In the mountainous archipelago of **Lofoten**, you can punctuate your paddling with a bit of climbing. Other areas to explore on water include **Hidra** (Norway's riviera), mountain-fringed **Flekkefjord**, the superb **Helgeland coast** and **Vega islands**. With many a rushing river, Norway attracts whitewater paddlers from all over the world to events such as the Ula Extreme Race, part of the **Sjoa River Festival** in the eponymous valley. Whitewater rafting can be done at **Voss** in Western Norway, **Mandalselva** in the south and on the **Driva** in Trøndelag.

Trail & Mountain Running

Brutal uphill-only races are popular in Norway, the most famous being **Skaala**, where competitors battle up a rugged mountain path from 29m above sea level to 1848m. That the world's top trail-running couple – Spaniard Kilian Jornet and Swede Emelie Forsberg – choose to live and train in the **Møre og Romsdal** area of northwest Norway confirms the region's position at the pinnacle of the mountain-running sphere. In 2014, Jornet and Forsberg launched the **Tromsø SkyRace** in Arctic northern Norway, a super-technical challenge.

Exploring the Lofoten Islands in Norway's north.

© Johner Images | Getty Images

Trail running in the Lofoten Islands.

DON'T LEAVE WITHOUT...
Visiting the Olympic Sliding Centre at Hunderfossen, just north of Lillehammer, where you can try bobsledding and even the skeleton, during which you'll travel headfirst at speeds of up to 70km/h with your nose inches from the ice.

Adventure Racing

Norway is infamous for masochistic physical challenges like the **Norseman**, one of the world's toughest triathlons. From Eidfjord, racers start the event by jumping off a ferry in darkness and try to end it almost 2000m above sea level at the top of Gaustatoppen mountain, with a huge amount of swimming, biking and running in-between. Other similar races are now springing up, with the **Fjord Extreme Ironman** being a notable rival.

Climbing

Norway's alpine epicentre is Romsdalen, from where you can scale peaks including Romsdalshorn (1550m), Venjetinden (1852m) and Kvanndalstind (1744m). Lofoten offers oceanside climbing under the midnight sun during summer, and in winter you can channel your inner Viking and go berserk swinging an (ice) axe into over 150 waterfalls at the ice-climber's Valhalla that is Rjukan (where an ice-climbing festival takes place in February).

Svalbard

Flung high in the Arctic Ocean, halfway between mainland Norway and the North Pole, this ice-encrusted archipelago is accessed by a three-hour flight from Oslo.

Camp Inside a Glacier

Longyearbyen is the base for most activities, including hiking and camping inside the Lars glacier, just behind town. Each summer, surface snow melts and seeps down the sides of the glacier, winding its way inside to form two rivers. Come winter, when the water has drained, these channels freeze and it's safe to walk along them and set up camp within. The experience starts with a two-hour climb to the entrance, pulling gear on pulks, before you plunge into the frozen underworld via a rope-assisted descent.

Mushing

In the absence of roads, many people use snowmobiles, but the adventurous will opt for a husky safari. Skimming along on sleigh-runners in winter and wheels in summer, most expeditions start east of Adventdalen, where you meet and harness your own team. Options include half-day trips to Foxfonna or Breinosa, where you might spy arctic foxes and Svalbard reindeer; overnight camps to Nordenskiöld National Park to watch the northern lights; and two-day expeditions to the Russian settlement of Barentsburg, with a population of 400 people, a hotel and a microbrewery.

Fatbiking

Cycle a fatbike under the midnight sun – rolling easily across riverbeds, beaches and snow – while eider ducks swoop overhead. A popular ride is to Bjorndalen (Bear Valley) to see the remains of the old WWII airport and defunct Mine 5.

Hiking

Polar bears outnumber humans here by more than a thousand, so you'll need a certified shotgun-wielding guide to accompany you on local trails. That sorted, options include climbing Plateau Mountain, fossil hunting at Deltaneset, and strolling to the Global Seed Vault, where millions of seeds from around the world are stored (so, in the event of a major disaster, lost crops could be regrown).

© Kai-Otto Melau/ Getty Images

OMAN

From the Musandam Peninsula and the Al Hajar Mountains in the north to the Empty Quarter in the southwest, everything about Oman's topography is extreme.

A dventure is never far distant in Oman. The rugged Al Hajar Mountains loom over the capital, Muscat; driving almost anywhere requires a 4WD; wadis serve up fine desert walking between oases and frankincense trees; and the coastline is full of surprises. Locals live largely traditional lives, particularly in the mountains, adding a wealth of cultural experiences.

Hiking & Desert Exploration

The **Al Hajar Mountains** are an almost undiscovered paradise for trekking. Hikers can follow ancient tribal routes between remote villages buried deep in wadis that in the past would have been used for trade or raiding. There are a few marked hikes, but most routes require guides. The **Empty Quarter** and the slightly tamer **Wahiba Sands** are amazing destinations for **4WDing** and **camping** beneath the stars

Climbing

In the north, the spectacular limestone cliffs of the Musandam Peninsula jut into the Gulf of Oman, and are an emerging destination for **deep-water soloing** – climbing without a rope over deep water (if you fall in, the main danger is giving yourself a saltwater enema).

Watersports

Musandam is also a sensational spot for **diving** and **snorkelling**, with superb reef diving, rich with soft and hard coral and marine life; it's quite common to see whale sharks, turtles and rays. The peninsula is popular with **sea kayaking** paddlers too. Further south, Masirah Island has world-class **windsurfing** from May to September.

DON'T LEAVE WITHOUT...
Exploring Jabal Shams and Wadi Ghul, 'Arabia's Grand Canyon', and daring to do the Balcony Walk.

Watching the sun set over Jebel Misht in the Al Hajar Mountains.

© Ross Taylor

225

Porters carry loads up the Biafo Glacier, Karakorum.

PAKISTAN

Pakistan offers enormous mountains, wild frontiers, harsh deserts and a rich culture.

S kiing, trekking, kayaking, desert crossings, climbing up mountains or soaring over them – Pakistan provides for a truly dizzying number of adventure pursuits. Even the drive up the remarkable Karakoram Highway is an adventure. However, all travellers should be aware of the risks involved in visiting Pakistan, which most Foreign Offices make clear.

Hiking & Climbing

The **Karakorum** in the country's north is absolutely magnificent, overwhelming in its scale and humbling in its beauty. It is the most heavily glaciated part of the world outside the polar regions and has four peaks over 8000m – including the world's second highest and arguably the most deadly mountain, K2 (8611m) – as well as endless so-called minor peaks. Even if you are not here to make a summit push, treks to K2 Base Camp and the more technical ascent of **Gondogoro La** are among the world's greatest high-altitude ambles.

Paragliding

Once you have climbed the mountains, the only thing left to do is fly over them. Paragliding in the Karakorum may not be for beginners, but if you have the skills then the soaring here is some of the best in the world. Pilots at 7000m need supplemental oxygen, but staying conscious brings vistas of endless jagged peaks and ancient valleys scoured out by vast glaciers.

Paddling

Steep slopes and snowmelt make for superb white-water kayaking in the north, where H2O hurries from the Himalaya and the Karakorum towards the Arabian Sea. The Indus, Ravi and Chenab rivers all offer skilled paddlers much excitement, especially between March and April.

UNCLAIMED ADVENTURE

Unlike Everest, skied by Davo Karničar in 2000, K2 has never seen a summit-to-base camp descent by a ski mountaineer. Hans Kammerlander skied the top 400m, and Luis Stitzinger and David Watson have skied large sections, but the complete challenge remains unclaimed.

PANAMA

With great hiking, surfing, diving, rafting and volcano climbing – plus sandy Caribbean beaches to hang out on – Panama offers a plethora of adventurous activities.

Panama is a country of curvy coastlines, idyllic Caribbean islands and coffee plantations. The coral reefs, pristine rainforests, beaches, surf and dive sites of Bocas del Toro archipelago make it the nation's most popular destination, while the fertile Chiriquí highlands to the west offer adventures, too, particularly for volcano lovers.

Hiking

Panama's best hiking is in the coffee-scented, mist-covered hills of the hyper-fertile **Chiriquí highlands** and **Volcán Barú National Park**. Clambering to the top of the seven-cratered Volcán Barú (3474m), the country's highest point (and only volcano), can be muddy and misty, but vast views from the top – including the unique sight of both the Caribbean and Atlantic oceans – plus encounters with resplendent quetzals en route, make it worthwhile. Get there for sunrise. Volcán Barú is also home to pumas, tapirs and the *condo pentad* (painted rabbit), a large spotted rodent. **Sendero Los Quetzales**, perhaps the country's most beautiful trail, is also in the park. Though it's only 8km long, allow four to six hours hiking time. Accessible via the Caribbean coast, the Talamanca mountains of **La Amistad International Park** are a bona fide wilderness and a wildlife-watcher's wonderland, with 90 mammal species, six cat species (including jaguars), and 450-plus bird species. In the stunning **Bocas del Toro** archipelago, Isla Colón has a network of trails, past caves, caverns and textbook jungle.

Surfing

Panama's up-and-coming surf scene embraces both coasts. Killer waves can be had at relaxed fishing village **Santa Catalina** – enjoy it while it remains underdeveloped. **Bocas del Toro** has mostly reef breaks, with Playa Punch throwing a combination of lefts and rights. Playa Bluff is **Isla Colón**'s most infamous wave, producing barrels with a reputation for breaking boards.

Paddling

Kayak between the thickly forested islands and uninhabited coves of the **Bocas del Toro** archipelago. Both **Ríos Chiriquí** and **Chiriquí Viejo**, near Boquete, offer superb whitewater rafting trips along narrow canyons and past hidden waterfalls, on Grade II–III rapids.

© worldswildlifewonders | Shutterstock

DON'T LEAVE WITHOUT...

Making the effort to get to Isla Coiba where near-perfect marine conditions offer world-class diving. The emerald-green sea around the Bocas del Toro archipelago doesn't offer the same visibility, but it is home to stingrays, dolphins and grey nurse sharks.

Panama is famous for its wildlife, including the red-eyed tree frog.

PAPUA NEW GUINEA

Papua New Guinea – beautiful, wild, friendly and exotic – is one of Earth's final frontiers.

There are few wilder places on the planet than Papua New Guinea (PNG) – a land of dense jungles, rugged terrain, surging rivers and vast swamps, soaring peaks, big surf and thundering deluges. Vast tracts remain roadless; even the capital, Port Moresby, is not connected by road to any major town. The only way in is to fly, sail or walk. Because of the logistical difficulties and (valid) safety concerns, adventure-seekers largely visit PNG with guided groups.

Hiking & Climbing

Most visitors come to trek; most of them, in turn, come for the famed **Kokoda Track**: a 96km rollercoaster of thigh-searing climbs and slick, muddy descents, all in air so thick and wet you can nearly swim in it. Military history is the prime drawcard, particularly for Australians interested in WWII, but Kokoda also offers a fascinating glimpse into village culture. The rhythms of life remain slow,

kids and adults alike wander barefoot, chickens strut around stilted houses, laughter fills the air and there's still no electricity. Also popular, particularly with peak baggers, is 4509m **Mt Wilhelm**, Oceania's highest mountain. It's a glorious climb, starting through montane rainforest with hundreds of wild orchid species and going up into alpine grasslands. Elsewhere, the **Blackcat** and **Bulldog Tracks** (the former offering finer scenery than Kokoda and more military artefacts) can be linked to make a superb coast-to-coast transect, although recent 'incidents' mean that no guided groups are currently doing this adventure.

Wreck Diving

Diving is popular in PNG, which has phenomenal coral formations and hundreds of wrecks, many of which haven't been explored. In Milne Bay it's possible to do a wreck dive around an eerily intact sunken fighter plane, a P38 Lightning shot down during WWII, which lay undetected for 50 years.

ULTIMATE ADVENTURE...
Combine a cruise on the wildside with a sea-kayaking expedition up the Sepik River, around Manus Island and along PNG's gorgeous coastline, guided by experts from Southern Sea Ventures.

Dawn light on the Kokoda Track; walking the route is a rite of passage for many Australians.

© Andrew Peacock | Getty Images

PARAGUAY

Landlocked and largely unloved by the travellers who flock to the rest of South America, Paraguay nevertheless offers adventure pursuits with a paddle and in the saddle.

K nown as el Corizón de Sudamérica (the Heart of South America) for its position in the middle of the continent, Paraguay is one of South America's least visited countries. The nation is split in two by the eponymous Paraguay River, separating the densely populated east from vast and sparse Región Occidental, known as The Chaco.

Paddle the Paraguay

Rivers have long been the romantic setting for exploration and adventure, and the Paraguay River is ripe for a modern multiday paddle. The navigable waterway is the landlocked nation's backbone, having provided shipping and trade access to the Atlantic. Today you can hop into a kayak in Bahia Negra, on the country's northern border with Brazil, and paddle 885km to Concepción. Camping on the bank, passing small villages or just floating through the jungle ringing with a cacophony of animal sound, this seven- to 10-day river trip passes through a wilderness inhabited by caiman, flamingoes, kingfishers, eagles, toucans, vultures and tuyuyu, not to mention piranha and golden dorado.

Pedal The Chaco

The Chaco is a vast plain and it's pretty much empty of people. Less than 2% of Paraguay's population live in an area that accounts for 60% of the country, and many of those who do are Mennonites, famous for their hospitality. But you're not here for the people. Instead, from your bike's saddle you'll be engulfed in a land teeming with animal life. You'll set off early every morning to beat the day's heat through forest echoing with the squawking of thousands of birds. As dawn breaks and your wheels roll silently down the road, you might see ocelot, puma, tapir, giant armadillo, spiny anteater, maned wolf, guanaco and, if you're very lucky, a jaguar will slink across your path. Add in the large, flightless rhea, millions of insects, 60 known species of snakes and at least six types of poisonous tree toad, and your ride is pretty much a zoological tour.

© tane-mahuta | Getty Images

ICONIC EVENT
Expedición Guarani, the Paraguayan leg of the Adventure Racing World Tour, is a 400km jungle thrash by foot, mountain bike and kayak.

If you're lucky, you might spy Paraguay's most spectacular predator, the jaguar.

PERU

Peru is a land of diversity and extremes, marked by the remnants of ancient cultures whose power still resonates throughout the land today.

Glorious and proud Peru stands as both a monument to ancient cultures and a wonderland for modern adventurers. Snowy Andean mountain peaks call climbers and trekkers, surfers seek out endless point breaks on a vast coastline, while the nigh-on-impenetrable Amazon wetlands and rainforests are teeming with life and ripe for exploration. The hardest thing about Peru is deciding what to do first.

Surf the Longest Left

Rolling in from the Pacific, consistent swells clatter into Chicama, near Trujillo in the country's north. They push in at such an angle and force that even when the swell is small the wave formed will stand up perfectly for more than 2km. So for about two and a half minutes barrels form and banks rise again and again on a ride so long you'll either utterly blow your legs or enter a mental state unlike any you've known before. Tucking into the 'longest left-hander in the world' is not all Peru has to offer surfers, though. Boasting 3000km of wild coast that is littered with point breaks, Peru is primed for a killer surf safari. Between morning and afternoon sessions don't miss out on ceviche – Peru's delicious raw fish lunch.

Boat into the Dark Jungle

The jungle explorer is one of the classic archetypes – swatting bugs in sweltering heat, lost in a maddening forest bursting with greenery and bristling with animals, full of sound and thick with smells. And there is no better way to penetrate deep into jungle than on the water. The Río Tambopata gives an opportunity for intrepid rafters to live this romantic ideal on a river journey through some wonderful and wonderfully isolated parts of the Amazon rainforest. As more and more tributaries feed into the Tambopata, the volume of water increases and the river throws up some super fun Grade III–IV rapids to get rafters' hearts racing. The

SPIRITUAL HOME OF...
Chewing coca. It's not an adventure in itself, but it is for the adventurous and using it will mean you can go harder, higher and longer. To combat the effects of altitude, suppress hunger and give themselves a straight shot of energy, Peruvians have been chewing the sacred crop for millennia.

© Philip Lee Harvey | Lonely Planet

Amazon is famed for its rich biodiversity and when the water calms the wildlife-spotting comes into its own. Eagle eyes can spy giant river otter, macaws, tapirs, spider monkeys, bright birds and, for the very lucky, jaguars and caiman. Rafting Amazonian rivers is a mystical journey of wildlife, wilderness, and wild water not to be missed.

Bag Peaks in Ancash

The majestic **Cordillera Blanca** is a magnet for trekkers and climbers with a huge number of options on offer near Ancash's capital, Huaraz. Trekkers favour either the **Santa Cruz** or **Quilcayhuanca and Cojup Valleys** treks, both of which are four fabulous days of walking among jagged, snow-covered peaks, skirting valleys, marvelling at glaciers and bright turquoise lakes. Though the Cordillera Blanca has 25 summits that reach more than 6000m into the heavens, the most coveted objective for mountaineers is **Huascarán** (6768m), the roof of Peru and the highest mountain anywhere in the tropics. Any ascent of Huascarán

is serious – this is not a mountain for the inexperienced. That said, there are loads of nearby summits screaming out to be stood on. Classic, more moderate peaks include **Pisco** (5752m), **Ishinca** (5530m) and **Vallunaraju** (5686m). A stout constitution, strong legs and an even stronger mind will see you rewarded with some of the most spectacular views in South America.

Sandboard the Dunes

Sand might shift more slowly than the ocean, but with the right board you can drop a big dune like it's a crashing wave. The wind-sculptured dunes of **Huacachina** are spot on for sandboarding – probably the most obscure of the board pursuits. It is a unique feeling to be zipping down a slope, blossoming with a yellow glow as it catches the softening afternoon sun – one that you are not likely to forget. For the uninitiated the clutching sand can be difficult to handle and you're bound to catch an edge and go head-over-heels, but the sand is soft (enough) so that all you have to do is dust yourself

A tiny village on the Alto Madre de Dios river, of which the Río Tambopata is a tributary.

off, spit the grains out from between your teeth and march back to the top to try again. Hot tip, cover up your skin as the sand can be unforgiving.

Trek with Ancients

There's a reason why the **Inca Trail** is so popular – it's an excellent adventure that just about anyone can complete. The four-day trek follows an ancient thoroughfare worn by the passage of thousands of feet, rising out of the Urubamba Valley, through cloud forests, over lung-busting high passes and along dramatic ridges, culminating in an early morning passage through the Sun Gate to finally gaze upon the implausible ruins of Machu Picchu. The site is spectacular and moving, and the massive structures built into such a wild and dramatic landscape cannot but leave visitors in awe of the toil and vision of the builders. The Inca Trail combines the power of the journey with the magnetism of the destination to create one of the world's great attractions. While the Inca Trail is a classic modern pilgrimage, it is only the most popular of such treks in Peru, there are more ruins in the country's mountains and deserts that can be equally rewarding for those who seek something a little different. For history, beauty, exertion and adventure, the ruins of Peru are hard to beat.

The grand finale of the Inca Trail, Machu Picchu.

© Philip Lee Harvey | Lonely Planet

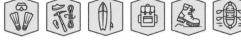

PHILIPPINES

If tropical jungles and steaming volcanoes are too hot for your taste, you'll find plenty of places to cool down along the world's fifth longest coastline.

A vast archipelago, the Philippines is best known for tropical island vistas – palm trees, white-sand beaches and temperate waters. Though it is a nation of water, it is also one of fire; situated on the edge of the Pacific Rim, the volcanic landscape gives rise to verdant rainforests and turbulent rivers beckoning explorers to discover their primordial secrets.

Diving & Snorkelling

Diving and snorkelling in the Philippines is sensational. Below the clear, calm waters you'll find a dazzling array of coral reefs and atolls, sheer submarine walls and an impressive collection of WWII-era shipwrecks. **Apo Island** is particularly famed for its vast coral gardens and abundant marine life. The wrecks of the *Morazán Maru* in **Coron Bay** and the USS *New York* in **Subic Bay** are particularly popular, as is snorkelling with whale sharks off **Cebu**.

Canyoning

The dense jungle canopy hides tropical treasures in the form of world-class canyoning. Beginners can tackle the relatively mild **Kanlaob River**, while experienced canyoneers will enjoy descending 15 individual waterfalls on the **Sampao River**.

Surfing

'Discovered' by surfers working on *Apocalypse Now*, the Philippines boasts some of the world's best breaks. On **Siargao Island** you'll find powerful, barrelling reef and beach breaks in more than a dozen locations, best for intermediate to advanced riders. Beginners may have more luck at **Zambales** or **Baler**.

Trekking

Landlubbers are equally spoiled for choice thanks to many stellar mountains to trek. For an easy, accessible ramble, the **Taal Volcano Trail** on Luzon affords incredible views. At the other end of the spectrum, remote and challenging **Mt Guiting-Guiting** awaits the committed. But, if you only do one hike, make sure you check out the unforgettable, postcard-worthy vistas of the terraced rice fields at **Banaue** in Ifugao Province.

DON'T LEAVE WITHOUT...
Rafting the country's roaring rivers. Whitewater paddling is a popular pursuit, with a multitude of venues spread across the country – the most famous being Cagayan de Oro.

Snorkelling with a whale shark off Cebu.

© soft_light | Shutterstock

233

POLAND

Poland's precipitous mountains, lovely lakes and resplendent rock formations provide ample outdoor opportunities.

Paragliders soar on summer breezes over the Żar and Szybowcowa mountains; kayakers enjoy autumn in the Masurian Lake District; ice divers crack the frozen sheen of northeastern Lake Gáladuś during winter; and in spring, climbers' frozen digits thaw for action on the sheer limestone pillars in the Kraków-Częstochowa Upland, 30km north of Kraków.

Hiking & Climbing

It's both a blessing and a curse that the 600km of trails in the **High Tatras** are easily accessible. The blessing: small backpacks, because many summits can be scaled in a single day. The curse: madding crowds, although refuges dotted around the mountains mean it's possible to construct DIY multiday hikes and escape the throng somewhat. Clamber 1200m up fixed chains to summit Poland's highest mountain, **Rysy** (2503m); scramble over **Orla Perć's** dozen cloud-poking 2000m-plus summits; boulder-hop a section of the 46km

Magistrála Ridge; and finish with a brandy in the Bilikova Chata, where photos of annual race competitors who haul 90kg up a nearby mountain adorn the walls.

Skiing

Zieleniec's 22km of north-facing slopes provide the longest white season, while **Skrzyczne** (1257m), the loftiest peak in the Beskid Mountains, has 13km of runs. Cross-country crusaders crunch along **Magurka Wilkowicka's** four tracks. The season is typically mid-December to early April.

Kayaking

Twenty lakes, two canals and six nature reserves are spread across 109km on the seven- to eight-day **Krutynia River kayak trail** in the Masurian Lake District, which presents the country's best paddling adventure. The upper section has a swift current that slows as the river flows, although nothing moves between December and April, when the river usually freezes.

© gubernat | Getty Images

DON'T LEAVE WITHOUT...

Snowmobiling in Zakopane. Make like James Bond – day or night – through pine forests and valleys of virgin snow beneath the looming Tatras in the Gubałówka Range.

A rare day of solitude in the High Tatras.

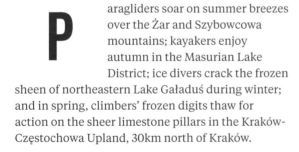

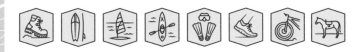

PORTUGAL

This Atlantic-facing Iberian nation may be best known for food and wine, but there's plenty for the outdoor enthusiast, with world-class watersports and terrific trails.

With a whopping 830km of wind-whipped coast, interspersed with cliffs, dune-covered beaches and charming islands, Portugal is perfect for watersports enthusiasts, especially surfers, and the country's unusual river beaches are ideal for wild swimming. Hiking, mountain biking and trail running conditions are sensational, particularly around the granite peaks of Peneda-Gerês and Serra da Estrela. Group all that with the sublime climate and cuisine, and it's easy to see why Portugal's outdoor industry is growing faster than Cristiano Ronaldo's head.

Hiking

Clifftop dunes, pleasingly anachronistic villages, wild orchids, rare black storks, sunshine and surprisingly few walkers make the **Algarve** awesome for hiking; Monchique and Rocha da Pena are good bases. In northern Portugal, trails tiptoe through the mountainous terrain of the country's only national park, **Peneda-Gerês** (which also offers excellent climbing), where huge granite domes protect medieval castles and monasteries, Roman milestones, step-back-in-time villages, fast-flowing rivers, lively vegetation, boulder fields, plus occasional Barrosã cows, roe deer and Iberian wolves. Several lesser-visited natural parks also have great hiking, especially underrated **Serra da Estrela** and its glaciated valley of Vale de Zêzere at the foot of the country's highest peak, Torre (1993m).

Long-distance walks

Rota Vicentina is comprised of two hiking trails: a 120km section of beautiful southwest coast between Santiago do Cacém and Cabo de São Vicente, and the 'historical way', which winds 230km through Sudoeste Alentejano e Costa Vicentina Natural Park, visiting cork-tree forests, villages and valleys. Guided options are available, but both are served by guesthouses. The 300km **Via Algarviana** follows unpaved roads from Alcoutim and Sagres across the width of Portugal via the wooded hillsides of Serras do Calderão and Monchique, while beautiful 540km **GR-22** is a circuit of historic villages in the Beiras region.

DON'T LEAVE WITHOUT...

Embracing Portugal's enigmatic equestrian tradition by riding an iconic Pure Blood Lusitano through the Ribatejo region. These sturdy steeds are used in Portuguese bullfighting, but it's possible to ride them on a far more peaceful adventure.

Paddling amid sea stacks off Praia Dona Ana on Portugal's Algarve coast.

Surfing & Windsurfing

Portugal has surf for all. The gentle warm waves of the Algarve are perfect for learners, whereas, at the other end of the scale, fearsome Nazaré, north of Lisbon, is one the world's biggest surfable waves. Beyond the Algarve, however, you'll need a decent wetsuit, thanks to the cold Atlantic current. **Lisbon** is one of Europe's great surf cities, with urban breaks such as **Carcavelos** and classic surf spots such as **Ericeira** and **Peniche** a short drive north. These breaks get busy, but to the north, away from major centres such as Porto, it's possible to score quiet, quality waves that vary from mellow beach breaks to reeling points. South of Lisbon, you'll find long stretches of empty coastline too. The lovely bay at **Arrifana** with its beach and point breaks is a classic Atlantic experience. Further south, the **Algarve**'s jade green waters are best during winter, when they pick up big swells and make a great break from northern Europe's cold waves.

Praia do Guincho and **Portimão** are world-class windsurfing sites, while the flat seas and strong winds of **Sagres** (the Algarve) also attracts pros. For the less serious, the **Lagoa de Óbidos** is a lovely lagoon frequented by both windsurfers and sailors.

Kayaking

Containing 80 islands and many rivers, Portugal is popular with paddlers. Organised trips and independent sea kayakers explore coves and beaches along the sheltered southern **Algarve coast**, while the **Mondego** offers excellent river boating – launch near Penacova for a relaxing half-day float downriver towards Coimbra. For a bigger challenge, paddle the **Douro**, which flows right across the country (guided trips available).

Diving

There's diving off the mainland, in places including Praia do Carvoeiro, but the **Azores** offers an extraordinary underwater experience. Here, you can go reef, wreck, seamount and cave diving, and potentially encounter manta and devil rays, various sharks (blue, mako, whale), dolphins and whales. Highlights include Rosais Reef (off São Jorge Island) and the Underwater Archaeological Park of the Bay of Angra do Heroísmo (Terceira Island), where the 'Cemetery of Anchors' includes the bones of ships spanning centuries.

Trail Running & Mountain Biking

Portugal's growing trail-running pedigree led to **Peneda-Gerês** hosting the 2016 IAU Trail World Championships, where the world's best rough runners duked it out over a rugged 85km course with 4500m of vertical gain. The beautiful island of **Madeira** stages the country's biggest annual trail race, the Madeira Island Ultra Trail, part of the Ultra-Trail World Series.

Joyous mountain-biking trails can be found in **Peneda-Gerês**, plus **Monchique** and **Tavira** in the Algarve, and **Sintra** and **Setúbal** in central Portugal.

© Juampiter Getty Images

© infografick | Shutterstock

RÉUNION ISLAND

This tiny Indian Ocean island is proof that good things come in small packages.

There ain't much in the way of outdoor activities you can't do on Réunion – a très remote region of France, between Madagascar and Mauritius – thanks to the island's combination of volcanic mountains (soaring up to 3069m), tropical rainforests and wonderful wave-washed coastline.

Les Hauts High Jinx

Réunion has two long-distance **hiking** routes (GR1 and GR2) and more than a thousand kilometres of marked trails, many that traverse the spectacularly diverse World Heritage-listed Réunion National Park, which sprawls across Les Hauts, the island's mountainous interior. The park's steep gorges and tropical rainfall also make for great **canyoning** and **rock climbing**, and in the rainy season (November–March) you can enjoy excellent **whitewater rafting** and **kayaking**.

Mountain Biking

There are rugged routes all over Réunion – Le Maïdo (which reaches 2205m) has 150km of trails on its slopes alone. The island is famed for the annual **Mégavalanche** race, which starts at 2000m and ends on the beach at St Paul on the northwest coast.

Surfing

At St Leu, **surfers** will find one of the world's best left-hand reef breaks. The island also has fine windsurfing and kitesurfing.

ICONIC EVENT
Every October, the Grand Raid ultramarathon sends trailrunners along a brutal 162km route with 9643m of elevation.

Looking out over Cirque de Mafate, which hikers pass on the GR2.

237

ROMANIA

Forget bloodied fangs and dictators, modern Romania offers gorgeous canyons, snow-capped peaks and a delta rippling with adventure.

Rambling through Romania you'll traverse volcanic cones in the Oaş and Harghita ranges, explore copious caves in the Apuseni Mountains, kayak 80 glacial lakes in the Retezat Mountains and meander through meadows swaying with wildflowers on the Moldovan Plains. Heading east, the Buzău River's narrow gorge gushes whitewater, while waterways are calmer in the southern Danube Delta.

Canyoning

Nestled in the Apuseni Mountains, the **Galbenei Canyon** carves deep into a limestone massif creating a gorge with natural arches, caves and hundreds of metres of rock walls. The narrow and chilly channel is fed by an underground spring, creating a canyoner's wet dream with nine waterfalls and abseils up to 15m long. Plucky adventurers can plunge into potholes in places, while underground tunnels add to the allure. The three via ferrata sections can be challenging if it's humid, as steel cables get slippery. Winter wading is a no-no (unless pneumonia's on your 'to-do' list); summertime splashing is the go-go.

Hiking

It would be rude to hike in the Southern Carpathians and not complete one of Europe's longest mountain traverses along the razor ridges of the **Făgăraş Mountains**. The country's highest point, Moldoveanu Peak (2544m), is here, along with more than 150 glacial lakes.

Kayaking

The huge Danube Delta is an ever-changing aquatic labyrinth where guides are essential. Paddle down side-canals, dangle a rod, scythe through swathes of reeds, camp on secluded islands amid sand dunes, and spy a wealth of wildlife, including millions of Egyptian pelicans. A twitcher's dream, the delta has Europe's highest concentration of bird colonies.

DON'T LEAVE WITHOUT...

Rafting the river Buzău (Grade II-III+ rapids), or going one better and kayaking/ canoeing its pretty tributary, Basca, where experienced paddlers can tackle an extra 15km of Grade III-IV rapids in spring.

Retezat National Park in the Southern Carpathian Mountains offers idyllic hiking terrain.

© starush | Getty Images

RUSSIA

The largest country on Earth offers almost unlimited adventure potential, much of which is still relatively unexplored.

R ussia's vast landmass holds everything from epic rolling plains, rugged mountains, colossal forests, endless tundra and active volcanoes. And, though years of communist rule made Russia a closed shop, international tourists, albeit in limited numbers, are slowly starting to gain access to its natural wonders. If you take the trouble to look, you can find extreme mountain bike rides, volcano hikes, challenging trail runs, unique dive locations and some of the biggest, least explored whitewater on the planet. Moscow and St Petersburg are the main entry points, but the 2014 Winter Olympics also put Sochi on the map. Siberia's Lake Baikal and wild Kamchatka are accessible but harder to reach, while the far northern wilderness is one of the world's most remote places. Crimea has huge potential, but it is currently a disputed region (see Ukraine on p291).

Hiking

Kamchatka's remote fumarole fields and bubbling geysers are a challenging, exciting destination. Most of the region is impossible to access, but Gorely and Mutnovsky volcanoes can be reached on a bumpy two-hour drive from Petropavlovsk–Kamchatsky, while Uzon volcano is reachable by helicopter.

    Lake Baikal, the world's oldest and deepest, has a growing trail network, including a three-day route from Listvyanka to Bolshoye Goloustnoye on coastal bluffs, sandy beaches and deep forest. Further east, **Altai** has routes through glacial mountains, river canyons and pristine blue lakes, particularly around Mt Belukha, though serious wilderness and poor trails make a guide essential.

Animal trekking safaris are on offer in **Siberia**, where the Sayansky Canyon leads to **Sayano-Shushensky Reserve** and the (remote) chance to spy rare snow leopards. In **Durminoskoye**, **Lazovsky** and **Zov Tigra** (Tigers' Call) national parks, guided treks seek Siberian tigers and Amur leopards. **Lake Kurile**, in Kamchatka, is a good bet for finding bears; there are so many around that an armed guard is essential.

Lake Baikal is a popular hiking destination, and in winter hikers can venture onto the ice.

© tolstnev | Getty Images

Skiing & Snowboarding

Given Russia's vast size, you might expect more ski resorts than there are – indeed, the only real 'world-class' resort in the country is **Rosa Khutor**, and that's only after a cash injection for the Sochi Winter Olympics (Sochi is actually roughly 40km south of the resort on the Black Sea). Snow conditions here can be hit and miss, while the resort infrastructure and visitor hospitality are, well, Russian, so they're often equally hit and miss. Still, there's an impressive 1760m of vertical, 18 lifts, a terrain park and a good mix of pistes, and some acceptable freeride terrain, too, with few of the rules and regulations of Western resorts (though there are few rescue services if things go wrong). Locals are friendly and happy to ski with overseas visitors, but you do need to be slightly wary of being ripped off, and savvy to the fact that, on occasion, paying a backhander may make things run more smoothly.

Away from Russia's leading resort there's relatively little to tempt visiting skiers unless you like it wild and exciting and have a deep pocket, in which case **heli-skiing** down the spectacular active volcanoes of the Kamchatka Peninsula on the country's Pacific coast is a truly unforgettable, once-in-a-lifetime ski experience.

Cycling
Mountain Biking

In the green season, well-developed downhill MTB operations exist at Sochi's **Gorky Bike Park**, Krasnodar's **Sober Bike Park**, the **Magnitogorsk City** resort and **Metallurg**, near lake Bannoe. Moscow's **Kant Sports Complex** has open trails, whereas the **Mashuk** and **Chaget** mountains are more remote options.

Road

Bike touring is relatively new to Russia, but there are testing climbs in the **Altai Mountains**, lakeside rides at **Baikal** and **Ladoga**, and Arctic adventures under the midnight sun on **Kola Peninsula**. The famous 643km **Golden Ring** tourist trail northeast of Moscow can also be done by bike in about 11 days.

Paddling

The **Altai Mountains** are Russia's top whitewater destination, combining long sections of Grade I–VI rapids with reasonable infrastructure and road access. The Chulyshman, Shavla and Chuya-Katun rivers challenge varying skill levels, but the ultimate test is the 20km journey through Mazhoy Gorge, one of the world's finest sections of whitewater.

The well-populated **Caucasus** region has easily accessible short day runs, while, on the opposite end of the scale, **Putorana**, above the Arctic Circle, is only reachable by helicopter and runnable in July. Virtually unexplored, it is a place for heli-kayaking and expedition-style waterfall hunting.

Climbing

Europe's highest mountain, 5642m-high **Mt Elbrus** is a natural destination for climbers, particularly Seven Summit collectors. Siberia's highest point, the three-peaked **Mt Belukha** (4506m), is extremely remote, but well worth all the planning required.

The big walls of **Bilibino**, in the Chukotka region of Siberia, have only recently been discovered by climbers. These superb granite crags are home to a growing number of trad routes up to 300m high, with almost endless potential remaining for those willing to brave the solitude and mosquitoes. Siberia's **Stolby Natural Reserve** is another, more historic climbing area, where the local ethic is to climb unroped. Try this at your own risk. The disputed region of Crimea is also a fine climbing destination, with many sport and trad routes.

Caving

Russia has unique caves, including **Kungurskaya** in the Urals, which has amazing ice sculptures and an underground lake. Equally beautiful is Kamchatka's 1km-long **Mutnovsky volcano ice tunnel**, created by a hot spring running through the glacier. **Tavdinsk**, in the Altai Mountains, has 30 connected caves for hikers and spelunkers to explore, while Siberia's 200m deep **Bolshaya Oreshnaya Cave** and the 62km-long **Botovskaya Cave** in Irkutsk are more exploratory destinations.

Trail running

A number of popular races have opened up trails, including the **Golden Ring Ultra in Suzdal**, the **Desert Steppes marathon** around Lake Elton, the **TransUral** in the Ural mountains and the **World Elbrus Race**, which uses four permanent marked trails. There are also permanent marked trail runs around **Moscow, St Petersburg** and in the **Urals**.

DON'T LEAVE WITHOUT...
Diving in the Black Sea, which teems with ancient wrecks. Elsewhere, Cape Tarkhankut's 'Alley of the Leaders' is filled with busts of ex-Soviet rulers, while The Barents Sea is home to giant groupers and huge crabs. Hardy sub-sea explorers dive inside the Arctic Circle at Nilmoguba.

Getting up close to a mountain gorilla is an unforgettable experience.

© USO | Getty Images

RWANDA

Gorillas in the mist may rightfully be front and centre, but the brooding volcanoes, flowering forests and hooting chimpanzees will definitely get a word in.

The 'Land of a Thousand Hills' it surely is, though it's a chain of conical-shaped volcanoes in the country's far northwest that really captures visitors' attention. The thick forests on their slopes support numerous species, including almost half of the world's remaining mountain gorillas.

Mountain Gorilla Walks

No matter how exhausting and challenging the steep hike up the volcano is, your energy and excitement levels will hit stratospheric heights the second you catch sight of the first mountain gorilla. Encounters with these incredible creatures in the forested depths of **Volcanoes National Park** last a single hour only, but it will be one of the best of your life. Whether you're watching a baby beat its chest, sharing thoughtful glances with observant females

or marvelling at the sheer scale of the silverbacks, your mind, heart and soul will be united and solely focused. The smallest details of their faces, human-like hands and enchanting eyes will be permanently engraved into your psyche. And then, before you know it, the spell will be broken by three short words: 'Time is up.'

Trekking

The same volcanoes that host Rwanda's gorillas are also brilliant for treks in their own right. You'll climb up through scenic sections of thick bamboo forest, past giant lobelia and flowering hagenia before popping out onto verdant alpine meadows. En route you may spot bushbucks, duikers, genets, forest pouched rats and a plethora of birdlife. And if the weather gods are shining down on you, the views over the rest of the **Virunga** chain volcanoes will be spellbinding.

DON'T LEAVE WITHOUT...
Tracking the newly settled chimpanzees as they make their way across the lofty canopy in Nyungwe Forest National Park.

SAMOA

The classic South Pacific island, Samoa's warm waters offer a permanent invitation to get wet.

S amoa consists of two large islands, Upolu and Savai'i, and eight small islets. The balmy South Pacific climate and warm water make this sublime destination an ideal destination for watersports, with the surfing especially excellent – hardly surprising given the islands' Polynesian culture and exposure to consistent swells – and open-water swimming, snorkelling and diving also popular. When you want to dry off, try climbing to the crater of Savai'i's active volcano on Mount Matavanu.

Surfing

Popular surf spots on **Savai'i** include Lano and Ananoa Beach in the southwest, and Manase and Fagamalo in the north; on **Upolu** check out the breaks from Apia east to Cape Utumauu, and on the south coast from Matautu to Matatufu. The south shores of both islands work all year round, while the north shores are best in the northern hemisphere winter, when you'll be surfing the same swells that hit Hawaii's North Shore – but without the crowds.

Information can be readily accessed at one of several surf camps on both islands, which, as well as ensuring you score the best waves, also use some of your 'fees' towards developing youngsters' education in local villages. They also organise 'surfaris' to ensure you make the most of swell and wind direction.

Samoan waves are not suitable for novices – they usually pack a punch and often break over coral reefs, and the rips and currents can be tricky; it's well worth getting a bit of local advice before you paddle out, especially on bigger swells. Alternatively, try **stand-up paddleboarding** on the calm lagoons inside the reefs.

Diving & Snorkelling

Samoa also has world-class diving and, with water temperature hovering around 25°C, you'll rarely need anything other than a shortie wetsuit. Most dive centres also run organised snorkelling trips if you're not open-water dive qualified. The ocean is home to about 900 species of fish and marine life – including spinner dolphins, stingrays and whales, along with 200 types of coral – and the reefs that surround the islands create beautiful lagoons with easy access for diving. Sites vary from colourful

© Martin Valigursky | Alamy, © Paul Kennedy | Getty Images

DON'T LEAVE WITHOUT…

Going underground in one of Samoa's incredible caves, such as Pa'ape'a Cave on Upolu (with its population of Polynesian swiftlets) or Dwarf's Cave on Savai'i, a surreal subterranean lava tube leading into the underworld.

Left, catching waves near the village of Luatuanuu, Upolu. Opposite page, Samoa is every bit the South Pacific paradise. Overleaf, snorkelling off Savai'i.

hard-coral gardens to dramatic canyon-revealing swim-throughs. One of the best and safest spots is **Apia's Palolo Deep Marine Reserve** at Vaiala Beach, where you'll find a spectacular deep blue hole flanked by steep coral walls that are home to brilliantly coloured tropical fish.

At the fringing reef of **Nuusafee** you can dive on two good, fish-rich sites, the Terraces and the Garden Wall. **The Fish Bowl** near Faleolo International Airport also has a wealth of marine life, while an easily accessible offshore site on **Savai'i** is the wreck of the *Juno*, a three-masted missionary sailing ship that was sunk in 1881.

Kayaking

You can also explore the coast by sea kayak, independently or with organised trips taking in several of the smaller islands. While you're gliding across lagoons the reef is visible beneath the boat, and when open-ocean paddling plenty of sea life can be observed, including turtles.

SAN MARINO

Lose yourself among the rolling green meadows and narrow lanes of this 61 sq km medieval microstate.

Something of an oddity and an anachronism, San Marino – a landlocked island state in the middle of Italy – is Europe's oldest republic and the world's fifth smallest country. Tiny it may be, but active travellers will find ample ground to explore, with steep escarpments and medieval fortresses towering over a chequerboard of neat fields, gentle hills and quaint villages. San Marino might have more vehicles than people, but its topographical tapestry is perfect for hiking, biking and horseback riding. A signature trek traces the steep ridgeline of the republic's tallest peak – **Mt Titano** (756m), a protruding tooth in the Apennine Range – where a trio of looming fortresses and the best view in the country await.

SÃO TOMÉ & PRÍNCIPE

Specks of green in a big blue ocean it may be, but this little-known island nation off West Africa is full of hard-earned jungle adventures.

Where? Exactly! What's more adventurous than visiting a country that nobody you know has ever heard of? The two tropical islands of São Tomé and Príncipe, afloat in the Gulf of Guinea, make up Africa's second-smallest country and provide some intense activities.

Summiting **Pico de São Tomé** (2024m), with its vertical jungle, vines and fallen trees, requires two tough days of trail blazing, and trekking the **Volta à Ilha** along the roadless southwest coast of São Tomé is no walk in park either. To cool off after all that hiking, try walking on water instead at one of the world's most beautiful SUPing spots: the remote **Baía das Agulhas** (Bay of Spires) on Príncipe's wild shoreline.

© Paul Kennedy / Getty Images

A baobab tree in the Siné-Saloum delta, an area best explored by kayak.

SENEGAL

The lifeblood of Senegal, its people and its astounding biodiversity arc its waterways, and for adventure seekers it is much the same.

S enegal's coast and its various river deltas are water-filled wonderlands that provide fulfilling kayak adventures. Inland is a much drier affair, with deserts taking hold of the north and mountains rising in the southeast. The latter provides some great mountain biking terrain, as well as opportunities to learn about unique local cultures.

Kayaking

The mangrove-lined waters of the **Casamance River** and its delta can be explored by kayak, allowing you unparalleled access to the area's habitats and local communities on remote islands. Get a brief taste over a day, or delve deeper with a week-long expedition. You'll be able to meet fishers in the shade of the mangroves, learn how oysters are harvested and begin to understand the Casamance way of life.

More wildlife-oriented kayak trips can be sorted north of The Gambia in the **Siné-Saloum**, part of which is protected as **Parc National du Delta du Saloum**. Also lined with mangroves in areas, this delta is punctuated with salt marshes, islands and thick sections of woodland that host some 36 species of mammal, including spotted hyenas, warthogs and red colobus monkeys. Birdlife is phenomenal here – keep an eye out for goliath herons, dimorphic egrets and dwarf flamingoes.

Mountain biking

Mountain bike across the varying landscapes of **Bassari** country, linking the region's villages by singletrack that has been carved out by locals over decades. Located in the country's southeast, near the borders with Guinea and Mali, the mountainous region is home to the fascinating Bassari, Fula and Bédik peoples.

DON'T LEAVE WITHOUT...
Swimming (or rather floating atop) Lac Rose – its ultra-buoyant and often-pink waters are 10 times more salty than the ocean.

© Robert Harding Productions | Getty Images

SERBIA

Home to four mountain ranges, well-marked trails and spectacular canyons, this relatively tourist-free destination has much to offer the intrepid traveller.

The Dinaric Alps, Carpathians, Balkan and Rilo-Rhodope mountains all cut through this picturesque nation, fast recovered from its war-torn past. Serbia is rich in history, with a mix of cultures, ethnicity and religions, and its remote regions are home to welcoming locals, traditional wooden huts and wholesome home-cooked food. Belgrade is the ideal starting point to access the country's national parks and nature reserves, which number more than 65. In winter, mountain resorts deliver top-quality skiing – indeed, Kopaonik on the Kosovo border is one of Europe's best skiing secrets, with 70km of runs, a good lift network and a long, reliable season.

Hiking

Serbia's highlands are a hikers' paradise. A good starting point is the 13km trek through the karst mountains of **Gradac river gorge**, with wood bridges, old dams and resident otters. For a wilder experience, hit the peaks, canyons and waterfalls of **Tara National Park**. **Medvednik Mountain**, **Trešnjica Gorge**, the high route above **Drina**

Canyon, the circle route around **Tara Mountain** and the 1675m ascent of **Veliki Stolac** are popular routes. **Iron Gates gorge**, in Djerdap National Park, the pyramidal **Rtanj Mountain** and **Midžor peak**, Serbia's highest at 2169m, also offer good trekking.

Cycling

Western Serbia is the place for bikers, with the peak-circling 35km ride from **Mt Divčibare** to **Mt Povlen** a popular option. **Mt Bobija** has some impressive viewpoints, **Trešnjica Gorge** offers short downhills, **Tara National Park** has routes in forest and meadows, and **Mt Radan** has access to the stone pyramids at Djavolja Varoš (Devil's Town). For a longer ride, the **Danube Bike Trail** runs 1040km right through the country.

Paddling

The **Drina River** offers a 22km paddle, taking in Vrelo waterfall and skirting the famous house on the rock. The unique meanders of **Uvac River**, dubbed the 'Serbian Colorado', are a good gentle option, whereas the **Ibar River** has Grade II–IV rapids, which are big and feisty in spring.

ICONIC EVENT
The Fruškogorski maraton is an annual ultramarathon held around Fruška Gora, where trail runners cover distances up to 125km.

Serbia's mountainous terrain is perfect for mountain biking.

SEYCHELLES

The Seychelles may be picture perfect and primed for luxuriating, but dip your head into its cobalt-blue waters and there is a high-voltage world awaiting.

With so much hype about these islands' hypnotic honeymoon beaches, the fact that the Seychelles is one of the Indian Ocean's great diving destinations seems to have been lost among all the superlatives. Revel in this knowledge as you explore beneath the surface at will. You'll have similar feelings atop the country's mountains.

Diving

There are incredible dive opportunities off the three main islands – Mahé, Praslin and La Digue – as well as off the other inner and outer islands. Particularly special is the underwater scenery, which is scattered with seamounts and mammoth boulders of granite.

The signature dive on **Mahé** is Shark Bank, where strong currents around a 30m-tall granite plateau foster incredible encounters with innumerable barracuda, batfish, yellow snapper, round ribbon-tailed rays and 9m-long eagle rays. Despite the name, it's not known for sharks. Disappointed? Don't be. Hit Shark Point where nurse sharks, grey reef sharks and whitetip reef sharks are common. Nearby is Jailhouse Rock, a thrilling drift dive with prolific fish life.

At the exposed seamount of Booby Islet off **Praslin**, you'll experience frenetic action, with Napoleon wrasses, moray eels, parrotfish, turtles, eagle rays and even nurse sharks. White Bank off La Digue features a marvellous series of tunnels and arches to go with its teeming shoals of jacks and other aquatic life.

Near Alphonse Island is the **Arcade**, a magical dive site known for its phenomenal coral gardens and spellbinding variety of fish and huge sea turtles. Another site in this area is the **Pinnacles**, where the reef – festooned with large seafans – plummets into the abyss.

Bouldering

La Digue isn't just good for diving and snorkelling, the granite boulders you swim around are also found on the beach, where multiple problems can be explored with a pair of climbing shoes and a chalk bag. Soft sand makes pads optional.

© RainervonBrandis | Getty Images

> ### DON'T LEAVE WITHOUT...
> Hiking up Morne Blanc (667m), a short but very steep (45% gradient) ascent. The staggering views make every step worth it.

The Seychelles has abundant world-class diving.

SLOVAKIA

From soaring mountains to subterranean mystery, the diversity of the Slovak landscape makes it one of the hidden gems of Eastern Europe.

Stretching across the country, the Carpathian Mountains define the Slovak landscape, just as they define most adventures here. A fantastic venue for climbing and skiing, the Carpathians also hide a myriad of valleys and tarns (alpine lakes) that feed a vast network of rivers. Each changing season brings a new character to the landscape and different opportunities for outdoor enthusiasts.

Hiking

Close to a national obsession in Slovakia, hiking can be as easy or as hard as you make it: guided or solo, winter or summer, hut-based or braving the elements in a tent. Some may be inclined to stick to the lowlands, visiting enchanting forests (40% of Slovakia is forested) and fairytale castles. For the more adventurous, a day hike to the summit of Slovakia's highest point, **Gerlach Peak** (2654m) is a classic target (a guide is recommended). If you like your adventures epic, try an extended traverse of the **High Tatras**, an undertaking that demands excellent levels of fitness.

Climbing

Climbing is a year-round sport on all mediums here, from bouldering to mountain climbing and everything in-between, and the country has produced some top-end alpinists, including Blažej Adam, Tono Krizo and Franktišek Korl, who in 1984 established 'Slovak Direct', widely regarded as the hardest route on North America's highest mountain, Denali. The **Sulov Rocks** – often called the 'Slovak Dolomites' – a jumbled collection of needles and spires composed of a delightful frictional conglomerate, which evoke the turrets of medieval castles, offer good rock climbing. Boulders can be found right across the country, including in the capital **Bratislava**. When the long Slovakian winter takes hold, the mountains truly come into their own with many ice and mixed lines forming

DON'T LEAVE WITHOUT...
Enjoying a relaxing experience with a historical bent, by cruising through Pieniny National Park on wooden raft, a tradition that takes place between May and October, and extends back as far as the 11th century.

© gribernat | Getty Images

Hiking in the High Tatras is close to a national obsession.

in the Tatras. That said, mountaineers seeking the freedom of the hills will unfortunately become the victims of red tape – insurance and membership to a mountaineering club is required.

Skiing & Snowboarding

The long winter is also a key reason behind the popularity of another of Slovakia's favourite mountain sports – skiing. The scope of this sport is staggering, with over 470km of slopes and more than 500 lifts spread over 100 individual resorts. **Tatranská Lomnica** holds the distinction of having the largest vertical drop (1302m).

Even with such expansive infrastructure, ski resorts are just the beginning. If you have the skills to go off-piste, the opportunities for backcountry touring and ski mountaineering are endless. Again, guided or self-guided options abound in the High, Low and Western Tatras. Competent skiers will find varied terrain consisting of open ridges, wooded slopes and steep couloirs.

Paddling

All things must come to an end, even Eastern European winters, and once the sun comes out and the snow melts away, the rivers swell and foam – putting a spring spark into the eyes of the nation's kayakers, canoeists and rafters. Whitewater slalom is modern Slovakia's most successful Olympic sport, and the country has some world-class paddling. The towns of **Liptovský Mikuláš** and **Čuňovo** boast artificial whitewater courses, while the **Dunajec** and **Belá** rivers have natural rapids.

Caving

More adventure can be found below ground in Slovakia in its impressive collection of World Heritage–listed caves. Only a small selection are open to the public, but they offer unique underground experiences, from boating along the 'River Styx' in Domica Cave to ladder and rope traverses in Krásnohorská Cave, and even a natural auditorium where concerts are held in Belianska Cave.

SLOVENIA

Green, rugged, picturesque and surprisingly focused on the outdoors, Slovenia punches far above its weight when it comes to adventure.

Slovenia is a gem. How it has remained off the global adventure radar for so long is astounding. A compact country of preposterously beautiful mountains, thick forests, clear lakes, green meadows, rushing waters and some of the planet's deepest caves, Slovenia has set more of its land in reserves than any other nation in Europe – 60% of the country is still covered in forest. If it's reminiscent of anywhere, it is Switzerland, except that Slovenia, if anything, is more focused on its mountains. Well, actually, one mountain in particular: Triglav. At 2864m it might not rank high in global terms, but that hasn't diminished its importance in Slovenian eyes. The peak is the subject of songs and poems, the namesake of financial institutions and it graces Slovenia's national seal and flag – all of which is emblematic of a culture fixated on the outdoors. Skiing is widely claimed to be the national sport, but it's rivalled by hiking. More than 10,000km of trails criss-cross Slovenia, astonishing for a country no bigger than Wales or Israel. Cycling is also incredibly popular, whether on road or singletrack, touring or bikepacking. On the water, canyoners jump, slide and rappel down plunging creeks; further downstream, rafters and kayakers run turquoise rivers. And there is climbing – a pastime that's the subject of national pride. The big wall and alpine ascents are focused on the spectacular, jumbled terrain of the Julian Alps (pronounced 'Yoolian'), but the Kamnik-Savinja and Karawanks mountains also offer serious alpine routes, and there are sports crags dotted around the country.

Hiking

Presented with 10,000km of trails, Slovenian hikers are spoiled for choice. There are gentle strolls through neat farmlands and quiet forests; conversely, up peaks and across monstrous cliff faces there are sketchy goat tracks blurring the line

DON'T LEAVE WITHOUT...
Scaling Triglav and stating a claim to become an honorary local. According to the adage: 'To be a true Slovenian, you must climb Triglav at least once in your life.'

between hiking and climbing. Many could double as BASE jumping launch pads. Not that this deters the locals. No matter their age or shape – young or old, lean or fat – Slovenians flock to trails of all levels of craziness. Nor does length daunt them. Long-distance paths lace the country, the most popular being the **Slovenian Mountain Trail**, the first national trail in Europe. Over 599km long, it begins in Maribor in the country's east, traverses the Kamnik-Savinja, Karawanks and Julian Alps (including an ascent of Triglav) before weaving through the Karst Region to the Adriatic Sea.

Undoubtedly the jewel in Slovenia's hiking crown is the trail network in **Triglav National Park**. Although Triglav itself is frequently climbed in two days, the park deserves a week. The Julian Alps are monumentally cragged and seriously stunning, far more rugged than their height suggests. For adrenaline-seeking hikers, traversing Kanjavec's north face is recommended, as is ascending Škrlatica, Queen of the Julian Alps; no prizes for guessing the King. And for those preferring not to hike above death-defying drops, the Seven Lakes Valley offers a succession of larch-studded meadows and crystal lakes.

Skiing

More than 40 ski areas are spread across Slovenia. As popular as skiing is, however, most areas are small compared to many found in nearby Austria, Italy or Switzerland, although this is often more than compensated for by Slovenian friendliness and low prices. **Kranjska Gora** is an internationally renowned area, but freeskiers and boarders wanting decent off-piste are advised to head to **Vogel** or **Kanin**. Even then, hardcore chargers may be left wanting more. The backcountry, however, is a different story. Although mellow routes exist, sphincter-clenching lines abound through the **Karawanks**, **Kamnik-Savinja** and **Julian Alps**. It's no coincidence that the first skier to descend Everest was Slovenian.

Cliffs overlook Seven Lakes Valley in Triglav National Park.

© Matic tojs | Alamy

Road Cycling

With its quiet country roads, luscious vistas and challenging mountain passes, Slovenia is a roadie's delight. Not surprisingly, the **Julian Alps** are a highly recommended destination. Cyclists seeking alpine epics can tackle the passes of Predel or Vršič or even the 20km ascent to the Mangart Saddle (2040m), one of Europe's most stunning climbs. For cyclists wanting easier days in the Julians, the Soča River valley is insanely beautiful – a mix of emerald waters, lush meadows and stupendous peaks.

Mountain Biking

Slovenia is riddled with superb singletrack, but there's a catch: riding on most forest trails is technically illegal. That said, the rules are rarely enforced, although they can be, especially in Triglav National Park. Nonetheless, the illegality is one reason MTBers tend to keep quiet about local trails, and discovering great Slovenian singletrack is best done via a guide – dozens of companies offer excellent trips of up to a week. Alternatively, visit one of the many MTB parks. Both **Maribor** and **Kranjska Gora** have high gnar-factor trails, although you can dial it down at both if you wish.

Bikcpacking

The **Slovenian Mountain Bike Route** (STKP) loops the entire country. Completed in 2016, this signposted mix of quiet roads, farm paths, forest trails and logging tracks covers 1800km and visits all of Slovenia's major mountain groups and passes. Although rarely technically demanding, with 50,000m of climbing it's certainly challenging physically. Along the way, 52 mountain huts offer accommodation, and it frequently passes railway stations so riders who don't have the time (or stamina) to complete the whole route can use trains.

Climbing

Kotečnik in the country's east is Slovenia's largest climbing area, with 330-plus routes. But clustered in the southwest corner, not far from the Adriatic Sea, are a trio of cragging areas just kilometres apart: **Črni Kal** (the country's second largest area), **Osp** and **Mišja peč**, which has Slovenia's hardest sports climbing, with routes to 9a+.

Historically, however, it's big wall climbing that's captured the country's attention. Three classic climbs are the north faces of **Travnik**, **Špik** and **Triglav**. The latter – breathtakingly immense at 3km wide and 1200m high – is so well known it is simply called Stena (The Wall). There have been at least 100 ascent variations, from the Slovenian Route (II+) to the legendary čop Pillar (VI) to Ulina Smer (IX), first climbed in 2011.

Water Sports

Canyoning has exploded in popularity in recent years. It's not just that Slovenian canyons are beautiful – they're downright fun. More than many areas, canyons here are natural water parks, and slides and jumps abound. The area surrounding **Bovec** is particularly popular with guided operators, which offer everything from easy descents of the **Sušec Gorge** to far more demanding trips down the waterfalls of **Globoški Potok**. In fact, Bovec is probably *the* place for watersports in Slovenia; not only canyoners but kayakers and rafters flock here, most notably for the exquisitely turquoise **Soča River** (with Grades I–IV).

Below, rafting the Soca River. Left, expect plenty of climbing while bikepacking through Slovenia, particularly in the Julian Alps.

© Sean Cooper; Simonkr d.o.o. | Getty Images

SOUTH AFRICA

The Rainbow Nation offers a dazzling spectrum of adventure sports and outdoor challenges, from extreme paddling events to epic overland trails.

For outdoor types, there's something tangibly exciting about visiting South Africa (SA). It's not simply the variety of terrain – although that is stunning, from the untamed Wild Coast and the gorgeous almost-tropical Garden Route to Drakensberg Mountains and the remote Richtersveld, the oldest mountain desert in the world. Nor is it down to the sublime weather or wonderful wildlife, it's because you know you're among kindred spirits. Every dawn, people all over the country can be found outdoors – mountain biking through Cape Town's Table Mountain National Park, catching waves at Jeffreys Bay, cycling up Chapman's Peak or training for the Comrades Marathon. They love their sports here and the evidence is all around you, from well-marked trails to incredible events and the inescapable fact that Saffas box well above their population weight and have produced world champions in almost every discipline imaginable, from mountain biking and surfski to paragliding and trail running.

Mountain Biking

Multi-stage races such as the Cape Epic – an eight-day, 700km-plus challenge often referred to as mountain biking's Tour de France – have put South Africa on the MTB map, but there's more to riding in SA than gruelling challenges. The country boasts many miles of mind-blowing singletrack and has an ever-growing cycling community. One of the few downsides to South Africa is the security situation and the biggest dilemma visiting bikers face is knowing where it's safe to ride. Nine times out of 10 you'll be OK, but often it's best not to ride on your own – you're simply inviting trouble. This is one reason why so many mountain bike clubs exist, adopting the 'safety in numbers' approach. So if you don't know anyone, simply contact a local club and ask if you can join their weekend ride – they're almost guaranteed to say yes.

Western Cape

With Cape Town at its centre, the Western Cape is the stuff of off-road dreams. As soon as you get off the plane, bikers will be drawn to **Table Mountain National Park** like moths to a flame. **Silvermine Nature Reserve**, **Black Hill** and **Cape Point** are ever popular locations (note: you'll need a day permit from the SANParks to ride anywhere within the National Park). And once you've exhausted Cape Town, head to **Stellenbosch** where a selection of singletrack, including the Dirtopia Trails, awaits.

The Drakensberg

The longest mountain range in South Africa is littered with trails. The Northern and Central Drakensberg have some of the best trails, from **All Out Adventure**'s farm near Bergville, where 150km of groomed singletrack has been created, to the more established and challenging trails around **Cathedral Peak**. Downhill purists will love the notorious **Bezuidenhouts Pass** – a rock-strewn skill-testing descent.

Johannesburg

Naturally, South Africa's largest city, Johannesburg, has an extremely active MTB community and you only need to head 50km north of the city to find some of the country's best mountain biking, between Jozi and Pretoria. The standout is **Northern Farms** in Lanseria, Gauteng – Jo'burg's best kept MTB secret, it's good for beginners and experts with a series of marked trails and some super technical sections for those looking to scare themselves. Another top spot is the **Van Gaalen**

Cheese Farm, situated about an 80-minute drive north of Jo'burg at the foot of the Magaliesberg Mountains, which boasts over 100km of purpose-built trails, including lots of sensational singletrack.

Singletrack Safaris

South Africa has more multi-stage bike races than any other country (more than 50 at last count) such as the **Joberg2c** (900km paired race between Heidelberg in Gauteng and Scottburgh on the KwaZulu-Natal coast) and **Sani2c** (Sani to Scottburgh). The **Tour de Tuli** – a 300km, four-day ride through the Tuli Block of southern Africa, connecting Botswana, Zimbabwe and South Africa – is essentially a safari on two wheels, with a competitive edge. For a more immersive, but equally quintessentially African MTB experience, head to

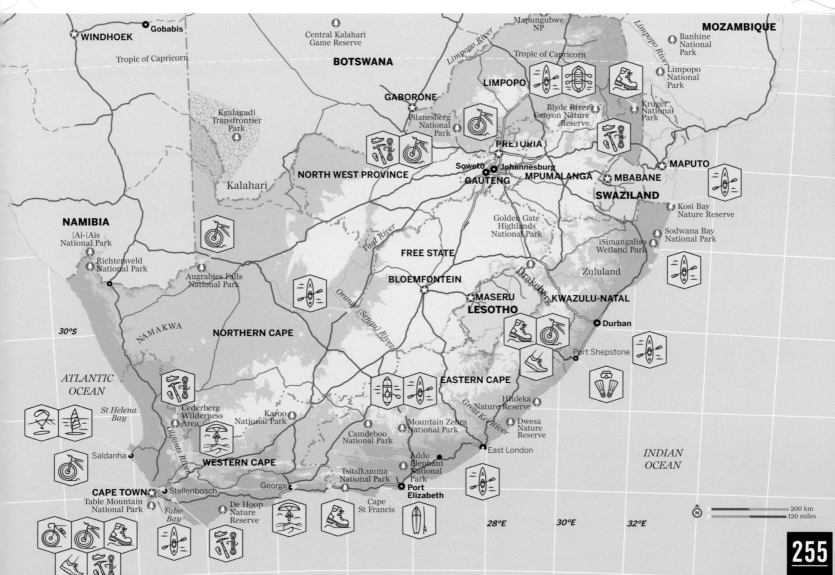

Cape Town has great trail running only a short distance from town.

the Green Kalahari and explore the lunar rockscapes of **Augrabies Falls National Park**, where you'll ride in tranquillity along a 36km trail in the company of giraffe and springbok. Another park that allows bikes is the **Garden Route National Park**, where the Harkerville, Diepwalle and Farleigh trails are highly rated.

Road Riding

South Africa is home to the world's largest individually timed race, the **Cape Town Cycle Tour**. Every March, some 35,000 cyclists take on the 109km route (which you can independently ride at any time of the year), pedalling a scenic loop of Cape Town and the Table Mountain National Park. Cape Town may not have the cols of the Alps or Pyrenees, but cycle up **Chapman's Peak** in high winds, and you'll think you're on the Col du Tourmalet, until you look up and suck in the spectacular coastal views stretching off across the Indian and Atlantic Oceans. No ride is complete without a cake and caffeine stop, and South Africa offers many enticing cycle-friendly coffee shops where you can sip on lattes in the company of other lycra-clad enthusiasts. It's worth noting that most of Cape Town's inhabitants ride at first light, getting their training done before work while simultaneously making the most of the quiet roads and cooler temperatures.

Hiking

Although you're likely to be in the company of a guide (safety and logistics play a large part in this), South Africa is home to some spectacular trekking trails that figure on many people's bucket lists. For a truly authentic South African experience, try a walking safari in **Kruger National Park**, where local guides lead small groups on foot through the bush in search of the Big Five, staying overnight in tented camps. South Africa's most famous hiking experience is the coast-hugging **Otter Trail** on the Garden Route. Guides take trekkers along the 45km route over five days, which sounds slow, but when you see the technical rocky terrain and the Bloukrans river crossing, you'll understand. Adventure seekers will be seduced by one of South Africa's newest trails, the **Rim of Africa**. This guided 650km traverse of the Cape Mountains, stretching from the Cederberg to the Outeniqua mountains, can be split into nine seven-day through-hikes, or tackled as one epic amble between September and November.

uKhahlamba–Drakensberg Park

The highest mountain range in South Africa, the Drakensberg is a three-hour drive from Durban. This surreally dramatic section of southern Africa's Great Escarpment allegedly inspired Tolkien's Middle Earth, and one look at the Amphitheatre will certainly get your imagination running wild. There are literally dozens of hikes to choose from, but the pick of the bunch is the **Drakensberg Traverse**, a 220km-ish route that crosses many of the 'Berg's biggest peaks, all of which are over 3000m and sport evocative names such as Champagne Castle and Mont aux Sources. It takes most hikers 12 days to complete this unmarked, life-changing trail. For those less adventurous or more time-poor, the numerous day hikes around **Giant's Castle Nature Reserve** offer an opportunity to explore caves and admire ancient cave paintings or, if time allows, head up the escarpment to get one of the world's best views.

© subman | Getty Images

© George Brits | Getty Images

Trail Running

Take a casual glance at a South African running magazine and you'll think the country is in the grip of a trail-running fever. You could race every weekend for several years and still not repeat the same event. Again, the fact that it's often wise to run in the company of others – especially in remote locations that you're unfamiliar with or in tourist hotspots like Cape Town, where muggings are a frequent occurrence – is one reason why so many trail running events exist, with 50% of the competitors being women. Certainly another reason, though, is the outstanding topography, with dramatic coastlines, ancient forests, mountain deserts, ridgelines and wild beaches all screaming out to be scampered across. Sections of many iconic hiking routes, such as the Garden Route's **Otter Trail** and the **Drakensberg Grand Traverse**, are used by off-road runners; famously, in 2014, South Africa trail runners Ryan Sandes and Ryno Griesel completed the super-technical 220km Drakensberg Traverse in just 41 hours 49 minutes.

Western Cape

One of the most active trail running communities can be found in **Cape Town**. With **Table Mountain** as a backdrop, it's hard not to be inspired to venture off onto the waymarked trails of the national park. Keep your wits about you, though, as the terrain is fairly technical and during the summer months, snakes such as the cape cobra are a regular sight.

Eastern Cape

If golden sandy beaches, grassy headlands and coastal forests pique your interest then head to the **Wild Coast**, named after the numerous ship wrecks dotted along the coastline. It's a fairly under-the-radar location (possibly thanks to the lack of phone coverage), but the **Jikeleza Route** is a good way to get a taster of this beautiful location.

Paddling

Thanks to warm weather encouraging year-round aquatic adventures along myriad majestic rivers and the country's curvaceous 2735km of coastline,

Rugged cliffs and high peaks line the Injisuthi Valley in the Drakensberg mountains.

South Africans are big into their boats, and the country has some of the planet's most prestigious paddling challenges.

River Racing

South Africa has more high-profile marathon races than you can point a paddle at, from the four-day **Berg River Marathon** in the Cape to the **Hansa Fish** in Cradock, but the most famous is the **Dusi**. Founded in 1951, the 120km run from Pietermaritzburg to Durban attracts almost 2000 kayakers, paddling everything from K1s (solo boats) to K3s. Taking place in mid-February, when the rivers are at their fullest due to late-summer rainfall, this four-day adventure is high on many paddlers' bucket lists. The two-day 67km **Umkomaas marathon** is another challenging event, with multiple rapids making it arguably the world's roughest kayaking race.

ICONIC EVENT
First run in 1918, Comrades Marathon is the oldest ultra-marathon in the world. The 90km race between Durban and Pietermaritzburg changes direction each year, and attracts almost 20,000 runners and five times that many supporters.

Safaris

To test your whitewater skills outside of a race, go kayaking or rafting down the crystal clear **Blyde River Canyon** in Mpumalanga, a beautiful but boisterous bit of riparian paradise. But it's not all about chasing rapids. For something a little more relaxing, try a canoe safari, where you can paddle among hippos in the waters of Maputaland's coastal lakes – **St Lucia**, **Sibaya** and **Kosi Bay** – or take an open boat down the **Orange** or **Breede** rivers in the Western Cape.

Surfski

Ocean skis and surfskis – long, super-sleek, ultra-light, fast-moving sit-on-top kayaks used to harness currents, winds and ocean swells – evolved from craft paddled by surf lifesavers. Arguably the art was defined and refined in South Africa, and the country continues to produce champions, from Sean Rice

and 12-time Molokai champion Oscar Chalupsky, to the legendary Mocké family. In the Cape Town suburb of **Fish Hoek**, you can take lessons with four-time Surfski World Champion Dawid Mocké and his wife Nikki (women's world champ) at their Varsity College Surfski School. Fish Hoek is also the finish of possibly the toughest one-day surfski race of the year: the 50km **Cape Point Challenge**. No matter when you visit, it's possible to tackle a small section of this event – the **Miller Run** – a famous downwind paddling route from Millers Point to Fish Hoek. And there are plenty of other events to choose from: masochists might be tempted by the biannual 250km four-day race from **Port Elizabeth** to **East London**, while travelling paddlers will be interested in the **Pete Marlin Surfski Race** on East London's Wild Coast. And those looking for a taste of history will head to **Durban** for the world's oldest surfski race – the **Illovo Pirates Umhlanga Pirates Surfski Race**.

Surfing

Flanked by the Indian and Atlantic Oceans, and with hundreds of beaches and breaks along its near-3000km coastline, South Africa is one of the most popular places on the planet for surfing. Ever since Bruce Brown's 1966 classic documentary *The Endless Summer*, one particular section along the Garden Route in the Eastern Cape has drawn surfers in search of the perfect wave. **Cape St Francis** is certainly worth a visit, but carry on down the coast to **Jeffreys Bay** – one of the world's finest surfing spots, host to Billabong Pro ASP World Tour surfing events and home to arguably the best right-hand point break on Earth.

Alternatively, for white-sand beaches, head to the Western Cape, where you'll share the chilly surf with dolphins and penguins. Many head to trendy **Camps Bay**, but to escape the crowds try **Llandudno** or False Bay-facing **Muizenberg**.

Further west still, **Saldanha Bay** offers excellent **kitesurfing** and **windsurfing**, and superb **stand-up paddleboarding**.

Climbing

Thanks to its vast mountain ranges and rocky shorelines, South Africa is home to some of the southern hemisphere's most beautiful and interesting crags. (Note: within conservation areas,

such as the Cederberg, you need a bouldering/climbing permit.)

There's near-enough a lifetime's worth of routes to explore around Cape Town, with Table Mountain and the national park dominating the landscape, but two-and-a-half hours' drive north will take bouldering fanatics to the **Cederberg Wilderness** area, where you'll find the **Rocklands**, one of the world's best bouldering areas, which is home to an enormous variety of beautiful sandstone boulders, including one of the world's hardest (and highest) lines, Nalle Hukkataival's Livin' Large (V15). Sites in the nearby **Rooiberg**, **Sanddrif Crag** or **Truitjieskraal** offer sport climbing.

For dedicated sport climbers, though, there's only one place to dine out in South Africa: The Restaurant (at the end of the Universe) crags, aka **Waterval Boven**, two-and-a-half hours east of Jo'burg. With more than 700 graded routes up to Grade 33, this isn't simply South Africa's premier sport-climbing spot, it's one of the best in the world.

Kloofing

You may not have heard of a kloof, but this is the name South Africans give to what we call a canyon. And South Africa has a lot of kloofs to explore. Kloofing is typically a guided activity, and one of the best places to whet your appetite is

Above, Wolfsberg Arch in the Cederberg Wilderness. Left, boys paddle out from Cape Town.

© stdman | Getty Images. © Sara Winter | Alamy

Cage diving with great white sharks at False Bay.

the Western Cape's **Hottentots Holland Nature Reserve** near Grabouw. Beginners will first tackle Riviersonderend Canyon, which takes them hiking, swimming and jumping along a 15km river trail, before perhaps progressing to steeper Suicide Gorge, with its majestic waterfalls and a 14m jump. Another cracking adventure can be had in Grootkloof near Johannesburg, home to some of the best kloofing in the **Magaliesburg** region. What begins as a gentle hike leads to a two-hour adrenaline-filled experience, abseiling down waterfalls and bum sliding down chutes, all while taking in the spectacular views.

Diving

With two oceans and thousands of kilometres of coastline to explore, South Africa is a divine diving destination. Thanks to the Mozambique Current,

the warm waters of the **east coast** are packed full of kaleidoscopically colourful fish, not to mention sharks, dolphins, whales and turtles. Head to the colder waters surrounding **Cape Town** and you'll see a whole new world, full of flourishing kelp forests including several species endemic to the Western Cape. **False Bay** has one of the most remarkable kelp forests, home to Cape fur seals and a large variety of unusual sharks, including pyjama catsharks, puffadder shysharks, spotted gully sharks and, rather unusually, the sevengill broadness shark. South Africa is famous for the incredible **sardine run**, which takes place between May and July, when millions of fish make the baffling journey from the Cape to KwaZulu-Natal, followed by droves of fishermen, sharks and, of course, divers. With its cool waters and large seal population, South Africa has a large population of **great white sharks** and people with a desire to look an apex man-eating predator in the eyes can do **cage dives** (for which you don't actually need to be open water qualified, and will probably only wear snorkelling equipment). At **Protea Banks**, off the coast from Margate, you can come out from the cage and dare to dive with the remaining 'Big Five' sharks: tiger, sand tiger, bull and hammerhead. For something a bit different, you can even try **Crocodile Cage Diving** at Cango Wildlife Ranch in Oudtshoorn – where you'll meet 4m Nile crocodiles, animals with a bite pressure four times more powerful than a great white shark.

Paragliding

Hosting 300 paragliding sites spread among the nine provinces and all-year flying, South Africa is a thermal paradise for paragliders. Almost half of the world paragliding records are set by South Africans, so it's clearly a good place to earn your wings. (Note: the South African Hang Gliding and Paragliding Association – SAHPA – requires all foreign pilots to get a temporary three-month licence, on the basis that licence qualification standards are built around local conditions.) If you're experienced, Cape Town's **Table Mountain** is one of the most spectacular places to fly, offering panoramic views of the Cape Peninsula. Two hours north you'll find **Porterville**, a town practically built around paragliding, with **Dasklip Pass** being a must. Head along the Garden Route and you'll find **George**, which offers plenty of paragliding spots from Hersham to Pencils.

© Danita Delimont | Alamy

SPAIN

Between its ocean beaches and alpine reaches, Spain is a deliciously diverse paradise for conquistadors of the great outdoors.

Whatever your adventure tipple, there's something very alluring about Spain. Perhaps it's the balmy climate and copious sunshine. Or the fact that the Spanish have perfected the art of having fun and challenging themselves, all amid utopian-esque scenery and fine cuisine. But probably the main reason is this: Spain is a topographical marvel, often described as Europe's second-most mountainous country (after Switzerland). Whatever the veracity of that bold claim, it's certainly got more than enough lumpy bits – from the Pyrenees in the north to the Sierra Nevada in the south – to satisfy adventurers of every persuasion. Within an abundance of cycling routes, it boasts some of the best climbing in Europe, as epitomised by the multistage road race, Vuelta a España, with the Catalonian centre of Leida hosting a lifetime's supply of rides. On 60,000km of waymarked footpaths, hikers will want to take it slow, while trail runners won't know what to do with themselves. Then there's the cornucopia of rivers speeding their way to the enormous coastline – both Atlantic and Mediterranean – making it a diving and paddling paradise. The final cherry on

the adventure cake is Spanish culture and history, from drinking sangria and dining on tapas after a long ride to hiking ancient byways in the footsteps of pilgrims – adventure here is part of an rich and varied tapestry.

Trail running

If you've ever done a European trail race, there's a high likelihood you'd have come across a Spaniard on your travels. More often than not, they're the ones laughing as they deftly spring from one rock to another with baffling ease and confidence. Despite this being a somewhat deflating experience for flatlanders, there's a good reason for this prowess on the trails. Spain is a geographical conundrum of opposing worlds – from the desert-like conditions in Andalucía to technical mountain trails in the Pyrenees, the Spanish are fortunate enough to have every type of terrain you could dream of.

Although the country can trace its trail running roots to the 1920s, when it organised various mountain races called 'Copa de Hierro' (Iron Cup) in Madrid's National Guadarrama Park, it's only in the past couple of decades that Spain's prowess on the trails has exploded. Having produced multiple

HOMEGROWN ADVENTURE HERO

Super runner Kílian Jornet, raised in a Pyrenean mountain hut, explains what's special about Spain's trails: 'Everywhere in Spain is cool to run in. Firstly, year-round good weather. There are also ranges like the Pyrenees, Picos de Europa, Riglos, Sierra Nevada… And then there are mountains where no one would think – like in the Balearic Islands, where trails are accessible all year round but are still challenging.'

world champions, including Kílian Jornet and Luis Alberto Hernando, the Spanish are dominating the skyrunning and trail running scene.

It won't come as a great surprise to you that most of the trail running races tend to take place in the mountains, and your first port of call should be the **Pyrenees**. From the Ordesa and Monte Perdido National Park to the Aiguestortes and Lake Sant Maurici National Park, it's a labyrinth of mind-blowing trails. Which is probably why you'll find there are so many world-class skyrunning and trail running events, from the **Buff Epic Trail** and **Ultra Pirineu** to the legendary **Zegama-Aizkorri**. Or you could test your metal on the **GR11 national trail**, which crosses the entire mountain range.

Another notable hot spot is the **Sierra Nevada**

in Andalucía, which is home to the second highest mountain range in Western Europe outside the Alps, and includes the highest peak in Spain, the 3482m-high Mulhacén.

Hiking

If you're looking for good weather, a bit of sun and stunning scenery to match, then Spain is one of Europe's best places to lace up your hiking boots and hit the trails. And although recreational hiking is still relatively new in Spain, 60,000km of waymarked routes are more than enough to keep you busy.

Similar to France and other European countries, Spain has adopted the Gran Recorrido (GR) method of signposting its trails. These are the long-distance

Right, paddling through Seville on the Guadalquivir River.

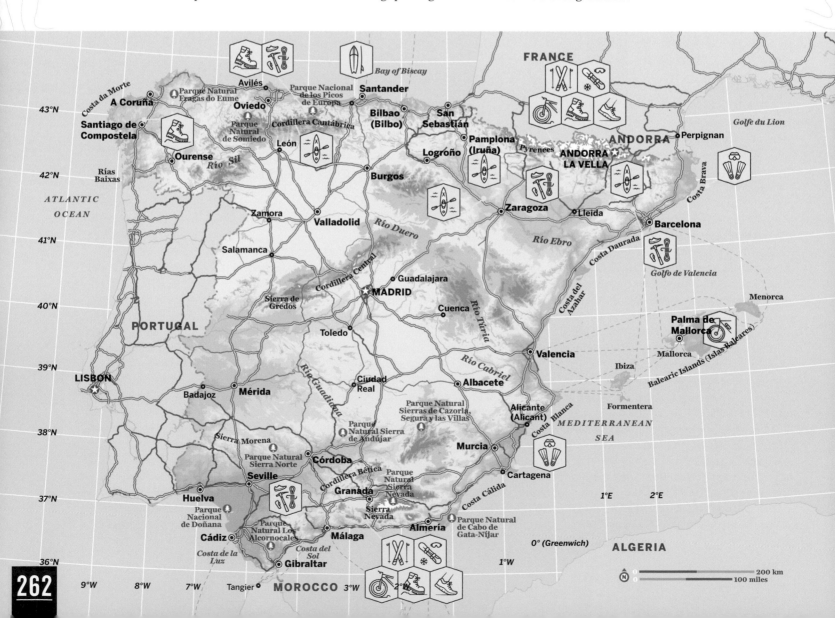

trails of 50km or more, marked by red and white stripes, which generally take a few days to a few weeks to complete. From a hiker's perspective, it might appear that all trails lead to Santiago de Compostela with a veritable conveyor belt of pilgrims heading along one of the ancient Caminos to the supposed burial site of Saint James. But there are, in fact, more than a hundred other long distance paths to choose from.

After the **Camino**, one of the most popular is the 820km **GR11**, Spain's version of the GR10 that traverses the Pyrenees. It passes through several national parks, including the glacial valley of the **Ordesa and Monte Perdido National Park**, home to Europe's deepest canyon. And slightly further along, you'll find **Aigüestortes National Park**, which is littered with fabulous paths and itineraries, including the **Carros de Foc**, which leads hikers through beautiful meadows and forests.

However, if you've not got a month to spare, then the Pequeno Recorrido (PR) are your next best bet. Ranging from 10km to 50km, and symbolised by yellow-and-white markings, these are ideal for those looking for a short break. The limestone massif of the **Picos de Europa** has some of the most spectacular routes and should certainly be added to any hiker's bucketlist, as should the Roman mines of **Las Medulas** in León province.

Speaking of lists, peak baggers will find it hard to resist heading to the **Sierra Nevada** to tackle the 3479m-high **Mulhacén**, the highest peak in the Iberian peninsula. It has panoramic views of the Mediterranean and you'll be able to cherry-pick your trails or pluck up the courage to negotiate the newly marked GR240 that encircles the park.

There are also shorter hiking trails – Sendero Local – indicated by green and white markers, or yellow and white for the Sendero de Pequeno Recorrido, but these tend to be in various states of disrepair, so come prepared to beat your path.

Paddling

Although whitewater rafting or kayaking might not be the first activities that spring to mind when you think of Spain, it's home to a plethora of awe-inspiring rivers and 8000km of coast, and should be on every paddler's destination list.

For those in search of rapids, one river sits head and shoulders above all others: the **Noguera**

Pallaresa, Spain's premier river for whitewater kayaking and rafting, and one of the top rivers in Europe. With 55km of Grade II–IV rapids, you'll be hard pressed to find more fun in such a short space of time.

If you're looking for something more relaxing, following the 'slow travel' theme, then the **Sella River** in Asturias will pique your curiosity. Outside the crazy carnival that takes place around the annual International Descent race, you'll usually have it to yourself.

The longest river in Spain, the **Ebro**, is an excellent option for those looking for a multiday adventure. Some rivers, such as the **Gállego** in Aragon, allow you to paddle all year round, but the best time is typically between spring and summer, when the rivers are at their fullest.

ICONIC EVENT
The International Descent of the Sella River is a madcap race, which, since 1929, has seen thousands of paddlers jostling for position during a 20km sprint down the river.

© Margaret Stepien | Lonely Planet

Mountain Biking

Spain has some of Europe's very best mountain biking – it's almost as if the valleys, hills and mountains have been geologically crafted into continuously flowing singletrack. One of the most impressive regions to ride is the **Catalan Pyrenees**. Culturally it's fascinating, but from a riding perspective it will blow your mind. There's massive variety, from technical and steep singletrack to rooty forested sections and everything in-between. What's more, there are dirt roads leading to most of the passes, meaning that if you have access to a van lift (through a tour operator or a willing friend), then you can avoid having to grind your way up the steep hills.

One of Spain's best-kept secrets is the **Transpirenaica**, a coast-to-coast traverse of the Pyrenees, which is a bikepackers dream. Those with a competitive streak, however, will want to tackle the **TransPyr MTB race**, but if you take it on, prepare for around 800km of racing laced with 20,000m of climbing.

Spain also has a large number of bike parks, with some of the best being **La Molina**, **La Pinilla** and **Zona Zero**. However, cross-country purists searching out sweeping singletrack will love the trails around the 860 sq km park in Andalucían **Sierra Nevada**.

Road Cycling

Cycling fanaticism reaches new heights in northern Spain – **Basque Country** – where roads are lined with red-and-green-flag-waving fans during the annual **Vuelta a España** race. Outside of that three-week tour (which is typically staged in September), this verdant corner of the country is an ideal landscape to discover on two wheels. There's art in Bilbao, food in San Sebastián and great wine everywhere. It's worth noting that the main roads in Spain tend to be wide and fast; equip yourself with detailed maps to stay off them. There are also a number of tour operators offering guided cycling tours in this corner of the country.

Another area that has a high concentration of on-the-ground cycling guides is **Andalucía**. Away from the coastal cities, this is an extraordinary place to explore as it is suffused with Moorish history, culturally rich cities such as Seville, and remote rural expanses. It's easy to thread together a week's worth of riding on the high-country roads through the whitewashed villages of the Alpujarras, and transport connections are excellent thanks to the coast's resorts.

In the Catalan northeast of Spain, beyond Barcelona, lies another cycling heartland. This is where many pro riders base themselves, particularly around Girona, for here the **Pyrenees** descend to the Mediterranean.

But it is Spain's **Balearic Islands** that hold the greatest promise for road cyclists. Mallorca, which receives frequent flights from Europe and ferries

Sierra Nevada has some of Spain's – not to mention Europe's – best mountain biking.

© Andy McCandlish

from mainland Spain, is one of the continent's top destinations for bike riders. Why? This compact island, 75km north to south, has every type of terrain from central plains criss-crossed with stone wall-lined lanes to the Tramuntana mountain range along the west coast. These hills are hugely popular winter training grounds for pro and amateur cyclists; base yourself in Sóller or Port de Pollença and you can follow sinuous roads through them. In winter, almond blossom brightens the lower slopes and later, as the weather warms, so the aroma of wild herbs permeates the air. Sea views add to the magic of this island, as do plentiful pretty villages, where cyclists can stop for snacks.

Snowsports

The Alps might hog the limelight when it comes to snowsports, but considering Spain's impressive peaks, it shouldn't surprise you to learn that there are one or two (34 to be precise), ski resorts begging to be explored.

Although spread all over the country, the vast majority sit high in the **Spanish Pyrenees**, with the biggest and most popular ski resorts situated 200km north of Barcelona in the Arán and Boi valleys of Catalonia. With 2166 hectares of slopes, Baqueira Beret, thanks to its excellent snow cover and extensive piste and off-piste skiing, is Spain's biggest and most popular resort.

However, if you're looking for guaranteed sun and snow then you'll want to head down to **Sierra Nevada** in Andalucía – the southernmost ski resort in Europe. Thanks to its proximity to the coast (which you can see from the slopes), it's one of the few places in Europe where you can surf in the morning and ski in the afternoon.

Surfing

If you're a fan of surfing, bodyboarding or even SUPing, Spain – with its fabulous selection of beaches, huge variety of waves and the all important sunny climes – is a happy haven.

Due to the country's colossal coastline, there are naturally plenty of options, from the beaches of **Mundaka** in the Basque Country down to **Yerbabuena** in Cádiz. But the current hot spot for anyone calling themselves a surfer is the **Cantabria** province on the northern coast, known as Green Spain. Regardless of whether you're looking for

a beach break in Los Locos or a point break at El Muro, at the southern edge of the Bay of Biscay you'll find it all – including the country's first and only surf nature reserve in **Ribamontan al Mar**. It was here that the first surfboards in Spain were made. And thanks to the long exposed coastline bordering the North Atlantic, there's guaranteed swell. If you don't mind the cold, then the best time to go is in the autumn and winter, where the deep lows track across the ocean, producing monster waves as high as 5m.

Hikers pass through the lovely Mallorcan towns of Sóller with Fornalutx on Ruta 13.

© Andrew Montgomery | Lonely Planet

Climbing

Thanks to its mountainous topography and excellent weather, Spain has become recognised as Europe's best sport-climbing destination, particularly during winter. Stretching from the limestone gorge of El Chorro in Andalucía, to the peaks of the Picos de Europa in Asturias, there is something for everyone. But perhaps the pick of the bunch is the autonomous community of **Catalonia**, in particular, the area to the north of Lleida, which has the highest concentration of crags in the region. Here you will find a roll call of the world's best crags: Oliana, Terradets, Riglos, Rodellar, to mention a few.

Also worthy of a visit is the mountain of a hundred summits – otherwise known as **Montserrat**. Offering 200m- to 300m-long routes, you'll be hard pushed to find better multipitch sport climbing in Spain.

Diving

It's not for nothing that Spain is referred to as the 'Caribbean of Europe'. There are literally hundreds of dive sites all over the country. One of the best can be found among the islands of **Las Medes**, along the Costa Brava. Brimming with marine life, from scorpion fish and octopus to stingrays and conger eels, you'll also find a plethora of shipwrecks.

However, one of Spain's best-kept diving secrets is the **Costa Calida and Islas Hormigas Marine Reserve**. Situated in Murcia province, this micro-climate boasts 315 days of sunshine a year and is subsequently teeming with marine life.

The main diving season is between March and November, but with water temperatures ranging from 10°C to 28°C, it's possible to dive year-round. For most of Spain you'll need diving insurance (and in Andalucía, you'll also need to have a dive medical certificate less than two years old).

Margalef, near Lleida in Catalonia, is one of the world's great sport climbing areas.

SRI LANKA

Once known as the Teardrop of India, Sri Lanka makes adventure chasers cry with joy as they explore the island's treasure trove of opportunities.

ith its sublime coastline, Sri Lanka has long been regarded as a delicious diving destination, due to a feast of great wreck and reef diving, but it's also a superb country for surfing and hiking.

Diving & Snorkelling

Where you dive in Sri Lanka depends on timing, since the monsoon seasons vary across the island. October–May is high season along the west and southwest coasts, and May–October is the best time to dive the northeast. Highlights include **Bar Reef** off Kalpitiya and **Pigeon Island**, just north of Trincomalee. There are dive centres all around the coastline, particularly in the south, although in many places – such as **Hikkaduwa** – the excellent snorkelling is an equally good way to enjoy Sri Lanka's turquoise water and kaleidoscope of tropical fish and sea turtles.

Surfing

As an introduction to tropical reef surfing, Sri Lanka is perfect, with (usually) forgiving waves combined with warm and very inviting water. Though well-established spots like Hikkaduwa and Arugam Bay get busy when a good swell hits, there are many quality quiet breaks to be discovered if you're prepared to explore. The area between **Hikkaduwa** and Mirissa on the southwest coast has its best surf during the northern hemisphere's winter, when hordes of European surfers hang out in surf camps and private lodgings. Small but consistent waves

roll ashore December–April, with the occasional overhead swell that will thin the numbers. The jewel in the crown, however, is the long right-hand point break at **Arugam Bay** on the southeast coast. It's best June–August, when you might discover a world-class wave breaking across the reef.

Kitesurfing

Consistent afternoon sea breezes and regular swells combine to create great kitesurfing conditions; **Negombo**, just north of Colombo, is a focal point.

Hiking

Sri Lanka's lush hill country contains epic trails. Good hiking areas include **Haputale** (check out Little Adam's Peak, Ella Rock and the Namunukula Mountains) and the **Knuckles Mountains** near Kandy, where you'll find five major forest formations and a wide variety of flora and fauna (Asian elephants, leopards, monkeys, mongoose, sloth bears, jackals, Sambar and chital deer, water buffalo, wild boars and 80 species of snake). The hikes here take you across clear rivers, through dense forests, past waterfalls and beside lush tea plantations, terraced paddy fields and colourful Kandyan home gardens.

Paddling

The **Kalu Ganga** (Black River) flows 129km from Sri Lanka's heart to the west coast town of Kalutara on the Indian Ocean. A canoe trip down the river will pass through ever-changing tropical landscapes and a fascinating variety of flora and fauna.

DON'T LEAVE WITHOUT...
Ascending Adam's Peak (2243m) to watch sunrise; you'll often see the peak cast a shadow across the clouds below.

Watch for wildlife, like this young macaque monkey, when hiking in Sri Lanka.

© Pete O'Donovan, © Matt Munro | Lonely Planet

SURINAME

A melting pot of ethnicities in a meltingly hot jungle, Suriname is remote, rugged and raw.

W elcome to the jungle. Suriname's population is incredibly diverse and its forests are unbelievably thick – this is a vast wilderness broken only by isolated Amerindian and Maroon settlements and illegal goldmines.

Canoe Expedition

Considering its thick, clutching jungle, the only real way to penetrate Suriname's interior is by river. A quick flight on a plane will get you to a grass runway somewhere in the middle of nowhere on the Lucie River. From here it's two weeks of paddling, fishing, camping and marvelling at the natural beauty of the Central Suriname Nature Reserve, which makes up 12% of the country. Harpy eagles, cock-of-the-rocks, scarlet macaws, jaguars, giant armadillos, giant river otters and eight species of primate make for unbelievable wildlife spotting as you drift down the jungle artery.

Climb the Voltzberg

Deep in the Central Suriname Nature Reserve, granite domes rise above the jungle and their summits afford outstanding vistas over a massive swathe of unbroken tropical wilderness. It's not easy to reach but the more you surrender to the country's rhythms the more incredible your journey. Take a bus to Witagron, a small Kwinti village on the Coppename River, then paddle a dugout to the outpost of Raleighvallen. From here it's two hours through a cacophonous animal soundscape to the base of the monolith, and another hour to the 240m summit and views of vibrant green canopy punctuated by more distant buboes of granite.

DON'T LEAVE WITHOUT...
Fishing for piranha; you won't easily forget catching the famous flesh-eating fish, nor fending off caiman trying to snaffle your catch.

SWAZILAND

It may be the second-smallest country on the African mainland, but Swaziland's lack of size in no way means a lack of adventure.

A frica's last absolute monarchy, Swaziland sits almost encased inside South Africa. It offers everything from spectacular hiking to powerful rivers.

Hiking

Hosting more than 200km of trails strung with 17 campsites, **Malolotja Nature Reserve** offers some of southern Africa's best hiking. Though Kruger National Park sits less than 70km away, and elephants inhabit a couple of the reserve's valleys, this experience isn't about big critters. Antelopes bounce about, and you may spy a few zebras, but mostly you'll see birds, wildflowers and open grasslands presenting wide views into deep canyons and across to Swaziland's second-highest peak, Ngwenya Mountain (1829m). The terrain is mountainous – the park ranges over 1200 vertical metres – and the hiking at times steep.

Rafting

The **Great Usutu River** burrows through Bulungu Gorge in Mkhaya Game Reserve, churning up Grade IV rapids that make for great rafting. Potentially more challenging than the rapids is the presence of crocodiles, though we've heard no reports of anybody being taken. In winter, trips can be spiced up with a 14m cliff jump (or 16m abseil) into a gorge.

DON'T LEAVE WITHOUT...
Seeing Malolotja from above on the Malolotja Canopy Tour, where a network of 10 ziplines connects 11 platforms through the lush canopy and cliff faces of one of the reserve's gorges.

SWEDEN

Twice the size of the UK, with a population comparable to London, most of Sweden is an adventurer's paradise of coast, lakes, islands, mountains and forests.

Instead of attempting to conquer nature, Swedes aim to harmonise with the outdoors through the philosophy of *friluftsliv* – 'open-air living' – that sees kindergarten classes playing out in sub-zero winter temperatures, and primary school kids learning how to light fires and whittle. The *allemansrätten* ('everyman's right') gives the Swedes (and you) the freedom to walk, paddle, ski and camp anywhere that isn't actually someone's garden. In a sparsely populated country where you can get lost, cold and dead quite easily, the Swedes believe the flip-side of the right to roam is self-responsibility: having the right clothing and kit, and real outdoor skills. However, Scandinavian efficiency means there's nearly always a keep-it-simple infrastructure of marked trails and accommodation – ranging from hut shelters to luxury wilderness hotels – and, of course, saunas.

The social and friendly Swedes are experts when it comes to running mass-participation wilderness events, too, from ski races and endurance SwimRuns to canoe marathons.

Stretching high into the Arctic Circle, Sweden has real seasons, with months of snow and ice for winter sports (and Northern Lights), and tundra for off-map expeditions under the midnight sun. In the south, hot summers are perfect for watersports. And there's a fifth Swedish season – winter-spring – when snow, sun and long days combine to make shirt-only cross-country skiing a great experience. Best of all is how little Sweden is known outside Sweden. Head into the outdoors and it'll just be you and the locals. Oh, and big wildlife that's only a mammoth short of the Ice Age – look out for wolves, bears, wolverine, lynx, reindeer and eagles.

Paddling

There's a lot of water in and around Sweden. Hundreds of rivers, thousands of lakes from pond-sized to Vänern, (the largest lake in the European Union, big enough to float two Luxembourgs), and the North Sea and Baltic coasts with their scatterings of islands. Canoe and kayak touring is a Swedish passion, and you can join clubs for city paddles, including night trips around the 14 islands that the capital is built across, or hire the kayaks and camping kit needed to set off for days of island hopping and wild camping through the **Stockholm Archipelago**. In the west, along the Bohus Coast running north of Gothenburg to the Norwegian border, you can paddle into small fishing villages for fabulous seafood, spot seals from the

© Johner Images | Getty Images

ULTIMATE CHALLENGE

The Havspaddlarnas Blå Band – Seapaddler's Blue Ribbon – has been established since 1990 to honour those who have successfully kayaked the 2300km of Swedish coast between the Norwegian and Finnish borders. So far it's been earned by more than 170 paddlers, ranging from teenagers to an octogenarian.

Ski-touring in Sarek National Park in Lapland in Sweden's north.

water, and (Swedish summers are hotter that you might imagine) drop overboard and follow a marked snorkel trail with its underwater guide-line and information boards in the 450 sq km **Kosterhavet Marine National Park**.

Every August, the 55km **Dalsland Canoe Marathon** tempts hundreds of paddlers, from hardcore competitors aiming to finish in less than four and a half hours, to have-a-goers who use the 11-hour window to enjoy the stunning views. Taking in the four lakes of Laxsjön, Svärdlång, Västra Silen and Lelång, with the necessary portages between them, the long course is open to K1s, K2s and canoes, while there are relay options, shorter courses and, now, SUP categories.

Rafting

Fancy rafting, Huckleberry Finn-style, down a river? You're in the right place. Logging companies were still floating timber down Värmland's Klarälven river as recently as 1991, and you'll be keeping old skills alive as you rope together the outfitter-provided logs, lash up an A-frame tent-cabin and push your raft off on a journey of anything up to eight days and 100km. There'll be periods of activity poling your craft off sand banks, out into the current and back into shore, but mostly you'll be moving at drift speed with time for swimming, fishing and keeping an eye out for beavers, moose and osprey. And, in best Swedish eco-friendly manner, you recycle your raft back into a pile of logs at the end of the trip.

Endless ice near Nynäshamn on the Stockholm Archipelago.

RunSwim

A Swedish invention, RunSwim is exactly what it says: you run to a lake, swim across it, get out, run to the next lake and so on. Based on a bet made in 2002 – now a sport that, like IKEA, is spreading across the world – the course for the original wager became the **ÖtillÖ** race and the World Championship event. The 75km distance is split into 65km of trail running across 26 islands, punctuated by a total of 10km of open-water swimming between them. One of the world's toughest one-day endurance races (if only for the chaffing), there's an even heavier-duty test in the new six-day **Stockholm Archipelago Ultraswimrun Challenge**, where competitors complete a total of 260km, of which 40km are swum between 70 islands.

Hiking

Home to forests, fells, lakes and Arctic Circle tundra, Sweden has some of Europe's emptiest, most challenging and least explored wilderness. In the south there are plenty of low-level, well-marked, beaten-track routes, but through central Sweden and northwards you need to be well prepared, properly equipped and often self-sufficient in food to take on days or weeks of remote walking. The challenges of wading deep rivers, dealing with sudden and extreme changes in weather (that can see summer sun turn to snow drifts in hours) and using navigation and lightweight-camping skills all tempt the adventurous. And it's the best way to spot Scandinavian wildlife, including reindeer, golden eagles, Arctic fox and moose – though you have to be lucky/unlucky (tick according to preference) to encounter bears or wolves.

The best long walk for experiencing the full splendour of Sweden's wilderness is the 440km **Kungsleden** (Kings Trail) above the Arctic Circle, which passes through the 5500 sq km Vindelfjällen Nature Reserve, and offers a detour option to the top of Kebnekaise, Sweden's highest peak (hurry, its 2000m height is being reduced by ice melt on its glaciated top), which demands stiff hiking and scrambling rather than actual climbing skills. Be prepared to be mostly self-sufficient on the Kungsleden, though there are huts at intervals along most of the trail, some with (expensive) supplies and food, and boats in summer cross lakes and big rivers.

© Lena Granefelt | Lonely Planet

© Matt Munro | Lonely Planet

Ice Skating

As their country has cold winters and close to 100,000 lakes, Swedes can usually count on skating from December to March. Arguably the best conditions are in the south and east near Stockholm, where hard freezes without snowfall produce clean ice for perfect skating. Non-skaters can develop skills and fitness using in-line skates and then join tours that can cover anything from 20km to 100km a day. Experienced guides, the right kit – particularly 'ice-claws' for hauling yourself back out of the water if the worst happens, and a waterproof rucksack with a change of clothes – and good technique are all essential.

The reward for the experienced is to head out onto the frozen waters of the Baltic Sea and skate between the islands of the **Stockholm Archipelago**, with landfall at darkness offering a sauna, good food and a hotel bed. Naturally the Swedes have a mass-participation event for good – or optimistic – skaters. The **Vikingarännet** (Viking Run) is an 80km race-tour between Uppsala and Stockholm with up to 2000 competitors.

Cross-Country Skiing & Ski Touring

Åre, in central Sweden's Jämtland province, is a snowsports magnet, famed for its down-hilling and partying, as well as the annual Red Bull **Home Run** race, which mixes 500 skiers and snowboarders in a no-holds-barred helter-skelter run from high on the slopes down into the town. Less chaotic and crowded is cross-country skiing on prepared trails, or touring on remoter marked routes while staying in huts, hostels or hotels. The classic Swedish ski tour is the **Jämtland Triangle**, a 47km, three-day route that starts and ends at Storulvån Fjällstation, and traverses the surrounding high ground with overnights in the mountain station at Sylarna and the Blåhammarens lodge with their restaurants and saunas. For the more sociable cross-country skier, the 90km **Vasaloppet** promotes itself as Europe's oldest/biggest/longest ski race, and attracts up to 15,000 skiers. Running on the first Sunday in March since its inauguration in 1922, popular demand has produced a non-competitive and less crowded tour using the same route on the Sunday before the competition.

In summer, the islands of the Stockholm Archipelago have superb hiking.

SWITZERLAND

Oft lauded as Europe's most mountainous nation, Switzerland has a not-so-secret bank account brimming with golden adventures.

Welcome to the country where adventure tourism was born just over 200 years ago, when rich Brits and feckless footloose troubadours like Lord Byron brainstormed the concept of the Grand Tour. Thomas Cook soon followed in Byron's bootsteps, sending travellers into the great white fins of the beautiful Bernese Oberland, and visitors have flocked to overexert themselves in the rare Alpine air ever since. Here you'll find some of the planet's premier climbing, skiing, biking and hiking routes, beneath bluebird skies where paragliders hover on thermals and BASE jumpers plummet from summits. Less well known are Switzerland's wild waterways – aquatic playgrounds for paddlers and canyoners. With some justification, Interlaken boasts about being Europe's adventure capital, but other less explored areas also offer escapades worthy of inclusion in a modern Grand Adventure Tour.

Hiking & Trail Running

The Bernese Oberland, especially the **Jungfrau Region**, offers some of the best hiking and running trails in the known universe. Accessed via the adventure hub of Interlaken, the area is overlooked by three towering peaks, characters locked in a perpetual fairy tale: 4158m Jungfrau (Young Maiden), 4107m Mönch (Monk) and the 3970m Eiger (Ogre). The latter might be shorter than its co-stars, but its black reputation as a cold-hearted killer has been well earned. During the past century, at least 64 climbers have died while attempting to ascend its infamous North Face, known as Mordwand (Murder Wall).

You don't need to be an advanced alpinist to appreciate the scale and beauty of these peaks from the paths that wend around their lower flanks and valley walls, though. Trails abound between the attractive train-accessed villages of Grindelwald, Wengen, Mürren and Lauterbrunnen, linking lakes such as the Bachalpsee and Sägistalsee, where the mountains are turned upside down in the cold water, and leading to glaciers, mountain huts, gorgeous cascades (the Staubbachfall and Trümmelbach waterfalls) and, obviously, eye-wateringly wonderful 360-degree vistas. Signature routes here include the **Eiger Trail** from Grindelwald to Alpiglen station; the longer trot from stunning Schynige Platte to the summit station of the Grindelwald-First cableway; and the ramble from Mürren to the Lauterbrunnen valley floor. A less-trafficked trek can be enjoyed on the path from Pfingstegg to the hut at Bäregg, above the lower Grindelwald glacier, or you can piece together a multiday meander such as the **Hintere Gasse** trekking route from Lauterbrunnen valley to Kandersteg, punctuated with overnight stays in super-scenic mountain huts.

Elsewhere, the **Four-Lake Hike** in the central **Jochpass region** – which loops around the picturesque puddles of Trübsee, Engstlensee, Tannen and Melch – is one of Switzerland's best boot-powered adventures.

In the east, **Toggenburg** is renowned for superb hiking routes through Alpine and riparian terrain, framed by the stunning Säntis massif and the seven Churfirsten peaks. Try the **Höhenweg** (high trail), a challenging multistage 87km trek through the magical mountains from Wildhaus to Wil.

Parc Naziunal Svizzer, Switzerland's sole national park, has 21 wonderful walking routes within its 174 sq km extent, all doable within a day (camping is forbidden). The most challenging and rewarding is the eight-hour one-way Macun Lakes Trek from Zernez to Lavin, via a high-hanging lake plateau beneath Piz Macun (2889m).

Skiing

Switzerland has some of Earth's most iconic and spectacular ski terrain. The big-hitters will always be the likes of Mürren, Wengen, Grindelwald and Zermatt, simply because of the incredible mountain panoramas that surround them, but there's plenty more on offer, and you can usually take a train right to the resorts. There's no better way of accessing the mountains than by the fantastically efficient and comfortable Swiss Rail network, which will literally take you halfway up the north face of the Eiger.

Cutting turns beneath the Matterhorn's awe-inspiring frame above **Zermatt** is one of skiing's great experiences, but here you'll also discover the downside of skiing in Switzerland – it's expensive.

Mürren, reachable only by cable car, hosts the world's biggest and longest amateur ski race, the 'Inferno' – a 15.8km beast that dates to 1928 and leaves you with serious thigh burn. **Wengen** and **Grindelwald** share with Mürren the fantastic backdrop of the Eiger, Mönch and Jungfrau mountains, along with a good mix of piste and off-piste skiing.

Swiss ski resorts often date back over a century. **Arosa**, for instance, was visited by Sir Arthur Conan

Doyle in the 1890s and still offers a great mix of piste and freeride terrain, especially since it was recently linked to neighbouring **Lenzerheide**.

Although Swiss resorts are typically very pretty, with traditional Alpine chalets and hotels scattered up steep hillsides and across mountainous pastures, well-known Davos (which boasts some of Switzerland's best skiing, whether you're a beginner or a freerider) offers a traffic-choked main street rather than Alpine chic. The linked resort of **Klosters**, popular with British royalty, offers a quieter and more traditional alternative.

And then there's **Verbier** – regular stopping-off point for the Freeride World Tour, and haunt of the rich, famous and not-so-famous – one of the world's great ski resorts, with the quality of skiing you'd expect.

Above, St Bernards at Musèe et Chiens du St Bernard; the last recorded rescue by St Bernards was in 1955. Overleaf, skiing the ridge between Pointe de Drône and Mont Fourchon in the Pennine Alps.

© Justin Foulkes | Lonely Planet

© Justin Foulkes | Lonely Planet

Climbing

Guides offer alpinists ogre-wrestling experiences on the **Eiger**'s frowning North Face, but even with expert guidance, this is a highly committing climb. An ascent of the stunningly steep **Matterhorn** – probably the planet's most recognisable peak – is more achievable, but still requires decent fitness and technical skill. Starting from Zermatt, most climbers ascend via the relentless Hornli Ridge, where the rock gives way to snow and ice as the summit approaches.

The **Western Swiss Alps** around Interlaken are full of limestone crags with bolted single-pitch and multipitch routes. Also investigate the **Jura Mountains** in the north, for everything from single-pitch sport routes to multipitch trad routes on limestone and occasional granite, or explore the **Eastern Alps'** gneiss-rock and limestone crags around Andermatt, Grimsel, Susten and Nufenen. Boulderers should head to the **Magic Wood** near Ausserferrera, **Kandersteg** in the Bernese Oberland, or **Grimselpass** and **Gotthardpass** in the east.

HOMEGROWN HERO

Most attempts on the Eiger's North Face in the 1930s took teams three or four harrowing days, but in 2015, double Piolet d'Or-winning Swiss climber Ueli Steck conquered it solo in two hours, 22 minutes, 50 seconds.

Road Cycling

Well-maintained roads, few vehicles and staggering scenery combine to create some seriously sexy cycling opportunities in Switzerland, which offers nine national and 123 regional bike routes. The country's undisputed grand climb is **St Gotthard**, with a series of sensational switchbacks that slither up the hillside via an old, cobbled traffic-free Roman road called the Tremola. Other top road rides include the **Grosse Scheidegg** and the **Albula**.

Mountain Biking

Switzerland puts the mountain firmly into MTB, and once the white stuff melts in spring, locals and biking blow-ins quickly swap sliding for riding. From the singletrack-striped skin of **Zermatt** and **Verbier,** to **Crans-Montana**'s park life and the less tyre-tracked trails around Saint-Luc, there's a multitude of mountain-biking adventures to be explored. If races are your bag, check out the annual **Eiger Bike Challenge** in August, or the **Nationalpark Bike-Marathon**, which provides

© Andrew Peacock

riders with the unique chance to cycle around Parc Naziunal Svizzer, where bikes are normally banned, before the 137km course sends competitors to Italy's Stelvio National Park. Otherwise, fill your hydration pack, hop on a funicular or lift, clip in and cruise down, tracing routes that blaze across the buxom nation's best bumpy bits.

Watersports

Sedate sailing, kayaking and stand-up paddleboarding can be enjoyed on many of Switzerland's lovely lakes. A canoe trail traces the length of languid **Lake Lucerne** – a waterway much beloved by Albert Einstein, a keen sailor – offering paddlers a range of route options between the canoe stations and campsites of Brunnen, Buochs and Rotschuo, from single day outings to overnight escapades. As sure as E=mc2, however, elevation plus snowmelt equals charging rivers ripe for riding in one way or another, and Switzerland offers paddlers plenty of whitewater highways to bomb along. Kayaking, rafting and riverboarding are all popular on **River Sarine** in the Pays-d'Enhaut, just outside Interlaken, where the furious flow threads the spectacular Vanel and Gérignoz gorges, rushing through Grade III–IV rapids. Other whitewater rivers include the **Rhine** (sometimes called the Swiss Grand Canyon, with Grade III–IV rapids) and the more benign **Aare** and **Arve**.

Canyoning

For a whitewater experience minus the boat, try canyoning, which marries down-climbing, abseiling and wild swimming, and arguably reaches its apex in Switzerland's steep streams, waterfalls and gullies. Standout Swiss canyons include **Chli Schliere** and the caves, cascades and slippery chutes of **Ticino**, where jade-green water stands out against the white walls like absinthe on ice.

BASE Jumping

With shockingly sheer cliff walls shooting 700m into the sky, Lauterbrunnen Valley has become the capital of Central European BASE and wingsuit jumping. There's even a diving board for jumpers to launch themselves from, and sometimes there's a queue. The inevitable consequence of wafer-thin margins of error (it only takes one unexpected wind gust for a jumper to become a ghost) combined with a spike in jumpers' numbers has prompted the press to brand Lauterbrunnen 'Death Valley', but the ultimate thrill–providing sports remain legal and surprisingly popular. Before you blow your dough on a wingsuit, however, be aware that all jumpers should have a skydiving licence and have completed a minimum of 200 dives before giving BASE a blast. In Lauterbrunnen, you're also required to purchase a 'landing card' (CHF25 a year) to compensate local farmers for the lumps left in fields.

Below, the historic Viamala links two mountain passes by a narrow gorge. Left, climbing the Tour d'Ai via ferrata in Vaud canton.

© Justin Foulkes | Lonely Planet

TAHITI & FRENCH POLYNESIA

For paradisical adventures, the islands of French Polynesia deliver – from Pacific Ocean water pursuits to tropical hiking, it's all here.

The 118 islands and atolls of French Polynesia, sprinkled across the Pacific Ocean, may be familiar to honeymooners, but for adventurers they tend to fly under the radar. Peer past the palm tree facade, however, and there's plenty of adventure to be found amid landscapes that vary from desert-like islets to soaring rocky ridgelines pocked with waterfalls, and an ocean frothing with wildlife.

Snorkelling & Diving

As you'd expect in a place where the sea temperature rarely drops lower than 25°C, underwater exploration is popular. Sharks, whales, giant manta rays and other exotic tropical fish abound. Reef dives are popular, but for a real thrill try Rangiroa where you can 'shoot the pass' on a drift dive in strong currents zipping past schools of grey, black tip or whitetip reef sharks, manta rays and dolphins.

Surfing & SUP

Conditions are epic, and the surfing is all about shallow reef breaks and tubes, so you have to know what you're doing. Teahupo'o is infamous for big, steep barrels (and crunchy wipeouts) – try to get away from the often-crowded main wave and explore one of six other less-frequented breaks nearby. Ava Mo'a Pass offers fine surfing and the island of Moorea throws up quality breaks. With lots of protected lagoons, there's also plenty of opportunity for stand-up paddleboarding: float calmly over coral gardens, catch a wave or go with the breeze on a down-winder.

Hiking

Polynesians rely on a network of footpaths to connect villages, especially on more remote islands. Choose from dedicated routes to informal networks that track through wild and impressive jungle scenery defined by jagged mountains, deep ravines, lush valleys and isolated lagoons. On the Marquesas, meander trails thousands of years old, past ancient tikis (stone or wood statues). Back on Tahiti, hike through the Papenoo Valley to Lake Vaihiria, or scale Mt Aorai, the island's third-highest peak.

DON'T LEAVE WITHOUT...
Trying outrigger paddling, which is a way of life in French Polynesia. You can still opt for the traditional dug-out experience, or go for the comfort of a modern sea kayak, so you can stow camping gear and set off to discover your own empty patch of paradise.

Surfing the legendary Teahupo'o.

© Gregory Boissy/AFP| Getty Images

TAIWAN

Cast aside preconceptions of tameness – Taiwan is a diverse, compact, adventure-friendly island.

Mention Taiwan and the mind's eye summons up cheap electronic goods and industrialised Taipei, but beyond the carapace of cities capping the west coast, the majority of the country is covered in thickly forested mountains reaching up to nearly 4000m. With everything in easy reach, explorers can easily hike into the mountains and be back in the bars of Taipei drinking *kaoliang* (fermented sorghum liquor) by evening.

Hiking

Taiwan's highest peak, **Mt Yushan** (3952m) – or Jade Peak – is one of its most popular hikes. Though the walk is short (just over 9km from the trailhead), most trekkers do it over two days so they can catch dawn at the summit and (hopefully) a cloud inversion in the valleys below. Beyond Yushan there are more than 200 peaks over 3000m, with many made accessible by Taiwan's extensive network of well-marked trails.

Climbing

Taiwan's best climbing is an hour of east of Taipei at **Long Dong**, a 2km stretch of golden and grey sandstone set above the wild Pacific Ocean. There are more than 2000 routes here, with a mixture of sport and trad routes for climbers to throw themselves at.

Watersports

The Pacific Ocean also delivers consistent (and warm) swells for **surfing** (typhoon season can produce some killer breaks). The south and east coasts offer the best surf. **Rafting** is another popular activity, particularly on the Xiouguluan and Laonong Rivers.

DON'T LEAVE WITHOUT...
Trying 'river tracing'. In summer, locals don wetsuits and follow rivers upstream – it's a great way to explore and stay cool.

TAJIKISTAN

Can you point to Tajikistan on a map? Time to explore one of Earth's most exciting hidden gems.

Tajikistan has some of the most impressive mountains to be found outside of the Himalaya, with peaks pushing 7000m, and 700 sq km of glaciers.

Cycling the Pamir Highway

An epic, high-altitude adventure, cycling the Pamir Highway is a breathtaking journey. Starting either in Tajikistan's capital, Dushanbe – or at the other end of the highway in Kyrgyzstan's vibrant second city, Osh – this 1300km route is unlike any other you've cycled before. Wending its way through the country's **Gorno-Badakhshan Autonomous Oblast** (GBAO) – an area that covers nearly half of Tajikistan's landmass yet holds just 3% of its population – the highway is a modern interpretation of the ancient Silk Road. Expect a lot of high mountain passes (up to 4655m) and a vast, empty, extraordinary landscape.

Whitewater Paddling

A country with such an impressive collection of lofty peaks will inevitably have incredible whitewater, if you know where to find it. Tajikistan's rivers are little explored and completely uncommercialised, so paddlers need to be independent and hardy souls who know how to get themselves into remote situations (the best way, besides putting your boat on the back of a donkey, is to rent a 4WD vehicle with a local driver) and get themselves out of trouble if things go pear shaped. However, the riches are great for those who dare. In the **Pamir Mountains**, whitewater can be found in abundance on the gorges that the Gunt and Vanch rivers rush through. April–September is best.

DON'T LEAVE WITHOUT...
Going dinosaur hunting. The Shirkent Valley, 60km west of Dushanbe in the Fann Mountains, is famed for having 400 dinosaur footprints preserved in the rocks that lie alongside some of the best walking trails in western Tajikistan.

TANZANIA

Kilimanjaro is but one of Tanzania's many mountains made for climbing, and the thrills don't stop at less lofty levels, where wild walking safaris and Indian Ocean diving can be enjoyed.

O ver millions of years, tectonic forces in Tanzania have ripped open the Great Rift Valley, thrusting up numerous mountain ranges and giving birth to a series of volcanoes, some of which are still active. This varied terrain offers impressive stomping grounds for trekkers of all abilities, and has provided a wealth of habitats for the country's flora and fauna, resulting in an enthralling cast to accompany any adventure pursuit, whether walking in the savannah or diving beneath the water's surface.

Trekking

Mention Africa to anyone with an adventurous spirit and **Kilimanjaro** won't be far from their thoughts. This ancient glacier-capped volcano is not only one of the continent's greatest sights, but also one of its biggest challenges. This has as much to do with the

lowly elevation of its base as it has with the 5895m height of its summit – the difference in altitude between the two is almost 5000m, making Kili one of the tallest freestanding mountains on the planet. On the positive side, this means your chosen route up will take you through a rich diversity of habitats, starting on the grassy plains and progressing up to lush rainforest (keep an eye out for elephants and buffalo), and eventually into alpine meadows before making your final assault on the summit across a barren, moon-like landscape. Only the masochists will revel at the thought of waking in the middle of the night for the last push, but the excitement of what lies ahead should keep your feet moving, one in front of the other, until you reach the roof of Africa for the crack of dawn.

But trekking in Tanzania can involve so much more than just conquering the biggest beast. Other volcanoes provide some surreal trekking

DON'T LEAVE WITHOUT...
Tracking chimpanzees through the Mahale Mountains' verdant, forest-covered slopes on the eastern shore of Lake Tanganyika.

© ithinair28 | Getty Images

Mighty Mt Kilimanjaro looms over the Marangu Route.

possibilities: walk the razor-edged crater rim of **Mt Meru** (4565m) and stare into its spectacular volcanic cone, or climb up the perilously steep, ash-covered sides of Tanzania's youngest (and still active) volcano, **Ol Doinyo Lengai** (2962m). If culture is calling, spend a week trekking from picturesque village to village in the lush **Usambara Mountains**. And if your inner David Attenborough wants a piece of the action, wade into the incredible biodiversity of the **Udzungwa Mountains**.

Walking Safaris

It's easy to marvel at the majesty of Earth's creatures from the safety of an open-topped 4WD, but one doesn't truly appreciate the raw power they possess until put on a level playing field with them. New walking safaris in the Serengeti are allowing you to do just that. What would be 'just another buffalo sighting' on a wildlife drive suddenly becomes an adrenaline-inducing, engrossing encounter – you'll hang on each and every word of your guide, and study intensely every minor detail and movement of the animal.

Diving

Who says all the action is above the surface? Dive into the waters of the **Zanzibar Archipelago** and you'll have a mask full of it – manta rays, sharks, barracuda, and hawksbill and green turtles patrol the depths, and vivid corals blanket sections of the ocean floor. Off the island of **Pemba**, north of Zanzibar, wall dives are particularly fulfilling. Inland there are also some unique freshwater diving opportunities in **Lake Tanganyika**, the world's longest (660km) and second-deepest (1436m) lake – it hosts an extraordinary number of endemic fish, including more than 200 species of brilliantly coloured cichlids.

THAILAND

From the islands and underwater reefs of the gulf to the jungle-strewn hills of the north, Thailand is a right royal paradise for ramblers, scramblers, runners, riders, climbers, cavers and divers.

W hen it comes to adventure travel, Thailand is a land of two halves, conveniently split between north and south by the country's sprawling metropolis, Bangkok. The south is largely defined by islands and beaches, formed around the Andaman Sea and the Gulf of Thailand. Underwater pursuits are the big attraction, but the islands and national parks also offer accessible jungle trekking, trail running and biking, while the limestone formations of Krabi province are a magnet for climbers. Northern Thailand is carpeted in jungle, creased by low mountain ranges and protected by national parks and reserves, where trekking, trail running, cycle touring, rafting, caving and waterfall rappelling are popular pursuits. Thailand's tropical climate can be hot and humid year-round in the south, but it gets chilly during the winter (dry) season in the hills of the north – a good time for trekking. Avoid the monsoon months of July–September.

Diving & Snorkelling

Diving, snorkelling and freediving are all popular and well-organised throughout Thailand's main islands and coastal resorts. From November to March is the prime time for diving in the Andaman Sea, but March to September offers the best diving opportunities in the Gulf.

Tiny **Ko Tao**, a two-hour catamaran ride from Ko Samui, is the most popular dive base in the Gulf; sheltered bays offer good year-round diving and shallow dive sites (and low-cost PADI courses) make it ideal for beginners. Experienced divers will love the diversity of marine life and underwater landscapes, with pinnacles, caves, coral gardens, wrecks and vertical swim-throughs such as Sail Rock. This is also one of the best places in Southeast Asia to see whale sharks.

Serious divers head to **Khao Lak**, the mainland gateway to the sublime islands of the **Surin** and **Similan** marine national parks, way out in the Andaman Sea. Book a place on a liveaboard dive boat and spend up to a week exploring Thailand's best dive sites.

Travellers gravitate to the drop-dead-gorgeous twin islands of **Ko Phi Phi Don** and **Ko Phi Phi Lei** for the powder-white beaches, while underwater adventurers will find coral reefs, submerged karst formations, crystal-clear water and a few wrecks; abundant marine life includes hawksbill turtles and leopard sharks. **Ko Lanta** is a more relaxed island with easy access to pinnacle dives at Hin Muang and Hin Daeng.

DON'T LEAVE WITHOUT...

Spelunking in the dramatic limestone caves of Chiang Dao in Chiang Mai province, or Tham Lot and Tham Nam Lang in Mae Hong Son Province, where you can raft the underground river systems and discover mysterious teak coffins. (Tip: stay at Cave Lodge).

Rich marine life off the island of Ko Tao.

© kampee patisena | Getty Images

Hill Trekking

Northern Thailand is a region of jungle-cloaked highlands, rich in protected national parks, minority hill-tribe villages, raging rivers and plunging waterfalls. The historic traveller hang-out of **Chiang Mai** is the epicentre of the trekking scene in Northern Thailand. Dozens of operators can organise jungle walks that might include an elephant ride, bamboo rafting and an overnight stay in a tribal village. Or just find a good guide and customise your own trek. About 15km from the old city, **Doi Suthep National Park** is blessed with some of Thailand's top hiking and mountain-biking trails. **Chiang Rai** is another major base for treks, with access to ethnically diverse minority villages and some remote jungle hikes.

Famous for the Thai-Burma Death Railway and Bridge over the River Kwai, **Kanchanaburi** is a ruggedly beautiful region easily accessible from Bangkok. Jungle trekking trips can take you to seven-tiered Erawan waterfall or further off the beaten path to Karen villages.

Climbing

While there's good climbing around Chiang Mai, most climbers head south to **Railay** in Krabi Province, where dozens of limestone towers and karst formations loom above the jungle and the Andaman Sea. It's a long-time climbing mecca, with more than 700 bolted routes to suit all levels of experience. Advanced – or just adventurous – climbers can try bouldering or deep-water soloing (DWS) where you climb sea cliffs without ropes, relying only on the water below to break your fall.

Bike Touring

Thais love getting around on two wheels and bicycle touring has exploded in popularity with travellers in recent years. With reasonably good road surfaces, manageable distances between villages or towns, roadside markets and impossibly scenic countryside, this is one of the best places in Southeast Asia to ride. You can explore Thailand entirely on paved roads, but excellent shorter cycling routes can be found on Phuket, around Ayutthaya, Chiang Mai, Kanchanaburi and in the highlands of Mae Hong Son.

Trail Running

Trail running is most popular – and most challenging – in Northern Thailand, where the higher elevation offers a break from the heat and humidity and hiking paths double as running trails. Most routes are unmarked, so it pays to hook up with a group or a guide. The dry season between January and April is the best time for running. The **Thailand Ultramarathon** in remote northeastern Thailand and **The North Face 100** (km) in Khao Yai National Park are both testing races.

With its large expat community and extensive network of mountain and forest trails, **Chiang Mai** is trail-running central in Northern Thailand; Pilgrim's Trail is a challenging 4.5km ascent in Doi Suthep National Park. In Southern Thailand, Phuket has a number of trails, or try the circuit trails on the islands of **Ko Samet** and **Ko Samui**.

Trekking in Chiang Mai.

© FredFroese | Getty Images

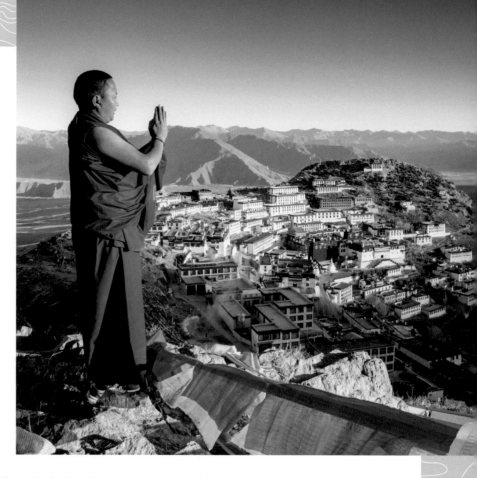

TIBET

Tibet is notoriously difficult to explore, but to experience trekking, biking and rafting on the roof of the world, it's worth the effort.

R ising more than 5000m above sea level in parts, the Tibetan Plateau is the highest and largest on Earth, fringed to the south by the mighty Himalaya and to the north by the high-altitude desert territories of Xinjiang and Qinghai, technically in China. Adventure and spirituality are ever-present here – the remoteness, permit rules and lack of transport infrastructure restrict most of Tibet to tour groups, professional mountaineers and the most intrepid travellers. Exploring Tibet is to enter a world of remote Buddhist monasteries, monks on arduous pilgrimage treks, sacred mountains and whitewater rivers barely touched by the outside world.

Trekking

Trekking in Tibet can be exhilarating and challenging, but you can't go it alone; all treks require booking with a recognised tour agency and a local guide. Some of Tibet's best treks link remote monasteries on ancient trade routes.

It's said that you will erase the sins of a lifetime if you complete the three-day *kora* (circular pilgrimage trek) around sacred **Mt Kailash** in far-western Tibet. Another reason is to witness the superb mountain views and prostrating monks.

Only 50km from Lhasa, **Ganden Monastery** is a must-visit for its magnificent high and low *kora*. It's also the start of the 80km, four-day trek to Samye Monastery, one of the best walks in Tibet.

Most people approach Everest from the Nepal side, but the views of the North Face from Tibet are far superior. Beyond Rongphu monastery – the world's highest at 4980m – the road from Tingri ends at a camp of yak-hair tents, from where it's a 4km hike to **Everest Base Camp** (5150m). Other treks in the region include the 10-day epic to the East Face and Karma Valley.

Top, a monk prays above Ganden Monastery. Left, trekking past a glacier near Shishapangma.

© Gabe Rogel; Matteo Colombo | Getty Images

Mountaineering

Although there are reams of red tape and permits associated with mountaineering, a few of the dozens of Himalayan peaks accessible from Tibet are open to climbers on officially recognised expeditions – including Everest (8848m), Cho Oyu (8201m) and Shishapangma (8027m).

Mountain Biking

Mountain-biking at this altitude is the ultimate challenge, but the roads from Lhasa to Kathmandu or Mt Kailash are gradually improving and the views are unsurpassed. A number of tour companies offer all-inclusive guided rides: the 20-plus-day tour from Lhasa to Kathmandu (via the Friendship Hwy) purportedly features the world's longest continuous road descent at over 150km.

DON'T ARRIVE WITHOUT...
A valid Chinese visa and a Tibet Tourism Bureau (TTB) permit. To travel outside Lhasa you'll also need a travel permit (from a tour agency) and a local guide.

Whitewater Rafting

As the Himalayan mountains provide the source of some of Asia's mightiest rivers, it's no surprise that there are thrilling whitewater adventures on offer in Tibet. Among the most popular rivers for rafting and kayaking excursions out of Lhasa are the Kyi-chu and the raging Reting Tsangpo and Drigung Chu.

TOGO

In mysterious Togo, a land often linked with voodoo, beauty may be found on the beach, atop a mountain or in the fluttering of forest butterflies.

Togo's wild beauty stretches from its powdery palm-fringed beaches on the Gulf of Guinea – where surfing opportunities abound – all the way to the parched golden savannahs bordering Burkina Faso. Caught between the two extremes are forested hills in the country's west, which spill off from Ghana's Volta Region – it's this environment that is a truly fulfilling (and ecofriendly) playground for trekkers.

Hiking

Mt Agou (986m), Togo's tallest peak, rises alone on the plains east of Kpalimé. The hiking trail will take you up through coffee and cocoa plantations, past terraced mountain villages and into some dense sections of forest. En route your guide will be able to explain the various flora and fauna you come across, as well as shed light on the local culture and history. From the summit you should be able to see Lake Volta's surface glistening in Ghana. Another option is to hike the verdant hills around **Mt Klouto** (710m), 12km northwest of Kpalimé. In the early mornings here the forest air is alive with butterflies.

Surfing

The country's Atlantic-facing coastline may be small, but the steeply shelving beaches along the Togolese coast offer plenty of excellent surf spots, not least around the lovely coastal capital **Lomé**. Also try **Aného**, further east towards Benin. The best breaks are found around sandbanks, created by natural or manmade features. Conditions are optimal July–October.

DON'T LEAVE WITHOUT...
Wild swimming in a plunge pool beneath Cascade de Womé, 12km from Kpalimé, accessed via Womé village and a 4km walk.

TONGA

The Kingdom of Tonga is a tropical paradise, which, at least for now, has largely escaped the attention of the masses.

Island Time' is an official metric in Tonga – far from the pressures of Western society, life moves at a slower pace in this South Pacific archipelago. Do as the locals do and resist the urge to rush as you wander along pristine beaches, bathe in azure waters or paddle between islands accompanied by magical marine life, including – if you time your trip right – humpback whales.

Diving & Snorkelling

Teeming with tropical marine life, Tonga's waters present a paradise for divers and snorkellers. Across more than 170 islands, there are plenty of submarine environments to explore, but notable highlights include the Arch of Ofalanga and Hot Spring Cavern in the **Ha'apai** group, as well as the wreck of the *Clan MacWilliam*, which lies in Davy Jones' Locker in the **Vava'u group**. Between July and October, humpback whales make their annual migration to breeding zones in the South Pacific, and Tonga is one of the last places on Earth where you can swim with these majestic creatures (ensure you book with a licensed whale operator).

Paddling & Hiking

Sea kayakers can explore the archipelago, camping on islands as they go, with local guides offering survival tips, from how to fish to picking a ripe coconut. On land, hikers will find the best trails in Eua National Park, which is dotted with well-marked trails.

DON'T LEAVE WITHOUT...
Taking a subterranean swim in Anahulu Cave, which has a small but particularly stunning underground lake.

Left, the thin air, steep climbs and bad roads make bikepacking in Tibet challenging, but the incredible mountains and friendly people are the pay off.

© aaabbbcccc | Shutterstock

TURKEY

If the bedrock of adventure is intriguing landscapes, then Turkey must rank highly on the list of must-explores.

Encircled by seas on three sides, Turkey features mountain ranges in the east that feed the mighty rivers of the Euphrates, Tigris and Aras, and a high plateau in the centre, plunging down to the mighty Bosphorus River, where Europe meets Asia, a union sealed by the metropolis of Istanbul. A moody tectonic and volcanic dynamic below is responsible for Turkey's hugely varied and constantly shifting landscapes, some of which, such as the famous and bizarre geology of the Cappadocia region, are found nowhere else on earth.

Trekking & Trail Running

A recent addition to the world's long-distance trail line-up, the Lycian Way on the Mediterranean coast in southwest Turkey has, since its inception in 2000, frequently been rated in the top ten by those who judge these things. The 540km route from Ölüdeniz to just shy of Antalya takes in both inland and ocean-side sections as it climbs mountain ridges and cliffs high above the water, passing ancient ruins en route. The full trail takes 20 to 30 days, but day hike sections are possible from towns including Demre, Kaş and Kemer. Or you can run it – the **Lycian Way Ultramarathon** traverses a 220km stretch over six days.

Paddling

In the **Çoruh River**, Turkey hosts one of the best paddling destinations for rafters and kayakers. A remote river relatively untouched by tourism, it passes through deep gorges, down steep valleys and on past rural heartlands and ancient ruined fortresses, running 440km from the Mescit Mountains to the Black Sea coast of Georgia. Go in May to June when snowmelt pumps up the volume.

Sea Kayaking

Dotted with hidden coves and inlets, soaring cliffs and deserted sandy beaches, Turkey's southern shoreline is ideal multiday kayaking territory. Many routes feature fascinating ancient ruins and Lycian tombs, far from tourist swarms. The Gulf of Gökova, the Gulf of Hisarönü and the Dalyan area are all notable places to float your boat, but don't miss paddling above **Kekova**, a sunken city, lying off a small island separated from the mainland hundreds of years ago during an earthquake.

© VichoT | Getty Images

DON'T LEAVE WITHOUT...

Paragliding from one of the highest commercial sites in the world, perched atop the 1960m Mt Babadağ. It's a 30–40 minute thrill ride back down, landing on the postcard-perfect Ölüdeniz beach. Almost as adrenaline-pumping is the 4WD journey up to the summit and the brief instruction session – 'Run. Fast. Don't stop.'

Mountain Biking

Perhaps most famous for its volcanic geography, balloon flights and cave hotels, the Cappadocia region in central Anatolia has recently established itself as a mountain biking hot-spot, a nomination promoted by the **International Cappadocia Bicycle Festival** in September. The event includes cross-country and multiday stage races, making best use of slick rock trails, lush green singletrack and a world of caves, canyons and secret paths.

Climbing

Mountaineering, climbing, canyoning, caving... Turkey's unique geological formations, from towering peaks to cavernous caves, make this a rock-hoppers dreamland.

Mountaineers will find some interesting summits to scale, including two inactive volcanoes, **Mt Erciyes** (3916m) and **Mt Agri** (5137m). The Kaçkar Mountains in the eastern Black Sea region, and the Cilo-Sat Mountains near Hakkâri in the Eastern Taurus are also worthy targets.

Sport climbers should head to the **Geyikbayiri** in Antalya, Turkey's most popular climbing area.

Caving

Some 35% of Turkey's terrain – especially in the Taurus region – consists of rock conducive to the formation of caves. There are an estimated 40,000 of them. Turkey's longest is Pinargozu Cavern, west of Beyşehir Lake, the deepest Çukurpınar Sinkhole, plunging 1880m at the south of Anamur.

Cappadocia offers mountain bikers incredible landscapes to ride.

TURKMENISTAN

Largely forgotten by the modern word, this intriguing and timeless land of shifting black sands is ripe for rediscovery.

O nce an integral part of the Silk Road, Turkmenistan has a colourful and mysterious history. Vestiges of its ancient past remain scattered throughout the black sand of the Karakum, in the shadowy shape of forlorn ruins that appear as timeless as the desert itself. The trekking – with and without horses – is sensational, and beyond its Caspian Sea coastline, the country offers an eccentric wild swimming experience, in a thermally heated underground lake complete with a resident colony of cacophonous bats. Who knows what secrets remain to be found its deepest canyons, valleys and caves?

Horse trekking

Turkmenistan has vast and largely untapped potential for adventure and exploration. One of the finest ways to travel is on the back of an Akhal-Teke, a horse with a local lineage that can be traced right back to the Mongols. Operators can facilitate horse-trekking trips, riding these metallic-sheened steeds that make magnificent companions with which to discover the rivers and gorges of the **Kopetdag Mountains**.

Hiking & Caving

Trekkers will undoubtedly gravitate toward the **Kugitang Mountains**, home to Turkmenistan's tallest peak, Aýrybaba (3138m). This range also houses the Kugitang Caves, once considered the most spectacular within the Soviet Union. Kopetang Cave is open for visitors who can embark on a three-hour spelunking excursion into the 60km abyss.

DON'T LEAVE WITHOUT...
Taking a dip in Köw Ata Underground Lake in a Bakharden cave. It's 65m below ground and naturally heated to a pleasant 35°C – but be prepared to share your bath with Central Asia's largest known bat colony.

TUVALU

White sands, green palms, turquoise waters – Tuvalu is the epitome of the South Pacific.

I f you've never heard of Tuvalu, don't beat yourself up too much, you're certainly not alone – however, you certainly are missing out. A small, secluded, far-flung and much scattered archipelago nation – comprised of nine atolls, two major islands (Funafuti and Nanumea) and 127 tiny islets, with a total landmass of just 26 sq km, spread out across a stretch of ocean measuring over 500 nautical miles north-to-south – this idyllic tropical paradise is perfect for paddling and sailing adventures, and endless hours of snorkelling and scuba diving in lagoons and open water.

Diving & Snorkelling

As the islands are comprised entirely of coral, you'll find expansive underwater gardens to explore, especially around the protected **Funafuti Conservation Area**. Across the islands, blast pits created beside the ocean by the US military during WWII have now become tidal pools where literally thousands of fish become trapped, offering a unique snorkelling experience.

Sailing & SUPing

Island hoppers should make their way to the island of **Nanumea**, which hides the wreckage of fighter planes and a landing craft scuttled upon the reef, where Neverland Yacht Charter can rent yachts and catamarans, and organise excursions. Paddlers will have to be more creative, transporting their own inflatable SUP boards, but the lagoons of **Nanumea, Funafuti** and the populated atoll of **Nukufetau** do offer sublime walking-on-water experiences for those who make the effort.

DON'T LEAVE WITHOUT...
Scuba diving into the 'House Under the Sea', an underwater cave near Nanumaga Island. Burned surfaces suggest that humans may have lived within the cave some 8000 years ago when sea levels were much lower.

UGANDA

Wildlife, glaciers and jungles, Uganda has the power to both stop you in your tracks and keep you running back for more.

H ome to the tallest mountain range on the continent and a lively section of the River Nile, the 'pearl of Africa' is a jewel for those looking for an escapade on the wildside.

Hiking

Where to start? Top of most people's wish list would likely be trekking into the forested depths of **Bwindi Impenetrable National Park** to share 60 unforgettable minutes with some of the last mountain gorillas on the planet. Other wildlife-related activities worth jumping into include tracking wild chimpanzees through the jungle at **Kibale National Park** or stepping onto the savannah of **Kidepo Valley National Park** for a walking safari, during which you can catch glimpses of cheetahs, lions, elephants, zebras, giraffes and more.

In the far west is Africa's tallest mountain range, where several of its peaks have permanent ice caps and three stand over 5000m. Treks in **Rwenzori Mountains National Park** are sure to be wet and cold, but extraordinary nonetheless. The much more gentle slopes of **Mt Elgon** in Uganda's far east are another worthwhile trekking option.

Paddling

And then you have the Nile. Base yourself in **Jinja** to wrestle with some of the continent's most boisterous whitewater (up to Grade V), either in a **raft** or alone in a **kayak**. The brave can even take it on rapids with just a **riverboard**. **Stand-up paddleboarding** is popular on some of the Nile's less gnarly stretches.

DON'T LEAVE WITHOUT...
Exploring some hardcore mountain biking along the tracks and trails of Mabira Forest Reserve, between Lugazi and Jinja.

UKRAINE

The shifting political landscape dictates the outdoor offering of Europe's second-largest country as much as its topography, but there's still plenty for adventurers to explore.

U kraine's outdoor pursuits have traditionally been concentrated around the Crimean Peninsula, with great climbing on coastal limestone crags, superb Black Sea kayaking and kitesurfing, and excellent mountain biking and paragliding. The peninsula is technically still part of the country, but it's been under Russian control and a dark security cloud since being annexed in 2014, forcing adventurous visitors to explore the rest of the country.

Hiking

Trekkers point compasses west to the Carpathians. Bare-sloped **Borzhava Mountains**, three hours south of Lviv, see sun for most of summer. The **Chornogora Range** is home to Ukraine's highest peaks and crystal lakes, and the sharp summits of the **Marmaray Ridge** on the seam with Romania are the most remote part of the Carpathians, accessible only with permission from Ukrainian border guards. Solitude-loving hikers also seek out the Gorgany mountains, the least populated part of Ukraine, which get their name from the sandstone scree or 'gorgany' littering the slopes of the range.

Paddling

May to September is when kayakers put-in on the **Cheremosh River** and follow the flow through the sandstone canyons of **South Bug**. Both have Grade II–III rapids. Melting snow ensures a whitewater spring.

DON'T LEAVE WITHOUT...
Exploring Eastern Europe's largest alpine resort, Bukovel, which has a mountain bike park with cross-country and downhill trails, and 50km of ski runs in winter.

UNITED ARAB EMIRATES

Better known for skyscrapers and luxury holidays, away from the cities the UAE's arid mountains are an adventure playground.

A land of manufactured dreams, the UAE was little more than sand dunes and fishing villages a few decades ago. Its cities of Dubai and Abu Dhabi are now pure constructed consumerism, but don't let that put you off – just think of it as a high-end starting point for some off-the-beaten-track adventures.

Mountain Biking

Hajar Mountains' arid red landscape is the activity hub, and Showka is where MTB first hit the UAE. Its popularity led to the creation of a dedicated centre in **Hatta**, with trails from beginner to expert. For a real tough ascent, hit **Jebel Hafeet** in Al Ain, where views of the surrounding mountains reward those who grind it out.

Road cycling

Closer to Abu Dhabi, the 5.5km harbourside race circuit **Yas Marina** is open to bikes on Sundays and Tuesdays. Just 20 minutes outside the city, **Al Wathba Cycle Park** is another option, with smooth purpose-built trails and solar lighting for desert night rides.

Hiking

Trekking in the UAE is best in winter. The **Hajar Mountains** offer several options, including ascents of Wadi Ghalilah and its popular but perilous Stairway to Heaven. **Hatta** also has a few short trails marked out through the hills.

Sea Kayaking

On the water, head away from the private city beachfronts to explore the meandering mangrove-forested coastline channels that are located just outside **Abu Dhabi**, on **Sir Bani Yas Island**, and in the **Kalba Nature Reserve** near Dubai. **Umm Al Quwain** has longer routes, with remote beaches and marine life including sharks, rays, turtles and flamingoes.

DON'T LEAVE WITHOUT...
Riding a camel into the desert and exploring an oasis such as Liwa in Abu Dhabi.

The beautifully sited town of Hatta has excellent hiking in the nearby hills.

Richard Watson | Getty Images

UNITED KINGDOM

Birthplace of many recreational outdoor pursuits, Britain boasts an almost baffling amount of wild terrain, despite its large population and small landmass.

The umbrella of the UK covers England, Wales, Scotland and Northern Ireland (NI), which all have their own heavily accented qualities, characters, contours and coastlines. These countries (and the counties within them) can be fiercely independent, with diverse and occasionally conflicting cultures, but a more homogenous and happier outdoor community exists here, blinded to political borders by a shared love of the landscape and the activities and adventures that can be explored within it.

That said, some age-old areas of aggravation persist – between landowners, ramblers and mountain-bike riders, for example, or fishing folk and paddlers – and the approach to these countryside conflicts varies. In England, Wales and NI, walking rights of way are enshrined within the Countryside Code, but cyclists and equestrians are restricted to designated bridleways; only 2% of rivers can be paddled year-round; and wild camping is only officially allowed on parts of Dartmoor. By contrast, Scotland takes a more permissive Scandinavian-style approach, and the Outdoor Access Code north of the border allows bikers, hikers, runners and horse riders to share wild trails, paddlers to explore most waterways and it also permits responsible camping on public land – rules all underpinned by a usually met expectation of mutual respect.

There are 15 national parks spread across England (The Broads, Dartmoor, Exmoor, Lake District, New Forest, Northumberland, North York Moors, Peak District, South Downs and Yorkshire Dales), Wales (Brecon Beacons, Pembrokeshire Coast and Snowdonia) and Scotland (Cairngorms, and Loch Lomond and The Trossachs), and moves are afoot to designate one around Northern Ireland's Mourne Mountains. Vast swathes of the countryside are also owned and maintained by the National Trust and other woodland, wildlife and forestry focused organisations – which juggle their environmental objectives with a generally genuinely enthusiastic approach to outdoor pursuits – and the entire country is covered by the world's best and most extensive mapping system, created and maintained by Ordnance Survey (OS), a government agency dedicated to the task since 1745.

The British are famously weather obsessed and, yes, it does rain. But this heaven-sent hydraulic power is what makes the landscape so luminously green and lovely, the rivers so exciting and real ale in the warm shelter of a proper old country pub at your adventure's end so very fine.

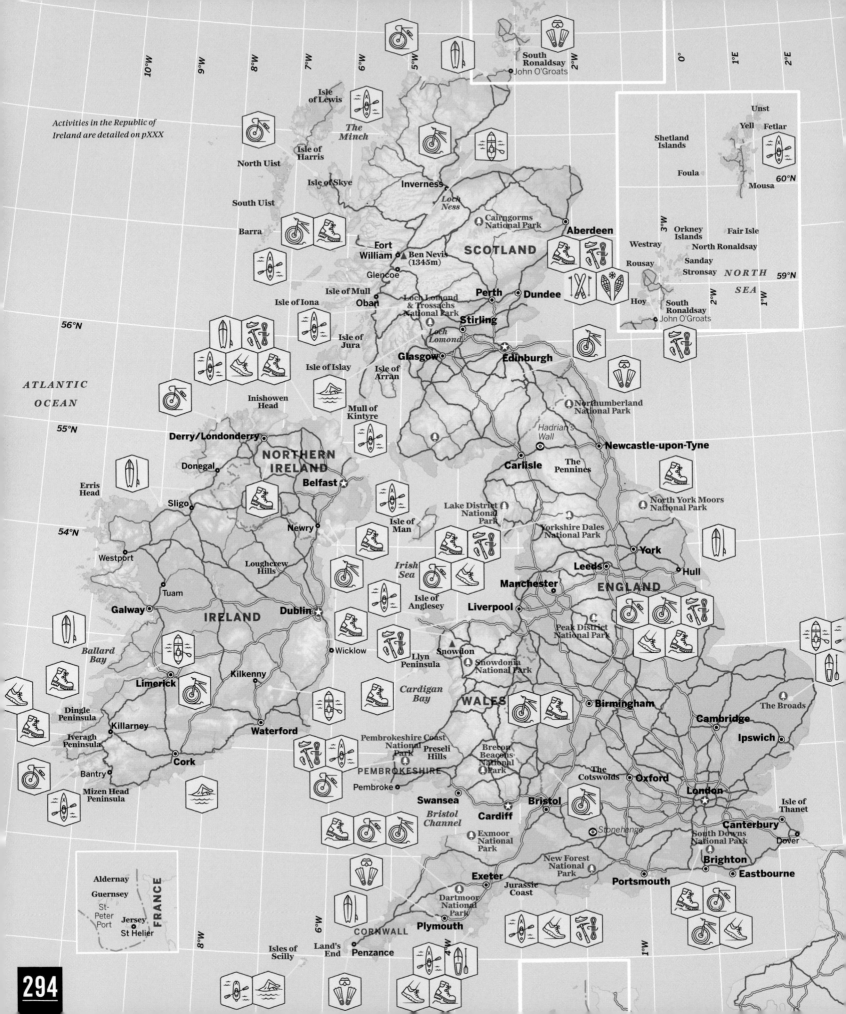

© Evocation Images | Shutterstock

Sailing

Sailing is in this island nation's DNA and it runs especially strongly along Britain's **south coast**. Sailing clubs and schools – from Plymouth and Dartmouth in Devon, through Weymouth and Portland in Dorset to Hayling Island and Lymington in Hampshire – populate the harbours along this shore. Cowes and Bembridge on the Isle of Wight, separated from the mainland by the sail-peppered Solent, are also salt-encrusted yachtie strongholds. The best are accredited by the Royal Yachting Association (RYA), which, despite the name, also represents dinghy sailors. The RYA runs sailing classes for people of all ages and abilities – most Britons start out getting a feel for the wind and tides in small one- or two-person dinghies, such as the Laser, before moving into larger, faster boats. RYA qualifications are recognised all over the world so you'll be equipped to skipper craft in places such as Australia or take part in regattas or competitions such as the annual Round-the-Island race.

Beyond the south coast, another sailing hotspot is the **Norfolk Broads** to the east of England, threaded with rivers and waterways. In the **Lake District** in Northwest England, Windermere and Coniston Water inspired Arthur Ransome's novel (and later film) *Swallows and Amazons*. Even the capital, London, offers sailing schools on the Thames.

The United Kingdom caters for all types of wind-powered fun, from messing about in dinghies to cruising in a chartered yacht. But for guaranteed sunshine you might need to set sail further afield.

The Round-the-Island race circles the Isle of Wight.

Walking

Britain's unique network of footpaths and byways is an ancient monument etched into the landscape that's every bit as important to the national identity as Stonehenge. Nowhere else is there such a dense and rich variety of walking routes, where your feet can retrace millennia of history along Roman causeways, medieval green lanes and Regency canal towpaths. Yet greater public access to England and Wales' peaks only came about far more recently, after hundreds of walkers wilfully trespassed onto Kinder Scout in the Peak District in 1932, clashing violently with local gamekeepers. It sparked a movement that would ultimately lead to the statutory opening up of the countryside after WWII,

and the creation of the national parks and national trails that remain Britain's crown jewels for outdoors enthusiasts. But wherever you choose to explore, any good British ramble should finish in the same time-honoured way: with a post-perambulation pint at a traditional pub. Cheers!

England

Thanks to Wordsworth's famous poetic wanderings more than 200 years ago, the **Lake District** became arguably the world's first mass tourism destination for recreational hikers. And while the likes of Windermere and Derwentwater can feel a bit manicured and twee, there are magnificently wild crags and isolated upland tarns all around you – particularly in the less-visited Northern Fells. Alfred Wainwright was the first to comprehensively document the dizzying array of fell-walks in his exquisite hand-drawn Pictorial Guides from the 1950s, and bagging all 214 '**Wainwrights**' is still a highly sought-after prize for any rambler.

Wainwright also masterminded the **Coast to Coast** walk: a 308km long-distance footpath across the neck of England from his beloved Lake District through the Yorkshire Dales and North York Moors to the North Sea. It's a challenging two-week traverse, showcasing some of the country's finest upland scenery. But it's far from England's longest trail – in every sense. That title belongs to the 1013km **South West Coast Path** around the glorious Cornish peninsula, from Somerset to Dorset. The National Trail is no seaside stroll, though: you'll climb the equivalent of Everest four times over along this epic rollercoaster of clifftops and bays.

Wales

Wales still boasts the only complete round-country footpath in the world, and it's a showstopper. In summertime, the 1400km **Wales Coast Path** around Pembrokeshire and the Llŷn Peninsula can be as pristinely azure and sand-swept as a Greek island. The inland leg along the English border follows the **Offa's Dyke Path**, along a 13th-century earthwork through the unspoiled and time-forgotten villages of the Welsh Marches.

Hillwalkers are spoiled for choice in Wales, with the highest, most technical climbs in the **Cambrian**

Perfect terrain for adventure; the Pembrokeshire Coast, Wales.

© Pete Seaward | Lonely Planet

Mountains to the north, extending to **Snowdonia National Park**. While scaling iconic **Mount Snowdon** is a must (choose the Miner's Track for the most scenic approach), extreme walkers could choose to do it as part of the **Welsh 3000s** challenge. Encompassing 14 other nearby summits over 3000ft (1000m) – all within 24 hours – the record for completing the 48km route stands at an astonishing four hours, 19 minutes.

Scotland

Arguably the UK's only true wildernesses are found north of the border, where Scotland's famous lochs, glens and mountains can be enjoyed without impediment, thanks to a presumed right of public access almost everywhere. Consequently, hiking here can be a far bolder, less path-bound affair than elsewhere in the UK. In winter, the **Cairngorms** mountain range in the east of the Highlands can feel like Lapland, as you encounter Britain's only free-ranging herd of reindeer on its vast, snowy plateau. It's a great place to learn ice-climbing and mountaineering too, using the National Outdoor Training Centre at **Glenmore Forest** as your hub to venture straight out onto the exposed granite peaks.

Many Scottish hillwalkers spend their lives '**Munro-bagging**', attempting to summit all 282 of the country's 3000ft (1000m) mountains, known as Munros after the pioneering mountaineer Sir Hugh Munro who first compiled a list of them all in 1891. And while wild camping is permitted on most open land, there's also a strong tradition of bothying in Scotland that shouldn't be missed. Usually a renovated old crofter's cottage or mountain hut with no running water, a bothy offers very basic shelter. But they're free to use and are often located in the most spectacular locations, miles from any roads. From a private beach overlooking Cape Wrath to a burnside cottage in the shadow of Ben Nevis, they're the perfect way to fully immerse yourself in a Scottish adventure.

Northern Ireland

The smash-hit TV series, *Game of Thrones*, has finally brought Northern Ireland's majestic natural scenery to the world's attention. It's not surprising the show's creators saw the perfect setting for the mythical Westeros among the dramatic granite tors and ancient woodlands of the **Mourne Mountains** – the highest range in Northern Ireland, with a wealth of tracks and trails. The tower-house castle ruins and ancient standing stones that scatter the coastal countryside around nearby Strangford Lough are also a fantastical sight for walkers enjoying the views out over the Irish Sea. The hardiest hikers could trek between these two regions via the **Ulster Way,** continuing along it through all six of the country's counties, across the heather-clad **Sperrin Mountains** and past the iconic **Giant's Causeway,** on a 1005km odyssey.

One of the best things about walking in the UK is that you're never far from a good meal and a beverage.

© Justin Foulkes | Lonely Planet

Climbing

Despite notoriously bad weather, the cliffs of the United Kingdom are the stuff of legend, and have produced some of climbing's most iconic names, the likes of Chris Bonington, Don Whillans, Jerry Moffatt, Ben Moon and 2016 bouldering World Cup champion Shauna Coxsey. The UK's climbing history is long and storied, dating back to the late 19th century, a time when it could be argued that climbing as a sport began.

The UK doesn't have the biggest crags or always the best rock, but it does have a diversity of rock types – slate and sandstone to limestone, grit, granite, rhyolite, gabbro and more – and a range of jealously protected styles, from trad climbing, sport climbing, bouldering, mixed climbing and deep-water soloing to obscure pastimes such as climbing soft chalk cliffs with ice axes and crampons.

But beyond the rock itself, the history and culture of UK climbing is a powerful mix: the stories of climbing's characters, the hard, bold routes, the close calls, the bad weather and the endless cups of tea all add to the rich (and often malodorous) stew that is climbing in the British Isles.

England

One of the cradles of climbing, the mountains and valleys of the **Lake District** are a trad climbing stronghold. Here, climbers can find everything from long, easy scrambles to short, desperate boulder problems and bold, hard 'death routes' best approached with great skill and caution. Some of the Lakes' more famous spots include spectacular crags such as **Scafell, Pillar, Gimmer** and **Dow**.

For many climbers around the world, the gritstone 'edges' (cliffs) of the **Peak District** epitomise UK climbing. Films like *Hard Grit* have cast the area as the home of mad, tea-drinking climbers who like nothing more than trusting their life to taped-down skyhooks. But the Peak has everything from scary, hard gritstone routes to well-protected trad routes,

as well as limestone sport and trad climbing – not to mention the endless bouldering. Gritstone Stanage holds pride of place in English climbing, and is home to hundreds of iconic routes and boulder problems. The nearby **Raven Tor**, a small limestone crag with some of the most polished holds you'll fall off anywhere, is another infamous destination and home of Hubble (8c+/9a), which, when it was climbed in 1990 by Ben Moon, was the hardest route in the world.

Wales

Variety is the spice of life in Wales. You'll find everything here: superb trad climbing on atmospheric sea cliffs such as **Gogarth** and **Pembroke,** sport climbing on sea cliffs like the **Diamond** and **Lower Pen Trwyn** to mountain crags such as **Clogwyn Du'r Arddu** and the slippery, weird climbing found in the abandoned slate mines of **Llanberis Pass**. Best of all, these crags are all within easy reach of one another.

Scotland

When it comes to winter climbing it's hard to beat Scotland. Here you'll find the UK's highest peak, **Ben Nevis** (1345m) and its 700m North Face, much beloved by alpine climbers. The Ben holds everything from easier classics such as Tower Ridge (Scottish IV), which was first climbed in winter in 1895, to hard modern classics like Centurion (VIII). But the Ben is just the tip of the ice climb; further east the more remote **Cairngorms** could rightfully be described as the epicentre of Scottish winter climbing.

Northern Ireland

Irish climbers think that **Fair Head** in County Antrim is the UK's best crag. Five kilometres long and up to 100m high, with superb grippy dolerite rock, soaring faces, stunning cracks and bold aretes to climb, Fair Head might just prove them right.

ULTIMATE CHALLENGE
Climbing onto the shoulders of the Old Man of Hoy. This iconic 137m-tall sea stack points at the bruised Scottish sky from the exposed archipelago that is the Orkney Islands, daring you to take it on.

Right, running up Ben Lomond with Loch Lomond below, Scotland.

© Andy McCandlish

Trail Running

All four corners of the UK offer great off-road running, with the country's numerous National Trails and many magical long-distance paths perfect for foot-powered adventures that are far from pedestrian.

Stand-outs include the 431km **Pennine Way** in Northern England, the gorgeous 240km **Offa's Dyke** path that traces the Welsh border, the 53km **Causeway Coast Way** in Northern Ireland, and Scotland's 155km **West Highland Way**, all of which host ultra-running races.

Clearly marked and well maintained, these paths are obvious targets for people setting FKTs (fastest known times), and even the longest of the long, the unbelievably undulating 1000km **South West Coast Path** has now been done in 10 days. More sensible runners bite them off in sections.

The UK's toughest running challenges are the **Dragon's Back Mountain Running race** – a five-day 300km journey with 16,000m of ascent across

ULTIMATE CHALLENGE

The Bob Graham Round is a historical challenge where self-sufficient runners try to traverse 42 Lakeland fells within a 24-hour period. Although Nicky Spinks has recently done a Double Bob Graham, no one has yet beaten Billy Bland's record.

the super-remote and often trackless terrain of the Welsh mountains – and the 400km **Cape Wrath Ultra**, which wends off-piste through the Scottish Highlands. A more eccentric event is found at the annual **Man versus Horse Marathon** in Llanwrtyd Wells, Wales, where runners compete against horse riders on a 35km off-road course.

Fell Running

In northern England, especially around the Lakes, trail running plays second fiddle to fell running, a more organic and less commercialised form of off-piste hill running defined by elevation climbed and lack of signage, with longer routes and races requiring competitors to self navigate. This sport, and Cumbria in particular, has produced characters including King of the Fells, Joss Naylor, a sheep farmer and running legend who set numerous records, including climbing 72 Lakeland peaks and running over 160km in under 24 hours in 1975.

Mountain biking

HOMEGROWN ADVENTURE HERO

Steve Peat, a legendary downhill MTB racer with a UCI World Championship and three World Cup titles, explains why he gets a buzz from riding in the UK: 'The addition of trail centres to the UK scene has been a huge success over the years. We may not have the elevation or lift-access trails, but we certainly have the variety of fun, technical, root-and-rock trails to match the rest of the world.'

For a relatively small place lacking really big mountains, the UK is an unlikely hotbed of off-road, two-wheeled action that has produced some of the very best riders in the world. Whether it's the carefully coiffured berms and rollers of the Surrey Hills or the wild and ragged boulder field descents of the Scottish Highlands, the sheer scope for mountain bike adventures is astonishing.

England

Just about every region in England has its MTB hot spots. The trails surrounding the small village of **Peaslake** and spidering through Surrey's **North Downs** are the closest to the capital and offer some good woodland riding. The chalky **South Downs** have more open, point-to-point routes. **The Forest of Dean** to the west is an old downhill haunt that over the years has matured perfectly to match the needs of today's long-travel trail bikes. Deeper into the southwest, Somerset's **Quantocks** and **Mendip Hills** both boast good singletrack tracing uncoiffured combes, and **Dartmoor** and **Exmoor** have some proper wild trails well worth exploring. Further north, small towns such as **Shrewsbury** and **Hebden Bridge** boast thriving MTB communities centred around stunning, often steep, singletrack. The **Peak District** and **Lake District** national parks are popular locations for tough, rocky rides. **Grenoside Woods**, on the outskirts of Sheffield, produced the prodigious talent Steve Peat.

Northern Ireland

An emerging star of the UK riding scene, the north of Ireland is really embracing MTBing thanks to an influx of new trail centres. **Rostrevor,** on the banks of Carlingford Lough, is the biggest with 46km of trail including two upliftable downhill tracks. It's the smaller **Castlewellan** centre, however, that is the real star, with trails mellow enough for new recruits intermingled with more challenging sections for the experienced. **Davagh Forest**, located 80km west of Belfast, is well worth a visit, too, for a more natural burst of singletrack action.

Scotland

The **Seven Stanes** network of trail centres arrived after the foot and mouth crisis of 2001 and put Scottish mountain biking on the map. The jewel in the crown is undoubtedly **Glentress**, near Peebles, which has more than 300,000 visitors a year. Those seeking 'hours from anywhere' wilderness trails need to look further north to the Highlands where ancient walking paths and Scotland's 'right to roam' access laws make for all-day adventures through breathtaking landscapes. **Fort William** hosts the only gondola-accessed riding in the UK in the form of the Red Giant descent and UCI World Cup track.

Wales

South Wales really is a trail centre mecca and offers some of the most well-established man-made trails anywhere in Europe. **Afan** and **Cwmcarn** offer reliable, all-year thrills but it's **Bike Park Wales** that has really captured the imagination of British riders. Pedal or uplift to the top then rocket back down pick-and-mixing blue, red, black and orange trails on your way. Further north, the scenery becomes increasingly mountainous with **Coed y Brenin**, **Coed Llandegla** and Snowdonia's gravity-focused **Antur Stiniog** and **Revolution Bike Park** offering up yet more brake-burning thrills.

© Andy McCandlish

© Joe Dunckley | Shutterstock

Road Cycling

You have to look a little harder for superlative road cycling in the UK compared with France, Italy or Spain, but it's there to be discovered. The first thing to understand is that there aren't the vast open spaces, massive mountains and valleys of other countries. Everything is smaller scale, but that just means it's more easily bitten off in 80-mile mouthfuls. There's a density to the road network (outside parts of Scotland) that means cycle tourists in the UK have the advantage of never being far from a town or village. The country is ideal for settling in one spot and exploring its environs in detail during day rides. The Sustrans organisation has pioneered safe cycling routes, with hundreds of numbered routes forming part of the National Cycle Network. They tend to follow quiet back roads and country lanes, and can also venture onto canal paths or gravel roads. They're mapped and signposted and are probably the easiest options for visitors. The country's biggest race, the Tour of Britain, takes place each September.

England is the most densely populated part of the UK, with national parks such as the South Downs, the Peak District, Dartmoor, Exmoor and the Lake District containing most of its steeper landscapes. There are pockets of idyllic countryside for cyclists to explore well within an hour's train ride from London, but the northeast, from the North Yorkshire Moors to Northumberland, arguably offers the country's best cycling. Yorkshire's cycling credentials have been increasingly recognised since it staged the Tour de France Grand Départ in 2014, and the county is hosting the Road World Championships in 2019.

In **Wales**, longer climbs may demand greater fitness but there are some flatter routes along the Pembrokeshire coast. There are similarly superb multiday coastal rides in **Northern Ireland**, for example from Ballyshannon to Larne. (Note that the UK's prevailing weather direction brings more rain to the west than the east.)

Scotland is heaven for more adventurous cyclists. The newest addition to its range of routes is the North Coast 500, but there are challenging cycle rides across the country, and heading to its islands, such as Skye, opens up more remote riding.

Above, climbing Chapel Fell in the North Pennines in England's northeast. Left, finding sweet singletrack in the Cairngorms, Scotland.

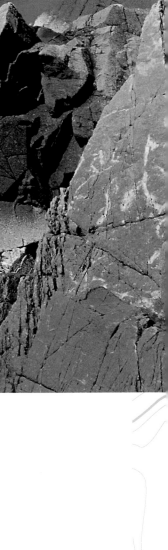

Paddling

The UK offers multiple paddling adventures, from somnambulant meanders along the country's canals (an interconnected network of waterways spidering 4800km across mainland Britain, including a new 240km cross-England canoe route between Liverpool's docks and the Humber estuary) to fast-flowing whitewater thrill rides. There's 12,429km of coastline to be explored, along with loads of lakes, lochs and loughs. Access to inland waterways can require a licence or be restricted; the best port of call for information is British Canoeing (www.britishcanoeing.org.uk).

England

You can paddle the **Thames** anytime, but the **Devizes–Westminster International Canoe Race**, run every Easter since 1948, appears on many must-do lists. Starting on the Kennet and Avon Canal and finishing opposite the Houses of Parliament 200km later, the race features 77 portages.

Canoe trails crisscross the **Broads**, a sprawling aquatic area that seeps across Norfolk and Suffolk, with waterside campsites and quintessentially British B&Bs providing overnight options. Unsurprisingly, the **Lake District** offers numerous flatwater paddling options, but **Cumbria** is also full

Top, sea kayaking at Porth y Ffynnon on the Pembrokeshire coast, Wales. Right, Scotland's rivers have excellent whitewater kayaking.

© Falk Kienas | Getty Images

of quality whitewater rivers, including the **Sprint** (Grade IV/V) and **Upper Duddon** (Grade IV).

In the South West, whitewater shenanigans can be enjoyed on dozens of Devon's rivers, including the **Erme** (Grade IV/V), **East Lyn** (Grade III–V), **Upper Tavy** (Grade IV+), **Upper Plym** (Grade V), **Upper Dart** between Dartmeet and Newbridge (Grade IV) and the more benign **Teign** (Grade III). Serious sea kayakers relish challenging surf conditions along the shipwreck-strewn coastlines of **North Devon** and **Cornwall**, including the **Roseland Heritage Coast** and **The Lizard**, while the spectacularly featured **Jurassic Coast**, running along South Devon and Dorset, is calmer, providing a playground for SUPers.

Scotland

The **Great Glen Canoe Trail** slices right through Scotland, from Fort William on the west coast to Inverness on the east, with the Caledonian Canal joining the dots formed by Loch Lochy, Loch Oich and monstrous Loch Ness. The 95km journey typically takes three to five days, with camping spots found lochside.

River Ness, which feeds the loch, has mild whitewater (Grade I–II), but real rapid runners are spoiled for choice in Scotland, where clear water constantly cascades headlong off the Highlands. Epic aquatic action can be found on rivers including the **Nevis** (Grade IV+), **Leven** in Kinlochleven (Grade IV–V), **Middle Etive** (Grade IV), **Garry** (Grade III) and **Orchy**, with its classic run between the between the Bridge and the Falls (Grade III–IV).

Around the craggy coast, superb sea kayaking can be enjoyed, from exploring the **Summer Isles** archipelago off Loch Broom to a full-on expedition along the **Scottish Sea Kayak Trail** skirting the wonderfully wild west coast between Gigha and Ullapool. The entire trail takes several weeks, but a highlight is paddling the picturesque **Lord of the Isles** section from Oban to Mallaig. Experienced sea kayakers can venture even further west, to **St Kilda**, or north to the **Shetlands**.

Wales

Britain's only coastal national park, the cove-punctuated 350km **Pembrokeshire** shoreline, provides a paddling paradise for kayakers, while inland the famous vales of Wales run white with

rivers charging towards the Irish Sea. Fast and furious highlights include the **Hepste** (Grade IV–V) and **Mellte** (Grade IV–V) in the Brecon Beacons; **Nantgrwyd** (Grade IV) and **Afon Glaslyn** (Grade IV) in Snowdonia; and the **Conwy** (Grade III–IV) in Betws-y-Coed, especially the Fairy Glen section.

Northern Ireland

Sea kayakers have plenty to ponder here, with the world-famous rock formations of the **Causeway Coast** and the mixture of sandy beaches and chalky cliffs that fringe the **East Coast Trail** further south, between Cushendall and Portaferry at the mouth of Strangford Lough. You can venture offshore to paddle around island groups like County Antrim's **Maidens** and the **Copelands** off County Down, or stick to the sheltered waters of **Larne Lough** and **Belfast Lough**.

Canoeists can explore the 58km **Lower Bann Trail** from Lough Neagh to the Atlantic, or follow the 53km **Foyle Canoe Trail**, which pokes its bow into the Republic of Ireland and drifts through Derry en route to the ocean.

© bikeriderlondon | Shutterstock

ULTIMATE CHALLENGE

As the Three Peaks tempt walkers and runners to tick off the mainland's highest peaks, so the new Three Lakes Challenge thrown down by British Canoeing dares kayakers to paddle the longest lakes in England (17.6km Windermere), Scotland (40km Loch Awe) and Wales (11.2km Llyn Tegid) in 24 hours (including travel).

ICONIC EVENT

The Scilly Swim Challenge sees competitors swim and walk/run across the Isles of Scilly. The event involves six swims averaging 2.5km each (total 15km) and six walks averaging 1.7 km (total 10km).

Surfing

Nowhere in the UK is much more than 100km from the sea, and most of the country's coastline gets surf, so it's little wonder surfing is a popular pursuit for climate-defying Brits. Cornwall and Devon have a surfing pedigree stretching back over 50 years, as does Wales, whereas northeast England, Scotland and Northern Ireland have only seen wave riding really take off relatively recently, largely thanks to improvements in wetsuit design.

Cornwall and Devon's north coast and the south coast of Wales have consistent waves all year round, although autumn is prime time (mild sea and air temperatures), whereas the North Sea coast and Scotland's north coast and Hebridean islands are best surfed in the late summer, when they're at their warmest.

Coasteering

An exciting combination of scrambling, jumping, wild swimming and free climbing, coasteering involves traversing the intertidal zone of a section of coast without using a boat, board or ropes. Participants expect to get wet and meet jagged rocks, and wear appropriate safety clothing: typically a wetsuit, helmet and footwear. The concept was coined in 1986 by Andy Middleton, director of TYF Adventure in **Pembrokeshire**, Wales. and now the pursuit is offered by hundreds of operators who guide groups on rugged shorelines all around the UK – especially Wales, Cornwall and Devon – and well beyond. It's also practised independently, but good local knowledge is crucial for safety.

Caving

Caving, or potholing as it's called here, can be done across the UK. The longest cavern is **White Scar Cave** in the Yorkshire Dales, but the most famous is the limestone labyrinth that burrows into the side of **Cheddar Gorge**, Somerset, which extends for 3.5km and has been attracting human attention for millennia. In 1903, near the entrance of Gough's Cave, the remains if a 9000-year man were found. Today you can squeeze on your knees and explore the cave system, straight after a subterranean abseil.

Diving

Though the UK doesn't have any live coral, it does boast a huge chalk reef at **Cromer Shoal** in Norfolk, which offers divers the chance to swim with harbour porpoises, plus grey and harbour seals. Elsewhere, excellent wreck diving can be done at **Scapa Flow** in Scotland, and **Lundy Island** has caves, a seal colony and more shipwrecks.

Wild Swimming

The chilly weather doesn't deter the UK's wild swimmers one bit, and new al fresco swimming places are being discovered all the time. Some standouts include **Waterfall Woods** in the Brecon Beacons, Wales; **Sharrah Pool** on Dartmoor; **Kailpot Crag**, Ullswater, in the Lake District; and the **River Thames** in Pangbourne.

Gorge Scrambling

Known as canyoning in most parts of the world, the Brits enjoy their best gorge scrambling in Wales and the Lake District, where it's more specifically known as ghyll scrambling. Like canyoning, the objective is to follow a gorge/ghyll/canyon, usually along the waterway that created it, employing skills such as climbing, abseiling, jumping and swimming.

Coasteering near Skrinkle Haven Beach on the Pembrokeshire Coast, Wales.

© Derek Phillips | Alamy

THE UNITED STATES

America is the land of the large – big cars, big appetites, big money – and its landscapes are no different: they're supersized, diverse and open for adventure.

Powerful topography more often than not goes hand-in-hand with adventure, and when it comes to big topography – monstrous mountains, huge gorges, dramatic deserts, colossal cliffs, raging rivers, cosmic coasts and enormous oceans – the US is, as it is in all things, a superpower.

In the contiguous US states alone you'll find all the elements and more for adventure: epic coastline, stunning mountain ranges like the Sierra Nevada and the Rockies, the gaping chasm of the Grand Canyon (and at its bottom the Colorado River), desert towers in Utah, vertiginous granite walls in Yosemite – the list is almost endless. To that you can add the non-contiguous states. To the north, Alaska holds vast, largely untapped wilderness to explore and North America's highest peak, Denali (6190m), to climb. To the west, pounded by enormous Pacific Oceans winter swells, Hawaii's waves are famous and feared, while beneath the waves there's an explosion of marine life.

When John Muir said, 'Keep close to nature's heart... and break clear away, once in a while, and climb a mountain or spend a week in the woods. Wash your spirit clean,' Americans took it to heart. From the Alaska Range to the Appalachians and beyond, they have followed in Muir's footsteps, retracing a multitude of hiking trails across the nation – including his iconic eponymous trail, which leads from California's Yosemite Valley all the way to the summit of Mt Whitney, the Sierra Nevada's highest peak, a journey of some 30 days.

But beyond Muir's favourite pastime, Americans have found a multitude of ways to wash their spirit clean. Ever the innovators, Americans have created many of the modes in which we love to spend our time outdoors: the modern mountain bike was born on the steep, dusty trails of Marin County; surfing (and SUPing) emerged from the sweet surging swell of Hawaii; BASE jumpers first tested their faith falling from the big walls of Yosemite Valley; while whitewater rafting started on the Snake River. The US even invented the notion of national parks, protecting the seething caldera that is Yellowstone National Park in 1872.

America is the supersized superpower of adventure; whatever your fix, you'll be sure to find it here in every form, from easy-to-access to epic-to-access. Tuck in.

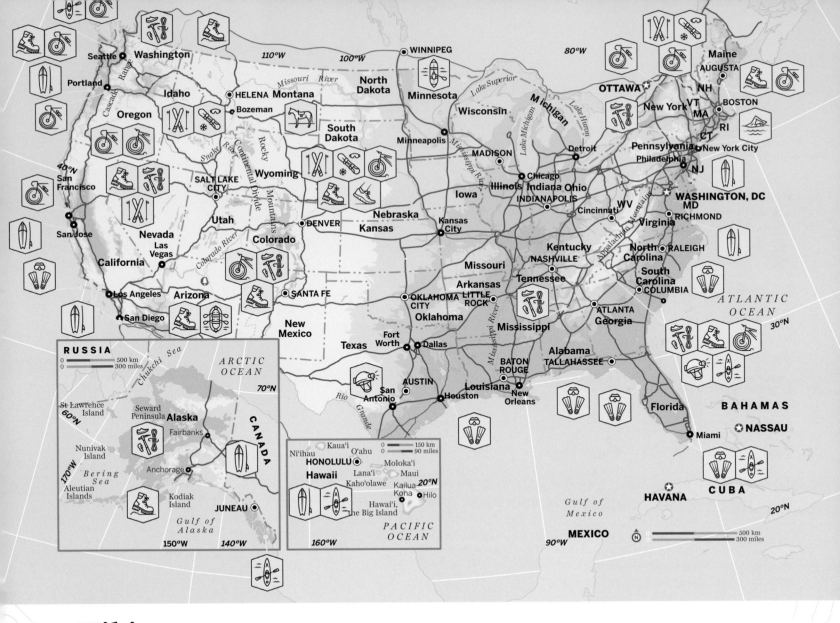

Hiking

The US is home to several epic hiking trails that take weeks or months to complete – including the Appalachian Trail, the Pacific Crest Trail, and the John Muir Trail – but you don't have to commit to anything like that distance to experience American landscapes. With iconic mountain ranges in the East and the West, desert terrain including the Grand Canyon, dozens of national parks (with trails managed by the National Park Service), and thousands of miles of trails through it all, the US offers adventure by foot from a half-day to a half-year.

Western States

Famed Scottish-American conservationist and writer John Muir made California's Sierra Nevada mountains famous as the 'Range of Light'. Striking clean white granite peaks ring alpine lakes along the 643km-long mountain range, which holds a number of the most classic hikes in the US: the 35km round-trip hike to the summit of **Mt Whitney** (4421m); the exposed and engaging route up the back of **Yosemite's Half Dome**, where hikers climb a cable ladder for the final 121-vertical-metres to the summit; and the 337km-long **John Muir Trail**, which joins the two, beginning near Half Dome and ending on the summit of Mt Whitney.

The deserts in the southwestern US provide a contrast to the mountains, and have gained notoriety in the past few decades as a premier adventure destination in the spring and autumn. The **Grand Canyon**, nearly 2km deep, cuts down through hundreds of millions years of geologic activity, and hikers can see that history in different

Right, gazing into the mighty abyss that is the Grand Canyon.

layers as they make their way to the bottom via several trails, some of which take only a day to descend (but often two days to ascend back to the rim). Though southern Utah's red rock desert doesn't have a Grand Canyon, it makes up for it in dramatic red sandstone walls, smaller canyons, fins, towers and arches – including the world-famous Delicate Arch in **Arches National Park**, only a 2.4km hike from the car park. Five desert national parks lie within a few hours' drive of each other here, all with distinctly different landscapes.

The Pacific Northwest's most famous mountains are volcanoes such as **Mt Rainier** (4392m) and **Mt Hood** (3429m), and although most require technical climbing experience, a summer day trip to Mt Rainier's **Camp Muir** requires only sturdy legs and good weather. Camp Muir is the base camp for the majority of summit attempts on Rainier, about halfway up the mountain. The route to Muir, even in the late summer, is usually snow-covered, and gives hikers a sense of the enormity of the mountain's glaciers and seracs. Of course, the Northwest has more than just volcanoes – the coast of Oregon and Washington offers sea-level hiking opportunities. Shi Shi Beach, a relatively easy stroll in Washington's **Olympic National Park**, starts in rainforest and ends on a beach lined with sea stacks. The 4265km **Pacific Crest Trail**, recently made famous in the bestselling book *Wild* (and accompanying Hollywood movie), runs from Canada to Mexico through Washington, Oregon, and California. Some of its most scenic sections pass by towering volcanoes in Washington and Oregon and are easily hikable in a day, or backpacked in two to four days.

The **Rocky Mountains** form the backbone of North America, and bisect the United States. Colorado has claimed the 'Rocky Mountain High' brand and is famous for its skiing, but when the snow melts in the summertime, its peaks and passes provide expansive views and solitude. Many of the state's highest mountains – the so-called '14ers', or peaks higher than 14,000ft (4200m) – are single-day walk-ups that will challenge both the legs and the lungs. The **Colorado Trail** traverses the Rocky Mountains from east to west, crossing eight sub-ranges over its 804km length, with an average elevation of over 3000m.

Colorado doesn't have a monopoly on hiking in the Rocky Mountains, however – those who have explored Wyoming's **Wind River Range** a few hours to the north will sing its praises. Although the driving and hiking takes a bit longer to access the 'good stuff', it delivers in spades, with sweeping batholithic granite faces and more than 150 named glaciers along the Winds' 160km length. Backpackers fill a pack and head to Titcomb Basin, a one- to two-day hike into a broad glacially carved valley lined with peaks reaching nearly 4000m high. Further north, Montana's **Glacier National Park** lies just south of the US-Canada border and boasts 160-plus-km of hiking trails connecting its many dramatic valleys between glacially striated peaks.

Eastern States

The mountains of the eastern US are not as high in elevation as their western counterparts, but the hiking is equally, if not more, celebrated. The 3508km-long **Appalachian Trail** is the country's original long-distance trail, completed in 1937, tracing the length of the Appalachian Mountains from south to north. Through-hiking the Appalachian Trail, or 'The AT', is a life goal of many hikers, and requires six months of walking,

DON'T LEAVE WITHOUT...
Hiking Zion National Park's Angels Landing Trail – just 8km long, but utterly unforgettable. The last 100m traverses a ledgy via ferrata route to a pedestal smack in the middle of the canyon, 460m above the canyon floor and the Virgin River below. Not for the faint of heart or the acrophobic.

© Matt Munro | Lonely Planet

Alaska's landscapes are made for adventure.

park, with five different trails leading to its summit.

Further north in the Appalachian Mountains is **Shenandoah National Park**, another place famous for its autumn colours, and also well-known for the adventurous hike and scramble up **Old Rag Mountain**. Old Rag is not the highest peak in the park, but is unique for its treeless, granite summit, which provides some of the best views in the park.

In the northeast US, New Hampshire's **White Mountains** only rise to 1917m, but thanks to their harsh weather and rocky topography can lay claim to being one of the training grounds for the US's most accomplished alpinists. **Mt Washington**, the high point of the range, is legendary for storms and 'the worst weather on Earth' thanks to the convergence of several storm tracks on its summit – it once registered wind speeds of 371km/h. All that said, those who venture into the White Mountains are rewarded with challenging trails to panoramic views. The 13km hike to Mt Washington's summit from the Pinkham Notch Visitor Center climbs out of a ravine and headwall to the top, gaining more than 1219m on the way up. Hikers hungry for more than one summit tackle the **Franconia Ridge Traverse**, a 14km loop hike up to and across the summits of Mt Lafayette (1603m), Mt Lincoln (1551m) and Little Haystack Mountain (1450m), before descending to the trailhead.

Alaska

Containing more acres of wilderness than the rest of the US combined, much of Alaska's terrain is daunting: glaciated peaks and massive national parks filled with big wildlife (bears and moose) but without roads, let alone trails. Veterans of Alaska backpacking would say some of the best scenery is accessed where there are no trails, and they might be correct, but there are plenty of trails that access wonderful Alaskan vistas. A few minutes south of Anchorage, the **Crow Pass Trail** climbs 5km to a public cabin, and descends from the pass through 28km of lush river valley. North of Anchorage, the 57km **Kesugi Ridge Trail** in Denali State Park follows a ridge with views to 6193m Denali and the Alaska Range to the west. Just west of Seward, the 13km **Harding Icefield Trail** climbs 1200m to views of its namesake icefield, more than 750 sq km of it. Alaska's Department of Natural Resources can provide information on trails in state parks.

and approximately five million steps. Thousands of backpackers attempt it each year, but many more hike shorter sections of the trail from various trailheads and road crossings along the route.

Great Smoky Mountains National Park, America's most-visited national park, straddles a sub-range of the Appalachian Mountains, and is named after not actual smoke, but a fog that rolls in and out of the peaks. The Smoky Mountains are famous for their forests, which cover the majority of the range's summits, and turn brilliant colours in the autumn months. **Mt LeConte**, at 2010m, is one of the tallest and one of the most popular peaks in the national

 © Justin Foulkes | Lonely Planet

Road Cycling

America's cycling culture has blossomed in certain states over the past decades. What the US lacks in riding history it makes up for with boundless options for Strava-obsessed road riders, casual tourers and backcountry bikepackers. Broadly, the vast country can be divided into three key cycling regions: the Northeast, the Northwest and the Southwest, and most visitors will focus on only one at a time, but there's great riding outside these hot spots too.

The Northwest

Comprising Northern California (NorCal), Oregon and Washington state, this is where to come to be dwarfed by giant redwoods, invigorated by sea-sprayed coasts and excited by progressive, cycling-friendly cities. There are probably more singlespeeds and cargo bikes per head in Oregon's **Portland** than anywhere else in the USA. But there are equally strong road-riding, cyclocross and bikepacking scenes in the green and foggy northwest. Classic excursions at the top of this region include the roads and bikeways around **Bend**, Oregon, and the **San Juan Islands**, easily reached from Seattle. Venturing south into Northern California brings riders into dark redwood and sequoia forests or, away from the coast's sea fogs, the **Sierra Nevada**, home of mountain lions and plenty of plaid shirts and pick-ups. The long-distance road route that links it all up is the Pacific Coast Highway. It's rideable but expect lots of tourist traffic too. After Portland, **San Francisco** is another epicentre of American bike culture with several places offering bike rentals. Bay Area riders embark on loops of **Marin County**, climbing Mt Tam for the kudos and views of San Francisco.

Bikepackers will relish pedalling around Washington's **Olympic Peninsula**, a rainy, moss-draped wonderland, or perhaps hitting Oregon's old wagon trails.

The Southwest

California gets drier and hotter the further south you go. **Los Angeles** has its own renegade riding culture, making the best of being in the city of the automobile, and **San Diego** is triathlete territory. Venture inland for mind-melting deserts, studded with Joshua trees, gnarled pines and cacti. **Arizona, New Mexico** and **Utah** may be best known for mountain bike trails over sticky slickrock, but roadies can easily compose loops from towns and cities on little-trafficked roads, so long as summer temperatures are treated with caution. But bikepackers will be in heaven. Dirt roads wind through desert and brush, and go as far as you care to – plenty have mapped these vast landscapes. New Mexico is particularly rich in routes: check out the **Organ Mountains** and **Jemez Mountains,** with Santa Fe making a great staging post.

The Northeast

For scenery that's slightly less arid, Vermont, Maine, Massachusetts, New England, Connecticut and New York State all have rich riding country, with roads passing clapboard barns and fiery fall leaves in the Green Mountains (Vermont) and the **White Mountains** (New Hampshire). Heading south to New York State, cyclists will find a wealth of opportunities with bikeways, canalways and hillier challenges in the **Adirondacks**. In **New York city**, cyclists take on cab drivers on the Five Boro Tour, but for adventures that are just as entertaining but less explctive filled, head out of the Big Apple.

© Matt Munro | Lonely Planet

ULTIMATE CHALLENGE
The 4800km Race Across America (RAAM) has been held annually since 1982, but why rush? Lots of established routes exist across the land of the free, west to east, north to south, all mapped by the Adventure Cycling Association.

Autumn cycling on the Blue Ridge Parkway, which passes through Virginia and North Carolina.

Mountain Biking

America is the birthplace of mountain biking, the free-spirited, devil-may-care mud-and-blood-splattered baby brother of civilised cycling that was dreamed up amid long, crazy, hazy afternoons of racing balloon-tyred cruisers in the hills of California's Marin County in the mid-1970s. Charlie Kelly and Fred Wolf organised the very first downhill race in 1976, riding modified cruiser bikes at breakneck speeds down a Mt Tamalpais logging-road route they named 'Repack', because of the repeated 'repacking' of grease into the molten-hot brakes required between races. After this Big Bang moment, the sport evolved enormously and its popularity rapidly spread across the globe. The US, however, with its spectacularly wild and varied landscapes, remains one of the best destinations on Earth for two-wheeled adventurers. All across the country, snow resorts have turned their green season slopes

into a booming wonderland of chairlift-supported bike parks for riders to explore, and beyond the groomed routes you will find an incredible diversity of off-piste trail riding and wilderness routes on both coasts.

Western States

The ochre-red trails of Utah's **Moab** are one of MTB's most iconic aesthetics. Just over 16km in length, the Slick Rock trail sets its sights rather loftily on being the best MTB ride in the world – and it's definitely up there, as is the nearby Poison Spider. The entertainment options are many: there are exposed cliff-top sections, super-steep slick rock descents and jeep tracks a plenty.

However, many Stateside rough riders rate Colorado's **Fruita** even higher than Moab as a trail hub. The town is surrounded by hundreds of miles of easy-to-access, fast-and-flowing canyon- ridge-

Riding the Flume Trail beside Lake Tahoe, Nevada.

© Andrew Peacock, © Cass Gilbert

ULTIMATE ADVENTURE
Riding the Kokopelli Trail, a 229km stretch of continuous double- and singletrack that rolls off-road all the way from Loma, near the trail town of Fruita, to MTB mecca of Moab.

and desert-style singletrack, with myriad route options available within the North Fruita Desert/18 Road trail system and from the Kokopelli Trailhead.

An affluent Colorado snow resort by winter, in summer Aspen's **Snowmass Bike Park** morphs into three-vertical-kilometres of chairlift-assisted downhill playground. There are four main bike park-style downhill runs as well as a smattering of more XC-focused offerings. It also plays annual host to the Enduro World Series if you fancy getting a racing fix. Want more pedalling? Nearby **Crested Butte** has one of the finest networks of trails in the country and hosts a claimed 750 trails.

The desert surrounding Nevada's Las Vegas can be a barren, arid place, but the Hoover Dam isn't the only thing worthy of a visit. The trails of **Bootleg Canyon** range from fast-flowing ribbons of hardpack singletrack right up to the forebodingly titled Armageddon Trail, which plummets right off the roof of the craggy canyon. Open all year round, the lower trails provide plenty of hardpack flow, while nearby Boulder City offers up plenty of eateries and bars to help you to refuel/rehydrate after a long day in the desert.

Oregon's **Bend** is one of those iconic American riding spots that feature on many a rider's bucket list. The town of Bend is at the heart of a sprawling network of trails, the majority of which can be accessed right from its centre. The sheer amount of riding in the area is staggering; there are even designated fatbike trails for when winter snow arrives. Fortunately, the Bend trails are some of

Discover Joshua trees on a bikepacking tour of the Southwest USA.

the most cared for in the US with up-to-date trail conditions and closures meticulously logged online.

Eastern States

Just a couple of hours from the Big Apple, **Windham** is a small town deep in the almost jungle-like Catskill Mountains in New York State. An upmarket ski resort in the winter months, it played host to the US's most recent UCI World Cup races and offers plenty of scope for chair-lift assisted downhill action, as well as the potential to take on an international-level race track. Resisting the urge to pretend that you're Aaron Gwin crossing the line on the way to his incredible 2015 victory may prove too tough to resist.

One of the US's newest bike parks, **Thunder Mountain** in Massachusetts roared onto the North Eastern scene back in 2015 and almost instantly made an impact. Everything about the park is designed to draw riders back. It may 'only' have 300 or so vertical metres of elevation but the hillside is packed with gravity-fuelled trails and is well worth a visit. The Hawley Wood trail is an expert-level jump-and-drop packed flow monster that's up there with the best bikepark trails in the country.

One of the most acclaimed areas for mountain biking on the east coast, North Carolina's **Brevard** flies in the face of thinking that stipulates you need to be out west to truly enjoy 'proper' trail riding. The stunning Appalachian Mountains hide a staggering array of cragged, muddy, natural riding, and there's a smattering of passionate, quality local shops and infrastructure to support it all. DuPont State Forest features some incredible riding with good beginner-friendly options, whereas more advanced mile-munchers will look to Pisgah National Forest for their thrills.

Alaska

Up in the far north, Alaska (home to the iconic **Iditarod**, a traditional dogsled race that's now open to fatbikes) has great wild riding at **Seward**, notably on the Lost Lake Trail. Just west of Anchorage, on the cusp of the Cook Inlet, you'll find 600-hectare **Kincaid Park**, where x-country skiing trails become rolling ribbons of MTB singletrack during the green season. **Matanuska Lakes State Recreation Area** has more beginner-friendly trails, still mostly along singletrack.

Skiing & Snowboarding

It's no surprise that US ski resorts do a great job of promoting themselves – after all, this is the home of the big sell – and the self-proclaimed 'best snow on Earth' (Utah) and 'champagne powder' (Steamboat Springs) is there to be enjoyed massively if you catch a big dump. American resorts are typically smaller than Europe's, but their catchment area is also comparatively small, so you'll rarely encounter the kind of 'lift lines' that you do in the Alps. Indeed, at more isolated ski hills such as **Lookout Pass** in Idaho or **Big Sky** in Montana, you may find yourself looking around for a ski buddy.

The best skiing is generally found in the Rockies, in the states of Montana, Idaho, Wyoming, Utah, Colorado and New Mexico. There are far more resorts in this enormous area than can be covered here, but you should treat that as an invitation to explore. The northern Rocky Mountain states look and feel very different from those in the south – both boast forested mountains, but the north is cleaved by valleys while dry plains and deserts characterise the south. One common denominator is that resorts tend to be based around old mining towns, which gives them a distinct Wild West feel. Butch Cassidy's first bank job was in the town of **Telluride**, Colorado, which offers some of North America's best skiing.

The country's high-profile resorts – such as **Deer Valley** in Utah, **Beaver Creek** and **Aspen** in Colorado and **Sun Valley** in Idaho – can be eye-wateringly expensive at times, but you do get

What goes down must first go up; ski touring in Alaska.

© Krystle Wright, © James McCormack

excellent service both on and off the mountain as well as superbly groomed slopes. At Beaver Creek the pistes are groomed and then the snow cannons are turned on to add a thin layer of 'fresh' snow over the top of the 'corduroy'; skiers are also provided with free hot cookies from 3pm.

If this kind of pampering ain't your thing, there are plenty of more downhome options. Many Rockies resorts focus as much on the authentic ski experience as the glitz and glamour, and lesser-known ski hills such as **Crested Butte** in Colorado, **Bridger Bowl** in Montana and **Schweitzer Mountain** in Idaho are more about what you can do on your skis than the size of your wallet, and consequently they offer some seriously testing terrain that more than makes up for their relatively small size.

Outside of the Rockies, California's Sierra Nevada range can provide excellent skiing for all levels of ability in resorts such as **Mammoth Mountain**, **Squaw Valley** and **Heavenly** (beautifully located above cobalt blue Lake Tahoe), although snowfall here seems to operate on a feast or famine basis – either massive dumps or hardly anything.

In the east, well-established destinations such as **Stowe** and **Killington** in Vermont (the latter the largest resort in the eastern US) and **Lake Placid** in upstate New York are well worth checking out if you're in the area, although they are renowned for having icy slopes and being bitterly cold.

Backcountry

Off-piste enthusiasts are spoiled for choice, especially in the Rockies. Towns such as **Bozeman** and **Whitefish** in Montana have fantastic backcountry terrain within easy reach of downtown, while at the south end of the range New Mexico/Colorado's **Sangre de Cristo mountains** offer idyllic skiing. **Colorado** also has a fine network of backcountry ski huts for multiday tours.

Off-piste at Jackson Hole, Wyoming.

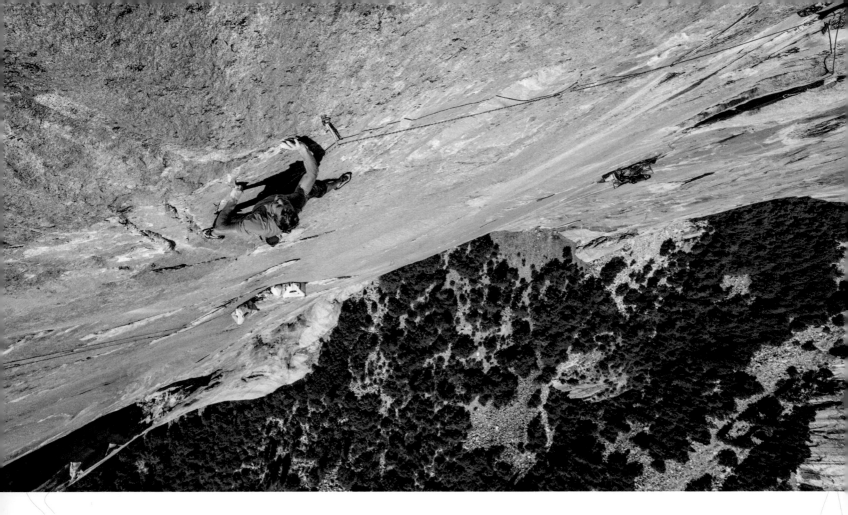

Climbing

Home to the planet's most famous climbing destination, Yosemite Valley, the US also offers everything from consumer-friendly sport climbing to frozen waterfalls, world-class bouldering and hardcore mountains. For climbers, this is the promised land: a place to buy a van, fill it with cheap petrol, and follow the seasons from climbing area to climbing area, living the dream.

Western States

Yosemite Valley, California, is the axis mundi of American traditional climbing. Home to some of the country's most-famous routes, such as the 900m Nose of El Capitan, this glacier-carved vale is hemmed with towering granite monoliths. These walls house hundreds of climbs, most of them splitter cracks that bolt upwards for hundreds of metres and require removable protection. Some routes take days to complete. The list of climbers who've left their mark here is a royal family tree of American climbing. John Muir, Royal Robbins, Lynn Hill, Alex Honnold and Tommy Caldwell cut their teeth on Valley granite and 'The Ditch' continues to be a proving ground for big-wall free climbers. The climbing itself is unreal – perfect cracks go on seemingly forever and offer ideal natural protection. The elfin forests of pines and dogwood, giant blonde rocks and waterfalls draw tourists, but once you're a couple of hundred feet above the din and campfire smoke, you'll see why Yosemite is America's best trad crag.

The high-desert cowboy town of **Bishop,** California, sits on the east side of the Sierra Nevada where it enjoys perfect climbing conditions – dry and cool – most of the year. The region is fat with all varieties of rock climbing, but the bouldering is standout. The Buttermilk boulders comprise a hillside of white and gold granite orbs settled into a quartz-pebble surface that cushions more-or-less flat landings. The Milks are often 'highball', a term that connotes anything from good fun to trouser-filling commitment. Luckily, there's great bouldering nearby for every level of hero. Check out the Druid Stones, the Happy and Sad Boulders and the cool-in-the-summer Rock Creek Boulders.

Above, big wall climbing on the Dawn Wall, El Capitan, Yosemite Valley. Right, climbing on one of Yosemite's smaller crags.

© Ben Ditto

HOMEGROWN ADVENTURE HERO

One of the best climbers of the 1980s and '90s, Lynn Hill is renowned for her first free ascent of The Nose (5.13 VI) on Yosemite Valley's 900m-high El Capitan face:

'The Nose route on El Capitan is the world's most famous big-wall climb. The first time I saw El Cap was at the age of 13 on a family camping trip. I couldn't believe that people were able to climb this gigantic granite monolith. But 20 years later, in 1993, I became the first person to make an all-free ascent of this historic wall. Many climbers manage to 'aid' the route, using gear to help them through hard sections, but since my free ascent only five people have freed the Nose, and only one, Tommy Caldwell, has freed it in a day, as I did in 1994. I'm grateful to have had the opportunity to demonstrate that with motivation, vision and preparation, a woman is as capable as a man.'

In winter 1991, two climbers in Ouray, Colorado – Bill Whitt and Gary Wild – got tired of waiting for waterfall ice to naturally form, so they tapped into a local hydro-electric waterline that runs on top of the Uncompahgre Gorge, a 1.6km-long, 30m-deep defile just south of town. Using a motley collection of garden hoses equipped with shower heads they started spraying the walls at night, 'farming ice' and creating ice climbs. From these humble beginnings arose **Ouray Ice Park**, a free ice-climbing venue with 200 established routes. If you're jonesing to swing tools, it's hard to beat the convenience of the park, and if you don't mind approaches and happen to catch good conditions, Ouray has nearby natural ice that'll blow your lederhosen off.

The variety of climbing in the Western states is enormous. Utah's **Canyonlands** are justifiably famous for their splitter sandstone cracks and spindly towers that poke the sky. **Indian Creek**, near Moab, offers hundreds of pure crack climbs that will test your jamming skills. Also in Utah is **Maple Canyon**, an area known for its unique conglomerate rock and steep sport climbs, which also boasts excellent ice climbing in winter.

Hueco Tanks, Texas, is famous to boulderers who have flocked here since the 1990s to explore its labyrinthine system of canyon walls and stand-alone blocks, adding hundreds of problems, some of which are world-class. Pocked with smooth, round holes called *huecos* (Spanish for hole) the syenite porphyry rock at the Tanks is distinctive and near perfect. Because of its popularity, reservations are required.

Eastern States

The US abounds with killer sport climbing but the best spot might be in the unlikely locale of rural east-central Kentucky. **The Red**, as climbers have dubbed it, is a system of canyons and sandstone escarpments carved by the Red River into steep and featured cliffs and caves. Climbers have been drilling sport routes here since the early 1990s, and now there are more than 1500 routes. The Red River Gorge Climbers' Coalition, an advocacy group for climbers, works to build trails, update hardware and implement rescue services, making the Red one of the most accessible and best-maintained climbing areas in the world. Comprising routes of all grades, great holds and a climber-friendly vibe, the Red is a mandatory tick on any sport-climber's American itinerary.

Four hours' west of the Red, **New River Gorge** in West Virginia has superb sport and trad climbing, while the sandstone slopers of **Horse Pens 40** in Alabama are justifiably famous among boulderers. Further north, **Rumney** in New Hampshire is one of America's best sport crags, while the **Gunks** in New York State has been home to trad climbers since the first routes were established in 1935.

Alaska

The **Alaska Range** is the crown jewel of North American mountaineering. Burly weather, proud glaciers and surrealistically rugged terrain define this remote and beautiful group of peaks that stretch 965km from Iliamna Lake in southwest Alaska to just over the eastern border into the Yukon, Canada. These mountains offer a plethora of climbing objectives, ranging from expeditions to **Denali** (6190m), North America's highest peak, to walk-ups in the Delta sub-range, where many mountains are just a kilometre off the Richardson Highway. Away from the snow and ice, **Ruth Gorge** offers mind-boggling big-wall climbs on a Yosemite-scale in an alpine setting.

Paddling

Expert paddlers pre-date the birth of the US. The Ojibwe started canoeing the lake they call Gitchigami (Lake Superior), the world's largest freshwater puddle, at least 8000 years ago. These sophisticated water-people built birchbark boats capable of cresting 3.6m-waves and withstanding 16km-long portages. While their paddling skills are legendary, John Wesley Powell – the one-armed Civil War hero who explored the Green and Colorado Rivers on separate expeditions in 1869 and 1872 – popularised the transcendent thrill and beauty of paddling in America, and revealed some of the risks: on his 1600km 1869 expedition through the Grand Canyon, Powell lost most of his provisions and three of his men. Today, paddlers in the US can explore 4.6 million kilometres of river terrain, 123,439 lakes and 153,000km of coastal shoreline. Whether it's the thrill of rafting the iconic whitewater rivers of the American West, the awe of sea kayaking past humpback whales in Alaska's Northwest Passage, the peace of canoeing a thickly forested wilderness in the upper Midwest, or the rush of kayaking Class V water in the southeast, the US is still the land of the free for paddlers.

Western States

Flowing 2333km from Colorado's Rocky Mountain National Park through the Grand Canyon and into the Gulf of Mexico, the **Colorado River** is the Holy Grail of American whitewater. Most paddlers, whether expert kayakers or novice rafters, negotiate the 477km Arizona stretch from Lees Ferry to Lake Mead, where red-rock canyons rise hundreds of feet and hydraulics such as Lava Falls, a Grade-10 (by Colorado River standards) rapid eats boats alive.

Below, rafters depart Lees Ferry on the Colorado River, Nevada. Right, paddling the Chassahowitzka River in Florida.

Private parties wait years to earn their coveted permits, which are chosen through a National Park Service lottery system (in 2016, only 472 permits were granted out of 4911 applications). For those who lack kayaking skills, but have desire and enthusiasm, many reputable rafting companies offer three- to 18-day journeys. Some still even use wooden dories, the rowboat John Wesley Powell steered with only one arm.

Washington's **San Juan Islands**, an archipelago just a short ferry ride from Seattle, are idyllic for paddlers. Protected from the Pacific by the Olympic Peninsula and Vancouver Island, the water between the 170 rugged islands teems with orcas, porpoises and sea otters. Paddlers can set out for a week or an overnight, but there always seems to be a sandy beach for camping with an excellent view of Mount Baker or the Olympic Mountains.

The Midwest

The Midwest isn't always associated with high adventure, but the 445,154-hectare **Boundary Waters Canoe Area Wilderness** is a paddling playground of 1000 lakes in the northeast corner of Minnesota, just south of Canada, which offers a backcountry camping experience like no other. Instead of Grade V rapids, the challenge lies in entering a roadless wilderness, accessible only by paddling lakes ranging in size from large ponds to immense stretches of water, in every kind of weather – temperatures can drop below 0°C in northern Minnesota even in summer. The lakes are separated by portages that range in length from a few metres to several kilometres. All the gear – from canoes to tents to paddles to PFDs to provisions – can be rented in Ely or Grand Marais, the two gateway communities into the Boundary Waters. Obtaining a permit from the National Forest Service is mandatory.

South East

Every September and October, during the famous Gauley Season, 60,000 paddlers from around the world capitalise on the Army Corp of Engineers' six-weekend dam releases that make the **Gauley River** flow like a runaway freight train through West Virginia. Dropping more than 203m through 40km of steep gorge covered in flaming hardwood forest, the Gauley has more than a hundred major steep and technical rapids, many of them Grade V, interspersed with stretches of calm pools. Solo runs are for experienced paddlers only, but seven commercial outfitters licensed by the West Virginia Division of Natural Resources offer whitewater rafting trips for novices. Just be prepared to paddle through your terror. A festival atmosphere prevails, especially on Bridge Day, the third Saturday in October, which features everything from BASE jumping (from nearby 267m New River Gorge bridge) to barbecues and beer.

Florida's **Biscayne National Park** is a sea kayaking and SUPing heaven just south of Miami. With more than 80km of designated water trails,

ICONIC EVENT

The annual Molokai Challenge, considered the pinnacle event in the world of surfski paddling, features competitors racing for 51km across the Kaiwi Channel, an expanse of open ocean between the Hawaiian islands of Molokai and Oahu, each May.

© Andrew Peacock, © Justin Foulkes | Lonely Planet

paddlers can explore inland lagoons, mangrove-choked channels and the calm waters of Biscayne Bay, while keeping an eye out for alligators, manatee, osprey and pelicans. In Mississippi, the 130km Pascagoula River drains an area of more than 12,800 sq km and is home to more than 300 bird species. The best way to see these bald eagles, brown pelicans, hooded warblers, swallow-tailed kites and more is by kayaking Rhodes Bayou near the mouth of the river with a trained naturalist from the Pascagoula River Audubon Centre in Moss Point, Mississippi.

North East

Spanning nearly 1200km from Old Forge in New York to Fort Kent in Maine, the **Northern Forest Canoe Trail** passes through 22 rivers, 58 lakes, a dozen watersheds and even dips into Canada. As the Algonquian and Wabanaki First Nations people knew centuries ago, this water route was the best way to wind through the Adirondack, Green and White Mountains. There are 63 portages, so it's wise to pack light. And plan on taking the trip from west to east in order to minimise paddling upstream.

Alaska

The route to the Klondike during the 1886–89 gold rush, the **Inside Passage** stretches 1868km from Washington's Puget Sound, north past British Columbia, before ending in Skagway, Alaska. The 926km Alaskan portion is particularly appealing. Like an aquatic Appalachian Trail, the path winds through 1000 islands, and mystical coves and inlets that harbour humpback whales, dolphins and walrus. Calving glaciers explode into the sea and Yosemite-like half-dome rock formations rise straight from the water in unexplored places such as the 55km-long fjords of **Tracy Arm-Fords Terror Wilderness**. The Inside Passage is more protected than the open North Pacific, but it stretches 185km wide from east to west in places, so be prepared for wind-bound days, tricky tides, wet weather (average annual rainfall is over 1524mm) and beaches inhabited by Alaskan brown bears. If that sounds too daunting in a kayak, there are easier options. Many small-expedition ships, like Lindblad Expeditions or UnCruise Adventures, offer seven- to 21-day trips on a luxurious vessel equipped with kayaks and standup paddleboards.

Hawaii

They may not have been invented here, but outrigger canoes arrived in the Hawaiian Islands around AD 200. Once the vessel of chiefs and a utilitarian vehicle for fishermen and voyagers, outrigger canoes play an important role in the islands' culture and the sport is imbued with tradition. Entire families, such as the Hawaiian clan of legendary surfer Dave Kalama, still compete together in local races, and there's no better place to learn the art of outrigger paddling.

Paddlers camp by a lake in Maine, New England.

© UpperCut Images | Alamy

Diving & Snorkelling

The US, which boasts coasts facing three oceans – the Atlantic, Pacific and Arctic – has underwater realms that would take even the most committed bubble-blower several tank-lugging lifetimes to explore, from Florida's fish-saturated coral reef to the drowned mines at Bonne Terre, Missouri, where a billion-gallon lake is apparently populated by one lonely carp.

Atlantic Coast & Gulf of Mexico

Off **Morehead** in North Carolina, the wreck of the U-352, a German submarine sunk during WWII – can be explored. Florida's **Panama City Beach** is home to the planet's biggest artificial reef, created after the 2006 scuttling of an aircraft carrier, the USS **Oriskany**, along with two Voodoo F101 fighter jets; now known as the 'Great Carrier Reef' the topmost section of the wreck is at 24m. On the peninsula, snorkellers can swim with manatees at **Crystal River**. Off the coast of Texas and Louisiana, in **Flower Garden Banks National Marine Sanctuary**, mantas and spotted eagle rays can be spied, amid reefs and underwater salt-dome mountains alive with thousands of fish. But it's the **Florida Keys**, dangling below Miami and beneath Biscayne Bay, that really unlock the door to the best diving in the US. Here, the country's only living reef is surrounded by marine life and scattered with shipwrecks. Sites are both easily accessible and sublime. John Pennekamp Coral Reef State Park has 40 living coral species and 650 fish species, including the goliath grouper. Wrecks include the 64m-long **Adolphus Busch** off Looe Key, the 57m **Thunderbolt**, lying upright and accessible 35m below the surface, off Marathon Key, and the 155m USS **Spiegel Grove** in 40m off Key Largo.

Pacific Coast & Alaska

Off California's coast, only 35km from LA, **Santa Catalina Island** and **Channel Islands National Park** have towering kelp forests, home to myriad marine species. Further north, **Point Lobos State Marine Conservation Area,** just below Monterey Bay, protects 4009 hectares of subaquatic terrain, offering excellent visibility and encounters with creatures including leopard sharks and harbour seals. A maximum of 30 people are allowed to dive per day, ensuring a special experience.

During summer, on the northeastern side of Alaska's **Baranof Island**, in a tight canyon at a site called Smudges, you can enjoy the surreal experience of diving amid hundreds of moon jellies.

Hawaii

The islands are rich with spectacular dives sites, offering encounters with dolphins, monk seals, sharks, turtles rays and countless fish species, amid a volcanic underworld. Off Oahu, at **Waikiki Wrecks**, it's possible to dive not one, but three sunken ships in a single day.

Diving off Santa Catalina Island, California.

© Kevin Panizza | Getty Images

Surfing

The US has good claim to be the home of surfing – spiritually in the form of Hawaii, and also culturally in the form of California.

Hawaii

Still the world's primo surf destination. Legendary spots such as **Pipeline** and **Sunset** on Oahu's north coast – and of course Maui's **Jaws** – produce the planet's best and most challenging waves, but you can also find more user-friendly walls of water at spots such as **Makaha Point** on the big island's west coast, **Hanalei Bay** on Kauai and all along **Maui's west coast**.

California

From the quality breaks around **San Diego**, on up past **San Onofre**, **Trestles**, **Laguna Beach** and **Huntington**, generations of surfers have flocked to the wide array of waves here. Further north are legendary point breaks such as **Malibu** and **Rincon**, while **Santa Cruz** has a vibrant cold-water surf community. The crowds tend to thin as you continue north – check out the fast, peaky beach breaks of **Cape Lookout,** Oregon, or **Westport** in Washington – both popular with Seattleites.

East Coast

Ocean City, New Jersey, has some of the eastern seaboard's best waves, while the consistent swells of **Virginia Beach** are the focal point for surfing in the Mid-Atlantic states. Florida's warm-water surf scene is well established, with **Ponce Inlet** at New Smyrna Beach offering some of the most rippable and consistent waves, while **Cocoa Beach**, to the south, produced Kelly Slater.

Alaska

The best breaks in the far north are found at Yakutat. They're brutally cold, of course, but dramatic and uncrowded, as the area is only accessible by boat or plane.

> **HOMEGROWN ADVENTURE HERO**
> A legendary Hawaiian waterman credited with popularising the sport of surfing, Duke Kahanamoku also swam for the US in three Olympics Games (1912, 1920 and 1924), winning medals each time. Duke was the first person to be inducted into both the Swimming and the Surfing Hall of Fame.

Trail Running

In a competitive sense, singletrack running history in the US goes back to 1905 and the Dipsea trail race in California, which still attracts competitors to the rolling forests outside San Francisco. Back then the trail calendar was sparse, unlike today when there are enough events to keep a runner sated for decades. From east to west, north to south, up to Alaska and across the seas to Hawaii, every type of landscape imaginable is represented here, from technical rocky mountain trails to lush forested corridors, harsh deserts and brutal canyonlands, volcanic tundras to ice-bound routes. The US truly has it all.

Colorado could be considered the spiritual home of trail running, anchored as it is to the mighty Rocky Mountains. It hosts the **Hardrock 100 Endurance Run** and the **Leadville Trail 100**, two of the most prestigious 100-milers on the planet, as well as a long list of shorter-distance trail events. The Rockies stretch 4800km across six states from Idaho and Montana down through Wyoming and Utah to Colorado and New Mexico, and there's running to be enjoyed all along the range.

In California's Sierra Nevada mountains, the **Western States 100** started as a man-versus-horse challenge in 1974, when Gordy Ainsleigh proved a man on foot, rather than sitting in a saddle, could complete the 100-mile (161km) distance in the 24 hours allowed for the horses. In 1977, the first official Western States footrace was inaugurated. It remains one of the world's most sought-after trail races.

The **Appalachian National Scenic Trail**, spanning 3500km and 14 states in the east, gets a lot of attention as a target for ultra record breakers – the current end-to-end record is 45 days, 22 hours by Karl Meltzer in 2016. It also offers plenty of easy-access runs on shorter highlight sections.

Beginner boards to rent at Waikiki Beach on Oahu, Hawaii.

© Matt Munro | Lonely Planet

Wild Swimming

Diving and snorkelling aren't the only ways to explore the endless aquatic environments of the US, where open-water swimming opportunities abound, from rivers and canyons to plunge pools beneath waterfalls and thermally heated natural baths. Ticklists commonly include **Hamilton Pool** grotto near Austin, Texas; **Havasu Falls** in Arizona's Havasupai Reservation; California's **Aztec Falls**; **Sliding Rock** in North Carolina; the **Blue Hole** in New Mexico; and Hawaii's jungle-fringed **Hali'i Falls**. The US is also home to some seriously scary open-water races, such as the **SharkFest** swim from Alcatraz to San Francisco, and an epic 45.5km lap around New York's Manhattan Island, now known as the **20 Bridges** swim.

Caving

The US has an extraordinary and expansive underworld to be explored by wannabe burrowers. Many locations offer a mixture of experiences, from entry-level cave tours for the average punter to more involved squeeze-on-your-knees adventures for serious spelunkers. Notable locations include monstrous **Mammoth Cave** in Kentucky, the world's longest cave system, where over 640km

of tunnels have been explored so far; **Carlsbad Cavern** in New Mexico, where more than 100 caves pockmark the Chihuahuan Desert; **Natural Bridge Caverns** in Texas and **El Capitan Cave** on Prince of Wales Island, Alaska. In Tennessee's **Craighead Caverns**, you can do an overnight subterranean tour to the shores of the Lost Sea – the largest underground lake in the US, and second-biggest on Earth – spotting rare anthodites (cave flowers) and a waterfall en route.

Horseback Riding

Home to horse-whisperers and huge horizons, the American West is the perfect place for equine-assisted exploration and adventure. Providers operate horse trekking experiences throughout the region, allowing visitors to trek through Tombstone in Arizona (home to the famous OK Corral), ride around Bighorn Mountain in **Wyoming**, meander beneath the big skies of **Montana** or gallop through Gila National Forest in southwest **New Mexico**.

Canyoneering

This activity – known to most of the world as canyoning, and involving a mixture of hiking, scrambling, rappelling/abseiling, jumping and

UNCLAIMED ADVENTURE

Washington State's North Cascades National Park has a number of thought-to-be-unexplored potentially awesome (possibly dangerous) canyoneering locations, including Agnes Gorge, created by a glacier-fed creek that's a tributary of the Stehekin River, and Hells Gorge, on a tributary of the Chilliwack River.

© Mark Read | Lonely Planet

© Matt Munro | Lonely Planet

*Left, going cowboy-style in Wyoming near the Grand Tetons. **Right**, shadows and light in Antelope Canyon, Arizona.*

occasionally swimming, in order to explore gorges – almost unarguably reaches its absolute zenith in **Zion National Park**, Utah, where wind and water have sculpted a series of breathtaking slot canyons in the dramatic desertscape. Nearby, quality canyons can be explored in **Moab**, **Cedar Mesa**, the **Escalante**, **Robbers Roost** and **North Wash**, all in Utah, and Arizona's **Antelope Canyon**. Further afield, other notable canyoneering locations include **Watkins Glen** in New York State and **Gulf Hagas** in Maine.

BASE Jumping

Above the slickrock and Wile E Coyote rockscape of **Moab**, where jeep drivers and mountain bikers get their buzz, another community of thrill-chasers plays a much more dangerous game, rock climbing to the top of the red cliffs and stacks, before BASE jumping or wingsuit flying back down. This is one of the few places in the US where BASE jumping and 'proximity flying' is legal. Other exceptions include **New River Gorge Bridge** in West Virginia, where jumping is permitted on Bridge Day each October; and **Perrine Bridge** above Twin Falls in Idaho, where no permit is required and novices can even do tandem jumps with experienced leapers.

Paragliding

Few experiences are quite as memorable as hovering like an eagle above the vast landscapes of North America, and while the sport doesn't provide the speed rush that BASE jumping delivers, paragliding offers aerial explorers the chance to truly absorb the scene between their shoes, while chasing thermals and sharing the sky with the continent's real raptors. Notable soaring sites include the wonderfully named Poo Poo Point on **Tiger Mountain** near Seattle in Washington state; **Sun Valley**, around Mt Baldy in Idaho, **Sedona Red Rocks** in Arizona and **Goodsprings**, near Las Vegas in the Nevada Desert.

URUGUAY

The big sky of Uruguay's interior offers authentic adventure.

W arm and temperate with vast plains and low hills that will drag your eyes and mind into the meditative middle distance, much of Uruguay has escaped the tourist inundations that many of its neighbours have suffered. That makes it perfect for those searching for something different.

Horse Riding

Live out your frontier fantasy by becoming a gaucho on a real working *estancia* (cattle ranch) in the unspoiled Uruguayan interior. Being an indentured labourer never felt so good – or so free – than when you're riding under the big sky of the rolling Pampas.

Kitesurfing

Get your kiting kicks on **Laguna Garzon** – either on the huge, flatwater lagoon inside the sand bar, or on the open ocean waves. When you're not kiting, you can marvel at one of the world's most unique bridges: the Laguna Garzon circular bridge.

Surfing

With swells crashing in from the Atlantic and a coastline marked by rocky capes, Uruguay has its share of surf breaks, but **Cabo Polonio** is special. This secluded spot is protected by the shifting sands of huge dunes across which there are no roads, meaning you either hike the 7km in or hitch a lift in a 4WD. The small fishing settlement has no running water or electricity and its isolation makes it a unique site of both environmental and cultural preservation as well as a quiet haven. As a bonus, it's likely that when you paddle out it will be just you and the sea lions vying for position in the lineup.

ICONIC EVENT: GRAN FONDO URUGUAY
Play pro cyclist for a day and brave the peloton as it flies around Punta del Este, one of the most action-packed towns in South America. If the 171km of the gran is too much for you, opt for the 84km medio fondo. Either way, pack your boldest Lycra knicks.

UZBEKISTAN

Once hidden by a veil of authoritarian restrictions placed on Western travellers, changes in government have finally opened up Central Asia's most populous country.

H istorically known as Transoxania, this Central Asian nation has lured for swashbuckling adventurers ever since the days of Alexander the Great. Today, busloads of tourists visit the architectural splendours of cities like Bukhara and Khiva. But don't be discouraged; there's still plenty left to see and do 'Along the Golden Road to Samarkand'.

Running with Camels

In the north of the country lies the 16th largest desert in the world, the **Kyzylkum** – the 'Red Sand'. A number of camps cater to inquisitive visitors, including Nurata Ecotourism Association and Sputnik Camp. These outposts have access to camels, relatively fresh supplies and bottles upon bottles of vodka. Through them travellers can arrange for multiday camel excursions, staying with Kazakh semi-nomads along the way. If riding or walking with these beasts doesn't put you off, then the truly eccentric can go for a run supported by the animals; enjoying an almost seaside feel while traversing the shores of the nearby Lake Aydarkul.

Hiking the Earthen City

Situated in the autonomous republic of Karakalpakstan, eastern Uzbekistan, is the **Toprak-Kala**, or 'Earthen City'. This ancient settlement – erected as the capital of the Khorezm state in the 3rd century AD – is an outstanding relic to a fallen civilisation. Organisations such as Advantour facilitate hikes up to and among the decaying ruins of this ransacked piece of history.

DON'T LEAVE WITHOUT...
Skiing in Beldersay. Snow sports don't immediately spring to mind in a desert-riddled double-landlocked destination, but Beldersay mountain resort, 80km southeast of Tashkent, has some good slopes and at less than $20 for a day pass, this is one of the cheapest and most unusual adventures to be had in the Western Tian Shan.

Snorkelling over a coral reef off Espiritu Santo.

VANUATU

From trekking fuming volcanic cones to diving WWII wrecks, Vanuatu is literally an adventure paradise.

A remote 80-island archipelago, strung out north–south on the South Pacific's Rim of Fire, Vanuatu's adventure offering is defined by the country's intimate relationship with the ocean and the volcanoes that gave it life.

Volcano Trekking

Begging to be climbed, the brooding twin peaks of **Mt Marum** and **Mt Benbow** loom large in the centre of remote Ambrym island. Often hazed by smoke, volcanic activity is constantly monitored and you must trek with a local guide. It's possible to do a day trek up and back from the north, scaling only Mt Marum, but a better choice is a cross-island trek with an overnight camp, visiting both volcanoes and hiking down the other side. Either way, you'll experience jungle trekking and a challenging ascent that delivers a view into a rumbling, spewing pot of magma, like looking into the very eye of planet Earth.

Wreck Diving

Vanuatu has some excellent reef diving around the main island of Efate, but the star of the show is found off **Espiritu Santo**, where the wreck of the SS *President Coolidge* lies less than 100m offshore. The luxury liner – commandeered as a troopship during WWII – was accidentally sunk when it hit a friendly mine. The wreck lies between 21m and 67m from bow to stern, offering divers a rare opportunity to explore a huge and complete ocean liner shipwreck from the shore.

Diving Million Dollar Point, just off the beach near Luganville, Espiritu Santo, is another highlight. The US dumped millions of dollars of equipment – including vehicles – here, when the British and French refused to pay rock-bottom prices for them at the end of WWII.

SPIRITUAL HOME OF...

Volcano surfing. Jeeps take you to within 100m of the crater of Mt Yasur on Tanna island, where spasmodic explosions ejaculate magma ominously into the sky, but it's the descent that really gets pulses racing. Volcano surfing was apparently invented here, by eccentric adventurer Zoltan Istvan in 2002. Go up for sunrise, rent an ashboard and surf down the western side of the crater. The soft ash is perfect for carving – you can make it from rim to the bottom in less than a minute.

© Andrew Peacock

VENEZUELA

Venezuela is a country of extraordinary natural beauty, hamstrung by political and civil unrest.

T here's no glossing over the turmoil that plagues Venezuela – and safety concerns are legitimate. That said, with caution and planning it's possible to visit and, if you do, the rewards are enormous. The country's natural beauty is astounding. Visions of the mighty tabletop *tepuis* will stay with visitors forever; the world's highest waterfall – the poetically named

Angel Falls – is take-your-breath-away majestic; there's sleepy Caribbean coast and clock-free islands, proud Andean peaks, steamy rainforests and big rivers. Venezuela is bursting with action for those with powerful legs, strong lungs and big imaginations.

Ascend a Tepui

Anyone who doesn't get giddy looking up at the *tepuis* (massive sandstone tabletops) looming like islands from the clutching tropical jungle in eastern Venezuela might need their head read. The trek up **Mt Roraima** on the Chimantá Massif is an all-time life highlight. It takes anywhere from five days, depending on how long you want to spend up there, and the top is amazing – 30 sq km of rock labyrinths and clear pools and, when the mist lifts, breathtaking vistas. No wonder Roraima inspired Arthur Conan Doyle's *The Lost World* (not to mention the landscape in the kids' film *Up*).

Tour by Mountain Bike

Merida is a hub for MTB action offering loads of dirt bombing options. Among the two-wheel delights is the **Travesia Merida-Barinas** – a 65km tour that starts in Gavidia at 3600m and traverses the Parque Nacional Sierra Nevada down to Canagua at 400m. The trek is easily broken into two days by spending the night in a rustic village along the way.

ULTIMATE ADVENTURE
The big Venezuelan climbing prize is free-climbing a *tepui*, spending days on the vertiginous walls battling bugs and mud and terror. This is not for the inexperienced: rope in some local guides and prepare for a wild ascent.

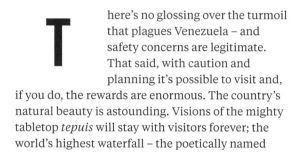

Left, Mt Roraima, the highest of the tepuis, is lined by 400m-high cliffs. Top, a hiker rests while climbing Mt Roraima.

© Arpad Benedek; David Santiago García | Getty Images

VIETNAM

Combining Asia's most famous karst landscape with 3000m-high peaks and the ruler-flat Mekong Delta, Vietnam is slender in shape but fat in adventure opportunities.

In Vietnam, appearances are deceptive. It's a country so narrow it might easily be just a layer of skin on the thigh of Asia, and yet it contains a remarkable range of landscapes and a wealth of adventure possibilities. At its southern end is the relentlessly flat delta of one of Asia's major rivers, the Mekong, fanning out towards the South China Sea. By the time you approach the Chinese border in the north, the wild Hoang Lien Mountains are breaking through 3000m to form the highest peaks in Indochina. Vietnam's quintessential landscape is the karst country, headlined by Halong Bay, arguably Asia's most recognisable natural landscape. Tourism is huge here, but the adventure possibilities are still somehow only in their infancy, with remarkably low-key climbing and kayaking. Inland, through Ninh Binh and Hoa Binh provinces, the karst country creates a made-for-cycling landscape of flat-bottomed valleys running between stark limestone peaks. Also in this limestone landscape are two of the world's three largest caves, bored into Asia's oldest karst mountains.

© Matt Munro | Lonely Planet

Cycling

Think of cycling in Asia and almost certainly this is the place that first comes to mind – the image of bikes among the rice fields is classic Vietnam. Riding here can be all things to all people. The **Mekong Delta** is custom-made for novice cyclists, or just those who abhor the idea of hills, providing gradient-free pedalling across a country that's almost as much water as land. In the north, the area around **Mai Chau** provides an archetypal karst experience, with its rice-terraced valleys reaching out from the town like fingers. Unmarked paths across the rice levees create an infinite wealth of biking opportunities.

The impressive karst formations of Halong Bay.

Touring

Vietnam's ultimate long-distance ride is an extended journey through its narrow central strip, pedalling between the former capital of Hue and the seaside resort of Nha Trang. Follow the coast from Hue to cutesy Hoi An then flirt with the highlands as you roll south to Dalat and a magnificent final descent into Nha Trang.

Mountain Biking

There's good singletrack off-road riding around **Dalat**, which also hosts Vietnam's first international MTB stage race, the three-day **Vietnam Victory Challenge** (held every March).

Hiking

Home to a long string of jungle-clad mountains running along its borders, and around 30 national parks, Vietnam abounds with walking possibilities. Headlining the options for most visitors is the country's highest peak, 3143m **Fansipan**, rising above the popular tourist town of Sapa in Vietnam's northwest. Though it's just 19km from town to summit, it's typically hiked over three days, heading out of Sapa through hill-tribe villages and then up into the thick forest and steep, slippery slopes. It

can be climbed year-round, though the best season is mid-October to mid-December and in wildflower-blooming March.

There's a fine option to get off the beaten hiking path in **Cuc Phuong National Park**, where a remote 16km track pushes through thick jungle to the Muong village of Khanh. Less than 300 people hike this track each year, and it can only be walked with a park guide, who will probably need to clear the way with a machete at times. Expect a legion of leeches and storybook jungle scenery, with the chance to stay a night on the floor of a Muong stilt-house at day's end.

Other good hiking destinations include **Cat Tien** and **Cat Ba** national parks.

Caving

Stumbled upon by a local farmer only in 1990, and first explored in 2009, **Son Doong** is the world's largest cave by volume. In 2013, the first visitors were allowed into the cavern, but it's no simple spelunking jaunt. Located in Phong Nha-Ke Bang National Park in central Vietnam, near the Laos border, the remote cave can only be entered on guided trips run by Quang Binh-based Oxalis Adventure Tours, which rightly claims that fewer

> **DON'T LEAVE WITHOUT...**
> Kayaking through sea caves and arches in Halong Bay. Many Halong tour boats carry kayaks, or they can be hired from operators and hotels on Cat Ba Island.

A doline lights up the massive interior of the world's biggest cave, Son Doong.

© Mike Rowbottom | 500px, © withGod | Shutterstock

people have entered the cave than have stood on the summit of Mt Everest. The challenging trip involves more than a day of trekking to the cave entrance, passing through swift-filled **Hang En** cave (the world's third-largest) along the way. Visitors here spend three days in Son Doong cave, camping inside it each night. The dimensions of the cave are extraordinary, comprising passages as high as 200m and as wide as 150m – it is said that you could fly a 747 through it. The journey involves underground river crossings and strands of jungle nurtured by the sunlight that pours through the cave's two large dolines.

Climbing

With its rim of limestone cliffs, **Halong Bay** looks cut from the pages of a climbing magazine, and yet it remains very much in the shadow of Railay (Thailand) in the pantheon of Asian climbing destinations. **Cat Ba Island** has the most developed and accessible climbing scene, with a range of bolted routes. The best-known climbing area here is Butterfly Valley (Lien Ming), about 10km from Cat Ba Town, while Moody's Beach and Hai Pai are good for beginners. The small limestone islands and stacks strewn through **Lan Ha Bay** around Cat Ba Island also provide a good range of climbing. Located in Cat Ba Town, Asia Outdoors pioneered many of the local routes and offers climbing instruction and trips.

Deep-water soloing

As at Railay, deep-water soloing (DWS) is big in Lan Ha Bay. This involves climbing unroped as you hang over the sea; when you're done, you simply let go, plunging into the water. Just watch the tides – the safety of DWS here is very dependent on them.

Canyoning at Datanla waterfall near Dalat.

ZAMBIA

Victoria Falls is a household name, but it's the wild delights of Luangwa and the Lower Zambezi that will have you coming back for more.

Z ambia is cut and bordered by a series of rivers, the legendary Zambezi being but one. The valleys hewn from these waters vary from shallow to sharp and deep, and the experiences they hold for the traveller are just as varied – absorb the majesty of wildlife on safari, or bow down to the power of Mother Nature while being whitewashed on a Grade-V rapid.

Walking Safaris

South Luangwa National Park is the birthplace of the walking safari, and it's still the top spot in Africa to enjoy one. Follow highly trained, armed guides through the bush as they expertly track wildlife, leading you to incredibly intoxicating sightings of wild dogs, elephants, buffaloes and, yes, even lions and leopards. But these walks aren't always about the high-adrenaline encounters – it's often the quiet moments in-between that you'll truly marvel at, such as when your guide delves into the minutiae of life in the wild, revealing how lion ants capture and kill their prey, for example.

Canoe Safaris

With each stroke of the paddle you'll know that you are stirring a river where giants lurk. And although the canoe is gliding ever-so-silently across the water's still surface, you quickly get the feeling that you are being watched. Eyes of hippos and crocodiles pop up here and there, vanishing beneath the surface as swiftly as they appear. The mighty river's banks in **Lower Zambezi National Park** are no less dramatic, with prowling lions, hulking elephants and a plethora of birdlife. Considering the closeness of the encounters, the experience feels as intimate as it does alarming. Unforgettable.

> ### DON'T LEAVE WITHOUT...
> Hopping into a whitewater raft in Africa's adrenaline capital – Victoria Falls – and taking on the Zambezi's epic series of Grade V rapids.

The lucky may catch a glimpse of a leopard on a walking safari in South Luangwa National Park.

© Philip Lee Harvey | Lonely Planet

ZIMBABWE

Tempestuous whitewater, many a mountain high and active safaris on land and water, Zimbabwe has a fantastic habit of surpassing all travellers' expectations.

Most of Zimbabwe resides atop a high plateau and forms the watershed boundary between two of Southern Africa's greatest rivers: the Zambezi and the Limpopo. Though the rivers sustain incredible wildlife and provide legendary safari and whitewater opportunities, numerous mountains, particularly in the Eastern Highlands bordering Mozambique, provide innumerable trekking opportunities.

Trekking

With verdant pine-covered hills and rounded quartzite peaks cloaked in mist, Zimbabwe's **Eastern Highlands** are an African aberration, seemingly transported straight from Scotland. This region proffers countless trekking trails that will take you past waterfalls (Mtarazi Falls plummets 762m), along tranquil rivers and up to stunning panoramas of Wizard Valley in Mozambique.

It's a stiff and steep three-hour hike from base camp to reach the mountain refuge hut within **Chimanimani National Park**, from where you can strike out to sites such as Skeleton Pass, Mt Binga (2436m) and the Bundi Valley. The latter is dotted with rock overhangs and caves, many of which make for great shelters to spend your nights. There are also some great, albeit frosty, pools to cool off in nearby. Infrastructure is at its most basic, so bring everything you'll need with you.

Whitewater Rafting

There is rafting elsewhere in the country but nothing compares to the all-out fury of the **Zambezi** immediately downstream of Victoria Falls – it is one of the world's finest whitewater rafting destinations. Best at low water from July to mid-February, the 21 rapids (many of which are Grade V) stretched over 25km will take you off some huge drops. Want more? Overnight and multiday options are possible.

DON'T LEAVE WITHOUT...
Visiting World Heritage–listed Mana Pools National Park for enthralling walking and canoe safaris along the banks of the Zambezi.

There are few more exhilarating experiences than rafting the Zambezi River.

© Chad Ehlers | Alamy

INDEX

ACKNOWLEDGMENTS

Published in October 2017
by Lonely Planet Global Limited
CRN 554153
www.lonelyplanet.com
ISBN 978 1 7865 7759 7
© Lonely Planet 2017
Printed in Malaysia
10 9 8 7 6 5 4 3 2 1

Managing Director, Publishing
Piers Pickard
Associate Publisher Robin Barton
Commissioning Editors Patrick Kinsella, Ross Taylor; **Editor** Nick Mee
Art Direction Daniel Di Paolo
Design Hayley Warnham; **Icons** Jacob Rhoades
Cartography Wayne Murphy
Print Production Larissa Frost, Nigel Longuet

Contributors: Alf Alderson, Andrew Bain, Robin Barton, Dominic Bates, Catherine Best, Chelsea Broderick, David Cauldwell, Tarquin Cooper, Damien Gildea, Will Gray, Damian Hall, Paul Harding, James Henderson, Jeff Jackson, Patrick Kinsella, Brendan Leonard, Antz Longman, Simon Madden, Jamie Maddison, Jonathan Manning, Leon McCarron, James McCormack, Sean McFarlane, Ric McLaughlin, Anna McNuff, Tobias Mews, Derek Morrison, Chris Ord, Flash Parker, Stephanie Pearson, Matt Phillips, John Shepherd, Ryan Siacci, Phoebe Smith, Ross Taylor, Justin Walker, Denby Weller, Jasper Winn

All rights reserved. No part of this publication may be reproduced, stored in a retrieval system or transmitted in any form by any means, electronic, mechanical, photocopying, recording or otherwise except brief extracts for the purpose of review, without the written permission of the publisher. Lonely Planet and the Lonely Planet logo are trademarks of Lonely Planet and are registered in the US patent and Trademark Office and in other countries.

STAY IN TOUCH lonelyplanet.com/contact

AUSTRALIA
The Malt Store, Level 3, 551 Swanston St, Carlton, Victoria 3053 T: 03 8379 8000

USA
124 Linden St, Oakland, CA 94607
T: 510 250 6400

IRELAND
Unit E, Digital Court, The Digital Hub, Rainsford St, Dublin 8

UNITED KINGDOM
240 Blackfriars Rd, London SE1 8NW
T: 020 3771 5100

Although the authors and Lonely Planet have taken all reasonable care in preparing this book, we make no warranty about the accuracy or completeness of its content and, to the maximum extent permitted, disclaim all liability from its use.

MIX
Paper from responsible sources
FSC™ C021741
www.fsc.org

Paper in this book is certified against the Forest Stewardship Council™ standards. FSC™ promotes environmentally responsible, socially beneficial and economically viable management of the world's forests.